D0772802

THREE MAGIC
LETTERS

Michael T. Nettles
and Catherine M. Millett

THREE
MAGIC
LETTERS

Getting to
Ph.D.

The Johns Hopkins
University Press
BALTIMORE

The Johns Hopkins University Press
2715 North Charles Street
Baltimore, Maryland 21218-4363
www.press.jhu.edu

Library of Congress Cataloging-in-Publication Data

Nettles, Michael T., 1955–
  Three magic letters : getting to Ph.D. / Michael T. Nettles, Catherine M. Millett.
    p. cm.
  Includes bibliographical references and index.
  ISBN 0-8018-8232-X (hardcover : alk. paper)
  1. Doctor of philosophy degree—United States.   2. Doctor of philosophy degree—
United States—Statistics.   3. Graduate students—United States.   4. Educational
surveys—United States.   I. Millett, Catherine M.   II. Title.
  LB2386.N48 2006
  378.2′42—dc22

                                                                    2005006472

A catalog record for this book is available
from the British Library.

To the Nettles and the Milletts

CONTENTS

FIGURES

TABLES

PREFACE

IN THE SPRING OF 1995, Catherine Millett appeared at the faculty office of Michael Nettles and asked a critical direct question: "How do doctoral students find the financial resources to support their academic interests and see themselves through timely completion of their Ph.D. degrees?" At the time, Catherine was halfway through the first year of her doctoral program, and Michael was a professor of education at the University of Michigan–Ann Arbor in the department in which Catherine was enrolled. Even though Catherine raised the question in the third person and framed it as an academic issue, it was clear to Michael that her concern was also personal. She was faced with the need to pay the tuition, fees, and her personal subsistence (more than $35,000 a year at the time) to carry her through the remainder of her Ph.D. program. Detecting Catherine's anxiety, Michael handed her a report from his 1980s Educational Testing Service research of doctoral student funding and progress that had been supported by the U.S. Department of Education and the Graduate Record Examinations Board. He encouraged her to read the report and draft her own ideas in the form of a research proposal. Michael retrieved proposals from his files and handed them to Catherine to view as prototypes. He advised her to study them, work on a proposal of her own, and report back in a couple of weeks. They marked a time and date on their calendars.

Two weeks later, Catherine returned with her draft proposal. Thus began our collaboration, with a free exchange of ideas and decisions about research procedures, methods, and strategies. We devoted quite a bit of time to thinking of criteria that we could rely on as the best for selecting universities that we would invite to participate in the research. Our attention then turned to revising the proposal and thinking of ways of raising funds to conduct the research. In essence, we were addressing Catherine's academic and personal requirements. That was the beginning of the project that grew to become this book.

The merit of our proposal attracted a planning grant from the Lilly Endowment. This initial support enabled us to visit half a dozen graduate deans across the United States and communicate our ideas and solicit advice and suggestions from many more by telephone, fax, and e-mail. We sought their opinions about financial assistance for doctoral students and the relationship of finances to other aspects of doctoral program experiences. We sought also to learn how demographic backgrounds of Ph.D. students altered patterns of funding, performance, and progress. Through this journey we gained the participation of many people and institutions, and that has remained constant throughout our research.

The Lilly Endowment grant, supplemented by a modest grant from the Department of Education's Office of Educational Research and Improvement (now the Institute of Education Sciences) through the National Center for Postsecondary Improvement, allowed us to further refine our proposal. Meanwhile, we obtained a major grant from the Spencer Foundation to conduct the next four years of research. This grant permitted us to launch the full-scale research, the findings from which constitute the substance of this book. Subsequently, we were fortunate to win a major grant from the National Science Foundation (NSF) to complete our analyses, convene our collaborators to discuss our findings, and write this book.*

Although the initial focus of our research was financial support for doctoral students, as the far-reaching effects of financial support became more clearly defined in our minds we broadened the scope of the study, allowing it to take on new directions, exploring the variety of experiences and performance of doctoral students beyond funding. We went from the idea of finding out how doctoral students are funded generally to a search for variations among institutional types, fields of study, students' personal backgrounds, and their scholarly development. These, in turn, raised many other issues involving nearly every conceivable aspect of the doctoral student experience: faculty relationships, research productivity, satisfaction, and academic progress. As the variables multiplied, the connections became more complex.

The research model, then, evolved from a very general goal of extending our knowledge of the doctoral experience in terms of its possibilities to the goal of improving the experience for students and their institutions. We cast the problem as follows: Students with individualized "endowments" enter their various institutions and programs from an array of background experiences and for a variety of reasons. They encounter a range of academic and social situations. They achieve various levels of financial stability. They demonstrate varying capacities for research and scholarly productivity. They perform and progress at different rates. And they experience various levels of satisfaction. Overall, we surmised that each of these variables could signal effective progress toward degree completion. Ultimately, we hoped to discover whether our respondents achieved their doctorates within the time frame of the study. For those who did, we wanted to know how long it took.

* Any opinions, findings, conclusions, or recommendations expressed in this material are those of the authors and do not necessarily reflect the views of the National Science Foundation.

We recognized at the onset that though the student characterization of the doctoral experience is important, it is only one consideration. Faculty and other university officials may share some of the same convictions but are also likely to have a distinctive perspective. Our focus is the student experience. Because we surveyed only students, we are not able to add faculty or institutional viewpoints to our analyses, although we rely on our own experience and the published research literature to interpret our results in light of what is known about the other parties' intentions. Also, we focused the study on students who had successfully completed one year of doctoral study and were in their second year or beyond. By doing so, we miss capturing some of the first-year angst that colors beginning doctoral students' ratings of their schools, their programs, their own intellectual capacity, and their career goals. Estimates of dropout rates during the first year of doctoral study average at least 10 to 15 percent (Bowen and Rudenstine 1992), and so we are missing a portion of the doctoral experiences of the small proportion of students who enter doctoral programs but decide before starting a second year to throw in the towel.

We attend to the demographic aspects of doctoral programs such as the race, citizenship, and sex distinctions of their participants. While approximately forty-five thousand students achieved a doctorate in the United States in 1999 (NCES 2002), these success stories belie widespread evidence of problems. Not all race groups are gaining doctorates at the same pace; international students are responsible for the largest increase in the doctoral growth rate; doctorates are increasing in some fields and declining in others; and some racial groups and women and men are participating unevenly in the various fields, foretelling an equally uneven distribution by sex and race in academe and in research professions. One note: while we have aimed at inclusiveness, many readers will note no references to Native Americans. Quite simply, there were too few, despite our surveying tactics, for productive analysis.

Overall, we sought to construct a survey in which a Ph.D. student or prospective student might recognize himself or herself and go on to discover those factors most clearly involved in the various kinds of success. For many graduate students, pursuing a Ph.D. means putting large chunks of their lives—childbearing, community service, family support and relations—on hold as completion times inexorably stretch out. Even those who finish, after eight to twelve years of study in some fields, may well end up with debt the size of a home mortgage. We hope our questions have quantified those aspects of the doctoral process so that students, faculty, and administrators are able to visualize the prospects and pitfalls. Students should be able to recognize themselves in the data, envision the situation, calculate their relative advantages and disadvantages, and pay heed to those factors identified with success. An administrator or faculty member should be able to reverse the thinking and focus on those aspects by field where institutional, departmental, or adviser support has been found deficient. In the end, this work contributes to the chronicles about development of doctoral education in the United States that date back to the mid-nineteenth century. In particular, it gives definition and measurement to the way students prepare and experience their doctoral studies in U.S. graduate schools.

HIGHLIGHTS OF THIS BOOK

The research on which this book is based was a comprehensive assessment of the backgrounds, lives, and experiences of doctoral students in the United States. The 9,036 students who participated represent contemporary doctoral students as they experience doctoral programs. The book presents a historical context in which to study doctoral students today, including historical and present trends. It also presents the details of our research design and a thorough description of our sample by its demographic and academic background characteristics. All of that is presented in the first four chapters of the book to give readers a sense of both who pursues doctoral degrees generally and who constitutes the focus of our research in particular.

Beyond the institutional and research contexts are the findings that emerged from both our descriptive and relational analyses about the finances of doctoral students and about the quality of their educational and social experiences and performance as they go through the doctoral education process. Our analyses, which are presented in fine detail, give attention to numerous findings about the students generally and many distinctions among them, especially by race, major field, and sex. Here we present some of the principal overall findings along the nine key dimensions that we studied: financing; socialization; research productivity; satisfaction, performance, and progress; rate of progress, completion, and time to degree; predictors of student experiences and performance; predictors of major distinction by field; predictors of major distinction by race and sex; and implications of the findings for policy and practice. These summary points give just a flavor of the focus and emphasis of the research, and the nuances are presented in great detail in the main text.

Financing

—About two-thirds of doctoral students entered their doctoral programs free of financial indebtedness.

—Slightly more than two-thirds of the students were offered financial assistance at the time they were admitted.

—Nearly half (48%) of the students who were offered aid received fellowship offers when they were admitted, 44 percent were offered research assistantships, and 60 percent teaching assistantships.

Socialization

—Student social interactions with faculty appear to be highest among engineering, sciences and mathematics, and education doctoral students and relatively low among doctoral students in the humanities and the social sciences.

—Peer interactions are positive for students of the social sciences, the humanities, and the sciences and mathematics. In contrast to their social interactions with faculty, students of engineering and education have rather low peer interactions.

—Consistent with their positive social interactions with faculty, engineering and education doctoral students rate their academic interactions with faculty relatively high. Humanities students also give faculty a positive rating, despite their relatively low social interactions with faculty. Doctoral students in sciences and mathematics and the social sciences rate the quality of their faculty academic interactions relatively low.

—The majority (69%) of students in each field and for both sexes and all races appear to have a mentor.

—Most students in the humanities (73%), sciences and mathematics (59%), and the social sciences (55%) are preparing to become college or university faculty or to seek postdoctoral research or academic appointments. Only 28 percent of engineering and 38 percent of education doctoral students expect to become college or university faculty or postdoctoral research fellows.

Research Productivity

—Just over one-half (51%) of the students indicated having achieved some type of research productivity during their doctoral programs.

—Only 30 percent of the students reported that they had published in a refereed journal—15 percent published one article and another 15 percent published two or more.

—In engineering, the humanities, and the sciences and mathematics, more men than women have published articles.

—African Americans reported lower rates of having published research articles than their peers in education, the sciences and mathematics, and the social sciences.

Satisfaction, Performance, and Progress

—Engineering students appear to have the highest level of satisfaction with their doctoral programs, while students of the social sciences reported the lowest.

—Our sample achieved grades that are consistent with general expectations about doctoral student course performance. The average grade-point average was 3.81 on a four-point scale or slightly higher than an A−.

—Because we surveyed only students who were enrolled, we have stop-outs rather than dropouts. Twelve percent of the students we surveyed stopped out of their programs at some time.

Rate of Progress, Completion, and Time to Degree

—In our sample, engineering students were making the fastest progress, followed by students in the sciences and mathematics, education, the humanities, and the social sciences.

—Overall, nearly 62 percent of the sample of students who had completed at least their first year of doctoral study at the time they were surveyed completed their doctorates within at least the six-year time frame covered by the study. Engineering had the largest share of completers (75% of the original respondents), followed closely by sciences and mathematics (72%).

—The mean elapsed time to degree for completers was 5.97 years. Engineering students who completed their doctorates within our measurement frame averaged the least time to degree, at 5.23 years. This was significantly different from the mean for students in sciences and mathematics (5.71), education (6.28), the social sciences (6.35), and the humanities (7.41).

Predicting Experiences and Performance

—While several elements contribute to receiving a fellowship offer at the time of admission to graduate school, three appear to tell the big story across the fields. Having relatively high scores on the verbal part of the Graduate Record Examination (GRE), being a member of an underrepresented race-ethnicity group, and being initially enrolled as a full-time student appear to enhance student prospects of being offered a fellowship when they are admitted into their doctoral programs.

—Two common elements of teaching assistantship and research assistantship offers upon entry involve being a full-time student and being older.

—African Americans are less likely than whites to be research assistants over the course of their doctoral program in every field except the humanities. Hispanics, who did not appear to be at a disadvantage with regard to receiving research assistantships in any field at the time of admission, appeared in the long term to be disadvantaged only in the field of education.

—Three elements of doctoral programs are prevalent in relation to overall student research productivity. Students who achieve productivity are more likely to be enrolled longer, to have a mentor, and to have an assistantship. With the exception of the humanities, research assistantships are preferable, and in the humanities, teaching assistantships are favored.

—Aside from continuous full-time enrollment, research productivity proved to be an important predictor of doctoral degree completion in all five fields.

—Aside from continuous full-time enrollment, which, as we might expect, was a significant predictor of faster progress in all five fields, the other significant predictors vary by field. Students with higher GRE verbal scores took significantly longer to finish their degrees in the fields of education, engineering, sciences and mathematics, and the social sciences. Conversely, higher GRE analytical scores predicted shorter time to degree in education, sciences and mathematics, and the social sciences. How students financed their doctoral degrees played a limited role in determining time to degree. None of the three major forms of student support—fellowships, teaching assistantships, and research assistantships—predicted time to degree. Student research productivity was also not a predictor.

Interpretation and Implications of Field Differences

—In every field, students with relatively high GRE verbal scores were more likely to receive fellowships on initial enrollment. In receiving teaching and research assistantships on initial enrollment, performance on the GRE General Test was also important.

—Students in fields such as engineering and sciences and mathematics tend to be liberally supported with research assistantships during their doctoral work, while humanities and education students appear to receive relatively few of these opportunities. Conversely, nearly three-quarters of the students in the humanities and sciences and mathematics and two-thirds of the students in the social sciences received teaching assistantships.

—The benefits that students derive from assistantships go beyond better peer connections or faculty interactions to include research productivity. For students of education and the humanities, serving as a teaching assistant may lead to opportunities to publish research articles during the course of one's doctoral program. In contrast, sciences and mathematics teaching assistants may have fewer opportunities to publish articles. This field-dependent conclusion about the value of teaching assistantships is somewhat novel, primarily because until now researchers have not broken apart the fields to examine the contribution of teaching assistantships to research productivity.

—The main contradiction we found with prior research is that teaching assistantships did not seem to lead to a slower rate of progress in any field of study, and for the 62 percent who completed their doctoral degrees, being a teaching assistant was not associated with a prolonged time to degree.

—In the area of socialization, students with mentors felt more positive about their relationships with faculty both outside and inside the classroom. Similarly, we found that having a faculty member who served as both adviser and mentor resulted in higher ratings of student interactions with their faculty advisers.

—In the fields of education, engineering, and the social sciences, having a mentor was positively related to degree completion as well as to a faster time to degree in the humanities and the social sciences.

—Faculty mentors also impacted research productivity, increasing the likelihood as much as two times for humanities and social sciences students. Individuals with mentors in all fields except sciences and mathematics were more likely to present papers at national conferences than peers without mentors.

—Students with higher ratings of student and faculty interactions were more satisfied with their doctoral programs.

—Students appear to become less enchanted in both academic and social interactions with faculty the longer they are enrolled.

—In contrast to mentoring, research productivity has drawn little attention from researchers—and obviously from students, if our 51 percent overall participation rate accurately represents their activities in this area. This suggests that research productivity is neither an established standard nor an expectation of doctoral programs—at least not on a par with writing a dissertation, a requirement of all who receive a doctoral degree.

—Although students may perceive the time required for research productivity as impeding their progress toward a degree, our data show research productivity to have the opposite effect. In all fields, students with research productivity were more likely to complete their degrees, and for those who earned their doctoral degrees, research productivity did not impede their progress.

—Two additional clues to the lack of productivity lie in the close relationship we found between mentoring and research productivity and between research assistantships and research productivity. Quite possibly, many of the students did not understand the short- and long-term benefits of writing and presenting papers and similar activities. That having a mentor and a research assistantship are so highly predictive of research productivity across disciplines and demographic groups suggests that this should become a departmental benchmark for creating optimal doctoral student experiences. For students aiming at academic or research careers, it is likely that research productivity may come to be viewed as an indicator of success in doctoral programs to rival degree completion and time to degree.

—Examining the factors that contribute to the rate of progress, we found little support for a view that financial hardship is slowing some respondents. Household income was only a weak predictor of slower progress in engineering and sciences and mathematics. Only in the social sciences were students with educational debt progressing at a relatively slower pace.

Group-Specific Implications of the Study

—Lower GRE scores of African Americans and Hispanics result in a different experience for them in their programs compared with their white counterparts. Unlike our findings of higher scores yielding fellowships, being African American or Hispanic was related to a greater likelihood of receiving fellowships despite lower GRE scores.

—The overall alarming differences by race relating to students' perceptions of their academic interactions with faculty in engineering appear to be corrected when such elements as GRE performance, mentoring, funding, and job expectations are addressed. The bad news is that engineering schools appear to be troubling places in need of improvement for the success of many of their African American students. The good news is that we have identified tangible elements such as mentoring, funding, and full-time enrollment status as targets for engineering schools to focus on in order to correct the racial differences in experiences.

—Academic interactions with faculty are one area where there appear to be some differences by race and field. In engineering, Asian Americans tend to rate faculty relationships positively. By contrast, Asian Americans in education viewed their academic interactions with faculty less favorably.

—One sign of African Americans' struggle in sciences and mathematics is their lower rate of research article publication. Our analyses show that in sciences and mathematics, African Americans were more than three times less likely than whites to publish. African Americans in education and the social sciences were also less likely than whites to publish an article. No other race group faced comparable challenges, although Hispanics in the social sciences were less likely to publish than whites.

—African Americans were less satisfied in their doctoral programs than white students in engineering and in sciences and mathematics. When their experiences and backgrounds are comparable, however, their lower satisfaction disappears.

—The principal difference between international students and their peers is their rate of progress, which may well have its roots in the visa requirements. International students in our study were moving at a faster pace than their American peers in each of the other race groups.

—An area of concern for women is in research productivity in engineering and sciences and mathematics. Adjusting for several background and experience factors, men showed a significant advantage in paper presentations, publishing research articles, and, consequently, overall research productivity. The most consistent contributors to these productivity measures are having a mentor and being a research assistant during the course of one's studies. Our findings indicate that women are not deficient in either measure in these two fields, so we are not able to explain the lower productivity of women with our data.

—Overall, the finding that men rated student-faculty social interactions higher than women is the most troubling observation.

—That older students were less likely to receive fellowships and research and teaching assistantships during the course of their studies did not surprise us. This situation held true for all fields. Only in engineering were older students less likely to complete their degrees, and only in education was age a small predictor of requiring less time to degree.

—Marital status was not found to be an impediment to student research productivity.

—Married students were less likely to stop out than their unmarried counterparts. Similarly, in education, engineering, and sciences and mathematics, being married or in a partnership proved to be a good predictor (twice as likely in engineering) of completing one's degree. Married and partnered students also had a faster elapsed time to degree than their single peers in engineering, the humanities, and sciences and mathematics.

—By and large, doctoral students with children under the age of eighteen have similar experiences as their peers without children. They reported similar social interactions with peers, social and academic interactions with faculty, and levels of research productivity. Perhaps not surprisingly, students with children were more likely to stop out of their programs. Our findings in engineering, the humanities, and the social sciences are that students with children under eighteen who complete their degrees take longer to do so.

ACKNOWLEDGMENTS

WE ARE GRATEFUL TO MANY PEOPLE for investing time, love, kindness, and money throughout the eight years of this project. First and foremost, we are thankful to Samuel Cargile, who provided the initial support for the project. At the time, Sam was a program officer at the Lilly Endowment (grant 950437), and he liked our initial idea enough to invest money from his precious discretionary fund account to launch our one-year planning activities at the beginning. We wonder what alternative pursuits we might have been forced to undertake without Sam's initial support. Thanks also to our colleagues Patricia Gumport and William Massy, of Stanford University, and Robert Zemsky and Peter Cappelli, of the University of Pennsylvania, who made up the Executive Committee of the National Center for Postsecondary Improvement (NCPI) in 1997, for providing bridge funding from the NCPI (grant R309A60001) to keep the research alive after our planning year. They appreciated the value of the research, and, being seasoned academic researchers themselves, they empathized with our needs at a critical juncture, having found themselves in similar circumstances from time to time in their own research endeavors. In addition to their collective support, each one weighed in substantively with helpful suggestions about design and implementation. We also appreciate the support of Carol Lacampagne, a former director of the Office of Educational Research and Improvement, for standing behind the decision of the NCPI Executive Committee.

The Lilly Endowment and the NCPI were important for launching the planning, but we designed an ambitious project for implementation that also required major grants. Patricia Graham and John Barcroft, together with their colleagues at the Spencer Foundation, provided the first major grant for the study through the Spencer Foundation's Major Grants program (grant 19980004). We can still recall the funny combination of euphoria and relief that we felt when learning from Pat Graham about the Spencer Foundation's decision to support our research. Thanks to the National Science Foundation (NSF), we received our second major grant for the study (NSF grant REC 9903080). Elizabeth VanderPutten, our NSF program officer, has encouraged us and cheered for us throughout. Along with her NSF colleagues Susan Hill and Mary Golladay, Elizabeth also gave us substantive advice throughout the project that helped enrich the results.

Our grant from the NSF provided the resources that we needed for convening graduate deans in a symposium in October 2002 to discuss the results, findings, and implications. While we are grateful to the individuals at both the Spencer Foundation and the NSF, we also appreciate both organizations' rigorous grant review processes, which yielded ideas to help us improve our research.

The backing of one's home institution is especially important in conducting research, and the University of Michigan was outstanding in its support. Various units and people throughout the university helped. First, we appreciate the folks in the Horace H. Rackham Graduate School, beginning with a succession of four deans, the late John D'Arms and his successors, Robert Weisbuch, Nancy Cantor, and Earl Lewis. Each one was a great colleague and friend in substance, spirit, wisdom, and encouragement. Their careful critiques of content and their endorsement of our work gave us the added credibility that we needed with their peers and colleagues in the graduate schools throughout the United States as we sought institutions to participate in the research. We were fortunate also to receive the advice and counsel of several other Michigan colleagues, especially Cynthia Cross, formerly of the Rackham Graduate School, and Marvin Parnes, the associate vice president of the Division of Research Development and Administration. Marvin provided modest but important bridge funding for our research during the first summer, while we awaited a response from the Lilly Endowment. Although modest in dollar amount, Marvin's support was monumental in the grand scheme because it gave us time to seek external grant support.

We are indebted to our friends and colleagues at the Educational Testing Service (ETS), John Yopp, Robert Durso, and Paul Ramsey. Even while we were working at the University of Michigan before joining the ETS, they provided data from the Graduate Record Examinations program that we used to confirm the self-reported scores of our student sample, giving us confidence in the self-reported data from our survey. This collaboration was extremely important for establishing the credibility of self-reported cognitive data. We also appreciate ETS President Kurt Landgraf's recognition of the importance of this work as well as his encouragement and support for its completion.

The Council of Graduate Schools (CGS) also played a helpful and supportive role. Thanks to Peter Syverson, Anne Pruitt-Logan, Jules LaPides, and Debra Stewart, we were able to present and discuss findings at the CGS annual programs throughout the project. This allowed us to get reaction and advice from the leaders of the nations' graduate schools. Debra Stewart continues to keep us connected with CGS-related activities, and we find that to be a valuable link for this project.

We extend our sincere gratitude to those who participated in our invitational conference in October 2002. Their reactions and suggestions to our initial draft were fundamental in structuring this publication. We would like to acknowledge them individually. They are Ann Austin, Michigan State University; Keith Baker, Stanford University; Sharon Brucker, Andrew W. Mellon Foundation; Paul Courant, University of Michigan–Ann Arbor; John Cross, Woodrow Wilson National Fellowship Foundation; Susan Dauber, Spencer Foundation; Nathan Daun-Barnett, University of Michigan–Ann Arbor; Stephen Director, University of Michigan–Ann Arbor; James Duderstadt, University of Michigan–Ann Arbor; Linda Dykstra, University of North Carolina–Chapel Hill; Linda Edwards, City University of New York Graduate Center; Yolanda George, American Association for the Advancement of Science; Edie Goldenberg, University of Michigan–Ann Arbor; Marc Goulden, University of California–Berkeley; Susan Hill, National Science Foundation; Carol Hollenshead, University of Michigan–Ann Arbor; June Howard, University of Michigan–Ann Arbor; Rita Kirshstein, American Institutes for Research; Charlotte Kuh, National Academy of Sciences; George Langford, Dartmouth College; Joan Lorden, University of Alabama–Birmingham; Ernest Middleton, Clark Atlanta University; Jeffrey Mirel, University of Michigan–Ann Arbor; Claudia Mitchell-Kernan, University of California–Los Angeles; Lester Monts, University of Michigan–Ann Arbor; Ann Mullen, U.S. Department of Education; Arie Nettles, University of Michigan–Ann Arbor; Dennis O'Connor, University of Maryland–College Park; Judith Ramaley, National Science Foundation; Paul Rasmussen, University of Michigan–Ann Arbor; Thomas Rochon, ETS; Homer Rose Jr., University of Michigan–Ann Arbor; Larry Rowley, University of Michigan–Ann Arbor; William Russel, Princeton University; Mark Schneider, Temple University; Lewis Siegel, Duke University; Catherine Snow, Harvard Graduate School of Education; Debra Stewart, CGS; Orlando Taylor, Howard University; Beatrice Terrien-Somerville, Columbia University; Elizabeth VanderPutten, NSF; John Vaughn, Association of American Universities; Harvey Waterman, Rutgers University–New Brunswick.

We have been very fortunate and are most appreciative for the high caliber of work and the fervent commitment of Kathy Devereux, our administrative assistant at the University of Michigan. Kathy assisted us in every aspect of this project from proposal to final draft. She has helped us communicate with all the staff and external participants and supporters of the research. Her knowledge of publication styles and rules and her attention to administrative details of all types from finances to publication requirements proved to be indispensable. We are also grateful to Kim Fryer and David Ohls at ETS. Kim and David took over where Kathy left off when we moved from Michigan to ETS. Kim Fryer assisted us with editing and presentation of data and figures, and David provided invaluable help in a variety of library and proofing tasks. We also appreciate the assistance of Amy Lallier, who provided the important support for our last push.

Many students contributed to this research in various different ways and also benefited from the opportunity to work on all aspects of the project. Typical of university- and ETS-based research, this project has been a continuous process of teaching and learning. The students include Doug Ready, Steven Culpepper, Su Bang Choe, Anne Feng, Phil DeCicca, Jean Waltman, Damon Williams, Lisa McRipley, Denise Williams, Gail Drakes, Sarah Welchans, Lindsay Holmes, Karen Thundiyil, Andrea Reinkemeyer, Heather Kent, Gina Kim, and Jennifer Beyer. They reviewed literature, analyzed data, prepared survey administrations, retrieved data and information about participating institutions from worldwide websites, and stuffed envelopes.

This research has involved, in addition to the University of Michigan, twenty-one universities, each one of which contributed the time of key officials, faculty, and students in activities ranging from conceptualizing design features to helping to administer surveys. They also helped to champion the study among their colleagues, who provided data and information about the institution and its students. To each of the following universities and representatives to the project we express the highest appreciation for collaboration:

—Sam Baldwin and Trevor Turner of Clark Atlanta University,

—Eduardo Macagno and Deborah McCoy of Columbia University,

—Frances Horowitz, Pamela Reid, and Charlotte Frick of the Graduate Center of the City University of New York,

—Margot Gill, Jerome Murphy, Marisel Perez, and Russell Berg of Harvard University,

—Orlando Taylor and Gwen Bethea of Howard University,

—George Walker, Donald Cunningham, and Juliet Frey of Indiana University,

—Juan Corradi, Catherine Stimpson, Ann Marcus, and Thomas James of New York University,

—Susan Huntington and Amy Edgar of Ohio State University,

—John Wilson and David Redman of Princeton University,

—Harvey Waterman, Richard Foley, and Ron Mallon of Rutgers University,

—Roni Holeton and William Weiler of Stanford University,

—Karen Zumwalt and William Baldwin of Teacher's College,

—Peter Goodwin and Elizabeth Bradley of Temple University,

—Jonetta Davis and William Destler of the University of Maryland–College Park,

—Virginia Hinshaw and Joanne Nagy of the University of Wisconsin,

—Teresa Sullivan and Richard Cherwitz of the University of Texas–Austin,

—Joseph Cerny and Judy Sui of the University of California–Berkeley,

—Claudia Mitchell-Kernan and Ellen Benkin of the University of California–Los Angeles,

—Linda Dykstra and Paul Ilecki of the University of North Carolina–Chapel Hill, and

—Russell Hamilton and Peter Reed of Vanderbilt University.

We express our great appreciation also to Carol Stimpson Stern of Northwestern University and Carolyn Thompson of the State University of New York–Buffalo, both of whom assisted us with the pilot testing of our survey instrument.

We have benefited also from the advice of two of the nation's leading education statisticians, one at the beginning and the other at the end of the process. Eugene Johnson was first involved when he was at ETS and later at the American Institutes for Research. He advised us on sampling, weighting, and types of statistical tests to employ. Shelby Haberman at ETS advised us on the critical elements to include in the analyses and the suitability of our models and methods.

Finally, we are very grateful to our families, whose loving support and free-flowing candid comments and opinions we relied on to keep us moving forward. First, we thank the Milletts, Catherine's parents Joan and John and siblings Margaret and Daniel. And we thank the Nettles, Michael's parents Harriette and Willie, siblings Evelyn and Francine, wife Arie, and three daughters Ana, Sabin, and Aidan. Each one has heard and read enough about the contents of this book that reading it in its published form will seem like déjà vu.

THREE MAGIC
LETTERS

CHAPTER ONE

A Map from the Past to the Present

AFTER NEARLY A CENTURY OF CONTROVERSY in political and academic arenas over the feasibility, value, and design of doctoral education, the first Ph.D. degree was established in the United States at Yale University in 1860. A year later, Yale awarded the first Ph.D. degree. It was sixteen years later, in 1876, that the Johns Hopkins University established the first graduate school. The history of doctoral education in the United States from those times onward has been written as fascinating narratives that trace the roots of the American doctorate to the German universities and the notion that a university should be "the workshop of free scientific research" (Brubacher and Rudy 1968, 175), an idea that originated in late-eighteenth-century universities in Halle and Göttingen and culminated in the founding of the Universities of Berlin, Breslau, Bonn, and Munich. In the late nineteenth century, Basil Lanneau Gildersleeve, a professor of Greek and one of the key figures in the development of graduate education at Johns Hopkins, recalled that as a youth he had fled to Germany to prepare himself for a professorship, "for to have prepared himself in the United States would have been impossible and to have argued for the necessity of professional preparation would have opened himself to ridicule and charges of absurdity" (Rudolph 1990, 334).

Historians have chronicled the lives of pioneering academicians of doctoral education at such places as Yale, Johns Hopkins, Michigan, Clark, Columbia, and Western Reserve and within such professional academic societies as the American Association for the Advancement of Education, the American Association for the Advancement of Science, and the American Philosophical Society (Storr 1953, 7, 70, 82). Initially modeled after the German Ph.D., the American doctorate was conceived as the degree awarded to an elite cadre of serious students for extended study as they prepared for careers as scholars and researchers. According to Anne Buchanan and Jean-Pierre Hérubel (1995, 2), the American doctorate, like the German Ph.D. and doctorates granted by universities in medieval Paris and Bologna, would be the qualifying degree that permitted scholars to become full participating members of the guild (Berelson 1960; Brubacher and Rudy 1968; Cordasco 1973; Storr 1953). This high status and challenge of pursuing the degree provoked William James to refer to it as "three magic letters" (James 1971, 341).

Two topics that are as important as the narrative history, although far more neglected, are the statistical history of doctoral education and the experiences and performance of present-day doctoral students. These are topics that tell us how far doctoral education has grown from its roots. Commonly sought vital statistics about doctoral education are aimed toward answering such questions as the following: What is the rate of doctoral education growth in the United States? How many people are pursuing and completing doctoral degrees? What is the demographic composition of the people pursuing and completing doctoral degrees? What types of universities are awarding doctoral degrees? What are doctoral students studying? What levels of success are doctoral students achieving? What careers do they pursue after earning doctoral degrees?

THE CURRENT LANDSCAPE

Now is a particularly interesting time for research on doctoral students. More than a dozen years have passed since the publication of William Bowen and Neil Rudenstine's (1992) careful examination of the doctoral education landscape and the people who pursue doctoral degrees. Because of the tremendous growth in the size and diversity of graduate programs and enrollments in the United States during the intervening years, there is no clear sense of the characteristics of the people who are pursuing doctoral degrees or the experiences of the expanded population of students. These issues vary in intensity for women, international students, Asian Americans, African Americans, Hispanics, and Native Americans. As in earlier stages of the education pipeline, underrepresented students in doctoral programs, especially African Americans and Hispanics, appear to be lagging behind whites and Asian Americans on major indicators of success (in this case, research publication and presentations, socialization within the fields, and timely progress toward the degree). The research about these groups of students and their doctoral experiences, however, has been sparse, probably because of difficulties researchers encounter in obtaining sufficiently large samples. One feature that makes our research distinctive is our ability to compare the experiences of doctoral students on a variety of demographic characteristics. The size of the respondent base allows these analyses by race, citizenship, and sex, finally doing justice to the evolving diversity.

A National Science Foundation (1996, 98) report, Indicators of Science and Mathematics Education, 1995, states that "more systematic research is needed on the quality of education received by students as well as research on ways to reduce student attrition." National data on degree achievement are generally available, but they lack key dimensions of students' educational, personal, and cultural backgrounds; financial support arrangements; student behaviors; and student attitudes and experiences related to their performance and development. Such bare-bones data cannot fill doctoral students' needs for information. At least one researcher (Lovitts 2001) has linked students' lack of information about their program requirements to the growing numbers of individuals who are "ABD" (all but dissertation) and to attrition rates. Here, we attempt to demystify the process by revealing the details of the lives behind the statistics, filling in the blank spaces with the factors that contribute to the quality of doctoral student development, achievements, and experiences.

Included among the contentious issues for the nation's diverse population of doctoral students are the following:

—the varying characteristics, preparation, and intellectual capacities of students

—the different outside-of-school lifestyles of students and the extent of overlap with their doctoral studies

—the various ways students experience their curriculum and training

—the variety of relationships between students and their faculty, advisers, and mentors

—the amount of time it takes for students to progress through their programs and complete their degrees

—the variety of types and amounts of funding students rely upon to support their doctoral education

—the variety of postdegree career plans, opportunities, and pursuits

—the variety of levels of student satisfaction with their doctoral educational experiences

BROADENING THE SAMPLE

In many areas we are indebted to researchers whose earlier work provides some clues to how a variety of measures interact for particular groups or within particular circumstances (Baird 1976, 1990b, 1993a; Berelson 1960; Bowen and Rudenstine 1992; Lovitts 2001; Nerad and Cerny 1993; Stein and Weidman 1989b, 1990; Weiler 1991, 1993). But to date no study exists that is both as comprehensive in its variables and as numerically strong in its sample base as ours. We undertook what turned out to be one of the largest surveys yet of American doctoral students. The result is a sample of 9,036 students drawn from twenty-one of the nation's major doctorate-granting institutions and representing eleven fields of study. To ensure broad applicability of our findings, we imposed strict demands on the designated sources, not resting until we had achieved a 70 percent return on the twenty-eight-page, eighty-eight-item survey instrument. The result is a database of unparalleled currency, presenting observations of students while they are actively involved in the doctoral process. The survey design also provided a sufficient number of students of all major racial backgrounds and allows analyses of our dependent variables in terms of race-ethnicity, citizenship, and sex.

Our intention was to explain how individual, institution, field, faculty, and financial characteristics helped students progress through and achieve during their doctoral program. We accomplished this in two stages: First, we compiled descriptive statistics from the responses and organized them by field of study. Second, we undertook relational analyses to explore the connections among our many variables. In this book, consistent with our initial goal of extending our knowledge of the Ph.D. process in terms of its possibilities, we attempt to interpret our findings, being sensitive to the silences and gaps in the narrative that may also be full of meaning.

AN ONGOING CONCERN

Sorting out the realities of the doctoral process has been a challenge for researchers as far back as Bernard Berelson and his 1960 landmark study, *Graduate Education in the United States*. Berelson (1960, 1) observes the following about graduate education: "Since the establishment of graduate work at Johns Hopkins in 1876, the graduate school has lived through a number of phases in responding to a variety of educational and social pressures; it has become the major home of research and scholarship, and the training therefore; it has incorporated both foreign and domestic features in its organization and programs; it has affected and been affected by the undergraduate program; it has moved and sometimes been torn between scholarly and professional emphases; it has grown from a few disciplines in a few institutions to many in many; and it has always exercised its own influence at a pivotal point in the system of higher education."

Berelson projected that graduate education would also face a "controversial future." Among the factors he foresaw as providing fuel for controversy was the increase in the number of students. Even with his thorough knowledge of the past and what turned out to be a perceptive general outlook of the future, Berelson could not have imagined the extent of growth in size, diversity, and complexity of graduate education that would occur over the ensuing four decades.

Nevertheless, graduate education has attracted less public attention than many other educational issues. The challenge of attracting public interest is what led Bruce Smith (1985) of the Brookings Institution (with the support of the National Science Foundation) to convene a special conference on graduate education. In his report on that conference, Smith (1985, 1) observes that the most far-reaching changes in education were appearing at the graduate level: "Changes in student demographic trends, in the life-styles of faculty, in the rapid advance of knowledge and the proliferation of new fields, in the capital intensity of the research effort, in the transformation wrought by new information technologies, in the traditional career expectations of advanced students, and in other areas."

This book addresses the topics that may command the public's attention. Certainly, the nation's nearly nine hundred thousand college and university faculty and 13 million undergraduates have a vested interest in looking beyond the growth trends and changing demographics to issues like socialization, expected and actual styles of performance and productivity, doctoral program duration, financing of the degree, and the relationship between finances and the quality of doctoral student experiences. Our findings offer new insights into the influences and limitations of the Ph.D. experience, as well as new questions for future exploration.

THE BOOK'S STRUCTURE

The first section of the book develops the context and specifics of the study. Chapter 2 begins the presentation of context of U.S. doctoral education in the form of both a statistical history and an introduction to the conceptual model we followed in conducting the research that constitutes the heart of the book. Chapter 2 presents much of the available data on long-term trends, showing the numerical increase in doctorate-awarding institutions, graduate enrollment, and degrees awarded. The relationship of growth in graduate institutions and enrollment to the numbers of doctorates attained is also addressed in chapter 2. The data are presented, wherever possible, by field of study, race-ethnicity, citizenship, and sex. We examine the choices of postdoctorate employment made by doctoral degree recipients, and we present our conceptual framework for the research that is the main focus of the book. We make the case that the vast growth and diversification of doctoral education in the United States make this a prime time to take stock of the student experiences and outcomes of doctoral education.

In chapter 3, on the logistics of the research, we explain how we developed an entirely fresh database, and we elaborate on the conceptual model presented in chapter 2 by describing and providing rationale for each of the various data elements. Also in chapter 3 we introduce the survey instrument that we developed to collect the data. We illustrate how our need to know shaped the choice and development of our variables. Even the strongest social science research has limitations, and at the end of chapter 3 we describe what we view as the limitations of our research.

Succeeding chapters focus specifically on the seldom-chronicled experiences and performance of students as they progress through their doctoral programs. We address such frequently raised questions as the following: What are the demographic characteristics beyond race-ethnicity, sex, and field of study of today's doctoral students (chapter 4)? What are the academic and financial assets and liabilities of students upon entering doctoral programs (chapter 5)? How do doctoral students finance their education (chapter 6)? How do students interact with peers, faculty, and mentors (chapter 7)? What is the scholarly productivity of students during their doctoral programs (chapter 8)? How do students assess themselves in terms of their performance, satisfaction, and progress (chapter 9)? What are the rates of progress, degree completion, and time to degree of doctoral students (chapter 10)?

In chapter 11 we use the same structure to discuss the relational analyses: demographics, preparation and screening, financing, socialization, research productivity, rate of progress, satisfaction, and degree completion. In chapter 12 we begin our interpretation of the findings by examining such general issues as financing and mentoring and their implications for doctoral study. In chapter 13 we continue our interpretations and discussions of implications, focusing on specific groups defined by race-ethnicity, sex, and personal background characteristics. We conclude in chapter 14 by summarizing our new knowledge and understandings, raising questions to be addressed in the future, and offering ideas for improvements in doctoral education.

CHAPTER TWO

Context, Trends, and Conceptual Framework for Research

FOR THE FIRST HALF CENTURY after the American doctorate was founded, both the number and the types of higher education institutions offering doctoral degrees grew steadily. The growth accelerated dramatically toward the end of each of the two subsequent half centuries, especially during the latter half of the twentieth century. By 1924, just sixty-three years after the first U.S. doctorate had been awarded, 61 universities awarded doctoral degrees, and by 1964—just after the centennial anniversary of the American doctoral degree—that number had risen to 208 (see table 2.1). By the year 2000, 528 universities—around one-third of the nonspecialized four-year colleges and universities in the United States—were awarding doctoral degrees.[1] Accompanying the growth in number of institutions has been the variation in the number of degrees awarded. From 1977 to 2000, the number of degrees awarded per institution ranged from fewer than eleven to more than one hundred (see table 2.2). In 2000 half of the doctorate-granting institutions awarded no more than thirty degrees; the proportion of institutions in that range has been stable over the past three decades. Yet in the same year, the 133 institutions that granted more than one hundred degrees awarded 77.9 percent of all U.S. doctoral degrees awarded (see table 2.3).

The sixty most prestigious and arguably most important universities in the United States awarding the highest-quality doctoral degrees constitute the membership of the Association of American Universities (AAU). In 2000 roughly half of all U.S. doctoral degrees awarded, and an even larger percentage in the science fields that are attracting the largest share of international students, were granted by AAU institutions. In that year AAU member institutions awarded most of the nation's doctoral degrees in arts and music (66.4%), humanities (65.3%), communication and librarianship (63.4%), social sciences (63.1%), engineering (62.4%), mathematics and computer science (61.7%), physical sciences and geosciences (60.4%), social service professions (55.2%), and life sciences (53.5%) (see table 2.4). At the same time, they awarded less than half of the nation's doctoral degrees in several fields: business and management (42.3%), ed-

1. In 2000–2001 the number of Title IV postsecondary institutions with doctoral degree–granting status was 654 (Knapp et al. 2002).

Table 2.1
Higher Education Institutions Awarding Doctorate Degrees in the United States, 1920–2000

Year	No. of Universities Awarding Doctoral Degrees
1920–24	61
1930–34	87
1940–44	107
1950–54	142
1960–64	208
1970–74	307
1977	371
1981	402
1991	468
2000	528

Sources: Data before 1977 from Harmon 1978; data for 1977 to 2000 from HEGIS (1977, 1981) and IPEDS (1991, 2000) completion surveys.

Table 2.2
Universities Awarding Doctorate Degrees in the United States, 1977–2000,
by the Number of Degrees Awarded per Institution

No. of Degrees Awarded per Institution	No. of Universities			
	1977	1981	1991	2000
<11	120	145	143	155
11–20	45	41	70	73
21–30	19	28	34	43
31–50	42	36	44	54
51–100	43	50	59	70
>100	102	102	118	133
Total	371	402	468	528

Sources: Data from HEGIS (1977, 1981) and IPEDS (1991, 2000) completion surveys.

Table 2.3
Doctoral Degrees Awarded by Higher Education Institutions, by Level of Doctoral Degree Production, 2000

No. of Doctoral Degrees Awarded	No. of Universities	No. of Degrees	% of Total Degrees
1–10	155	722	1.6
11–20	73	1,080	2.4
21–30	43	1,087	2.4
31–50	54	2,087	4.7
51–100	70	4,920	11.0
>100	133	34,922	77.9
Total	528	44,818	

Source: Data from IPEDS (2000) completion survey.

ucation (30.6%), psychology (21.4%), and religion and theology (8.6%)—fields that require less financial investment in scientific and technological equipment, have higher community service and practice demands for faculty, and require less complex research infrastructure to operate. These relatively low cost elements make it possible for non-AAU universities to carry out doctoral education and often with comparatively simple infrastructure.

Table 2.4
Doctoral Degrees Awarded by Association of American Universities Institutions, by Major Field, 2000

Field	Total Doctorates	No. of Doctoral Degrees Awarded by AAU	AAU Degrees as % of Total Degrees
Arts and music	1,136	754	66.4
Humanities	3,668	2,397	65.3
Communication and librarianship	415	263	63.4
Social sciences	3,983	2,514	63.1
Engineering	5,384	3,357	62.4
Mathematics and computer science	1,856	1,145	61.7
Physical sciences and geosciences	4,023	2,429	60.4
Social service professions	270	149	55.2
Life sciences	8,427	4,506	53.5
Other[a]	1,297	588	45.3
Business and management	1,245	527	42.3
Education	7,171	2,191	30.6
Psychology	4,163	891	21.4
Religion and theology	1,780	153	8.6
All disciplines	29,162	17,514	60.1

Source: Data from IPEDS (2000) completion survey.
[a]"Other" includes science and engineering technologies, interdisciplinary or other sciences, architecture and environmental design, law, vocational studies, and home economics.

Table 2.5
Historical Trend in Bachelor's, Master's, and Doctoral Degrees Awarded by U.S. Universities

Year	Total	Bachelor's Degrees		Master's Degrees		Doctoral Degrees	
		Number[a]	% of Total Degrees	Number	% of Total Degrees	Number	% of Total Degrees
1869–70	9,372	9,371	100.0	—	0.0	1	0.0
1879–80	13,829	12,896	93.3	879	6.4	54	0.4
1889–90	16,793	15,539	92.5	1,105	6.6	149	0.9
1899–1900	29,375	27,410	93.3	1,583	5.4	382	1.3
1909–10	39,755	37,199	93.6	2,113	5.3	443	1.1
1919–20	53,516	48,622	90.9	4,279	8.0	615	1.1
1929–30	139,752	122,484	87.6	14,969	10.7	2,299	1.6
1939–40	216,521	186,500	86.1	26,731	12.3	3,290	1.5
1949–50	496,661	432,058	87.0	58,183	11.7	6,420	1.3
1959–60	476,704	392,440	82.3	74,435	15.6	9,829	2.1
1969–70	1,030,473	792,316	76.9	208,291	20.2	29,866	2.9
1979–80	1,260,113	929,417	73.8	298,081	23.7	32,615	2.6
1989–90	1,414,016	1,051,344	74.4	324,301	22.9	38,371	2.7
1999–2000	1,739,739	1,237,875	71.2	457,056	26.3	44,808	2.6

Source: Data from NCES (2002).
Note: The data present numbers of degrees awarded in a single year for the last year of the decade.
[a]First professional degrees are included with bachelor's degrees until 1960.

RELATIVE GROWTH
IN DOCTORAL DEGREE PRODUCTION

Doctoral education saw steady growth from 1870 to 2000, similar to trends for bachelor's and master's degrees. At the end of the first decade of the twentieth century, fewer than four hundred doctoral degrees were granted, representing 1.3 percent of all degrees awarded (see table 2.5); bachelor's degrees accounted for 93.3 percent of the total, and master's degrees, 5.4 percent. Even then, leaders of American higher education were concerned about the proliferation of doctoral degrees. William James (1971), in *The*

Ph.D. Octopus, expressed concern—shared by many scholars of his time—over the growing requirement by colleges and universities that every one on their faculty possess the doctorate. James primarily feared the consequential broadening (that is, lowering) of talent that would enter Ph.D. programs, something he saw as a dangerous precedent for higher education.

The fears of some distinguished scholars notwithstanding, the doctoral degree has grown steadily. Of all the bachelor's, master's, and doctoral degrees awarded in 2000, doctoral degrees made up 2.6 percent (table 2.5). In 2000 more than 1.2 million bachelor's, 457,000 master's, and almost 45,000 doctoral degrees were awarded. In a more recent forty-year period, the proportion of master's degrees awarded increased dramatically, from 15.6 percent of all degrees in 1960 to 26.3 percent in 2000. Allan Cartter (1976, 76) attributes the growth in doctoral programs, in part, to "the post-Sputnik expansion of graduate education, triggered by exciting developments on the scientific front and strongly assisted by rapidly expanding federal programs of student support, [which] encouraged growth in doctoral programs." Other factors include the relative shortage (until about 1968) of Ph.D.s in sufficient numbers to meet expanding teaching and research needs and the incentive provided by Selective Service policy that, until the summer of 1969, granted draft deferments to students attending graduate school (Cartter 1976). Contrary to predictions of decline (Veysey 1978), the upward trend of graduate education has been steady.

DOCTORATE REPRESENTATION
AMONG THE ADULT U.S. POPULATION

Despite increased access to graduate education, only a small portion of Americans have attained a doctoral degree. According to the Census Bureau's (2002) *Current Population Reports,* in 2000 a mere 1 percent of the nation's adult population—approximately 1.5 percent of the men and 0.6 percent of the women eighteen years and older—had earned a doctoral degree (see table 2.6). The proportion varies by race group, with only 0.3 percent of African Americans, 0.4 percent of Hispanics, 1.1 percent of whites, and 2.6 percent of Asian–Pacific Islanders having earned doctoral degrees. A smaller share of white women (0.6%) than of white men (1.7%), and a smaller share of Asian–Pacific Islander women (1.4%) than of Asian–Pacific Islander men (3.9%), has achieved a doctoral degree. The comparable sex distribution for African American and Hispanic doctorates in the adult U.S. population is about even.

In 2000 women represented 52.0 percent of the adult population in the United States but only 29.5 percent of the earned doctoral degree population. A similar imbalance is observed by race-ethnicity. Some groups are overrepresented among doctoral recipients, and others are underrepresented. For example, whites accounted for 81.6 percent of the earned doc-

Table 2.6
Doctoral Degree Recipients among the U.S. Population Eighteen Years and Older, by Race-Ethnicity and Sex, 2000

Race-Ethnicity and Sex	Total U.S. Population Eighteen Years and Older			Total U.S. Population Eighteen Years and Older with Doctoral Degree			
	N (in thousands)	% within Race Group	% Overall and within Sex	*N* (in thousands)	% of Total Doctoral Degree Recipients	% within Race Group	% Overall and within Sex
Overall							
Total	201,762		100.0	2,032	100.0		1.0
Male	96,901		48.0	1,433	70.5		1.5
Female	104,861		52.0	599	29.5		0.6
African American							
Total	23,308	100.0	11.6	72	3.5	100.0	0.3
Male	10,400	44.6	10.7	37	1.8	51.4	0.4
Female	12,908	55.4	12.3	35	1.7	48.6	0.3
Asian–Pacific Islander							
Total	7,859	100.0	3.9	207	10.2	100.0	2.6
Male	3,753	47.8	3.9	148	7.3	71.5	3.9
Female	4,106	52.2	3.9	59	2.9	28.5	1.4
Hispanic							
Total	21,109	100.0	10.5	84	4.1	100.0	0.4
Male	10,443	49.5	10.8	51	2.5	60.7	0.5
Female	10,665	50.5	10.2	33	1.6	39.3	0.3
White							
Total	148,091	100.0	73.4	1,659	81.6	100.0	1.1
Male	71,674	48.4	74.0	1,195	58.8	72.0	1.7
Female	76,417	51.6	72.9	464	22.8	28.0	0.6

Source: Data from U.S. Census Bureau (2000).
Note: Totals in each race category account for 2,022 of the total 2,032 doctoral degree recipients.

torates in the United States that year, compared with their 73.4 percent representation in the population; Asian–Pacific Islanders, 3.9 percent of the total U.S. population, had 10.2 percent of all doctoral degrees; and Hispanics, 4.1 percent of the population, 10.5 percent of doctorates; whereas African Americans, representing 11.6 percent of the population, held a mere 3.5 percent of doctoral degrees (see table 2.6).

DOCTORAL GROWTH BY DEMOGRAPHICS

Many experts such as Cartter (1976) and Laurence Veysey (1978) failed to anticipate the broadening of doctoral education by race-ethnicity and sex that occurred in the 1970s. Women and minorities, despite their continuing underrepresentation, have been key factors in the overall growth in doctoral enrollment and degree recipients. More recent forecasters accounted for the growing interest and participation of women and, to a lesser extent, African Americans but gave little consideration to the role that Asian Americans, Hispanics, and Native Americans would play. This is understandable, given that much of the U.S. population growth during the past two decades was propelled by the recent immigration of East Asians and Mexicans. As for the projections of increased participation by women, underestimates owed in part to generational differences in the behavior of women of childbearing age. Over the 1980s and 1990s, having children became less of an impediment to career development and to graduate school attendance. Similarly, there was little historical precedent for the increase in international students that occurred during the latter years of the twentieth century.

Sex Gains

In the century and a quarter since Helen McGill White became the first woman Ph.D. recipient in the United States (at Boston University in 1877), women have made tremendous gains in representation among earned doctorates, with most of the increase occurring during the past thirty-five years (see table 2.7). From 1960 to 1970, the number of women doctoral degree recipients quadrupled, while the number of men tripled. From 1980 to 2000, the enrollment of women in U.S. graduate education increased by 60.0 percent, compared with 15.5 percent for men (see table 2.8). Similarly, 93.0 percent more women received doctoral degrees in 2000 than in 1981, compared with a mere 10.1 percent increase among men (see table 2.9). Even though in 2000, women accounted for most bachelor's degrees awarded (57.1%) and graduate enrollments (57.9%), they continued to be underrepresented among doctoral degree recipients (44.2%). Nevertheless, the overall gains made by women were remarkable, given that at the beginning of the twentieth century they represented only around 10 percent of the nation's doctoral degree recipients annually.

Race-Ethnicity Gains

Although African Americans figured among the earliest recipients of doctoral degrees—Edward Bouchet, the first African American recipient of a doctorate at Yale in 1874, and W. E. B. DuBois, the first at Harvard in 1885—their numbers represented a tiny fraction of the available talent in the African American population who were eligible by virtue of having earned a bachelor's degree. The U.S. Department of Education first gathered race data in 1976, in the Higher Education General Information Survey (now called Integrated Postsecondary Education Data Systems); therefore, we are able to present trend data by race only beginning with 1976.

In 1976 the National Board of Graduate Education appointed a special advisory group, which comprised prominent graduate education leaders of the time, to examine the status of underrepresented minorities in graduate school. The group's report characterized the underrepresentation of minorities enrolling in graduate school and receiving doctoral degrees as "striking" (National Board on Graduate Education 1976, 3). The report revealed that while African Americans and Hispanics represented more than 16 percent of the nation's population, together they accounted for only 6 to 7 percent of the graduate school enrollment and around 5 percent of the doctoral degrees awarded each year. Regarding the need to increase minority representation, the board stated the following:

Table 2.7
Historical Trend Analyses of Doctoral Degrees Awarded to Men and Women by U.S. Universities, 1869–2000

Year	Total	Men	% of Total Degrees	Women	% of Total Degrees
1869–70	1	1	100.0	0	0.0
1879–80	54	51	94.4	3	5.6
1889–90	149	147	98.7	2	1.3
1899–1900	382	359	94.0	23	6.0
1909–10	443	399	90.1	44	9.9
1919–20	615	522	84.9	93	15.1
1929–30	2,299	1,946	84.6	353	15.4
1939–40	3,290	2,861	87.0	429	13.0
1949–50	6,420	5,804	90.4	616	9.6
1959–60	9,829	8,801	89.5	1,028	10.5
1969–70	29,866	25,890	86.7	3,976	13.3
1979–80	32,615	22,943	70.3	9,672	29.7
1989–90	38,371	24,401	63.6	13,970	36.4
1999–2000	44,808	25,028	55.9	19,780	44.1

Source: Data from NCES (2002).

Table 2.8
Opening Fall Graduate Enrollment by Sex and Race-Ethnicity, 1980, 1991, and 2000

Race-Ethnicity and Sex	1980 No.	1980 %	1991 No.	1991 %	2000 No.	2000 %	% Change 1980 to 2000	Proportional Representation of Change
All races								
Total	1,344,073		1,638,900		1,850,271		37.7	
Female	669,220	49.8	878,021	53.6	1,070,655	57.9	60.0	79.3
Male	674,853	50.2	760,879	46.4	779,616	42.1	15.5	20.7
Black								
Total	75,086	5.6	88,876	5.4	146,147	7.9	94.6	14.0
Female	46,927	62.5	57,924	65.2	101,561	69.5	116.4	
Male	28,159	37.5	30,952	34.8	44,586	30.5	58.3	
American Indian–Alaskan Native								
Total	5,198	0.4	6,636	0.4	9,529	0.5	83.3	0.9
Female	2,723	52.4	3,892	58.6	6,044	63.4	122.0	
Male	2,475	47.6	2,744	41.4	3,485	36.6	40.8	
Asian								
Total	31,611	2.4	57,637	3.5	85,032	4.6	169.0	10.6
Female	12,974	41.0	25,880	44.9	44,995	52.9	246.8	
Male	18,637	59.0	31,757	55.1	40,037	47.1	114.8	
Hispanic								
Total	32,108	2.4	50,811	3.1	86,140	4.7	168.3	10.7
Female	16,370	51.0	28,474	56.0	53,568	62.2	227.2	
Male	15,738	49.0	22,337	44.0	32,572	37.8	107.0	
White								
Total	1,104,696	82.2	1,257,947	76.8	1,141,574	61.7	3.3	7.3
Female	566,174	51.3	707,285	56.2	689,147	60.4	21.7	
Male	538,522	48.7	550,662	43.8	452,427	39.6	−16.0	
Temporary residents								
Total	92,177	6.9	176,993	10.8	232,247	12.6	152.0	27.7
Female	23,503	25.5	54,566	30.8	90,282	38.9	284.1	
Male	68,674	74.5	122,427	69.2	141,965	61.1	106.7	
Unknown race								
Total	3,197	0.2		0.0	149,602	8.1	4579.4	28.9
Female	549	17.2			85,058	56.9	15393.3	
Male	2,648	82.8			64,544	43.1	2337.5	

Sources: Data from HEGIS (1980) and IPEDS (1991, 2000) enrollment surveys.

Table 2.9
Doctoral Degrees Awarded, by Field of Study and Sex, 1981, 1991, and 2000

Academic Discipline and Sex	1981 No.	1981 %	1991 No.	1991 %	2000 No.	2000 %	Percent Change 1981 to 2000
All disciplines							
Total	32,982		39,350		44,818		35.9
Female	10,261	31.1	14,575	37.0	19,806	44.2	93.0
Male	22,721	68.9	24,775	63.0	25,012	55.8	10.1
Engineering							
Total	2,561	7.8	5,262	13.4	5,384	12.0	110.2
Female	104	4.1	484	9.2	835	15.5	702.9
Male	2,457	95.9	4,778	90.8	4,549	84.5	85.1
Physical science and geosciences							
Total	3,145	9.5	4,289	10.9	4,023	9.0	27.9
Female	378	12.0	843	19.7	1,026	25.5	171.4
Male	2,767	88.0	3,446	80.3	2,997	74.5	8.3
Mathematics and computer science							
Total	980	3.0	1,654	4.2	1,856	4.1	89.4
Female	139	14.2	280	16.9	405	21.8	191.4
Male	841	85.8	1,374	83.1	1,451	78.2	72.5
Life sciences							
Total	5,633	17.1	6,687	17.0	8,427	18.8	49.6
Female	1,548	27.5	2,625	39.3	4,037	47.9	160.8
Male	4,085	72.5	4,062	60.7	4,390	52.1	7.5
Psychology							
Total	2,964	9.0	3,450	8.8	4,163	9.3	40.5
Female	1,280	43.2	2,113	61.2	2,804	67.4	119.1
Male	1,684	56.8	1,337	38.8	1,359	32.6	−19.3
Social sciences							
Total	3,276	9.9	3,179	8.1	3,983	8.9	21.6
Female	904	27.6	1,129	35.5	1,710	42.9	89.2
Male	2,372	72.4	2,050	64.5	2,273	57.1	−4.2
Humanities							
Total	2,383	7.2	2,405	6.1	3,668	8.2	53.9
Female	1,098	46.1	1,197	49.8	1,855	50.6	68.9
Male	1,285	53.9	1,208	50.2	1,813	49.4	41.1
Religion and theology							
Total	1,276	3.9	1,075	2.7	1,780	4.0	39.5
Female	101	4.2	138	5.7	417	11.4	312.9
Male	1,175	49.3	937	39.0	1,363	37.2	16.0
Arts and music							
Total	654	2.0	836	2.1	1,136	2.5	73.7
Female	258	39.4	370	44.3	594	52.3	130.2
Male	396	60.6	466	55.7	542	47.7	36.9
Education							
Total	7,900	24.0	6,706	17.0	7,171	16.0	−9.2
Female	3,736	47.3	3,900	58.2	4,611	64.3	23.4
Male	4,164	52.7	2,806	41.8	2,560	35.7	−38.5
Business and management							
Total	845	2.6	1,452	3.7	1,245	2.8	47.3
Female	125	14.8	366	25.2	384	30.8	207.2
Male	720	85.2	1,086	74.8	861	69.2	19.6
Communication and librarianship							
Total	253	0.8	315	0.8	415	0.9	64.0
Female	115	45.5	153	48.6	233	56.1	102.6
Male	138	54.5	162	51.4	182	43.9	31.9
Social service professions							
Total	433	1.3	430	1.1	270	0.6	−37.6
Female	173	40.0	240	55.8	192	71.1	11.0
Male	260	60.0	190	44.2	78	28.9	−70.0
Other							
Total	679	2.1	1,610	4.1	1,297	2.9	91.0
Female	302	44.5	737	45.8	703	54.2	132.8
Male	377	55.5	873	54.2	594	45.8	57.6

Sources: Data from HEGIS (1981) and IPEDS (1991, 2000) completion surveys.

Increased minority participation in graduate education is an important national goal to be realized for the social, economic, intellectual and cultural well-being of all persons. It is for the collective benefit of society that the representation of minority group persons among those earning advanced degrees be increased.

Individual equity is a fundamental concern. Distinctions that confer opportunity and status according to race, religion, sex, or national origin must be removed so that minority persons may be afforded a full opportunity to pursue graduate study according to individual motivation and intellectual potential. (National Board of Graduate Education 1976, 1–2)

In 1977, one year after the National Board of Graduate Education released its seminal report, the nation's universities awarded 33,244 doctoral degrees (see table 2.10). Only 3.8 percent of them (1,253) were awarded to African Americans, and another 1.6 percent (534) to Hispanics, for a combined 5.4 percent (1,787) to the two major American minority groups, which were also the most underrepresented among graduate enrollments. A little more than two decades later, 4.8 percent (2,140) of the doctoral degrees granted in 2000 were awarded to African Americans, and another 3.1 percent (1,384) to Hispanics, for a combined total of 7.9 percent (3,524).[2] The alarm bells sounded by the National Board of Graduate Education in 1976 continue to ring today, nearly three decades later.

The demographic profiles over the past two decades show extraordinary growth for women, international students, and Asian Americans. The most noteworthy growth has been among Hispanics, Asian Americans, and international students. The number of Hispanics receiving doctoral degrees increased by 188.9 percent from 1981 to 2000, the number of Asian Americans by 162.5 percent, and that of international students, 157.6 percent (see table 2.10). The increase in that period for African Americans was nearly 69.2 percent, and for Native Americans, 18.5 percent.

In terms of graduate enrollment and numbers of doctoral degrees awarded over the same period, the increase in the number of women of every race-ethnicity group exceeded the increases for men. The only declines in graduate enrollments and doctoral degrees awarded were a 16.0 percent decline in white men enrolled in graduate school, a 21.1 percent decline in white men among doctoral degree recipients, and a 42.1 percent decline in Native American male doctoral degree recipients (see tables 2.8 and 2.11).

The distribution of men and women among doctoral degree recipients

2. Analyses conducted through the National Science Foundation's WebCASPAR system arrived at 48,818 doctorates in 2000 compared with a figure of 48,808 provided by the *Digest of Education Statistics, 2001* counts (NCES 2002). The numbers from the National Center for Education Statistics are restricted to individuals in the fifty states plus the District of Columbia.

Table 2.10
Doctoral Degrees Awarded, by Race-Ethnicity, Selected Years, 1977–2000

Year	African American	Alaskan Native	Asian or Pacific Islander	Hispanic	White	Temporary Residents	Unknown Race	Total
1977								
No.	1,253	95	658	534	26,851	3,747	106	33,244
%	3.8	0.3	2.0	1.6	80.8	11.3	0.3	100
1981								
No.	1,265	130	877	479	25,908	4,204	119	32,982
%	3.8	0.4	2.7	1.5	78.6	12.7	0.4	100
1987								
No.	1,016	102	1,057	906	23,373	6,358	1,414	34,226
%	3.0	0.3	3.1	2.6	68.3	18.6	4.1	100
1991								
No.	1,210	104	1,452	800	24,902	9,824	1,058	39,350
%	3.1	0.3	3.7	2.0	63.3	25.0	2.7	100
2000								
No.	2,140	154	2,302	1,384	26,366	10,831	1,641	44,818
%	4.8	0.34	5.1	3.1	58.8	24.2	3.7	100
	Percent Change in the Number of Doctoral Degrees Awarded for Selected Periods							
1977–87	−18.9	7.4	60.6	69.7	−13.0	69.7	1234.0	3.0
1977–2000	70.8	62.1	249.8	159.2	−1.8	189.1	1448.1	34.8
1981–2000	69.2	18.5	162.5	188.9	1.8	157.6	1279.0	35.9
1987–2000	110.6	51.0	117.8	52.8	12.8	70.4	16.1	30.9
	Percent Change in Racial Composition of Doctoral Degrees Awarded for Selected Periods							
1977–87	−21.2	4.3	56.0	64.8	−15.5	64.8	1195.7	
1977–2000	26.7	20.2	159.5	92.2	−27.2	114.4	1048.3	
1981–2000	24.5	−12.8	93.2	112.6	−25.1	89.6	914.8	
1987–2000	60.9	15.3	66.3	16.7	−13.9	30.1	−11.4	

Sources: Data from HEGIS (1977, 1981) and IPEDS (1987, 1991, 2000) completion surveys.

varies by race. In 2000, the ratio of men to women, overall, was 55.8 to 44.2 (see table 2.11). Men were the majority for some groups, women for others. Men earned a larger share of doctorates among Asian Americans and Asian–Pacific Islanders (56.0 to 44.0), whites (51.8 to 48.2), and international students (70.7 to 29.3). African Americans and American Indians–Alaskan Natives were the groups in 2000 for which the majority of degree recipients were women (among African Americans, the ratio was 38.8 to 61.2, and among American Indians and Alaskan Natives, 35.7 to 64.3).

In 2000 international students represented just 12.6 percent of the graduate school enrollments but nearly 24.2 percent of doctoral degree recipients (see tables 2.8 and 2.10). This suggests that international students have been much more concentrated in doctoral programs than in the master's component of graduate education and that they may have a higher completion rate than other groups. International students accounted for 27.7 percent of the enrollment increase from 1980 to 2000 but 56.0 percent of the increase in the number of doctoral degrees awarded (see tables 2.8 and 2.11).

From 1980 to 2000, graduate enrollment in U.S. universities increased by 37.7 percent (see table 2.8). The growth in minority graduate enroll-

Table 2.11
Doctoral Degrees Awarded, by Sex, Race-Ethnicity, and Citizenship, 1981, 1991, and 2000

Race-Ethnicity and Sex	1981 No.	1981 %	1991 No.	1991 %	2000 No.	2000 %	% Change 1981 to 2000	Proportional Representation of Change
All races								
Total	32,982		39,350		44,818		35.9	
Female	10,261	31.1	14,575	37.0	19,806	44.2	93.0	80.6
Male	22,721	68.9	24,775	63.0	25,012	55.8	10.1	19.4
Black, non-Hispanic								
Total	1,265		1,210		2,140		69.2	7.4
Female	571	45.1	634	52.4	1,310	61.2	129.4	
Male	694	54.9	576	47.6	830	38.8	19.6	
American Indian– Alaskan Native								
Total	130		104		154		18.5	0.2
Female	35	26.9	46	44.2	99	64.3	182.9	
Male	95	73.1	58	55.8	55	35.7	−42.1	
Asian–Pacific Islander								
Total	877		1,452		2,302		162.5	12.0
Female	222	25.3	474	32.6	1,014	44.0	356.8	
Male	655	74.7	978	67.4	1,288	56.0	96.6	
Hispanic								
Total	479		800		1,384		188.9	7.6
Female	193	40.3	395	49.4	767	55.4	297.4	
Male	286	59.7	405	50.6	617	44.6	115.7	
White								
Total	25,908		24,902		26,366		1.8	3.9
Female	8,598	33.2	10,643	42.7	12,714	48.2	47.9	
Male	17,310	66.8	14,259	57.3	13,652	51.8	−21.1	
Temporary residents								
Total	4,204		9,824		10,831		157.6	56.0
Female	639	15.2	1,993	20.3	3,176	29.3	397.0	
Male	3,565	84.8	7,831	79.7	7,655	70.7	114.7	
Unknown race								
Total	119		1,058		1,641		1279.0	12.9
Female	3	2.5	390	36.9	726	44.2	24100.0	
Male	116	97.5	668	63.1	915	55.8	688.8	

Sources: Data from HEGIS (1981) and IPEDS (1991, 2000) completion surveys.

ment during the 1990s was mixed among the race-ethnicity groups.[3] Despite a 3.3 percent increase in the number of white students enrolled from 1980 to 2000, their representation declined from 82.2 percent to 61.7 percent in 2000. Each of the other race groups increased both in number and as a percentage of the total enrollment. Asian Americans, Hispanics, and international students experienced the most dramatic increases, followed by African Americans and American Indians.

Overall, the number of doctoral degree recipients increased by 34.8

---

3. Given the U.S. Department of Education's National Center for Educational Statistics present data collection methods, it is not possible to distinguish master's students from doctoral students.

percent from 1977 to 2000 (see table 2.10). The vast share of the growth in the number of doctoral degrees conferred annually over the 1980s and 1990s was concentrated in the international student population. Between the years 1976 and 2001, the number of doctorates awarded to international students grew approximately 189.1 percent, representing 11.3 percent of total doctorates in 1977 and 24.2 percent in 2000. Over the same period, whites' share of total doctoral degrees awarded declined from 80.8 percent in 1977 to 58.8 percent in 2000. During that time, African Americans' representation among doctoral degree recipients increased from 3.8 percent in 1977 to 4.8 percent in 2000, and the Hispanic and Asian American shares grew from 1.6 to 3.1 percent and from 2.0 to 5.1 percent, respectively.

On the surface, this appears to indicate enormous progress for Asian Americans and international students and comparatively little progress for African Americans and Hispanics. But it is progress, nonetheless. The percentage of total doctoral degrees awarded to African Americans (4.8%) and Hispanics (3.1%) in 2000 was not much different from that in 1977. However, the number of African Americans receiving doctorates annually (2,140) was 70.8 percent more in 2000 than it had been in 1977, and the increase for Hispanics over the same period was 159.2 percent. The number of whites receiving doctoral degrees in 2000 (26,366) was nearly 1.8 percent less than in 1977; and while they represented 80.8 percent of doctoral recipients in 1977, by 2000 that number had decreased to 58.8 percent.

Who completes doctoral degree programs? Doctoral student attrition is a vexing issue for higher education. Comparing enrollment and degree completion data, the 26,366 white doctoral degree recipients in 2000 represented around 2.3 percent of the white graduate enrollment (1,141,574), but the African American (2,140) and Hispanic (1,384) doctorates were each closer to 1.5 percent their total graduate enrollments (146,147 and 86,140, respectively). This is a crude yet best available indication that attrition from graduate school may be higher among African Americans and Hispanics. The rival explanation is that African American and Hispanic graduate students are relatively more concentrated in master's than in doctoral programs. Much of the challenge for the nation's graduate universities is to ensure that the numbers and representation at the finish line (receiving doctoral degrees) are as large as the numbers and representation at the starting line (receiving bachelor's degrees, taking the Graduate Record Examination [GRE], and entering doctoral programs).

In the twenty-five years since the National Board of Graduate Education report, the nation's graduate institutions have awarded nearly twenty-five thousand doctoral degrees to African Americans and more than fourteen thousand to Hispanics. These numbers resemble the number of African Americans (29,222) and Hispanics (16,498) who occupied full-time instructional faculty positions in the nation's colleges and universities in 1999. Although African Americans and Hispanics represent roughly 11 percent each of the U.S. adult population, they make up just 4.9 and 2.8 percent, respectively, of the nation's faculty (NCES 2002).

In summary, the overall changes in doctorate patterns by race, sex, and international participation from 1980 to 2000 can be attributed primarily to the 162.5 percent increase of Asian Americans, the 157.6 percent increase of international students, the 188.9 percent increase of Hispanics, and to a lesser extent the 69.2 percent increase of African Americans, as degree recipients. During the same period, the increase for whites was 1.8 percent (see table 2.10). These trends reveal that overall, and relative to their representation in the U.S. population, African Americans, Hispanics, and women represent a disproportionately small share of graduate enrollments and doctoral degrees awarded by U.S. universities. On the other hand, women experienced steady growth in receipt of doctorates from 1981 to 2000, outpacing men of their same race group. Though they still represent only around one-third of U.S. doctoral degree holders in the U.S. population, in 2002 women were, for the first time, awarded more doctoral degrees than men in a single year (Smallwood 2003). This suggests that the gender balance in doctoral degree recipients is improving. Hispanics also experienced rather dramatic growth, though eclipsed by international and Asian American students.

Trends by Field of Study

A defining characteristic of the doctoral experience and another important way to examine the trends in doctoral education is by major field of study. The fields that experienced the greatest growth in doctoral degrees awarded between 1980 and 2001 were engineering (110.2%), mathematics and computer science (89.4%), art and music (73.7%), communication and librarianship (64.0%), and humanities (53.9%) (see table 2.9). Comparatively, rather modest growth in doctoral degrees awarded in the fields of life sciences (49.6%), business and management (47.3%), psychology (40.5%), religion and theology (39.5%), physical sciences and geosciences (27.9%), and social sciences (21.6%). Education doctorates represented 24 percent of all doctoral degrees awarded in 1981, compared with 16 percent in 2000.

Between the years of 1980 and 2001, the most impressive growth for women occurred in the field of engineering, with 104 doctoral engineering degrees awarded to women in 1981, and 835 in 2000—a 702.9 percent increase (see table 2.9). Women represented only 15.5 percent of the doctoral recipients in engineering in 2000, however, and while this is a vast improvement over their 4.1 percent representation in 1981, it is far short of their 44.2 percent representation among doctoral degree recipients overall in 2000. Other fields in which women recipients showed exceptional growth include the physical sciences and geosciences, where the number of women increased by 171.4 percent, and mathematics and life sciences, in which women doctorates increased by 191.4 percent and 160.8 percent, respectively. In every broad major field, the number of women receiving doctoral degrees was larger in 2000 than in 1981; by contrast, the number of men receiving doctoral degrees declined by 70.0 percent in the social service professions, 38.5 percent in education, 19.3 percent in psychology, and 4.2 percent in the social sciences. In 2000 women received most of the doctoral degrees awarded in the social service professions (71.1%), psychology (67.4%), education (64.3%), communication and librarianship (56.1%), art and music (52.3%), and humanities (50.6%).

In addition to the increased number of African Americans and Hispanics receiving doctorates each year, another sign of their progress, albeit modest, is the change in the major field distribution. In 1981, for example, 1.9 percent of the African American doctoral degree recipients received their degrees in the field of engineering, 8.3 percent in the life sciences, and 9.2 percent in psychology (see table 2.12). By the year 2000, 4.3 percent of African American doctoral degree recipients received their degrees in engineering, 10.3 percent in the life sciences, and 10.0 percent in psychology. African Americans were best represented among degree recipients in religion and theology (11.0%), education (11.0%), and social service professions (10.0%), but even these shares appear to be changing and reaching a more balanced distribution. In 1981 48.5 percent of African American doctoral degree recipients received their degrees in the field of education, but by 2000, that share had declined to 36.8 percent. For adequate representation among total doctoral degree recipients to be achieved, the number of doctoral degrees awarded to African Americans needs to increase in every field, especially among research doctoral degrees in education.

In contrast to other race-ethnicity groups, the increasing number of doctoral degrees among Asian Americans has been evenly distributed across the fields. The growth in degree receipt among international students has been concentrated in engineering, mathematics, and the sciences. In 2000 international students constituted a relatively large share of the degree recipients in engineering, mathematics and computer science, and the physical and life sciences. For example, from 1981 to 2000, the number of international students increased among engineering doctoral degree recipients by 185.4 percent, from 37.3 to 50.7 percent of the doctoral degrees awarded.

Despite the rather large rate of increase in doctoral degrees awarded to Hispanics from 1981 to 2000, Hispanics made up a small share of doctoral degrees awarded in every field. In 2000 Hispanics were best represented in the field of psychology, where they received 6.4 percent of doctoral degrees awarded. Like African Americans and American Indians—Alaskan

Table 2.12
Doctoral Degrees Awarded, by Race-Ethnicity and Field of Study, 1981, 1991, 2000

Academic Discipline and Race-Ethnicity	1981 No.	Race represen-tation (%)	Within-Race Represen-tation of Total Degrees	1991 No.	Race Represen-tation (%)	Within-Race Represen-tation of Total Degrees	2000 No.	Race Represen-tation (%)	Within-Race Represen-tation of Total Degrees	% Change 1981 to 2000
All disciplines										
All races	32,982			39,350			44,818			35.9
Temporary resident	4,204	12.7		9,824	25.0		10,831	24.2		157.6
Black	1,265	3.8		1,210	3.1		2,140	4.8		69.2
American Indian– Alaskan Native	130	0.4		104	0.3		154	0.3		18.5
Asian	877	2.7		1,452	3.7		2,302	5.1		162.5
Hispanic	479	1.5		800	2.0		1,384	3.1		188.9
White	25,908	78.6		24,902	63.3		26,366	58.8		1.8
Unknown race	119	0.4		1,058	2.7		1,641	3.7		1,279.0
Engineering										
All races	2,561			5,262			5,384			110.2
Temporary resident	956	37.3	22.7	2,726	51.8	27.7	2,728	50.7	25.2	185.4
Black	24	0.9	1.9	45	0.9	3.7	91	1.7	4.3	279.2
American Indian– Alaskan Native	5	0.2	3.8	7	0.1	6.7	5	0.1	3.2	0.0
Asian	191	7.5	21.8	355	6.7	24.4	380	7.1	16.5	99.0
Hispanic	23	0.9	4.8	50	1.0	6.3	86	1.6	6.2	273.9
White	1,352	52.8	5.2	1,959	37.2	7.9	1,948	36.2	7.4	44.1
Unknown race	10	0.4	8.4	120	2.3	11.3	146	2.7	8.9	1,360.0
Physical sciences and geosciences										
All races	3,145			4,289			4,023			27.9
Temporary resident	530	16.9	12.6	1,431	33.4	14.6	1,466	36.4	13.5	176.6
Black	32	1.0	2.5	36	0.8	3.0	68	1.7	3.2	112.5
American Indian– Alaskan Native	4	0.1	3.1	9	0.2	8.7	14	0.3	9.1	250.0
Asian	106	3.4	12.1	171	4.0	11.8	201	5.0	8.7	89.6
Hispanic	27	0.9	5.6	73	1.7	9.1	76	1.9	5.5	181.5
White	2,445	77.7	9.4	2,480	57.8	10.0	2,016	50.1	7.6	−17.5
Unknown race	1	0.0	0.8	89	2.1	8.4	182	4.5	11.1	18,100.0
Math and computer science										
All races	980			1,654			1,856			89.4
Temporary resident	225	16.6	5.4	808	48.9	8.2	868	46.8	8.0	285.8
Black	10	0.7	0.8	14	0.8	1.2	27	1.5	1.3	170.0
American Indian– Alaskan Native	3	0.2	2.3	2	0.1	1.9	2	0.1	1.3	−33.3
Asian	45	3.3	5.1	75	4.5	5.2	127	6.8	5.5	182.2
Hispanic	6	0.4	1.3	19	1.1	2.4	25	1.3	1.8	316.7
White	691	51.1	2.7	705	42.6	2.8	745	40.1	2.8	7.8
Unknown race	0	0.0	0.0	31	1.9	2.9	62	3.3	3.8	n.a.
Life sciences										
All races	5,633			6,687			8,427			49.6
Temporary resident	720	12.8	17.1	1,689	25.3	17.2	2,183	25.9	20.2	203.2
Black	105	1.9	8.3	113	1.7	9.3	220	2.6	10.3	109.5
American Indian– Alaskan Native	16	0.3	12.3	9	0.1	8.7	18	0.2	11.7	12.5
Asian	194	3.4	22.1	289	4.3	19.9	652	7.7	28.3	236.1
Hispanic	68	1.2	14.2	97	1.5	12.1	218	2.6	15.8	220.6
White	4,530	80.4	17.5	4,317	64.6	17.3	4,870	57.8	18.5	7.5
Unknown race	0	0.0	0.0	173	2.6	16.4	266	3.2	16.2	n.a.

(*table continues*)

Table 2.12 (*continued*)

Academic Discipline and Race-Ethnicity	1981 No.	1981 Race represen- tation (%)	1981 Within- Race Represen- tation of Total Degrees	1991 No.	1991 Race Represen- tation (%)	1991 Within- Race Represen- tation of Total Degrees	2000 No.	2000 Race Represen- tation (%)	2000 Within- Race Represen- tation of Total Degrees	% Change 1981 to 2000
Psychology										
All races	2,964			3,450			4,163			40.5
Temporary resident	95	3.2	2.3	125	3.6	1.3	154	3.7	1.4	62.1
Black	116	3.9	9.2	128	3.7	10.6	214	5.1	10.0	84.5
American Indian– Alaskan Native	10	0.3	7.7	16	0.5	15.4	27	0.6	17.5	170.0
Asian	33	1.1	3.8	60	1.7	4.1	181	4.3	7.9	448.5
Hispanic	73	2.5	15.2	148	4.3	18.5	267	6.4	19.3	265.8
White	2,637	89.0	10.2	2,878	83.4	11.6	3,168	76.1	12.0	20.1
Unknown race	0	0.0	0.0	95	2.8	9.0	152	3.7	9.3	n.a.
Social sciences										
All races	3,276			3,179			3,983			21.6
Temporary resident	437	13.3	10.4	846	26.6	8.6	1,058	26.6	9.8	142.1
Black	106	3.2	8.4	115	3.6	9.5	200	5.0	9.3	88.7
American Indian– Alaskan Native	13	0.4	10.0	11	0.3	10.6	15	0.4	9.7	15.4
Asian	78	2.4	8.9	95	3.0	6.5	174	4.4	7.6	123.1
Hispanic	53	1.6	11.1	69	2.2	8.6	104	2.6	7.5	96.2
White	2,589	79.0	10.0	1,958	61.6	7.9	2,220	55.7	8.4	−14.3
Unknown race	0	0.0	0.0	85	2.7	8.0	212	5.3	12.9	n.a.
Humanities										
All races	2,383			2,405			3,668			53.9
Temporary resident	208	8.7	4.9	398	16.5	4.1	437	11.9	4.0	110.1
Black	65	2.7	5.1	53	2.2	4.4	127	3.5	5.9	95.4
American Indian– Alaskan Native	8	0.3	6.2	3	0.1	2.9	13	0.4	8.4	62.5
Asian	27	1.1	3.1	57	2.4	3.9	116	3.2	5.0	329.6
Hispanic	56	2.3	11.7	88	3.7	11.0	167	4.6	12.1	198.2
White	2,019	84.7	7.8	1,720	71.5	6.9	2,611	71.2	9.9	29.3
Unknown race	0	0.0	0.0	86	3.6	8.1	197	5.4	12.0	n.a.
Religion and theology										
All races	1,276			1,075			1,780			39.5
Temporary resident	90	7.1	2.1	116	10.8	1.2	265	14.9	2.4	194.4
Black	45	3.5	3.6	66	6.1	5.5	196	11.0	9.2	335.6
American Indian– Alaskan Native	1	0.1	0.8	1	0.1	1.0	1	0.1	0.6	0.0
Asian	33	2.6	3.8	45	4.2	3.1	92	5.2	4.0	178.8
Hispanic	7	0.5	1.5	21	2.0	2.6	29	1.6	2.1	314.3
White	993	77.8	3.8	812	75.5	3.3	1,148	64.5	4.4	15.6
Unknown race	107	8.4	89.9	14	1.3	1.3	49	2.8	3.0	−54.2
Art and music										
All races	654			836			1,136			73.7
Temporary resident	37	5.7	0.9	102	12.2	1.0	224	19.7	2.1	505.4
Black	17	2.6	1.3	14	1.7	1.2	30	2.6	1.4	76.5
American Indian– Alaskan Native	2	0.3	1.5	2	0.2	1.9	1	0.1	0.6	−50.0
Asian	7	1.1	0.8	26	3.1	1.8	49	4.3	2.1	600.0
Hispanic	4	0.6	0.8	8	1.0	1.0	21	1.8	1.5	425.0
White	587	89.8	2.3	666	79.7	2.7	756	66.5	2.9	28.8
Unknown race	0	0.0	0.0	18	2.2	1.7	55	4.8	3.4	n.a.

22

Table 2.12 (*continued*)

Academic Discipline and Race-Ethnicity	1981 No.	Race represen- tation (%)	Within- Race Represen- tation of Total Degrees	1991 No.	Race Represen- tation (%)	Within- Race Represen- tation of Total Degrees	2000 No.	Race Represen- tation (%)	Within- Race Represen- tation of Total Degrees	% Change 1981 to 2000
Education										
All races	7,900			6,706			7,171			−9.2
Temporary resident	593	7.5	14.1	577	8.6	5.9	634	8.8	5.9	6.9
Black	614	7.8	48.5	463	6.9	38.3	787	11.0	36.8	28.2
American Indian– Alaskan Native	57	0.7	43.8	36	0.5	34.6	45	0.6	29.2	−21.1
Asian	105	1.3	12.0	127	1.9	8.7	185	2.6	8.0	76.2
Hispanic	140	1.8	29.2	164	2.4	20.5	322	4.5	23.3	130.0
White	6,391	80.9	24.7	5,136	76.6	20.6	4,981	69.5	18.9	−22.1
Unknown race	0	0.0	0.0	203	3.0	19.2	217	3.0	13.2	n.a.
Business and management										
All races	845			1,452			1,245			47.3
Temporary resident	161	19.1	3.8	519	35.7	5.3	410	32.9	3.8	154.7
Black	32	3.8	2.5	28	1.9	2.3	56	4.5	2.6	75.0
American Indian– Alaskan Native	5	0.6	3.8	2	0.1	1.9	5	0.4	3.2	0.0
Asian	25	3.0	2.9	57	3.9	3.9	61	4.9	2.6	144.0
Hispanic	2	0.2	0.4	9	0.6	1.1	18	1.4	1.3	800.0
White	619	73.3	2.4	785	54.1	3.2	655	52.6	2.5	5.8
Unknown race	1	0.1	0.8	52	3.6	4.9	40	3.2	2.4	3,900.0
Communication and librarianship										
All races	253			315			415			64.0
Temporary resident	29	11.5	0.7	60	19.0	0.6	96	23.1	0.9	231.0
Black	19	7.5	1.5	27	8.6	2.2	25	6.0	1.2	31.6
American Indian– Alaskan Native	1	0.4	0.8	0	0.0	0.0	2	0.5	1.3	100.0
Asian	5	2.0	0.6	9	2.9	0.6	5	1.2	0.2	0.0
Hispanic	1	0.4	0.2	2	0.6	0.3	11	2.7	0.8	1,000.0
White	198	78.3	0.8	209	66.3	0.8	269	64.8	1.0	35.9
Unknown race	0	0.0	0.0	8	2.5	0.8	7	1.7	0.4	n.a.
Social service professions										
All races	433			430			270			−37.6
Temporary resident	28	6.5	0.7	63	14.7	0.6	26	9.6	0.2	−7.1
Black	52	12.0	4.1	35	8.1	2.9	27	10.0	1.3	−48.1
American Indian– Alaskan Native	2	0.5	1.5	2	0.5	1.9	0	0.0	0.0	−100.0
Asian	11	2.5	1.3	10	2.3	0.7	12	4.4	0.5	9.1
Hispanic	10	2.3	2.1	13	3.0	1.6	11	4.1	0.8	10.0
White	330	76.2	1.3	302	70.2	1.2	186	68.9	0.7	−43.6
Unknown race	0	0.0	0.0	5	1.2	0.5	8	3.0	0.5	n.a.
Other										
All races	679			1,610			1,297			91.0
Temporary resident	95	14.0	2.3	364	22.6	3.7	282	21.7	2.6	196.8
Black	28	4.1	2.2	73	4.5	6.0	72	5.6	3.4	157.1
American Indian– Alaskan Native	3	0.4	2.3	4	0.2	3.8	6	0.5	3.9	100.0
Asian	17	2.5	1.9	76	4.7	5.2	67	5.2	2.9	294.1
Hispanic	9	1.3	1.9	39	2.4	4.9	29	2.2	2.1	222.2
White	527	77.6	2.0	975	60.6	3.9	793	61.1	3.0	50.5
Unknown race	0	0.0	0.0	79	4.9	7.5	48	3.7	2.9	n.a.

Sources: Data from HEGIS (1981) and IPEDS (1991, 2000) completion surveys.

Natives, Hispanics were underrepresented in every broad field in which doctoral degrees were awarded. In each of the remaining broad major fields, Hispanics constituted less than 5.0 percent of the degree recipients. American Indians and Alaskan Natives represented 0.3 percent of degree recipients in 2000 overall and less than 1.0 percent of degree recipients in every field.

Occupational Commitment

Our interest in doctoral students goes beyond their experiences while earning their degrees. We are also interested in their postdoctoral plans as a measure of their doctoral program experiences. The National Science Foundation's annual Survey of Earned Doctorates generates data on the postgraduation occupational commitments of recent recipients of doctoral degrees (see table 2.13). In 2000 51.8 percent of doctoral degree recipients were committed to academic appointments at the point of earning their degrees, compared with 52.8 percent in 1980. Another 21.1 percent were committed to employment in private industry or self-employment and 8.4 percent to government in 2000, compared with 17.0 percent and 12.6 percent, respectively, in 1980. In 2000 18.7 percent of new doctoral degree recipients were committed to some endeavor other than academe, private industry, and government, compared with 17.5 percent in 1980. Roughly half of all doctoral students were planning to work in the academy (Hoffer et al. 2001). What bearing, if any, should this have on their course work or noncourse training?

As with other aspects of the doctoral experience, employment commitments vary by race and sex. A higher percentage of women (55.4%) than men (48.4%) were committed to academic appointments in 2000, a sex gap that had remained constant over the two previous decades. Among the race groups, a smaller share of Asian Americans (36.0%) indicated a commitment to academe, and a much larger share to private industry (49.1%), than whites (52.4% and 20.1%, respectively), African Americans (52.9% and 12.4%, respectively), and Hispanics (57.5% and 17.6%, respectively). A larger percentage of African Americans indicated a commitment to other types of employment (25.6%) than the other race-ethnicity groups. International students and Asian American students had similar patterns; smaller shares of international doctorate recipients with permanent and temporary visas were committed to academic employment (45.1% and 34.3%, respectively) than United States citizens (52.1%).

Summary of Trends

The trends and status in doctoral education presented in this chapter reveal the following:

—a vast increase in the numbers of doctorate-granting institutions (table 2.1)

Table 2.13
Employment Sector of Doctorate Recipients with Postgraduation Commitments in the United States, by Demographic Group, Selected Years, 1980–2000

Sector and Year	Total	Male	Female	U.S. Citizen	Permanent Visa	Temporary Visa	Asian[a]	Black	Hispanic	American Indian[b]	White
All employment commitments											
1980 (N)	14,558	10,053	4,505	14,010	548	470	481	628	257	41	12,674
1990 (N)	13,396	7,603	5,793	12,899	497	1,205	416	536	382	50	11,891
2000 (N)	14,752	7,505	7,247	14,049	703	2,371	854	897	594	87	12,139
Employment commitments with responses to sector											
1980 (N)	14,540	10,042	4,498	13,994	546	470	481	626	256	41	12,659
1990 (N)	13,283	7,559	5,724	12,789	494	1,200	415	530	378	49	11,791
2000 (N)	14,550	7,407	7,143	13,858	692	2,324	831	884	581	85	11,992
Academe											
1980 (%)	52.8	49.0	61.3	53.3	41.4	48.3	30.4	60.1	59.0	51.2	53.3
1990 (%)	52.0	47.9	57.3	51.8	57.1	55.9	40.2	56.8	57.9	65.3	51.9
2000 (%)	51.8	48.4	55.4	52.1	45.1	34.3	36.0	52.9	57.5	63.5	52.4
Industry or self-employment											
1980 (%)	17.0	20.5	9.4	15.8	47.8	41.5	53.2	4.3	9.8	9.8	16.3
1990 (%)	20.4	25.8	13.2	19.9	31.6	39.0	43.9	5.3	12.7	14.3	20.4
2000 (%)	21.1	27.5	14.5	19.9	45.7	59.6	49.1	12.4	17.6	8.2	20.1
Government											
1980 (%)	12.6	14.2	9.3	13.0	3.8	4.5	8.1	14.2	12.9	17.1	12.7
1990 (%)	9.6	10.9	7.9	9.8	3.8	1.8	8.7	10.2	10.8	4.1	9.6
2000 (%)	8.4	9.8	6.9	8.6	3.8	1.7	6.5	9.0	9.1	11.8	8.3
Other											
1980 (%)	17.5	16.4	20.0	17.9	7.0	5.7	8.3	21.4	18.4	22.0	17.7
1990 (%)	18.1	15.4	21.6	18.5	7.5	3.3	7.2	27.7	18.5	16.3	18.1
2000 (%)	18.7	14.3	23.3	19.4	5.5	4.4	8.4	25.6	15.8	16.5	19.2

Source: Data from Hoffer et al. (2001).
[a]Includes Pacific Islander.
[b]Includes Alaskan Native.

—wide variations in numbers of degrees produced annually among doctorate-granting institutions (tables 2.2 and 2.3)

—a high proportion of degrees in high investment fields, such as science, granted by AAU universities (table 2.4)

—steadily increasing numerical growth in doctorates awarded over the past three decades (table 2.5)

—low representation of doctoral degrees (1%) among America's adult population (table 2.6)

—uneven representation by race and sex group compared with group's representation in the general population (table 2.6)

—vast gains in the representation of women among earned doctorates during the past three decades (table 2.7)

—increases in female, African American, and Hispanic enrollment in graduate programs (table 2.8)

—increases in female representation among doctorates in engineering, sciences, and mathematics (table 2.9)

—strong growth in doctoral degrees in the fields of engineering, mathematics, computer science, business, and art and music (table 2.9)

—low representation of African Americans and Hispanics among earned doctorates, relative to their representation in the general population (tables 2.6 and 2.10)

—high representation of international students, Hispanics, and Asian Americans among doctoral degree recipients (tables 2.10 and 2.11)

—modest indicators that distribution by field is changing among African Americans and Hispanics (table 2.12)

—trend away from a commitment to academic appointments among doctoral degree recipients (table 2.13)

Overall, the data indicate that the nation's doctoral degree production by field, race-ethnicity, citizenship, and sex is vibrant and growing.

Our Conceptual Analytical Framework

Researchers have explored demographic, financial, academic, and personal characteristics in search of the factors that promote success in doctoral education. Inevitably, observations about doctoral study and the people who succeed in attaining degrees take on the sanctity of theory. We have all heard a variety of theories: older students take longer to complete their programs, research assistantships are better than teaching assistantships, students from selective undergraduate institutions have a head start, and so on.

Bernard Berelson's *Graduate Education in the United States* (1960) forms the foundation for the present study. Berelson's research provides a basis for understanding the sea change that has occurred in the past forty years. When Berelson was conducting his research, doctoral education was primarily a white male experience, yet the issues he examines are ones that greet us with astonishing familiarity: Where did students earn their bachelor's degrees? What was their intellectual preparation for graduate school? How did they fund graduate education? How long did it take them to earn their degrees? The focus on field of study and the differential impact of teaching assistantships and research assistantships on time to degree completion in our work echoes Berelson's earlier findings.

When we were planning the study on which this book is based, William Bowen and Neil Rudenstine's *In Pursuit of the Ph.D.* (1992) had recently been published. Their focus on field of study and the different impact of teaching assistantships and research assistantships on time to degree completion influenced our thinking. For contemporary measures of doctoral student experiences and socialization, we relied on the categories of doctoral student experience studied by other scholars such as

Leonard Baird (1990b), James Blackwell (1981), Beatriz Clewell (1987), Ronald Ehrenberg (Ehrenberg and Mavros 1995), Corinna Ethington and Anoush Pisani (1993), Jean Girves (Girves and Wemmerus 1988), Chris Golde (Golde and Dore 1997), Barbara Lovitts (2001), Gary Malaney (1987), Maresi Nerad (Nerad and Cerny 1993), Willie Pearson (1985), Anne Pruitt and Paul Isaac (1985), Elizabeth Stein (Stein and Weidman 1989b), Vincent Tinto (1993), Howard Tuckman (Tuckman, Coyle, and Bae 1990), John Weidman (Weidman, Twale, and Stein 2001), and Kenneth Wilson (1965). The specific associations that our research has to prior work are illustrated throughout the book; at this stage we simply introduce and generally describe our conceptual model and its component parts.

The ingredients of our conceptual model resemble in name and positioning the models that social scientists use in examining the educational experiences and performance of students at all levels. As at other levels of education, however, the definitions, intention, and meaning of these concepts at the doctoral level are unique. For example, financial aid is arguably as important at the undergraduate level as at the doctoral level. But at the doctoral level, type of financial support (fellowships, research assistantships, and teaching assistantships) in many respects also defines the type of professional preparation that students receive rather than simply the source of the funding and whether it is to be repaid. Socioeconomic status, which is usually measured by combinations of parental or individuals' education, income, and occupation, is another good example of distinction in meaningfulness. At the undergraduate level, the typical student has a direct relationship with her or his parents, and students' human capital is a reflection of their parents' human capital. At the doctoral level, students tend to be relatively less dependent on their parents, and therefore their own household incomes should be considered in standard-of-living estimates. Each of the critical elements is defined and discussed throughout the book.

Figure 2.1 presents the elements of our framework. It suggests that personal and academic backgrounds, along with other acquired benefits, contribute to the quality of students' experiences and outcomes. In essence, the more highly valued students' personal backgrounds are to doctoral program faculty, we expect, the more positive their experiences and performance outcomes are likely to be. Our model conveys our interest in teasing out the unique effects of each background element and acquired benefit on experiences and outcomes while accounting for other characteristics and experiences that may also contribute to student experience. The model consists of a combination of conventional measures that have been included in prior research and some new measures that are examined here for the first time. In the case of the former, we contrast our findings with those in the existing literature. In this chapter, however, we simply present the elements of the model to introduce the comprehensive collection of variables and the types of relationships that we examined.

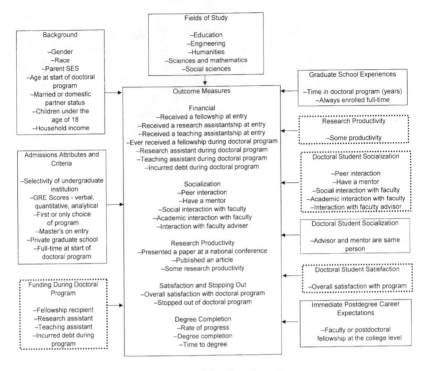

Fig. 2.1. Conceptual Model of Doctoral Student Experiences

The middle box in figure 2.1, Outcome Measures, contains the five major elements of the doctoral experience that are the main focus of our analyses: type of funding, socialization, research productivity, satisfaction and stopping out of a doctoral program, and doctoral degree completion. Listed under each of the five major headings are the specific elements we examine in our analyses. We recognize that these five areas do not represent an exhaustive list of the critical aspects of the doctoral experience; most arguably absent is teaching experience.

Surrounding the core outcome measures are other features of the doctoral experience that may influence the outcome. An important distinguishing characteristic of the surrounding boxes is whether they are framed with a solid or a dotted line. Boxes with solid lines include personal characteristics or aspects of the doctoral experience that we use only to predict an outcome. For example, we examine the relationship of GRE scores (which are in a solid-line box) with research productivity, but we do not predict GRE scores in this study. The boxes with dotted lines include aspects of the doctoral experience that may be determinants as well as outcomes of student experience. Receiving a research assistantship is an example of a doctoral experience that we first examine to estimate who will receive a research assistantship over the course of their doctoral student experience. In addition, we are also interested in how being a research assistant is associated with doctoral student research productivity. Our hypothesis is that the type of funding students receive is related to their research productivity. For many of these issues, we can think of the classic question, Which came first, the chicken or the egg? We do not attempt to estimate, statistically, the order of events; rather, we address the relationship. We do, however, suggest the most likely order in commentary that accompanies our analyses and interpretations.

The variables in the Background block constitute many of the personal and family attributes that may influence a student's doctoral experience. Gender and race-ethnicity are determined at birth, whereas such characteristics as parental socioeconomic status, age at the start of the doctoral program, marital or domestic partner status, having children under the age of eighteen, and household income may vary over one's lifetime. These background characteristics may have had a positive or negative influence on students' previous educational experiences and continue to influence their experience while they are enrolled in doctoral programs.

A crucial facet of the doctoral experience is the field of study. Unlike college, where the student experience is fairly similar regardless of academic major, specialization in a field of study at the graduate level defines the doctoral experience in several key ways. For example, the historical and cultural norms of a discipline often determine the style and type of scholarly productivity. In the humanities, books are frequently considered to be the highest symbol of achievement, whereas refereed journal articles may be the preferred mode in the sciences. The humanities are keen on narrative forms of discourse, whereas in the sciences quantitative illustrations are standard fare. Yet another distinction is the customs regarding funding resources and amounts. Humanities scholars are accustomed to relatively small sums for individualized research from a narrow range of philanthropic organizations and an even narrower range of governmental sources, while scholars in the sciences are represented in nearly every government funding program and typically receive large grants. Such factors may determine what is acceptable scholarship, funding patterns and types of financial support, and postdegree career options (Bowen and Rudenstine 1992; Lovitts 2001).

The block of elements entitled Admissions Attributes and Criteria represents different aspects of the graduate school admissions process. When students apply to graduate school, they typically present such credentials as the college or university where they earned a bachelor's degree, their GRE scores, whether they earned a master's degree before the start of their doctoral education, and whether they intend to pursue their study on a full-time or part-time basis. These credentials signal to graduate school admissions committees prospective students' potential to handle the work of a doctoral program and, to some degree, their potential to make a contribution to their chosen field. The latter becomes much more apparent during their doctoral studies, but initial estimates are made when faculty committees are selecting the students they will admit. The prevailing school of thought is that attending a selective undergraduate institution, having relatively high GRE scores, having a master's upon applying, and intending to enroll full-time make students most attractive to admissions committees. With the assumption that students who enroll in their first or only choice of graduate school may be happier, we asked students whether the doctoral programs in which they were enrolled had been their first choice when they were applying to graduate school.

Graduate school experiences such as the amount of time in program and full-time enrollment are other aspects of the experience that are likely to play a role in how students experience a doctoral program. Immediate postdegree career expectations—for example, interest in becoming faculty—are yet additional factors that relate to how students make decisions and experience their doctoral programs.

STATISTICAL ANALYSES

The analyses for this study are both descriptive and relational. In chapters 4 through 10 we present the descriptive analyses. The intent of these chapters is to provide a picture of the doctoral experience that reveals similarities and differences among the race and sex groups within fields of study on the various measures. These include analysis of variance for continuous outcomes and chi-squares (crosstabs) for dichotomous (binary) outcomes.

Databases often include multilevel information, providing data about both individual cases (level-1 data) and the organizations or groups in which they are located (level-2 data). A database may include, for example, information about both students and their schools, patients and their hospitals, corporations and the states in which they are located, or, in the case of this study, doctoral students (level 1) and the academic departments in which they study (level 2). For decades, quantitative researchers have aggregated level-2 characteristics onto level-1 data, resulting in numerous theoretical and methodological inaccuracies. Proper analysis of data involving "nested" components calls for hierarchical linear modeling (Bryk and Raudenbush 1992), which allows us to isolate the effects of level-2 characteristics on an outcome and to determine whether specific level-2 characteristics affect the relationships between level-1 characteristics and an outcome.

As with most quantitative research, greater variation in an outcome makes it more likely that effects will be found. Because the goal of hierarchical linear modeling (as with traditional ordinary least-squares regressions) is to "explain" differences among individuals' outcomes, little variation in the outcome means there is quite simply nothing to explain. Hierarchical linear modeling adds an additional element. An outcome may well vary among level-1 units (individual doctoral students), but that variation may be quite similar among level-2 units (academic departments); the result, in the case at hand, is that there is greater variation within departments than among them. For example, there may be more variation among history students in an individual department than there is among the twenty-one history departments in the study. If an outcome does not vary between level-2 units (departments, in this case), traditional ordinary least-squares regressions are appropriate. Our exploratory analyses found that little of the variance in doctoral student outcomes is related to the departments in which students are pursuing degrees.

The relational analyses consist of regressions by field of study. We performed both linear (continuous outcomes) and logistic (dichotomous outcomes) regressions. The regressions focus primarily on the complex relationship of student background characteristics, undergraduate preparation, and graduate school experiences with the dependent measures. The analyses permit us to assess how the variety of doctoral student characteristics and quality of experiences affect the dependent measures. Table F.21 (in appendix F) illustrates the variables we included in each analysis. The table shows the variables that were statistically significant contributors in any fields and variables that were not significant in any field.

Segue to Research

The historical context, with which we began this chapter, shows us how far doctoral education has progressed. It has grown in both size and diversity and has become an essential component of American higher education. Few people argue anymore about whether the Ph.D. should be a requirement for college and university faculty status. Every college and university seeks doctorate holders, and both regional and professional accreditation associations take their numbers into account when deciding the accreditation status of their member institutions, especially four-year colleges and universities. The growth in size and demographic diversity of U.S. doctoral education over the past forty-five years makes it timely to examine how it is working.

CHAPTER THREE

Survey Design
and Research Logistics

FOREWARNED IS FOREARMED: in most human endeavors, knowledge is power. Such is the case for students in the pursuit of doctoral degrees. Aside from becoming better educated ourselves about the variety of ways that students experience the process, our intent is to arm current and prospective students with the power to better structure their own doctoral experiences and to provide faculty and administrators with statistical support and strategies that broaden student successes and satisfaction.

Researchers focusing on the doctoral experience initially face handicaps. As noted in chapter 2, existing databases do not distinguish doctoral students from the mass of graduate students at all levels. As well, though some contain the characteristics of people who attend graduate school, none is sufficiently equipped to permit researchers to examine the full range of performance and socialization experiences, let alone relate these to issues like financing and time to degree.[1] Other longitudinal databases provide information primarily about the types of people who attend graduate school but do not include financial aid data.[2] Another source, the National Science Foundation's Survey of Earned Doctorates provides useful information about those who cross the finish line, especially how they financed their education; but by definition it includes only those participants who succeed in earning a degree and reveals little of their development and the quality of their experiences. Finally, the American Association of Universities and the Association of Graduate Schools collect data and information about the flow of students into and through doctoral programs but with a heavy institutional bias and a lack of personal input from the students on their development, achievements, or satisfaction.

All of these reasons suggested that broadly based advancement of our knowledge about the doctoral process could come only by developing a fresh database of such size and complexity that it would permit us to generalize to the entire U.S. population of doctoral students. We designed our

---

1. These include the National Center for Education Statistics databases such as the National Postsecondary Student Aid Survey (NCES 1998) and its follow-up surveys, the Beginning Postsecondary Survey (NCES 1992b) and Baccalaureate and Beyond (1992a), along with the Recent College Graduate surveys (NCES 1995).
2. These include the National Center for Education Statistics National Longitudinal Study of 1972 (NCES 2003) and High School and Beyond (NCES 2000).

study to capture those decisive experiences and backgrounds that produce the new Ph.D. It was a tall order. The survey instrument needed to cover the relevant issues raised by previous researchers, the graduate deans of participating institutions, and the participants in a series of focus groups that we conducted, and it was made possible by the exceptional breadth of the sample. These discussions helped reduce the main areas of interest to eight broad categories: demographics, preparation and screening, socialization, financing, productivity, personal satisfaction, rate of progress, and degree completion.

In preparing the survey, we used a kaleidoscope analogy, with the idea that different patterns would form when we twisted the lenses from looking at outcomes by sex, race, or field of study. For example, we wanted to be able to look across the range of financial support and view its ramifications for different groupings. The point was to design the initial structures with such clarity that in the end they would reveal where doctoral study is susceptible to improvement—those possibilities cited in the introduction. Where are the opportunities? Where are we hidebound? How can prospective Ph.D. students craft their own experiences in doctoral programs? How can universities contribute to their students' advancement?

THE VARIABLES OF INTEREST

Demographics

Our starting point emerged from revelations in the trend data we gathered (presented in chapter 2). The academic community never projected the look of today's doctoral classes—either numerically or in its growing diversity, which includes the dramatic increase in international student participation. We wanted to learn how the present composition of doctoral programs compares with the broader changes in society and how representative doctoral programs are. We know, for example, that women have been underrepresented in doctoral programs overall and particularly in science and engineering fields. At the same time, international students seem to be multiplying. All the while, the rates of doctorate attainment have been rising, with obvious implications for both the academic workforce and for higher levels of business, industry, and government.

Some phenomena require explanation. These include the underrepresentation of African Americans and Hispanics in doctoral education—severe in the case of African Americans. We need to know how much this underrepresentation is just a numerical imbalance and to what extent it is related to an imbalance in the whole achievement process. Similarly, the remarkable progress of Asian Americans raises a different set of issues. Does their strong presence in doctoral programs, for example, reflect broader society? To what extent is their representation, as well as that of other race-ethnicity groups, concentrated in a few fields and distributed through the various fields?

Family background is also of interest to us. To what degree are doctoral programs recycling the social order rather than expanding opportunities for higher education? Has there been an opening up? We wish to know whether a preponderance of the doctoral students grew up in families for whom graduate and postbaccalaureate study is a tradition. This concern applies also to the undergraduate colleges and universities attended by our sample. We want to identify what effect, if any, attending a selective college or university has on the quality of doctoral program experience.

Predoctorate Preparation

Because of the problem universities have had in sorting out doctoral students from master's students, there have been little clear data distinguishing them. Since we consider doctoral programs both as centers of intellectual excellence and as systems for creating knowledge, we can expect participants to have undergone rigorous and focused preparation. What exactly does this undergraduate preparation consist of?

Within the context of our survey, we seized on the opportunity to find out whether these doctoral students were locked into a formula of preparation. Is there still just a narrow set of feeder schools whose students pursue the most desirable institutions? When in their lives did these students know they were going to seek a Ph.D. or the equivalent? Did they all have to present 4.0 undergraduate grade point averages to gain admission? To what extent is family background part of the picture? What are the commonalities among people who made it into these programs, and what differences exist by race, sex, and age? When it came to learning how people prepare for the doctorate, however, we made choices in the interests of efficiency. For example, we could anticipate looking at undergraduate institutions by selectivity but not broadly in terms of the total undergraduate experience.

Predoctorate Screening

We have an abiding interest in the relationship of the Graduate Record Examinations (GRE) to postgraduate admission experiences and performance. The GRE is widely used by graduate institutions to identify talent. On how many different fronts does the exam deliver? As programs have become more formal, the GRE has become an increasingly important element in the application process. Scores are used differently, however, across the academic terrain; some programs require but ignore it; some make important decisions for admission or financing based on it. There has been no systematic study, and no one really knows the variety of ways the GRE is used across the landscape of graduate education nor the variation in weight attached to it when it is used. The availability of GRE scores for a large sample advances other research goals, enabling us, for example, to examine the relationship of test scores to such outcomes as research productivity and degree progress. How well does the GRE forecast the quality of the student experiences beyond the first year of doctoral study?

Although the extent of predoctoral screening poses its own challenges, we cannot examine the full effect here. The people who are screened out in the admissions process are not a part of our sample. Proxies, however, offer ways to examine the influence of the GRE in expanding opportunities for advancement. By asking whether the student obtained his or her first choice of doctoral program, we were able to discover some of the relationships among preparation, background, and even test scores. By asking about satisfaction with the program, we carried this a step further into the personal outcomes of the institutional screening decisions. However, because we do not know how wide the gate is open, we are unable to be conclusive about screening.

Socialization

A little more than a decade ago, Claude Steele wrote poignantly about a moment at which he began to feel that he belonged as an academic; many of us can identify with that small but vital epiphany: "I remember conducting experiments with my research adviser early in graduate school and awaiting the results with only modest interest. I struggled to meet deadlines. The research enterprise—the core of what one does as a social psychologist—just wasn't *me* yet. I was in school for other reasons—I wanted an advanced degree, I was vaguely ambitious for intellectual work, and being in graduate school made my parents proud of me. But as time passed, I began to like the work. I also began to grasp the value systems that gave it meaning, and the faculty treated me as if they thought I might even be able to do it. Gradually I began to think of myself as a social psychologist" (Steele 1992, 72). Although we describe this process as socialization, it can as easily be seen as professional "fit," with the student both consciously and subconsciously acquiring the knowledge associated with her or his field as well as the unique characteristics of its practitioners. We posit that professional fit can be demonstrated through the doctoral student's relationships within her or his department, through interactions with advisers, faculty, and peers. Although doctoral study is acknowledged as an individual endeavor, previous research (Arce and Manning 1984; Baird 1990b; Bargar and Mayo-Chamberlain 1983; Blackwell 1993; Hartnett 1976; Lovitts 2001) demonstrates that social connections—student to faculty, student to peers—also have an impact on the experience.

We wanted to know about the student relationships, as people move through the process, between mentoring and rate of progress and between mentoring and research productivity. We also wanted to probe the relationship between students' outside lives and their doctoral program experiences. Because of the variety of people in our sample, we expected the quality of their experiences to reflect their diversity. Our goal was to explore the range of their academic and social experiences alongside the quality of these experiences and then to relate these findings to other outcomes such as productivity and progress.

Financial Support

We assumed that the purely practical aspects of financing one's physical existence would either facilitate or impede all the other parts of the doctoral experience. For survey design, this meant seeking out those means of enabling persistence, supporting longer research in order to complete papers and publications, and developing teaching skills through assistantships, all the while maintaining a quality of life consistent with socialization and personal satisfaction. In addition, it required acknowledgment that undergraduate preparation has important implications for how students finance their doctoral studies, in terms of residual debt load and of potential fellowships and assistantships based on earlier achievements. Throughout the 1990s, graduate deans and researchers were concerned about the effects of growing debt loads, but other financial arrangements such as fellowships and assistantships, or even drawing on personal resources, may impinge in different ways on doctoral students' performance. Sharing these concerns, we sought to understand the effects of the various forms of support on students' experiences; whether, in the case of fellowships and assistantships, all students had the same opportunity to obtain these funding supports; and whether these funding supports had the same payoffs for students on other indicators, such as rate of progress, regardless of race, citizenship, or sex.

Research Productivity

Our measure of student performance comes from academe's valuation of research productivity. Certainly for novice scholars looking toward university teaching careers, publications and conference presentations constitute serious evidence of academic performance. They reveal an individual's ability to go beyond the minimum expected of a doctoral student and exhibit her or his skills and knowledge for public consumption. In academic terms, these little wins—a journal article, a poster session—can add early points on the job acquisition and tenure scoreboard, but many doctoral students learn about this form of self-promotion only after they have matriculated in a doctoral degree program. Does such research productivity come with an important trade-off—extended time to degree? As the foregoing suggests, with respect to rate of progress or time to degree, students can be caught between a rock and a hard place: Since the doctorate is a stepping stone to many careers, the sooner students begin to advance in their fields, the sooner they reap the benefits. On the other hand, in many fields, moving faster may be associated with lower research productivity.

This notion of research productivity has other benefits. Our own experience with doctoral programs has brought home the general limitations of a grading range of A+ to B−. When 45 percent of students rank themselves in the top 25 percent of their class (as was the case with our sample), other means need to be developed to measure performance, or broader variability in grading doctoral student performance is needed. Hence our focus on research productivity constitutes a useful way of helping students understand their departmental standing. By defining productivity in multiple ways—publications, presentations, and the like—we expect to be able to show the percentage of students in various fields who were taking the fullest advantage of their research opportunities and who were sharing academe's concern for public dissemination of knowledge.

Personal Satisfaction

As any doctoral candidate can report, the euphoria that follows a successful comprehensive examination and dissertation defense has few equals in personal satisfaction. We explored the role that personal satisfaction and the need for self-fulfillment play in the doctoral process. This concept also embodies appreciation and recognition that one's choice of doctoral program has been appropriate and comfortable. Although students may experience success on various performance indicators, a high degree of satisfaction and a sense of self-realization have currency in all their endeavors. In essence, doctoral students are trading off great parts of their present lives against an uncertain future. Without the glow of personal satisfaction, as the years pile up, we might expect to see students experiencing difficulties in other academic or even personal pursuits. At the very least, we might expect to see growing disdain for the process and perhaps failure to complete the degree.

Rate of Progress

While completion of the doctoral credential itself is acknowledged to be the ultimate prize, multiple factors contribute to that outcome. The first of these is persistence, fueled by the belief that achieving candidacy—the so-called ABD (all but dissertation)—is itself a step worthy of celebration. The ABD is a common, if unofficial, title bestowed on a student who has completed course work and usually a qualifying examination that declares her or him a candidate for the doctoral degree; all that is lacking is completion and defense of the dissertation. The ABD leaves students with just one more hurdle in the process of completion. Among other things, achievement of this level of success is a tribute to students' stamina and ability to cope with the challenges of academic life.

For decades, time to degree has been the whipping boy in doctoral education, both from the standpoint of efficiency and with reference to the creation of this new degree—the ABD—held by default or surrender by increasing numbers of students. Since doctoral education has significance beyond the academy as well as within it, it is important to know what the expectations for time on task should be. As well, by constructing milestones that mark the stages in the process, we hope to learn about related issues such as the role of financial support, mentoring, and program satisfaction. Aside from concerns about growing numbers of ABDs, time to degree is perhaps the most widely discussed, perplexing, and worrisome aspect of the doctoral student experience both within and outside the academy. Unlike the baccalaureate and first professional degrees, which carry prescribed time periods for completion, the doctoral degree is much more open-ended. The rate of progress and time to degree appear to depend more on disciplinary norms than many of the other factors, such as financial support.

Because students in our survey would not be able to supply their own completion date, we decided early on that another appropriate measurement might be rate of progress. Were all students in all fields making similar progress toward the degree, or were there important differences by field, race, and sex? Previous research suggests that sex, marital status, and number of dependents impede the rate of progress (Abedi and Benkin 1987; Nerad and Cerny 1993; Tuckman, Coyle and Bae 1990). We hypothesized that a series of questions related to the degree milestones—course work completion, qualifying examination, and candidacy achievement—would reveal important and previously undetermined differences among our study groups.

Degree Completion

The research in the field of doctoral education suggests a hierarchy of accomplishments of which obviously the most important is degree completion. Students enter the doctoral process fixated on the credential as the crowning achievement. Degree completion signifies successful fulfillment of the program requirements not only to academics within the field or discipline but also to the general public. Although our research is not longitudinal, we are able to examine both completion rates and time to completion.

We are able to make temporal pronouncements on completion rates by field of study, race-ethnicity, citizenship, and sex. Other researchers have suggested attrition rates in some fields as high as 50 percent and as low as 10 percent (Bowen and Rudenstine 1992; Lovitts 2001). Since our survey focused on students in their second or further year of doctoral study, we effectively cleared the decks of those who were merely testing the waters. As a result, we anticipated that the survival and completion rates for our sample might be considerably higher than previous studies have reported.

RESEARCH DESIGN

Selecting the Institutions

We selected key universities in such a way that the institutions that grant the majority of doctoral degrees were represented and the cooperation of their administrators was secured. We selected seventeen of the twenty-one participating universities for initial focus and used the remaining five to provide particular variety. We chose a purposive sampling plan that allowed us to generalize findings to the population of doctoral students attending the nation's largest research universities. The institutions in the sample are City University of New York, Clark Atlanta University, Columbia University, Harvard University, Howard University, Indiana University, New York University, Ohio State University, Princeton University, Rutgers University–New Brunswick, Stanford University, Teachers College, Temple University, University of California–Berkeley, University of California–Los Angeles, University of Maryland–College Park, University of Michigan–Ann Arbor, University of North Carolina–Chapel Hill, University of Texas–Austin, University of Wisconsin–Madison, and Vanderbilt University.

Six criteria guided the selection of this diverse and visible pool of doctorate-granting universities (presented in appendix A, table A.1). We drew from the top sixty doctorate-granting universities in the United States, selecting universities that were among the 120 to receive the highest current fund revenues from the U.S. government and offered degrees in a variety of fields.[3] From these, we selected institutions that represented the range of geographic regions in the United States. The selected universities were among the major producers of minority doctorates, according to the National Research Council Summary Report of 1994, and had highly ranked academic departments (see table A.2).

In addition, other sites were chosen to fulfill specific purposes. City University of New York, Temple University, and Teachers College provided a contrast to the mostly full-time, traditional enrollment of doctoral students at the other eighteen universities. Howard University and Clark Atlanta University were chosen because they are historically black universities and bolster the African American student representation in the student sample.

Fields of Study

We wanted to include in the research as many major fields as possible. As we sought a rationale to broaden the fields of study beyond the rather narrow range of disciplines covered in prior research, we used a combination of strategies in our selection. First, English, history, economics, math-

---

3. The top sixty universities award nearly 60 percent of doctoral degrees each year. In 1992–93 they granted 24,220 of the 42,132 doctoral degrees in the United States.

ematics, political science, and physics were selected to match the six disciplines in Bowen and Rudenstine's 1992 study, *In Pursuit of the Ph.D.* This allowed us to contrast some of our findings with those reached by Bowen and Rudenstine on some performance indicators, especially time to degree. Second, we selected the fields of engineering and education because they enroll students whose experiences and training have too often been omitted from research, despite the fact that they are also often training for research and academic careers. As well, these two fields provide a contrast to the doctoral experiences of students in the social sciences and humanities.

These disciplines were also the ones that the graduate deans advised us to include because of the challenges they face in ensuring that underrepresented students are successful. Hence the doctoral students in the sample were selected from the following eleven fields of study: biological sciences, which includes biochemistry, biophysics, and molecular biology; economics; education; engineering, which includes chemical engineering, electrical engineering, and mechanical engineering; English; history; mathematics; physical sciences, which includes chemistry and physics; political science; psychology; and sociology. For purposes of analysis, the eleven fields are collapsed into five major fields: education; engineering; humanities (English and history); sciences and mathematics (the biological sciences, mathematics, and the physical sciences); and social sciences (economics, political science, psychology, and sociology). (For a discussion on why we combined the biological sciences, mathematics, and the physical sciences, see appendix B.)

Building the Sample

Since the goal for the study was to create a fresh, purposive database, a sample of actively enrolled doctoral students had to be constructed in such a way that adequate representation was achieved for field of study, race-ethnicity, citizenship, and sex. To ensure the respondents' immersion in their fields of study, we focused on doctoral students who were beyond the first year of their doctoral course work and were actively engaged in their doctoral programs. The sampling design was carefully crafted to ensure unbiased representation of actively enrolled doctoral students within each of the participating universities and fields of study. To achieve this goal, a sample design was developed that included the entire census of African American, Asian American, Hispanic American, and Native American students, a random representative selection of white doctoral students, and an oversampled (50%) random selection of international doctoral students, all of whom were enrolled in either six credits of course work or dissertation work in the fall of 1996. The outcome was a stratified sample of 14,020 doctoral students, drawn from the twenty-one universities and the eleven disciplines or fields of study.

THE SURVEY INSTRUMENT

The Survey of Doctoral Student Finances, Experiences, and Achievements owes some of its underpinnings to Michael Nettles's previous research on black, Hispanic, and white doctoral students (1989). Nettles's earlier Doctoral Student Survey (1986) was developed in collaboration with associate deans at Florida State University, Ohio State University, Rutgers University, and the University of Maryland–College Park. We modified the instrument on the basis of new findings that had been published in the literature and correspondence and conversations with the twenty-one campus liaisons. We invited the campus liaisons, most of whom were associate deans, to incorporate administrative practices and contemporary graduate education policies that might not be grounded in the existing literature.

To refine the instrument, we conducted pilot tests at the State University of New York–Buffalo, Northwestern University, and the University of Michigan. The instrument was administered to doctoral students under timed conditions and followed up by hour-long focus groups, which asked respondents about the wording of the questions and the range of issues covered in the survey.

The new instrument consists of seven sections: application and enrollment process, current doctoral program experience, attendance patterns, financing doctoral education, future plans, undergraduate experiences, and background. In addition, students were asked to sign consent forms giving permission to the Educational Testing Service to provide us with their GRE scores. The instrument also contains space for students to provide the names and addresses of two relatives who are always likely to know their whereabouts. This information will be valuable for longitudinal student tracking. (For the survey instrument, see appendix C.)

Survey Administration and Data Gathering

The objective of the data-gathering phase of the study was to obtain a 70 percent response rate to our survey. To accomplish this objective, the survey was first administered to the entire sample and then twice more to nonrespondents. Each survey packet included a cover letter signed either by both of us, by a representative of the participating university, or by all three. Within a few days of each survey mailing, we sent a reminder in the form of a postcard to each student in the sample. We used cash payments as an inducement for students to complete the survey. The name of each doctoral student who returned a completed survey was entered in a pool to win one of thirteen cash payments (one of $500, one of $400, one of $300, and ten $100 cash payments).

Response Rates

The sample of 9,036 doctoral students represents a 70 percent overall response rate. The percentage of respondents varied among the race groups, by sex, and by field. Seventy-five percent of white doctoral students responded, followed by 72 percent of Hispanics, 66 percent of Asian Americans, 64 percent of African Americans, and 58 percent of international students. U.S. citizens had an 84 percent response rate, international citizens 58 percent. Seventy-four percent of women and 65 percent of men returned a completed survey instrument. By field of study, response rates were 79 percent of students in education, 69 percent in humanities and social sciences, 64 percent in sciences and mathematics, and 63 percent in engineering.

Weighting the Sample

The sample of respondents comprises four race groups of U.S. citizens and a fifth group made up of international citizens from around the world. Ten percent of the respondents were African American, 9 percent Asian American and Asian–Pacific Islander, 7 percent Hispanic, 58 percent white, and 16 percent international citizens. The respondents were evenly divided between women and men. The field distribution of the respondents was as follows: education, 27 percent; engineering, 10 percent; humanities, 15 percent; sciences and mathematics, 21 percent; and social sciences, 27 percent.

In an effort to achieve an approximate representation of the race distribution among graduate enrollments by field of study, our sample of respondents had to be weighted to correct for an oversampling or undersampling of students. As the standard against which the representativeness of our sample is judged, we chose the 1996 graduate student enrollment (master's and doctoral students) in the selected fields at the twenty-one institutions. Where this proved impossible, data from other years were obtained. Weights are referenced to this 1996 group, which should be more representative of the true population of doctoral students than is our sample (see appendix D, table D.2).

The oversampling of minorities was intended to produce a sample of individuals that was large enough for analysis. Since this was not an issue with respect to sex, women were not oversampled, and so the weight variable does not account for sex. This may be problematic if the proportion of women in our survey differs dramatically from that in our target population. However, there seems to be little empirical difference in the proportion of females in our survey and the proportion of females enrolled in graduate programs in 1996, our referent group for weight construction.

The actual weighting formula tries to match our sample's distribution exactly to that of the base:

$$W = \frac{\text{Total enrolled within race \& field (institution population)}}{\text{Total enrolled within race \& field (sample)}} * \frac{\text{Total enrolled (sample)}}{\text{Total enrolled (institution population)}}$$

Table 3.1
Unweighted and Weighted Distribution of the Sample

Variable	Unweighted		Weighted	
	No.	%	No.	%
Sex				
Female	4,533	50	4,086	45
Male	4,502	50	4,949	55
Ethnicity				
African American	943	10	570	6
Asian American	773	9	676	7
Hispanic	602	7	347	4
White	5,256	58	5,411	60
International	1,462	16	2,032	22
Field				
Engineering	2,507	28	2,633	29
Education	886	10	1,591	18
Humanities	1,326	15	858	9
Sciences and mathematics	1,853	21	2,341	26
Social sciences	2,464	27	1,613	18

Source: Survey of Doctoral Student Finances, Experiences, and Achievements.

This will match every proportion in our sample to that of the base and will eliminate the problem associated with oversampling of minority students. In the analyses presented in this book, the sample estimates are weighted. Table 3.1 shows the effect of the weighting on the distribution from the unweighted to the weighted sample.

Database Development

We supplemented the data by adding the *Barron's Profiles of American Colleges and Universities* (1999) ranking of the admissions selectivity of students' undergraduate college or university.[4] In addition, for the students who signed consent forms, we added the GRE General Test scores obtained from the Educational Testing Service. The predictor variables include both individual and institutional characteristics that may plausibly affect the experiences of doctoral students: race, sex, parents' socioeconomic status, student age at the time of enrollment, whether the student was married or had a domestic partner, whether the student had children under eighteen years of age, student's household income, student's GRE General Test scores (verbal, quantitative, analytical), whether the student graduated from a selective U.S. college or university, whether the student had a master's degree before entering the doctoral program, whether the student was attending her or his first or only choice of doctoral program, whether the student enrolled full-time when starting the doctoral program, whether the student's graduate department was in a public or private college or university, the amount of time in years since the student first entered the doctoral program, whether the student had always attended full-time, whether the student's adviser was also her or his mentor, and student's ex-

4. Barron's awards selectivity status of the basis of high school rank, high school grade point average, and median entrance examination (SAT or ACT) scores.

pectation of having a faculty or postdoctoral position upon degree completion. (Appendix D presents a more detailed description of these variables and the process by which variables such as socioeconomic status were standardized to allow comparison, as well as a detailed description of the factor analyses and regression tools.)

Limitations

Among the many tools for collecting evidence, we selected the large-scale survey route resulting in the database just described. Some respondents, however, fortuitously sent comments about their situations. Many of these are included in later chapters. Having such detailed accounts from all of our subjects would have enriched our understanding and appreciation of the survey results. While we chose the fields to include the majority of doctoral students, clearly we have not covered the proliferating range of disciplines and subdisciplines. We might have included business, foreign languages, and fine arts—such as music. But to do so would have necessitated important trade-offs in our goal of sampling for diversity. Quite simply, this study, if it were to be useful, demanded a racial mix in sufficient numbers to allow analysis. The need for substantial numbers of students in the designated programs also resulted in eliminating some smaller doctorate-granting institutions from consideration. Because of our concentration on major institutions, the selection of participants might be seen as being elitist, but that is an incontrovertible aspect of American higher education. At the graduate level, the most academically selective colleges and universities have the largest pool of qualified candidates from which to choose, and most also have prestigious departments in the fields under study.

The study's design coincided with the tentative beginnings of unionization among graduate students, who constitute a substantial campus workforce. Clearly, this is an important development for which we can envision repercussions in all of our areas of interest such as financial support, socialization, and research productivity. Nevertheless, most of the graduate students' contract activities followed the completion of our survey by at least months, if not years, and so, regrettably, these developments in the doctoral experience are not accounted for here.

An important area of the doctoral experience needing more focused attention is the dissertation process. The variability of this document, depending on institution, department, and individual committee members, seems to constitute a research project in and of itself. We are aware of a range of approved options, from the substitution of three journal articles for a full-fledged dissertation to the requirement that a dissertation represent totally original—ground-breaking, in fact—work. But as our survey became ever longer and ever more daunting, we decided to forgo these explorations, despite the refinements they would have added to the overall picture.

The study's focus on doctoral students meant that all of our attention was devoted to gathering student accounts of their experience and none to the opinions and perspectives of faculty and administrators. Their comments would certainly add texture and nuance to the findings presented here. Perhaps other researchers will seize the opportunity. Finally, the value of this database will be fully realized only when an effort is made to collect longitudinal data about these doctoral respondents. Only then will we be able to discuss how doctoral student experiences contribute to post-doctoral life and to society beyond the academy.

CHAPTER FOUR

Demographics
of the Sample

WHEN AN EIGHTY-YEAR-OLD Ph.D. student wrote us a short note about the bypass and prostate surgery he had endured before reaching candidacy, we began to recognize the extraordinary depth of our sample. We had identified people whose experiences are never tapped by conventional research. Such personal information was not requested, but the information that accompanied the completed surveys established an intimacy that reminded us that we were dealing not just with data but with the hopes and dreams of real people. Certainly, we had accounted for the traditional-age students, and we had included a number of nontraditional-age students, with a leavening of outliers that made us think we had accessed the full spectrum of doctoral students. When our eighty-year-old respondent concluded, "What one does with a newly minted Ph.D. at eighty is a real question. But the getting there is worthwhile and broadening," it was hard not to cheer.

The demographics of our sample resemble those of recent doctoral recipients in the United States as typically profiled by the U.S. Department of Education's National Center for Education Statistics (e.g., NCES 1994, 2001) and the National Science Foundation (e.g., Hoffer et al. 2001). Our sample, for example, has slightly more men than women (55% and 45%, respectively). Six percent of our respondents were African American, 7 percent Asian American, 4 percent Hispanic, 61 percent whites, and 22 percent international students. Proportions for the field of study were education, nearly 29 percent; engineering, 18 percent; humanities, 9 percent; sciences and mathematics, 26 percent; and social sciences, 18 percent.

Among the fields of study, there are real differences by race and sex representation. When we disaggregate the sample by sex and field, the sex composition of the sample shifts from a nearly even distribution to resemble the national profile of doctoral degree recipients by sex and field, with women representing 69 percent of doctoral students in education, 14 percent in engineering, 52 percent in the humanities, 32 percent in the sciences and mathematics, and 52 percent of social science students. Similarly, the racial composition of the sample (see table 4.1) resembles the national profile of doctoral degree recipients (see table 2.12). Hispanics are heavily distributed toward education and humanities and African Americans toward education and social sciences, while international students

Table 4.1
Race-Ethnicity Distribution of the Sample, by Field

Field	African American	Asian American	Hispanic	White	Noncitizen	Total
Education						
No.	279	144	150	1,841	219	2,633
%	11	6	6	70	8	100
Engineering						
No.	42	181	41	682	645	1,591
%	3	11	3	43	41	100
Humanities						
No.	52	47	40	660	60	859
%	6	6	5	77	7	100
Sciences and mathematics						
No.	60	219	51	1,298	712	2,340
%	3	9	2	56	30	100
Social sciences						
No.	136	85	66	930	396	1,613
%	8	5	4	58	25	100
Total	569	676	348	5,411	2,032	9,036

Source: Survey of Doctoral Student Finances, Experiences, and Achievements.

and Asian Americans have a sizable presence in engineering and in sciences and mathematics.

In the past three decades several researchers have raised concerns about the underrepresentation of black students in scientific fields (Malcom 1990; Malcom, Hall, and Brown 1975; Thomas 1980); others have voiced concern regarding the underrepresentation of women and minorities in general (CSEPP 1995). As seems apparent from our demographic data, these concerns are entirely justified. A close look at our sample by sex, race-ethnicity, and field of study brings attention to the small number of women and men of some racial backgrounds in specific doctoral programs. For example, the race and sex composition of the engineering sample is African American women 1 percent, African American men 2 percent, Asian American women 2 percent, Asian American men 9 percent, Hispanic women 1 percent, Hispanic men 2 percent, white women 7 percent, white men 36 percent, international women 4 percent, and international men 36 percent. The uneven distribution of men and women by race within fields limits our analyses. Similarly, the small number of Hispanics in our sample within each field of study prevents us from looking at particular experiences within this group. We are not able to address a concern raised by Abdìn Noboa-Ríos (1982) and Robert Ibarra (1996) that aggregating Hispanics clouds differences among various ethnic groups of Hispanics in the doctoral education process, such as Mexican Americans and Puerto Ricans.

AGE OF DOCTORAL STUDENTS

Age has been a common focal point in research on doctoral students. The research literature regarding age centers on investment in human development, receipt of financial aid, issues of productivity, student choice about completing their doctorates, and the effect of age on progress.[1] As the anecdote about the eighty-year-old candidate illustrates, age when starting the doctoral program varied considerably within our sample, students in sciences and mathematics being the youngest, on average, at twenty-five years old, and education students the oldest, on average, at just past thirty-five years old. With the exception of engineering, where women doctoral students were younger by almost a year, men and women in the specific fields were within a few months of the same age. In terms of race and citizenship, Asian American students in the sample were slightly younger than the average (twenty-six years compared with twenty-nine years), but by field they were not younger than Hispanics and whites. African American doctoral students tended to be slightly older than the average (thirty-seven years compared with thirty-five years in education; twenty-eight years compared with twenty-five years in sciences and mathematics). Ages of international students at the start of their doctoral programs ran close to the averages in all fields except education, where they were slightly younger than the norm (thirty-two years vs. thirty-five years).

AGE WHEN STUDENT
DECIDED ON A DOCTORATE

Our review of the literature did not uncover research that examined the age when students made what may have been at that point the most critical decision of their lives—to earn a doctoral degree. As noted, our interest in some questions presented here only as descriptive analyses is to see whether a profile of doctorate-minded individuals develops.

Field differences were confirmed when we asked students to identify the age at which they first decided to work on a Ph.D. Students in sciences and mathematics appear to have made this decision before they turned twenty, and education students, not until they were nearly thirty. Average age in other fields fell somewhere in between, for an average age in our sample of nearly twenty-four at the time the initial decision was made. Generally, women decided slightly earlier than men in the field of engineering but were slightly later in sciences and mathematics. In the other three fields, no sex differences surfaced. Again, differences among the races were reflected in the previous data about age of starting the Ph.D. program.

1. For research that examines the relationship of age to financial aid, see Malaney (1987) and Baird (1976); for the relationship of age to research productivity of doctoral students, see Hagedorn and Doyle (1993); for the relationship of age to research productivity of doctoral recipients, see Buchmueller, Dominitz, and Hansen (1999) and Clemente (1973); for research on the relationship of age and retention, see Girves and Wemmerus (1988) and Ott, Markewich, and Ochsner (1984); for the relationship of age to degree progress, see Tuckman, Coyle, and Bae (1990); and for research on the relationship of age to degree completion, see Baker (1998) and Cook and Swanson (1978).

Asian American Ph.D. students appear to have made these decisions somewhat earlier than their white peers in education, ahead of their white and international peers in engineering, and ahead of their international peers in sciences and mathematics. African Americans were close to the norm in all fields, as were Hispanics and international students.

MAKING THE DOCTORAL DECISION

More than 75 percent of the sciences and mathematics students decided either before or during their college career to pursue a doctoral degree, compared with doctoral students in engineering (nearly 60%), humanities (57%), and social sciences (57%). Only 25 percent of education students, however, decided either before or during college to earn a doctoral degree. In education, engineering, humanities, and sciences and mathematics, similar proportions of men and women made the decision during their baccalaureate period. In every field except education, the mode for women and men for deciding to work on a doctorate was during their undergraduate years (ranging from 38% in engineering to 48% in sciences and mathematics). In education, the modal time for both women and men was while working, after attaining a master's degree (39%). For men in engineering, the master's and postmaster's period was also an important time for deciding to pursue a doctoral degree (31%, compared with 20% for women). More women than men in engineering decided to pursue their doctoral degrees while working after graduation from college (13%, compared with 8% for men).

When we looked at the responses on the timing of the doctoral decision by race, we found that while the percentages varied, the mode for each race group in each field was during college, except for education, for which the mode time occurred after the master's degree, while the individual was working. Our findings were similar to Pearson's (1985) conclusion that most black and white scientists made the decision to pursue graduate studies during college.

PARENTAL EDUCATION LEVELS

Pursuing our initial query about whether the Ph.D. process was merely reproducing the existing social structure,[2] we looked at the sample's parental education. Examining the sample by the fields in which students were enrolled, we found that nearly 34 percent of humanities students were from homes in which at least one parent held either a Ph.D. or a first professional degree (e.g., J.D., M.D.). Students in sciences and mathematics and in the social sciences also had strong parental education backgrounds,

---

2. Given researchers' finding that doctoral degree recipients appear to have had parents with relatively high educational attainment (Smith and Tang 1994), we are not surprised about the relatively high parental attainment of our sample.

with 27 percent and 26 percent, respectively, having at least one parent with an advanced degree. Of the engineering students, 24 percent reported an advanced degree among their parents. This number fell to 16 percent for education students, who clearly came from the weakest family education backgrounds.

The sex differences by fields were even more instructive. In engineering, for example, 39 percent of the parents of women doctoral students had achieved a doctoral or first professional degree, compared with only 21 percent of the parents of male engineering doctoral students. The male engineering students were also more likely to have had parents whose highest educational attainment was a high school diploma (19%) than women engineering students (12%). This pattern—a higher proportion of male than female students whose parents' highest education level was the high school diploma—applied to all of the other fields.

In every field, the parents with the highest educational attainments were the mothers and fathers of Asian American and white doctoral students, and the field in which they had the highest educational attainment was humanities. In the humanities, just under 60 percent of the parents of both Asian American and white doctoral students had completed a graduate degree, compared with 40 percent of the parents of African Americans, 37 percent of the parents of international students, and nearly 32 percent of the parents of Hispanics. More than half the parents of Asian American and white doctoral students in the fields of engineering, sciences and mathematics, and the social sciences had completed graduate degrees. This level of parental educational attainment by far exceeds the parental educational attainment of the general U.S. population.

Across all fields, African American and Hispanic doctoral students in the field of engineering reported the highest percentages of parents with graduate degrees (40% and 48%, respectively), suggesting important implications for the engineering and the sciences and mathematics fields. Most (more than 60% of) African American, Hispanic, and international doctoral students in the field of education had parents who had not completed a bachelor's degree. By contrast, the parents of more than half (55%) of white doctoral students and two-thirds (68%) of Asian American doctoral students in the field of education had completed at least a bachelor's degree, and 34 percent of whites and 39 percent of Asian American parents had completed a graduate degree.

PARENTAL SOCIOECONOMIC STATUS

Another calculation from the data combined parental education levels and occupations to produce a measure of parental socioeconomic status (SES) that we applied to all fields. Given that doctoral students are typically at least several years removed from their parental nest, the relationship of parental SES to the quality of doctoral student experiences remains unclear.[3] Humanities students came from the highest parental SES back-grounds, followed by social sciences and sciences and mathematics stu-dents, with similar family backgrounds, and engineering students; educa-tion students had, on average, the lowest parental SES level. We are curious about why women in each field, with the exception of the social sciences, hail from higher socioeconomic status backgrounds than their male coun-terparts. Among the four fields in which this difference proved significant, women in engineering had the highest parental SES backgrounds, fol-lowed by women in the humanities.

Overall, African American and Hispanic students reported relatively low SES backgrounds compared with the other race-ethnicity groups and were not different from each other. Asian Americans and whites were not significantly different from each other in parental SES across the range of the five fields. Only in the field of engineering did African Americans have lower parental SES than Asian Americans and whites. In the humanities, African Americans had SES backgrounds similar to those of Asian Ameri-cans. Hispanic students reported lower SES than whites and international students in education and lower than whites in the humanities and social sciences. The international students in our sample appear to have had lower family SES than whites in all five fields.

DOMESTIC FACTORS

On the basis of his review of the work of R. B. Levin and A. L. W. Franklin (1984) and Marilyn Heins, S. N. Fahey, and L. I. Leiden (1984), Baird (1990b) reports that graduate students often have nonacademic roles that are as important to them as their roles as graduate students; many, for in-stance, are spouses or partners and parents. These multiple roles may com-pete with one another for students' attention and may be accompanied by numerous demands on students' time and energy as well as financial re-sources. Researchers have sought to determine the relationship between marriage or partnership and success in doctoral programs (Feldman 1973; Hawley 1993); marital status and productivity (Feldman 1973); marital sta-tus and social interactions (Feldman 1973); and marital status and degree progress (Girves and Wemmerus 1988).

Our marital status measure may not be comparable to prior studies be-cause we included in our definition both students who were married and students who had domestic partners. For ease of presenting and reading, we refer to this category of our sample as married, and both partners and spouses are referred to as spouses. Under this categorization, nearly 54 per-cent of the doctoral students in the sample were married. The largest per-centage of married students (62%) were from education (as one might ex-

---

3. In the one study (Mooney 1968) we have found that examines its influence on degree completion, parental socioeconomic status did not have a significant impact on doctoral stu-dents' degree completion.

pect from the higher ages of doctoral students in education), followed by humanities (54%), social sciences (52%), sciences and mathematics (50%), and engineering (49%). The only significant difference we observed was between education and most other fields. When we viewed marital status by sex, we found that 68 percent of the men and 59 percent of the women in education doctoral studies were married. In the humanities, a similar pattern occurred, with 57 percent of men and 51 percent of women being married. The opposite was true in sciences and mathematics, with 53 percent of women married compared with 49 percent of men. Differences in the marital status of men and women in the other fields were minimal.

Comparing the race-ethnicity groups, while there are varying percentages of students who were married, most of these are not different statistically speaking. One difference across several fields was observed in comparing African Americans and whites. A higher percentage of white students than African Americans in education, humanities, and social sciences were married. In education, a higher percentage of whites were married than their international counterparts, while in sciences and mathematics a higher percentage of international students were married than African Americans and Asians; in the social sciences, international students also had a higher percentage of students who were married.

Educational Attainment of Spouses or Partners

What is the benefit of having a spouse with a higher level of education? At least one group of scholars has found the higher educational attainment of black doctoral students' spouses to be associated with higher degree completion rate (Willie, Grady, and Hope 1991). The spouses of doctoral students in our sample are best characterized as having a high level of educational attainment. Only a few anomalies turned up when we examined the highest level of education reported for the spouse of our doctoral sample: only 12 percent of the spouses of the doctoral students did not have a bachelor's degree, and only 2 percent of the doctoral students had spouses whose education was a high school diploma or less. The highest percentage of students with spouses who did not have a bachelor's degree were majoring in education (15%), followed by social sciences (11%), engineering (10%), and sciences and mathematics (9%). Approximately 28 percent of the sample who were in domestic relationships had spouses whose highest attainment was a bachelor's degree; 45 percent of spouses had a master's degree, and 16 percent had a Ph.D., J.D., or M.D.

Our data seemed consistent with Helen Astin's (1969) and Saul Feldman's (1973) findings that in all fields of doctoral study women were significantly more likely than men to have spouses whose highest educational attainment was a Ph.D., J.D., or M.D. There is little race difference in the educational attainment of the spouses of doctoral students.

Student Status of Spouses

While many doctoral students' spouses have attained high levels of education, many others are pursuing their doctoral degrees at the same time. Although research has focused on dual-career couples, not much is known about dual-student couples and the effect of this occurrence on the doctoral student experience. Among the students who were married, nearly one-third (29%) had spouses who were also students. Education students least often had a spouse who was a student (17%); doctoral students in the sciences and mathematics were most likely to have a student spouse (40%), followed by students in engineering (34%), social sciences (32%), and humanities (31%). The differences between education and each of the other fields were statistically significant and are most likely attributable to the fact that their spouses are older and have income-paying jobs. In education, a higher percentage of male than female students (19% vs. 16%) had spouses who were also students. In sciences and mathematics, we found the opposite: a higher percentage of women students than men (45% vs. 38%) reported that their spouses were students. We observed minimal differences in spousal student status by race: a third of the noneducation doctoral students and around half of the international students in sciences and mathematics had spouses who were students.

Children under the Age of Eighteen

The effect on doctoral endeavors of having children under the age of eighteen has received limited research attention. One area of research has focused on the differential effect of having children on the stress of women's and men's graduate student experiences; married women graduate students with children in the home are believed to experience the greatest time pressures (Gilbert 1982). A more prevalent research issue has been the influence of children on degree progress (Abedi and Benkin 1987; Nerad and Cerny 1993; Tuckman, Coyle, and Bae 1990; Wilson 1965). The general conclusion is that having children—and, in a study by Howard Tuckman, Susan L. Coyle, and Yupin Bae (1990), having larger numbers of children—retards degree progress.

Among our sample, it appears that students in many fields are forgoing parenthood, at least temporarily. In the sciences and mathematics, 87 percent of respondents reported having no children under the age of eighteen, followed by students in the humanities (82%), engineering (81%), the social sciences (80%), and education (52%). In education, engineering, and sciences and mathematics, we discovered a difference between the percentages of men and women having children under eighteen. In each case, fewer women than men in our sample reported having children under the age of eighteen. There are few differences among the race groups with respect to the presence of young children. In sciences and mathematics, 30 percent of African Americans had children under eighteen, compared with 10 percent of whites. It is still interesting to observe, however, that in education, more than half of the African Americans and Hispanics reported having children under the age of eighteen, compared with just a little more than one-third of the Asian Americans and nearly one-half of the whites.

ANNUAL INCOME

Typifying what Marjorie Lozoff (1976, 142) describes as "genteel poverty," the incomes of our sample bear out reports of the financial sacrifices made by graduate students. Sixty-seven percent of the respondents reported that their own incomes (not including spouses' income) was less than $20,000; 24 percent had incomes between $20,000 and $49,999; and 9 percent reported annual incomes of more than $50,000. With the exception of education students, large proportions of the students in the other fields (70% in engineering, 73% in social sciences, 78% in humanities, and 88% in sciences and mathematics) reported annual incomes of less than $20,000. Education was the only field with a high proportion of students reporting incomes between $20,000 and $50,000 (38%) and more than $50,000 (24%), which may be explained by their older age and the greater probability that they have a full-time job. With the exception of education, the percentages of men and women who earned less than $20,000 are generally similar. Among education students, a larger share of women (42%) than men (30%) fell into this income category. In education and engineering, a larger share of men than women reported earning more than $50,000. Race differences appear to have been minimal in the income area. In the field of education, 27 percent of African Americans reported earning $20,000 or less, compared with 40 percent of Hispanics, 35 percent of whites, 55 percent of Asian Americans, and 70 percent of international students. We observed a similar pattern in the social sciences.

Spousal Annual Income

As we have seen, women doctoral students in several fields may be operating with lower incomes than their male colleagues; however, their spouses are more likely to earn more than $50,000 than the spouses of male doctoral students in all fields. When there are differences by race-ethnicity, it appears that international students' spouses are less often earning more than $50,000. This may be because of restrictions on the employment of student spouses. A smaller percentage of Hispanic spouses (27%) than whites (46%) in education have annual incomes exceeding $50,000.

Mean Household Income

These differences in spousal income are mirrored by differences in mean household income. Doctoral students in education have considerably higher mean household incomes than students in each of the other fields. But there are sex differences: except in the fields of education and humanities, the mean household income of women doctoral students is higher than that of their male colleagues. There are also race differences: white doctoral students in education report higher mean household incomes than both white students in other fields and their counterparts in other race-ethnicity groups in all fields. The major race-ethnicity differences in household income are in the field of education: between African Americans and whites ($57,000 and $67,000, respectively), between Asian Americans and whites ($49,000 and $67,000, respectively), between Hispanics and whites ($49,000 and $67,000, respectively), and between international students and whites ($24,000 and $67,000, respectively). Similarly, in sciences and mathematics, whites' incomes led those of Asian Americans ($30,000, compared with $26,000), and African Americans reported lower household incomes than whites ($22,000, compared with $30,000).

Among engineering students, each of the race-ethnicity groups reported higher annual household incomes than international students: for international students in the field of engineering, the average annual household income was $24,000, compared with $42,000 for African Americans, $34,000 for Asian Americans, $39,000 for whites, and $30,000 for Hispanics. The lower income of international students is largely a function of the visa restrictions on their earnings, which typically require them to be enrolled full-time, to remain in good academic standing, and to work no more than twenty hours a week on campus.

CONCLUSION

As with any research involving samples, it is important to know the characteristics as a context for understanding the results and findings. The demographics of our sample are useful in that they closely resemble the characteristics of doctoral degree recipients reported by the National Science Foundation and the U.S. Department of Education. Although this does not suggest that the experiences of our sample of students can be generalized to the population of all doctoral students at the nation's more than six hundred doctorate-granting institutions, it does give a general sense of connection. Because our sample is typical, perhaps doctoral students may see the findings as applicable to their own situations. The sample also reveals different demographics among fields and by race and sex that should be kept in mind for their relevance to the findings that are presented in the remaining chapters.

CHAPTER FIVE

Admissions
and Screening

FROM THE DATA PRESENTED IN CHAPTER 4, it is clear that all doctoral students are not created equal. They enter their doctoral programs with varying degrees of advantage. Some are from families in which a graduate education is uncharted territory and a cherished goal; for others, it is a family tradition. Many decide on doctoral work early in their school years or in college, while some heed the calling later, during their adult working lives. Some students' attention is diverted from their doctoral studies by the presence of young children in their homes. Some begin doctoral programs at retirement age and are much older than their classmates. Undergraduate education, performance on the Graduate Record Examination (GRE), the time between college and doctoral program enrollment, and program choice are other traits that appear to contribute to students' eventual experiences in their programs. Upon applying to a doctoral program, each student is screened by various field-oriented standards as well as department standards. Because of its prominence in the admissions process, and its role in forecasting student success beyond the admissions process, the GRE stands out as an especially important screening element.

SELECTIVITY OF
UNDERGRADUATE INSTITUTIONS

In *The Shape of the River,* William Bowen and Derek Bok (1998) give much attention to their findings regarding advantages that graduates of selective colleges realize in the labor market. It appears that the selective colleges also have an advantage in postbaccalaureate degree attainment.[1] The selectivity of doctoral students' undergraduate college has been linked to successful completion of graduate degree programs (Astin 1982; Baker 1998; Mooney 1968).

We are most interested in students who attended one of the 120 most selective colleges and universities in the United States, since the selectivity of students' undergraduate institutions may reveal something about

---

1. We were interested in research that examines the relationship between the selectivity of doctoral students' undergraduate college and their doctoral research productivity but were able to find only studies that examine the relationship between the undergraduate institution selectivity and the research productivity of doctoral recipients (Buchmueller, Dominitz, and Hansen 1999; Long, Allison, and McGinnis 1979; Wong and Sanders 1983).

their preparation for and inclination to enter a doctoral program.[2] We were able to ascertain the undergraduate selectivity of all but 240 students in our sample. Ratings do not exist for colleges and universities outside of the United States, however, so we counted students who earned baccalaureate degrees outside the United States as having not attended a most selective college or university.

More than 90 percent of doctoral students attended a different institution for their doctoral program from the one they attended for their undergraduate education. Around 36 percent of the sample attended one of the 120 most competitive or highly competitive undergraduate institutions in the United States. Within the major fields, the fields with the largest percentage of students from the most competitive or highly competitive undergraduate backgrounds were the humanities (55%), the social sciences (38%), sciences and mathematics (36%), engineering (35%), and education (28%).

With the exception of engineering and the social sciences, we found no discernible difference in the selectivity status of the undergraduate colleges and universities attended by men compared with women. In the fields of engineering and social sciences, women more often than men attended the most selective colleges and universities (44% of women and 33% of men in engineering, 41% of women and 33% of men in the social sciences). In engineering, this is noteworthy, given the severe underrepresentation of women in the field. Perhaps increasing the share of women from less selective colleges and universities to approximate the proportion of men could yield greater representation.

Given what we typically observe about undergraduate admissions test scores by race, it is not surprising that in every field, a larger share of Asian Americans attended the most selective undergraduate colleges and universities, while a larger percentage of African American students attended less selective colleges and universities.[3] With the exception of humanities, a smaller share of African Americans attended the most competitive colleges and universities than their Asian American, white, and international peers. In sciences and mathematics, more than half of the Asian American and white doctoral students attended the most selective undergraduate colleges and universities, compared with just 16 percent of their African American counterparts. The Asian American and African American difference, which is the largest, is also found in education (35% vs. 19%), engineering (64% vs. 34%) and the social sciences (53% vs. 33%). If doctoral

2. We developed a data file of selectivity, which we call the Nettles and Millett Enhanced Institutional Selectivity File, that is rooted in the *Barron's Profiles of American Colleges and Universities* (1999). The enhancement is an estimate of selectivity for colleges and universities that did not participate in Barron's.
3. In at least one study (Nettles 1990b), black doctoral students were less likely than Hispanics and whites to have attended selective undergraduate institutions.

programs in even the most prestigious graduate institutions, like the ones included in this research, relied only on the most selective colleges and universities for students, the underrepresentation of African American and Hispanic students that we observe would be even more acute. African Americans make up 5 percent of the degree recipients in the nation's most selective colleges and universities, and Asian Americans 11 percent. The pursuit by doctoral programs of greater African American representation may require several strategies, including continuing recruitment from a wider range of selectivity of colleges and universities, increasing African American student representation in the most selective colleges and universities, and perhaps even consideration of a broader array of selection criteria in the graduate admissions process for predicting their success.

First-Choice Program

Researchers for some time have speculated on the role program choice plays in later doctoral experiences. For students who are selecting their doctoral programs with the prospect of having a particular mentor, pursuing a particular intellectual focus, or joining a particular research initiative, first choice may be critical. For others who are less certain about their focus and are either more adventuresome or exploratory about their research endeavors, attending their first-choice program may be less important, unless, of course, geographical preferences or restrictions come into play. Are students who attend their first-choice or only-choice program more satisfied with their doctoral experience? Of our sample, more than two-thirds (69%) were attending either their first-choice or only-choice doctoral institution. More students in education (86%) were attending their first-choice institution than in other fields. Education is also the field in which students were relatively older and were more often studying part-time than the other fields and therefore more likely to have geographic preferences enter into their choices.

After education, engineering (70%) was the field with the next highest percentage of students in first- or only-choice programs, followed by sciences and mathematics (63%), social sciences (60%), and humanities (53%). A somewhat higher percentage of women than men in education and social sciences were attending doctoral programs of their first or only choice (88% vs. 84% in education, and 62% vs. 57% in the social sciences, respectively). This ordering may suggest that humanities, social sciences, and sciences and mathematics are the most competitive fields in which to gain admission among doctoral programs in the universities represented in this study. A somewhat higher percentage of women than men in education and social sciences were attending their first or only choice of doctoral programs (88% vs. 84% in education and 62% vs. 57% in the social sciences). Few race-ethnicity differences were apparent, as most of the doctoral students in each field seemed to be attending what they considered to be either their only-choice or their first-choice doctoral program.

MATCH BETWEEN UNDERGRADUATE
AND DOCTORAL FIELDS OF STUDY

Doctoral programs of different fields vary in the extent to which foundational knowledge and preparation are required, but familiarity with the field from prior preparation would seem to be advantageous in all fields. John Smart (1987) has found, for example, that students who elected to pursue the field of their undergraduate major adjusted better to graduate school, had better relationships with their faculty, and were more satisfied with graduate school than their counterparts who changed majors.

Given the quantitative and cumulative nature of the disciplines, it is not surprising that most students of engineering (88%) and sciences and mathematics (83%) retained their field of study when they moved from undergraduate to doctoral programs. For much the same reason, a high percentage of humanities (72%) and social sciences (63%) students were also majoring at the doctoral level in the field of their undergraduate degree. By contrast, only 22 percent of education doctoral students received their undergraduate degrees in education. Unlike engineering and sciences and mathematics, education is a professional field of study that draws on a range of disciplines and includes a much larger proportion of students who are further removed, by virtue of their age and work experience, from their undergraduate experience. There are some small differences between the sexes in both education and engineering. In education, 75 percent of women, compared with 85 percent of men, reported having an undergraduate major that was different from their doctoral major; in engineering, 18 percent of women reported not having majored in that field as undergraduates, compared with 11 percent of men. These are the two fields with skewed gender distributions, and in each case the dominant sex has a greater tendency to have matching undergraduate and doctoral major fields. This suggests that a larger share of the minority sex in each of these two fields (women in engineering and men in education) takes longer to see the field as appropriate for them.

Compared with other race-ethnicity groups, a much smaller share of Asian American (7%) education doctoral students chose for their doctoral degree the same field they had studied for their bachelor's degrees. This compares with 21 percent of whites, 22 percent of Hispanics, 30 percent of international students, and 30 percent of African Americans. Given the relatively large interest of Asian Americans who select postsecondary math, science, and engineering, and their relatively minor interest in teacher education, it is not surprising that a relatively small share of Asian American doctoral students had majored in education as undergraduates.

Attending a Public
versus Private Graduate School

The distinction between public and private programs may be less consequential at the doctoral level than at the undergraduate level. Indeed, the
hierarchical linear model analyses that we performed in this study reveal
greater differences within university programs than across the programs
in such ways as peer interaction and student-faculty interaction. Although
like undergraduate education, the tuition and other costs of doctoral programs at private universities is higher than those for the public universities, the extent to which doctoral students actually pay these prices, as opposed to having their costs covered by their fellowships and assistantships,
does not vary between the two sectors. More than 60 percent of our sample was attending public graduate schools, but this varied considerably by
field. More than two-thirds of the students in sciences and mathematics
(71%) attended public graduate schools, as did 68 percent of engineering
students, 66 percent of humanities students, and 62 percent of social sciences students. The high share of education students attending private
graduate schools (59%) occurs because of the large number of students in
our sample who were attending Teachers College of Columbia University;
in our sample, 68 percent of the education doctoral students attending a
private graduate school were enrolled at Teachers College.

Men and women in humanities, sciences and mathematics, and social
sciences did not differ in their attendance at private versus public graduate schools. Women were more likely than men to attend private graduate
schools in education (nearly 60%, compared with 56%) and engineering
(nearly 42%, compared with 30%). While most of the doctoral students
outside education attended public graduate schools, there were some race
differences. In education, a higher percentage of African Americans (62%)
than Hispanics (49%) and international students (51%) attended private
schools. Also in education, a smaller percentage of Hispanics (49%) than
whites (60%) attended private graduate institutions. Even given the rather
high demand among international students for engineering and sciences
and mathematics programs, white students (38%) in engineering were
more likely than international students (27%) to attend private graduate
schools, and in sciences and mathematics, a higher percentage of African
American students (57%) than Asian Americans (33%), Hispanics (24%),
or international students (26%) attended private schools. Nearly the same
percentage of African American doctoral students in sciences and mathematics were attending their first-choice institution as were attending private universities.

Graduate Record Examination Scores

Despite the significance of GRE scores, students and faculty were ambiguous about how GRE scores play out over the course of doctoral programs.

The following quotation, taken from an unsolicited letter submitted by one of our respondents, is illustrative of the ambiguity among students: "While I am happy to provide some of the requested information, I do not believe my GRE scores, GPA [grade point average] stats, or academic performance ratings are relevant to the aim of your study. (This is not a matter of protecting privacy.) I understand that such information is useful for categorizing and contextualizing the information elsewhere in the survey. I believe your survey's main purpose, as outlined on the cover page, is important and necessary. I just do not believe test scores and grade point averages are relevant. I feel quite strongly about this· (Yet, I was quite pleased to see some of the questions asked in the survey.)"

Warren Willingham (1974) suggests that the GRE is superior to the undergraduate GPA in the graduate admissions process because of the two weaknesses of undergraduate grades—their narrow range and the variability of their meaning across colleges and universities. Tuckman, Coyle, and Bae (1990) have tried to distinguish what GRE scores and grades represent. To them, the GRE is a measure of achievement, while grades are a measure of student ability. Whatever the distinctions, many graduate schools require students to take the GRE General Test, and they typically use the scores to forecast student success and to help make critical decisions such as who will receive the various fellowships and assistantships that are available.[4] To provide a clearer picture of our sample's prowess, we discuss each part of the General Test—verbal, quantitative, and analytical—separately and by field, sex, and race, characteristics that typically reveal differences in achievement on the GRE and other admissions tests.

The overall mean for our sample on the verbal test was 583. The highest verbal mean achieved among our five fields was in the humanities (669), followed by social sciences (601), sciences and mathematics (575), engineering (562), and education (556). With the exception of the field of education, this is a somewhat heartening ordering, given the nature of the work required in each of the fields. We expected humanities students to show relatively high verbal and relatively low quantitative skills. The scores of education students on the verbal section, while not surprising, may reflect the broader diversity of interests in the broad field of education as well as the broader demographic diversity, namely, by age and race. The differences in the GRE verbal scores of men and women in engineering and in sciences and mathematics were significant. Among engineering students, women averaged a higher score than men (587 to 557), while in sciences and mathematics men achieved a slightly higher score than

---

4. Researchers have examined the relationship of performance on the Graduate Record Examination to receiving fellowships (Malaney 1987), to graduate grade point averages (Morrison and Morrison 1995; Sternberg and William 1997), to the research productivity of doctoral recipients (Clark and Centra 1982; Schrader 1978, 1980), and to degree attainment (Ehrenberg and Mavros 1995; Rock 1972; Zwick 1991; Zwick and Braun 1988).

women (579 to 568). The engineering sex difference in verbal scores may be linked to the fact reported above, that women more often than men switched into engineering from other fields at the undergraduate level. Regardless of the field they are switching from, it is highly unlikely that their prior training placed more emphasis on quantitative and less on verbal skills than that of their counterparts who did not switch majors.

As we observed earlier, the highest verbal scores in our sample were achieved by the humanities students, with men and women nearly matched in performance (671 vs. 667), followed by men and women in the social sciences (597 vs. 605) and in education (559 vs. 553). White humanities students achieved the highest average verbal score (689), followed by Asian Americans (645), Hispanics (618), international students (576), and African Americans (569). This, too, is an ordering that we have become accustomed to in admissions testing during the past half century. The international student position in the ordering reflects in part the bias in favor of students in our sample for whom English is the native language. The position of last place for African American students in the verbal ordering is consistent with the other two parts of the test and presents a major challenge for African Americans competing for admissions and other benefits and awards conferred upon graduate students for which GRE scores are a criterion. The lowest GRE verbal scores for all race groups were in the field of education. Consistent with the other fields, white students reported the highest average scores (591) among education doctoral students, followed by Asian Americans (515), Hispanics (506), African Americans (461), and international students (446).

By comparison, the overall mean score for the quantitative test was 672, with engineering students achieving the highest mean at 757, followed by those in sciences and mathematics (731), social sciences (656), humanities (614), and education (567). However, the sex differences in GRE quantitative scores were significant in each of the fields, and in each case men achieved the highest scores (see fig. 5.1). The sex difference was narrowest in engineering, where both women and men achieved higher quantitative scores than in the other fields (750 for women, 758 for men). Although they more frequently entered engineering after pursuing a different major in undergraduate school, women doctoral engineering students displayed high quantitative ability. In sciences and mathematics, the field with the second highest quantitative mean, the sex difference was much wider than in engineering (743 for men and 704 for women). The gap between men and women continued to widen in social sciences (689 for men, 623 for women) and humanities (641 for men, 588 for women). In education there was a 42-point gap, with men averaging 596 and women 554.

While engineering students in all race-ethnicity groups achieved higher GRE quantitative scores than their counterparts in other fields, leading the

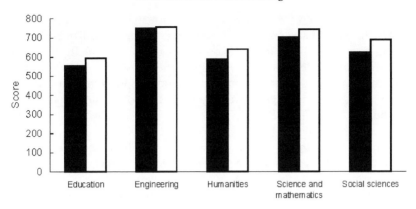

Fig. 5.1. GRE Quantitative Scores, by Sex and Field. GRE tests are scored on a scale of 200 to 800. *Solid bar,* women; *open bar,* men.
Source: Survey of Doctoral Student Finances, Experiences, and Achievements.

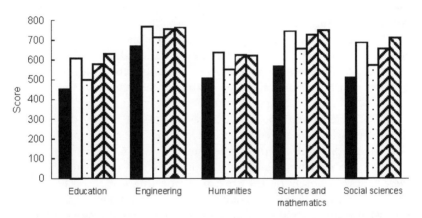

Fig. 5.2. GRE Quantitative Scores, by Race-Ethnicity and Field. GRE tests are scored on a scale of 200 to 800. *Solid bar,* blacks; *open bar,* Asians; *dotted bar,* Hispanics; *ascending hatching,* whites; *descending hatching,* international students.
Source: Survey of Doctoral Student Finances, Experiences, and Achievements.

engineering group were Asian Americans (769), followed by international students (764) and whites (755) (see fig. 5.2). These scores were higher than those of Hispanics (714) and African Americans (671). These relatively high scores reveal a challenge facing the GRE Board—to produce a quantitative test that discriminates better at the higher end of the score scale. With a score range of 200 to 800, averages that are so close to the top for engineering doctoral students reflect the high quantitative orientation of engineering doctoral students but also suggest that a more challenging test is needed. The same is the case in sciences and mathematics, although to a slightly lesser degree. In the sciences and mathematics, international students (751) and Asian Americans (745) achieved higher GRE quantitative scores on average than students of other race groups. Among the others in sciences and mathematics, the average quantitative score for whites was 728, for Hispanics 656, and for African Americans 566. Perhaps because of these high scores, several fields require applicants to take subject area tests in addition to the general test.

The mean scores both in engineering and in sciences and mathematics, however, continue to reveal the separation of Hispanic and especially African American students from the top performers in their field—at least, judging by their GRE scores. Again, in social sciences, African Americans had lower GRE quantitative scores than each of the other groups, 509 compared with 710 for international students, 687 for Asian Americans, 657 for whites, and 571 for Hispanics. In the field of education, international and Asian American doctoral students achieved the highest GRE quantitative scores, at 630 and 609, respectively. White students in education reported GRE scores averaging 578, followed by Hispanics at 499 and African Americans at 452. The scores of African Americans in education are the lowest scores of any race group among all five of the fields. This is a matter that must be of concern to African American students seeking doctorates in education as well as to the GRE Board and the colleges and universities that are enrolling and preparing African American students for such study.

Like the verbal test, the analytical test of the GRE is more discriminating, scores being more evenly distributed across the spectrum. The mean GRE analytical score for the entire sample was 645, with sciences and mathematics students achieving the highest group mean, at 679. They were followed closely by students in engineering (677), social sciences (646), humanities (645), and education (571). Sex differences did not appear to any great extent in the analytical scores, except among engineering students, among whom the average score for women exceeded that of men by 31 points (704 compared with 673). This is a much larger gap than in the quantitative section (8 points favoring men) and about the same gap as in verbal scores. Indeed, women in engineering achieved the highest GRE analytical scores of either sex among all fields. In each of the other fields, the average scores for men and women were similar: sciences and mathematics, 680 versus 678; social sciences, 647 versus 645; humanities, 648 versus 643; and education, 570 versus 571, respectively.

Among the race groups, GRE analytical scores followed much the same pattern as the quantitative scores. The highest scorers were found in engineering and in sciences and mathematics; and on average, the highest score recipients by race in these two fields were whites and Asian Americans. The analytical scores of white and Asian American doctoral students in engineering were 709 and 697, respectively, and in sciences and mathematics, 705 and 683, respectively. For African Americans in engineering, the average analytical score was 599, and for sciences and mathematics, 522. For Hispanics in these two fields the scores were 622 and 598, and for international students around 648 in both. As was the case with GRE verbal and quantitative scores, doctoral students in education achieved the lowest of the average GRE analytical scores in each race group, and African American students in education were the lowest among the groups, at 459. Among education doctoral students, whites achieved the highest GRE analytical scores (599), followed by Asian Americans (561), Hispanics (524), and international students (517). Consistent with the verbal and quantitative scores, the race group ordering on the analytical test for African Americans in our sample reflects a monumental education, measurement, and equity challenge for the nation.

PROGRAM TRANSITION
Role of the Master's Degree

Students arrive at their doctoral programs by different routes. Some pursue the doctorate immediately after receiving their baccalaureate degrees, while others wait years. Some complete a master's degree before proceeding to a doctorate, others enter directly into a Ph.D. program.

Far more education students (79%) than students in any other field completed master's degrees before pursuing doctoral degrees. This again reveals the professional nature of the education doctoral degree. To a lesser extent than education, but certainly more so than the other fields and disciplines, the engineering doctorate is also a professional degree and consequently is second to education with respect to the share of students in the sample who have already completed master's degrees (45%). Among the three remaining field groups, more than one-third had attained master's degrees in the social sciences (36%) and humanities (34%), and only a fifth, the smallest proportion, of students in sciences and mathematics (20%). The only fields in which men and women were different on this measure were engineering and sciences and mathematics. Nearly 47 percent of men in engineering programs had earned master's degrees, compared with 31 percent of their female counterparts, and in sciences and mathematics, 21 percent of men, compared with 18 percent of women.

As with practically everything else about the sample, there are race distinctions in the patterns and tendencies of students regarding their prior preparation and achievements. In education, a higher percentage of African Americans (85%) started from master's degrees than Asian Americans (69%) or international students (73%). In engineering, a higher percentage of international students (59%) had attained master's degrees, compared with Asian Americans (39%) and whites (33%). The same pattern was found in sciences and mathematics: nearly 39 percent of international students had master's degrees, compared with 18 percent of Asian Americans, 8 percent of Hispanics, and 10 percent of whites. In sciences and mathematics, a larger percentage of African Americans (27%) had first achieved master's degrees than had Hispanics (7%) and whites (10%). Whether having a master's degree before entering a doctoral program is advantageous is questionable, and outside of the field of education, it certainly does not appear to be the dominant occurrence. Some in our sample could still settle, in the end, for a master's degree as a consolation prize after giving up their doctoral pursuits before completing a dissertation, qualifying examinations, or even required course work. But to pursue graduate education with the intention of attaining a master's degree before the doctoral is a different matter. In the field of education, this approach appears to be the norm rather than the exception, and many programs are structured in that pattern. In the other fields, entering the doctoral program directly after completing a baccalaureate degree appears to be standard practice.

Time Off between Degrees

Another indicator of style of transition is the amount of time students take off between completing their undergraduate degrees and entering their doctoral programs. Time off, just as other styles of transition, has purposes and consequences. Given the professional nature of the field of education, for example, it is widely believed that time spent as a practitioner in the field has long-term benefit to education doctorates, whether they become scholars or leaders after achieving the degree. In contrast to education, it is widely believed that scientists and mathematicians experience prolonged productivity by beginning early and that, given the nature of the work, their most prolific years are likely to be during the first half of their careers. As with most characteristics of doctoral students, the amount of time students take off before attempting a doctorate also varies considerably by field. At slightly more than two years, sciences and mathematics students reported taking the least amount of time off between receiving their undergraduate degrees and beginning their doctorates.

At the opposite end of the continuum, with an average of nearly twelve years off, education students experienced the longest time lapse between receiving their baccalaureate degrees and entering doctoral programs. In the remaining three field groups (engineering, humanities, and social sciences), students took off, on average, 3.5 to 4.5 years. The differences between men and women on this measure are negligible. Even in the fields of engineering and the social sciences, where there is a gender difference in the amount of time taken off, the differences appear to be ever so slight. In the case of engineering, women took off half a year less than men (3.0 years compared with 3.5 years), on average. In social sciences, women took off about a half a year more (4.5 years compared with 4 years). In sciences and mathematics, the average time off was nearly 2.25 years for both sexes, and in humanities, nearly 4.5 years for both. The average time for education students, as we have seen, was nearly 12.0 years for both men and women.

In the field of education, African Americans and whites both took off more time (12.5 years) than their counterparts in other race-ethnicity groups: 8.0 years each for Asians and international students and 10.0 years for Hispanics. Besides education, the greatest race differences lay in the field of sciences and mathematics, where African Americans took twice as much time off, on average, as their counterparts in the other race groups (4.0 vs. 2.0 years). Such choices may have consequences. Beatriz Clewell (1987) suggests that minority students who enter graduate programs immediately after attaining undergraduate degrees may be more likely to persist to program completion.

As expected, the reasons students gave for taking time off between the baccalaureate and doctoral study differed across fields of study, although the three principal reasons—the need for work experience, the need for a break, and uncertainty about graduate school—were all relatively common. Unsurprising is that the more a field is tilted toward being a professional field, the more likely was work experience to be a factor, as was uncertainty about whether to pursue a doctoral degree. Among education students, more than a third (35%) were uncertain about whether they would pursue a doctorate when they completed their undergraduate degrees; this was followed by their need for work experience (32%) and an interest in starting a family (9%). For engineering students, the most important reasons were the need for work experience (31%), not knowing whether they would pursue a doctorate (17%), and the need for a break (10%). For humanities students, uncertainty about pursuing a doctorate was the principal reason (30%), followed by the need for a break (25%) and the need for work experience (13%). Sciences and mathematics students cited first their need for work experience (25%), followed by the need for a break (16%) and uncertainty about pursuing a doctorate (15%). For social sciences students, uncertainty loomed largest (28%), followed by interest in work experience (25%) and the need for a break (14%).

In education and the humanities, men and women do not appear to differ in their reasons for taking time off between the bachelor's degree and the doctoral program. In engineering, 20 percent of the women reported that they needed a break from school, compared with 8 percent of men, while 33 percent of men reported they wanted work experience, compared with 17 percent of women. Twenty-five percent of women in engineering indicated that they did not know whether they would pursue a doctoral degree, compared with 16 percent of men, and that seems to be in line with gender difference in the change of fields among doctoral students in engineering. The differences in the social sciences and in sciences and mathematics were less dramatic. In the sciences and mathematics, 19 percent of women did not know whether they would pursue a doctorate, compared with 13 percent of men, and this was the most frequently cited reason. Thirty percent of women, compared with 25 percent of men, in the social sciences reported that they had been uncertain about pursuing a doctorate when they graduated from college. The major differences among race-ethnicity groups in reasons for taking time off between programs occurred in education. A larger percentage of whites than African Americans and Hispanics gave uncertainty about pursuing a doctoral degree as their primary reason for taking time off.

FULL-TIME ENROLLMENT
AT THE START OF DOCTORAL STUDIES

In practically all ambitious pursuits, the more time and intensity one expends, the greater the likelihood of a positive outcome. Doctoral education is no exception. Attending graduate school as a full-time student has been found to be correlated with doctoral students' persistence and degree attainment (Clewell 1987; Girves and Wemmerus 1988; Ott and Markewich 1985).

Our data support the common perception that doctoral study is best approached as a full-time endeavor. With the exception of education, where a majority (63%) of students were full-time but less so than in other fields, the norm for full-time study was more than 90 percent: 95 percent in engineering, 95 percent in humanities, 97 percent in sciences and mathematics, and 94 percent in social sciences. To some extent, this is a reflection of the criterion of full-time enrollment used in selecting the sample and the requirements of the institutions included in the study. Men in humanities and social sciences started their doctoral studies as full-time students at a slightly higher rate than women. In every field but sciences and mathematics, whites and African Americans had equal rates of starting as full-time students. The lower rates of full-time enrollment among African Americans is yet another characteristic that is cause for concern and speculation about the extent to which their full-time status may be affected by other attributes of human capital, such as prior academic experience and GRE scores. International students generally had the highest rates of full-time enrollment at the start of the doctoral program, and this is strongly linked to their J-1 and F-1 student visas, requiring them to maintain full-time enrollment during the academic year.

ALWAYS BEING A FULL-TIME STUDENT

Full-time enrollment rates dropped over the course of doctoral studies for the students in our sample. As with full-time enrollment at the start of the doctoral program, education students reported the lowest rate of full-time enrollment over the course of their studies. Fewer than half (42%) of education students remained enrolled full-time, compared with 79 percent of humanities students, 81 percent of social science students, 86 percent of engineering students, and 91 percent in sciences and mathematics. Women in the social sciences reported a lower rate of full-time enrollment than men, 78 percent compared with 85 percent. The pattern of international students differing in their full-time enrollment status held when we looked at full-time enrollment over the course of doctoral studies.

CONCLUSION

The advantage students acquire before their doctoral programs comes in various forms, including the quality of undergraduate experience, whether they are attending the doctoral institution of their first choice, the GRE scores they achieve, and the style of transition they make. The most notable and alarming distinction among doctoral students revolves around GRE scores across fields and race. We examine the effect of GRE scores on a variety of experiences of doctoral students in chapter 11. Suffice to say at this point that the wide variation observed across fields and race-ethnicity and sex groups makes us wonder about the extent to which student potential is captured by the scores, especially the relationship of the scores to student performance. Regardless, one can appreciate the diversity of social and human capital of students who enter doctoral programs.

CHAPTER SIX

Financing
a Doctoral Education

WE BEGAN THIS RESEARCH searching for answers to Catherine's original question, "How do doctoral students fund themselves from the time they enter through the point of completing their degrees?" We have come to the conclusion that there are no simple answers to what appears on the surface to be a straightforward question. Doctoral students' financial conditions, circumstances, choices, and consequences are complex. In fact, the question itself is not as simple as it seems. To begin with, there are many different sources and types of financial assistance, and each one carries with it training and career implications. Here is a description of one student's circumstance: "My financial history is more complicated than it might appear. In general, my living expenses are met by support from my institution. I have in the past carried some non-educational credit card debt, but my balance is now $0. I took a federal loan out this year for the purchase of a computer, but that is unusual. I took some loans as an undergraduate, but my parents paid them off before I entered grad school. So it was a 'loan' that turned into a 'personal source.'" Finances are important for reasons that are broader than satisfying student needs. As well, they may contribute to determining the size of the eligible pool of students that universities consider admitting and may also shape policies of universities and the government in producing a supply of doctorates.

To explore students' financial conditions, we looked at students' undergraduate debt at the time they received their baccalaureate degrees and their outstanding undergraduate education debt at the time they began their doctoral programs. To consider how students finance their doctoral programs, we examined the types of financial support they were offered at the time of admission, the types of financial support they received over the course of their doctoral programs, and their personal resources and external work demands. The financial picture is made even more complex when one considers the differences among students by field of study and, within field, by the different experiences of women and men and differences in the characteristics and attributes of students of race-ethnicity.

For the past three decades, scholars have equivocated about the role played by finances in student access and persistence and in the quality of experiences in doctoral programs. Some researchers have established a link between the type of funding students receive during doctoral programs and their research productivity (Buchmueller, Dominitz, and Hansen 1999; Ethington and Pisani 1993; Roaden' and Worthen 1976); others find connections between funding and degree completion as well as time to degree (Bowen and Rudenstine 1992; Ehrenberg and Mavros 1995). The equivocating, we have learned, is justified. Finances are a complex matter involving both tangibles, such as cost, price, personal income, multiple types of assistantships, and fellowships, and many intangibles, such as various personal attitudes toward, understanding of, and psychological approaches to acquiring and using money.

Bowen and Rudenstine (1992, 178), in a tersely compelling understatement, write, "Money plainly matters." In the beginning, money calculations are often a part of the decision process that students move through when considering doctoral programs. As they decide to enroll in particular programs, students confront many of the same financial issues they will face throughout their doctoral experience, such as taking stock of personal resources, anticipating daily subsistence expenses, managing debt, and securing fellowships and assistantships.

Twenty years ago, Bruce Smith (1985) noted that students in the arts and sciences might already have been discouraged from attending graduate school by their large undergraduate debts. Perhaps Gary Malaney (1987, 85) best sums up the importance of financial considerations in graduate education with the following comment: "Without it (financial support), prospective students might not begin graduate study . . . and current students might not be able to finish their degree programs." He suggests that with the rising cost of graduate education and the increased burden of undergraduate indebtedness, financial support for graduate study may be necessary to entice many undergraduates to pursue advanced degrees.

Malaney's assessment appears to be as applicable to today's graduate students as it was to students of two decades ago. Since finances are a critical element in the experiences and achievements in doctoral programs, perhaps one way to untangle the conundrum is to examine student funding experiences across the major fields and by sex and race.

STUDENT DEBT
BEFORE STARTING A DOCTORAL PROGRAM

Undergraduate education debt burden has long been seen as a possible deterrent to student pursuit of graduate education. However, 65 percent of our sample had no undergraduate debt at the time they received their bachelor's degrees. The National Center for Education Statistics analyses of the data from the 1999–2002 National Postsecondary Student Aid Study (NPSAS:02) estimates that in 1999–2000, 60 percent of the those who completed their Ph.D.s in fields other than education, and 50 percent of those who completed doctorates in education, had not borrowed for their undergraduate education (Choy, Geis, and Malizio 2002). In light of that finding, our sample is comparable to the proportion of Ph.D. completers who did not borrow to finance their undergraduate education. Similarly, since 43.7 percent of all 1995–96 undergraduates borrowed (Berkner and Malizio 1998), it also seems that our students, at 35 percent, are somewhat typical.

Doctoral students' propensity to carry undergraduate debt appears to vary somewhat by field, race, and sex. In our sample, engineering majors represented the highest percentage of students who had no debt when they completed college (74%), followed by majors in sciences and mathematics (69%), social sciences (62%), education (59%), and humanities (58%). This ordering among the fields does not intuitively appear to be connected with socioeconomic status (SES), given that the humanities students in our sample rated highest on that measure—unless, of course, higher-SES students have less aversion to undergraduate loans.

Historically, women have been less likely to borrow for their undergraduate education (Nettles 1990a; Solmon 1976). Audrey Cohen and Alida Mesrop (1972) attribute the relatively high loan aversion of women students in the 1960s and 1970s to their hesitancy to borrow heavily against future earnings—which were expected to be lower than men's—and their relative difficulty in qualifying for loans, owing to sex discrimination in the banking industry. It is noteworthy that over the past decade, the sex representation among undergraduates has also shifted: in 2000, most undergraduates were women (56%). In contrast to the past, women and men today seem equally matched in their propensity to borrow for their undergraduate education. The National Postsecondary Student Aid Study (NPSAS:96) reveals that in 1996, 26.5 percent of women undergraduates, compared with 24.4 percent of men, received loans (Berkner and Malizio 1998). Our findings suggest that undergraduate borrowing behavior is not uniform across fields. A smaller percentage of women (60%) than men (65%) in the social sciences have no debt, as do a smaller share of men (56%) than women (61%) in education. In engineering, humanities, and sciences and mathematics we found no gender difference. In each case, however, the proportion of students in our sample who had borrowed for their undergraduate education, while slightly (5 to 10%) higher than the rates found for the general undergraduate population, are not out of line in comparison.

Many universities require international students to demonstrate a capacity to pay for their doctoral degrees, so it is not surprising that a larger share of international students than students of each of the other race-ethnicity groups indicated having no undergraduate education debt. In education, fewer African Americans (43%) and Hispanics (41%) were debt free than their counterparts of the other race groups. The same held in humanities, where only 33 percent of African Americans and 30 percent of Hispanics were debt free, compared with 59 percent of whites and 79 percent of international students. In sciences and mathematics, only 55 percent of African American and Hispanic students carried no undergraduate debt, compared with 86 percent of international students. In the social sciences, only 38 percent of African Americans were debt free, compared with 61 percent of Asian Americans, 57 percent of whites, and 84 percent of international students. These higher rates of undergraduate indebtedness for African American and Hispanic doctoral students may reflect their lower financial assets compared with whites and international students. It is yet another layer of mounting evidence of the disadvantage among African American and Hispanic doctoral students.

Whether students took on loan debt as undergraduates is the first level of analyses. The next is the amount of indebtedness. Among doctoral students who had undergraduate loan debt, 32 percent owed less than $5,000, 27 percent fell in the range of $5,000 to $9,999, and 40 percent had debt of $10,000 or more. The average amount owed was around $9,500. Education students had, on average, $8,828, while students in engineering had $9,924, in humanities $9,577, in sciences and mathematics $9,718, and in social science $10,191. The debt levels of women and men in all other fields were comparable to each other. In education, engineering, humanities, and social sciences, the mean undergraduate debt for students who had debt did not differ significantly by race. In sciences and mathematics, Asian American and white students had lower undergraduate loan debt ($6,824 and $7,352, respectively) than international students ($8,180). Given that doctoral education is an investment that eventually yields larger career earnings, these amounts of indebtedness seem modest, but the extent to which they affect low-SES students more than high-SES students may be a concern to graduate institutions and policy makers.

The highest percentage of students in our sample who were debt free were working toward doctorates in engineering (78%), followed by those in sciences and mathematics (73%), education (73%), social sciences (67%), and humanities (61%). Yet again, humanities, the field with the highest parental SES, had the smallest percentage of students who were free of education debt when they entered doctoral programs. In engineering and social sciences, a smaller percentage of women than men had no debt: in engineering, 71 percent of women compared with 80 percent of men, and in social sciences, 64 percent of women compared with 70 percent of men. In all fields, international doctoral students were most likely to carry no education debt at the start of their doctoral program. In education, humanities, and the social sciences, African Americans and Hispanics were more likely than their white peers to have education debt upon entering their doctoral programs.

On average, students with education debt began their doctoral programs owing slightly more than $11,000. We do not know the variety of types of service that students were making on their debts while working on their doctorates. Social sciences students had accumulated the most debt by the start of their doctoral programs, slightly more, on average, than $12,426. Engineering students, at slightly more than $10,510, had the lowest amount. The highest percentages of students with more than $10,000 in education debt at the start of their doctoral programs were for those majoring in humanities (18%) and social sciences (17%), followed by students in sciences and mathematics (13%), education (12%), and engineering (10%). Graduate schools need to learn more about the social class structuring of the amounts of debt within these fields. The difference in average loan debt for women and men with debt at the beginning of their doctoral programs was significant only in education ($12,086 compared with $10,085). We found no within-field differences by race in the average education debt owed by students with debt at the start of their doctoral programs.

Given that African American and Hispanic students accumulated higher amounts of undergraduate debt than the other groups, it is somewhat surprising that their overall debt upon entering doctoral programs was lower. Also interesting, but beyond the scope of this study, is the extent to which the underrepresentation of African American and Hispanic students can be attributed to the higher undergraduate debt and continuing debt burden at the point at which they would be entering doctoral programs. Since our study focused on students who had entered doctoral programs, we were not able to address this question in this study. Catherine Millett (2003), in a separate study, has found evidence to suggest that debt appears to have a large enough effect on the postsecondary decisions of low-SES students that it deserves more attention from graduate institutions seeking to increase the representation of African American and Hispanic doctoral students.

FINANCIAL AID OFFERS UPON ADMISSION

The type of financial support students are offered may be an indication of the quality and extent of their academic opportunities and may even predict the quality of their experiences. Fellowships seem to be the top prize because they often cover all student expenses and ordinarily come with no work requirements. Research and teaching assistantships, however, which often require students to work with faculty on research projects or instructional activities, can be most valuable for their associations and the apprenticeships they provide to students in preparation for professional careers. We were interested in whether students were offered financial support by their graduate institutions when they first enrolled in their doctoral programs. In our pilot study leading up to this research, several graduate deans told us they believed that many students were aware that their financial support came through their graduate institutions but often did not know the original source of funds. Students may be aware, for example, that they are working with a professor on a research project, but they may not know that the project is funded by a National Institutes of Health training grant and that their tuition, fees, and stipend are paid by that grant. Similarly, doctoral students with teaching assistantships may not be aware that the source of their support is undergraduate student tuition and fees. Consequently, we asked the students in our sample to indicate whether they received various types of graduate institution support, but we did not ask them to indicate the sources, assuming that, consistent with our pilot test results, they might not know.

Graduate Institutions' Offers

Graduate institutions offered financial assistance to 67 percent of the students in our sample at the time the students were admitted. At opposite extremes were sciences and mathematics, where 91 percent were offered aid, and education, where 46 percent received offers. Given the professional nature of education doctoral programs, the latter rate, though relatively low, is still impressive. One might assume that in sciences and mathematics the sources of support are mainly undergraduate tuition subsidies and research grants and contracts. In the field of education, given the large number of students who completed master's degrees on the way to their doctoral programs, we may assume that programs have the added subsidies provided by their master's degree program from which to produce financial offers to beginning doctoral students. In the other fields, offers of financial support were clustered around two-thirds of entering students: engineering (71%), humanities (61%), and the social sciences (66%). There were also some sex differences in these initial offers. A somewhat larger percentage of women in engineering and the humanities were offered financial assistance—77 percent versus 70 percent in engineering and 65 percent versus 57 percent in the humanities. In the case of engineering this is a larger percentage of a much smaller pool and perhaps the effect of women being in such short supply and high demand.

The race differences in offers of financial assistance at the time of admissions were mainly between international students and whites, and even there the differences were not dramatic. In every field, with the exception of the humanities, a somewhat smaller percentage of international students were offered financial assistance by their graduate institutions. In education and humanities, a higher percentage of both African Americans and Hispanics were offered financial support at admissions than whites: in education, 54 percent of African Americans and 64 percent of Hispanics, compared with 45 percent of whites, and in the humanities, 87 percent of African Americans and 82 percent of Hispanics, compared with 56 percent of whites.

In the sciences and mathematics, though African Americans in large numbers received offers of assistance when entering, they less often received offers with their admissions than their noninternational peers (82% compared with 95% for Asian Americans, 98% for Hispanics, and 92% for whites). This may be a function of the lower rate of offers to our sample's African Americans enrolled in sciences and mathematics doctoral programs at historically black colleges and universities. (See appendix E for a discussion on the differential effects of attendance at historically black colleges and universities.) This lower rate of offers is nonetheless significant, given the acute underrepresentation of African Americans in sciences and mathematics doctoral programs and the small supply of African Americans in the doctoral-trained workforce of the United States.

Fellowship Offers

Often, to be competitive with other doctoral programs, institutions offer fellowships to the students who present the most promising and accomplished academic records. Fellowship offers usually reflect the market forces of supply and demand by talent but also, to some degree, by demographics. Nearly half (48%) of the students who were offered aid received a fellowship offer when they were admitted to their doctoral program. Humanities had the highest percentage of students receiving fellowship offers (71%), followed by social sciences (52%), sciences and mathematics (45%), engineering (45%), and education (44%). A higher percentage of women than men were offered fellowships in engineering (54% vs. 43%) and in sciences and mathematics (52% vs. 42%).

In each field except education, more than two-thirds of our sample's Hispanic and African American students who were offered aid were offered fellowships at the time they enrolled in their doctoral programs (see fig. 6.1). These rates indeed reflect the high demand for the small supply of Hispanic and African American doctoral students in every field. Although these are important awards for attracting students, unless students undertake a broader range of support, they can be shut out of apprenticeship opportunities that may have a greater effect on their longer-term career success than the short-term benefits of fellowships.

Research Assistantship Offers

Research assistantships typically require students to work from ten to twenty hours a week with faculty members on internally sponsored or subsidized research or externally sponsored research. They provide students with hands-on training and experience that prepares them to become independent producers of research in their field. Often, faculty consider these to be precious slots with high stakes for the success of their own research projects. They are usually required to disseminate their findings in a timely fashion, and they rely on students to provide substantive assistance.

About 44 percent of the doctoral students who were offered financial

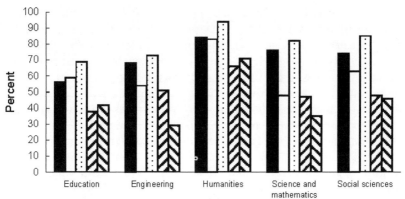

Fig. 6.1. Fellowship Offers at Time of Doctoral Program Enrollment, by Race-Ethnicity and Field. *Solid bar,* blacks; *open bar,* Asians; *dotted bar,* Hispanics; *ascending hatching,* whites; *descending hatching,* international students.
Source: Survey of Doctoral Student Finances, Experiences, and Achievements.

support upon admission were offered research assistantships. Engineering had the highest percentage of students who were offered research assistantships (69%); next were sciences and mathematics (55%), social sciences (30%), education (26%), and humanities (14%). The only statistically significant sex difference in the offers of research assistantships at admissions was in engineering, with a larger percentage of men (70%) receiving such offers than women (61%). This raises a question about the possibility of differential opportunity for women in engineering to gain valuable apprenticeship experiences.

Several researchers have examined education financing by race-ethnicity. Both Blackwell (1987) and Nettles (1990a) find that a higher proportion of whites than blacks had teaching and research assistantships. Pearson (1985) finds no difference in assistantships versus fellowships, but he does observe a higher proportion of teaching assistantships than research assistantships among blacks. Madeline Williamson and Robert Fenske (1994) report that Mexican American and Native American women experienced more financial difficulty than men and that such difficulties were related to their need to borrow.

Race differences in initial offers of research assistantships seem to derive from the lower frequency of offers to African American students in engineering and in sciences and mathematics. In our sample, 36 percent of African American engineering students were offered research assistantships, compared with 69 percent of Asian Americans, 70 percent of whites, and 71 percent of international students. Similarly, in sciences and mathematics, 33 percent of African Americans were offered research assistantships upon entering their programs, compared with 62 percent of Asian

Americans, 56 percent of whites, 56 percent of Hispanics, and 53 percent of international students. In the fields of education, humanities, and the social sciences, the patterns are similar, though the differences between race-ethnicity groups are less pronounced. The apparent disadvantage of African Americans in the valuable apprenticeship opportunities provided by research assistantships is especially alarming in sciences and mathematics and in engineering, where their underrepresentation is most severe. That the pattern is the same, though less dramatic, in other fields raises the question of the factors, race included, that are being taken into account when these decisions are made and the social dynamics that may be at play, given the severe underrepresentation of African Americans in graduate faculties. Hispanics until recently have been clustered closer to African Americans, but in the case of research assistantship offers, they are now much more akin to the other groups. These issues are explored further in the relational analyses.

Teaching Assistantship Offers

Graduate student teaching assistantships cover a broad spectrum of instructional activities, including assisting professors to prepare lectures, providing tutorial assistance to students, and delivering instruction directly. For students who are preparing to become faculty, the experience of teaching during their doctoral programs is invaluable. For all the criticism that college and university faculty receive for the unevenness and unsatisfactory quality of classroom teaching, it would appear that one solution—and perhaps the best solution—is for universities to improve the training provided to prospective teachers. As a short-term benefit for universities, having talented doctoral students help provide the teaching of undergraduate students is economically important for subsidizing doctoral training and research.

Approximately 60 percent of our sample who were offered financial assistance at admissions indicated that they were offered teaching assistantships. This is a larger share than were offered fellowships (48%) or research assistantships (44%). The share of teaching assistantship offers to students in engineering, sciences and mathematics, and social sciences conformed to the general average, offers were somewhat fewer in education (41%) and humanities (44%). Given the rather large undergraduate humanities requirements in the nation's universities, one might have expected offers of teaching assistantships to doctoral students in the humanities to rival those of social sciences students.

The sex differences in the offers of teaching assistantships were significant in the fields of sciences and mathematics and in the social sciences. In sciences and mathematics, 67 percent of women and 77 percent of men, and in the social sciences, 60 percent of women and 67 percent of the men, were offered teaching assistantships.

Of the students who were offered financial assistance at the time of admission, a relatively small percentage of African Americans were offered teaching assistantships in engineering, sciences and mathematics, and social sciences compared with whites. As with research assistantships, the African American challenge of receiving offers of teaching assistantships on par with other race-ethnicity groups appears greatest in engineering and in sciences and mathematics: in engineering, only 19 percent were offered teaching assistantships, compared with an overall 43 percent, and in sciences and mathematics only 53 percent, compared with 74 percent overall. We might conclude that African Americans were not getting teaching assistantships on par with their white counterparts because they were awarded fellowships instead. Indeed, they had a higher rate of fellowship offers than whites. Hispanics also had higher rates of fellowship offers than did white students, however, though they did not suffer the same low rates of teaching assistantship offers at admission as African Americans.

SOURCES OF FINANCIAL SUPPORT DURING THE DOCTORAL PROGRAM

The initial offers of student aid are important for student recruitment to doctoral programs. The offer of financial support can be a factor in choosing a particular graduate program. After the initial offers, however, doctoral students have multiple years of study and work ahead, making the aid they receive long-term probably more important for understanding the quality of their doctoral program experiences than initial offers. In our survey, we asked doctoral students if they had ever received any of twelve different sources of support: fellowships, research assistantships, teaching assistantships, administrative assistantships, residence hall or program assistantships, travel grants, dissertation grants, university research grants, research grants from a private foundation, federal- or university-sponsored loans, tuition or fee waivers, and employer tuition assistance. Of these, we focus on three: fellowships, research assistantships, and teaching assistantships. As the following discussion suggests, these forms of support are very much a product of field of study.

Fellowships

As far back as 1960, researchers have noted differences in how financial aid is allotted across the various fields of study. Berelson (1960) cites a 1957 survey, by the National Opinion Research Center, showing that more than three-quarters of the graduate students in the arts and sciences received stipends. As well, 53 percent of humanities, 51 percent of physical science, 48 percent of engineering, and 45 percent each of biological sciences and social sciences students received fellowships. Berelson (1960) also reports his own survey, finding that, with the exception of professional fields (such as education), fellowships and teaching assistantships were evenly distributed across fields to about half of the eventual recipients of doctoral degrees. Arthur Hauptman (1986) also finds that graduate students in the arts and humanities were most likely to receive institutionally funded fellowships.

Our sample substantially confirms these findings. Humanities students were more likely than other doctoral students to receive fellowships. Slightly more than 69 percent of humanities students received these awards, followed by students in social sciences (61%), sciences and mathematics (59%), engineering (50%), and education (46%).

In a study of the characteristics of people who received various types of financial support, Baird (1976) finds that men and women were equally likely to receive fellowships and assistantships. Our results corroborate Baird's findings in the fields of education, humanities, and social sciences but not in engineering or sciences and mathematics. In these areas, women were more likely to receive fellowships. In engineering, 69 percent of women, compared with 47 percent of men, received fellowships, and in sciences and mathematics, 67 percent of women, compared with 56 percent of men.

Baird (1976) and Malaney (1987) both find race to be a strong predictor of receiving fellowships. Our study seems to reveal a similar finding. When we looked at receiving a fellowship over the course of the doctoral program without distinguishing field of study, Hispanics were the most likely recipients (81%), followed by African Americans (67%), Asian Americans (60%), whites (55%), and international students (45%). When we added field of study to the picture, the race differences largely remained. In every field, a larger percentage of Hispanics than white students received fellowships during their doctoral programs, and in education, engineering, and social sciences, African Americans reported a higher rate of fellowships than whites. Education was the only field in which Hispanics had an advantage over African Americans in receiving fellowship offers over the course of their studies. Another notable exception was international students in relation to U.S. citizens. In engineering and in sciences and mathematics, African Americans, Asian Americans, and whites each reported a higher rate of fellowships than did international students. African Americans and Hispanics in social sciences had a higher rate than international students, whereas in education a higher proportion of Hispanic students than international students received fellowships. We are not able to judge the effect that the availability of fellowship support may have on attracting students to doctoral programs or contributing to retaining them beyond initial entry, since our sample consisted only of students who were pursuing their degrees and had successfully completed at least one year. These are important considerations for gaining a complete picture of doctoral student finances.

Research Assistantships

Berelson (1960) finds that research assistantships were limited mainly to the sciences and engineering, where most of the funds were concentrated at that time. Baird (1976) later determined that students in physical sciences, life sciences, and engineering were more often the recipients of research assistantships than their counterparts in other fields. A decade later, Hauptman (1986) reported that students in those three fields were more likely to receive research assistantships, while students in the arts and humanities and the physical sciences were more likely than students in other fields to receive teaching assistantships. These differences persist in the current study, research assistantships being most prevalent in engineering and in sciences and mathematics, with 82 percent of the doctoral engineering students receiving this form of support, followed by students in sciences and mathematics (69%), social sciences (49%), humanities (33%), and education (28%).

In our sample, men and women in all fields of study were equally likely to have received research assistantships. This finding is a departure from the work of other researchers who have found that while men and women received financial aid in the same proportion, men were more frequently recipients of research assistantships, while women were more likely to receive teaching assistantships (Solmon 1976; Wong and Sanders 1983). Lewis Solmon (1976) attributes the difference in assignments to male professors' preference for working with male students and expresses concern that men thereby benefit from greater professional development than women. This is also different from our finding that men were favored in research assistantship offers upon entering doctoral programs in the field of engineering. Given our finding of parity in research assistantships, it appears that during the course of doctoral studies the initial gender imbalance levels out, despite the lower representation of women on engineering faculties; this circumstance resolves a gender equity dilemma.

Different researchers have also asked whether research assistantships and teaching assistantships were spread evenly among race groups. Marian Brazziel and William Brazziel (1987) present data to show some minority groups were less than half as well represented among teaching and research assistants as their white peers, and in a later study Nettles (1989) confirms that black doctoral students were less likely to be teaching or research assistants than either their white or Hispanic colleagues. Pruitt and Isaac (1985) consider research and teaching assistantships to be key retention tools for minority students owing to their critical role in promoting apprenticeships through the research and teaching responsibilities. When we looked at the propensity ever to have been a research assistant (at some point in the course of doctoral studies) by race without adding the field dimension, African American doctoral students were the least likely to have been research assistants (28%, compare with 62% for Asian Americans, 44% for Hispanics, 51% for whites, and 61% for international students).

When we added field, however, the differences shifted (see fig. 6.2). Humanities was the only field with no race differences. In education, 19 percent of African Americans received research assistantships, compared with 37 percent of Asian Americans and 29 percent of white students. In engineering, African Americans, at 44 percent, trailed Asian Americans (81%), Hispanics (83%), whites (86%), and international students (81%) in ever having been research assistants. In sciences and mathematics, a higher percentage of Asian Americans (72%), Hispanics (67%), whites (71%), and international students (65%) reported having research assistantship experience during their doctoral programs than African Americans (38%). The problem of African Americans having assistantships is dire; not only are they underrepresented initially, but also their underrepresentation persists throughout their doctoral experience. How might this circumstance negatively affect their productivity during doctoral programs and their career preparation?

Our data dramatically indicate that international students are not being excluded from participation in research assistantships in U.S. universities. This is counter to the perception that international students are consumers paying their own way through doctoral programs and supports the competing popular notion that international students are among the elite talent that faculty seek to join them in their research pursuits. As early as 1976, Baird reported that while international students were less often recipients of aid awarded by American institutions, they were equally likely

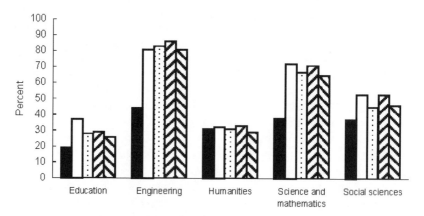

Fig. 6.2. Research Assistantships during Doctoral Program, by Race-Ethnicity and Field. *Solid bar,* blacks; *open bar,* Asians; *dotted bar,* Hispanics; *ascending hatching,* whites; *descending hatching,* international students.
Source: Survey of Doctoral Student Finances, Experiences, and Achievements.

as American students to receive assistantships. Ten years later, Malaney (1987) had a similar finding. Using the 1983 Survey of Earned Doctorates, Hauptman (1986) finds that 36 percent of American students received research assistantships, compared with 47 percent of foreign nationals and 52 percent of foreign students holding permanent visas. Hauptman acknowledges that because these students were enrolled mainly in the physical sciences and engineering, perhaps they had greater access to assistantships, but it appears that in the 1980s they were not being denied research assistantships because of their citizenship. Nor are they up to the present, as 80 percent of international students in our sample received research assistantships in engineering, 65 percent in sciences and mathematics, 46 percent in social sciences, 29 percent in humanities, and 26 percent in education. In each case, these rates were comparable to those of Asian Americans and Hispanics and only slightly below that of whites.

Teaching Assistantships

With the exception of the field of education, teaching assistantships are a ubiquitous form of financial support. The highest percentage of students who received teaching assistantships were majoring in sciences and mathematics (74%) and in humanities (74%), followed by social sciences (64%), engineering (51%), and education (29%). Indeed, over the long term the humanities students in our sample participated at the highest levels in teaching assistantships, despite having had among the lowest rates of participation at the start of their doctoral programs. It appears that humanities programs may engage doctoral students in the teaching function later in their programs than the social sciences. In the humanities, women and men reported comparable rates of having been teaching assistants. A larger percentage of women in engineering (61%) were teaching assistants than men (49%), as well as in education (30% of women compared with 27% of men). In contrast, a larger percentage of men in sciences and mathematics (76%, compared with 70% women) and in the social sciences (68%, compared with 60% women) reported having had teaching assistantships.

Similar to research assistantships, Hispanics had teaching assistant experience comparable to that of whites (see fig. 6.3). With the exception of humanities, African Americans tended to be teaching assistants less often than whites—18 percent versus 30 percent in education, 33 percent versus 61 percent in engineering, 50 percent versus 70 percent in sciences and mathematics, and 46 percent versus 66 percent in social sciences. African Americans also differed from Asian Americans in education, sciences and mathematics, and social science. In all, however, the research involvement of more than 50 percent of African Americans over the long term in humanities and in sciences and mathematics is perhaps the most encouraging level of involvement in the assistantship participation examined in

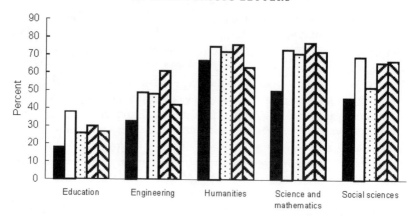

Fig. 6.3. Teaching Assistantships during Doctoral Program, by Race-Ethnicity and Field. *Solid bar,* blacks; *open bar,* Asians; *dotted bar,* Hispanics; *ascending hatching,* whites; *descending hatching,* international students.
Source: Survey of Doctoral Student Finances, Experiences, and Achievements.

this research. In 1986, Hauptman reported that 40 percent of foreign doctoral degree recipients had served as teaching assistants while they were graduate students, compared with 52 percent of American doctoral degree recipients. In our sample, 57 percent of international students had served as teaching assistants, although the proportion varied by field, from as high as 72 percent in sciences and mathematics to as low as 27 percent in education.

Except in engineering, where a smaller percentage of international students than whites had been teaching assistants (42% vs. 61%), the rates of teaching assistantships for international students were close to those of whites. International student participation as teaching assistants exceeded that of African Americans in sciences and mathematics (72%, compared with 50%) and in social sciences (67% compared to 46%). The relatively high involvement of international students in teaching assistantships overall, and especially in the fields of sciences and mathematics, where they are most heavily represented, is further testament to the high value of international students to the doctoral education enterprise. This raises questions about the level of reliance of U.S. doctoral programs on international students for maintaining their current levels of productivity and whether the quality of the supply of American doctoral students is adequate.

OTHER MEANS OF SUPPORT
DURING THE DOCTORAL PROGRAM

Doctoral students rely on other sources of support, in addition to an abundance of fellowships, research assistantships, and teaching assistantships, to finance their doctoral programs. These include loans, personal resources, and jobs unrelated to their doctoral programs.

Education Debt

Hauptman (1986) reports that among doctoral students, those in the social sciences, the arts and humanities, and education were more likely to borrow than students in the physical sciences, life sciences, and engineering. Overall, 30 percent of doctoral students in our sample incurred debt during their doctoral programs. Across fields of study, the range differed dramatically, with the highest percentage of students who took on debt majoring in the humanities (47%), followed by education (44%), social sciences (40%), sciences and mathematics (14%), and engineering (12%). In our sample, a higher percentage of women than men students in the social sciences (44% vs. 35% men) incurred debt.

International students, not unexpectedly, rarely took on debt. Within this group, the highest incidence of incurred debt in any by field was 16 percent of humanities students. Otherwise, in education and in sciences and mathematics there seems to be a higher tendency for African Americans and Hispanics to borrow, compared with international students, adding to their cumulative profile of disadvantage. This concurs with Earl Smith and Joyce Tang's (1994) analyses of the Survey of Earned Doctorates and Survey of Doctorate Recipients. In most cases, despite the higher rates of African American and Hispanic borrowing, the difference is not significant in comparison with whites.

Having debt is one issue; the amount of debt is yet another. In addition to his finding that students in the arts, social sciences, humanities, and education are more often borrowers, Hauptman (1986), citing a study of Pennsylvania graduate and professional borrowers (David 1983), reports that the average level of accumulated debt doubled from 1976–77 to 1982–83, from $5,000 to $10,000. The range for our sample was very wide, with education doctoral students who had debt reporting the highest mean graduate school–related debt ($22,286) and sciences and mathematics students reporting the lowest ($12,920). However, on average, the education debt of doctoral students was $19,343. Overall, women with debt had a higher debt level—$19,843, compared with $18,731 for men. The sex difference disappeared when we examined the debt burdens of women and men within the same field.

Overall, there were no race-ethnicity differences in mean education debt. Within fields of study, race differences in debt burdens among students who incurred debt during their doctoral programs followed a different pattern from the one seen in their undergraduate debt burden. Education, humanities, and social science students had similar levels of debt across race groups. In engineering, however, international students reported a significantly higher level of debt than their white peers ($23,214, compared with $15,236). We observed a similar pattern in sciences and mathematics, where international students had $23,182 in debt compared with $12,143 for Hispanics and $11,738 for whites. Given their higher rates of participation in assistantships, the debt levels of international students raises questions about the prospect of higher costs of living that requires them to accrue such high levels of indebtedness in engineering and in sciences and mathematics.

Personal Resources

The prevailing popular sentiment is that doctoral students use little of their own personal resources to pay for their doctoral education and instead rely almost exclusively on fellowships and assistantships to cover the costs. Put another way, any doctoral student worth her or his salt will not need to rely on personal resources to pay for a doctoral education, and doctoral programs of high quality generate sufficient resources to sponsor their students from start to finish. Little research exists on how much of the cost of their own doctoral education bill students actually pay. Gita Wilder and Nazli Baydar (1991) provide some data in their longitudinal study of 2,521 men and women who took the Graduate Record Examination. Of the 56 percent of these who actually went on to graduate school, only 14 percent indicated that they had paid none of the cost themselves. The others who enrolled in graduate school paid, on average, one-half of the cost out of their own pockets. Since Wilder and Baydar's sample also included students in master's programs, where financial aid may be less plentiful, one might expect the out-of-pocket cost for doctoral students to be much less.

In the year of our survey, nearly 40 percent of the doctoral students in our sample indicated having used their personal resources to pay tuition and fees, apart from money they received for assistantships or fellowships. On average, students who used personal resources spent nearly $4,500 a year. Sciences and mathematics students used the least amount of personal resources (on average, less than $2,628 a year), with education students spending an average of $5,255. Across fields, men and women reported similar experiences using personal resources to pay for their doctoral education.

In 1990 Nettles began the process of identifying race differences in students' use of personal resources. At that time, he found both black and white students to be more likely than Hispanic students to rely on personal resources to pay most of their doctoral education expenses (Nettles 1990a). The presence of international students in our study somewhat reshaped the mix. International students in the field of education appear to have used a larger amount of their personal resources to finance their doctoral educations. In education, the differences in the amount of personal resources relied on by international students ($9,739) exceeded each of the other race-ethnicity groups. In engineering, the higher dependence on personal resources by international students ($6,600) is significant when viewed alongside out-of-pocket expenses of Asian Americans ($3,008) and whites ($3,073). In the social sciences, the higher international student reliance on personal resources ($6,273) is significant compared with both African Americans ($2,830) and whites ($3,810).

Jobs Unrelated to the Academic Program

Concerns have been raised that working at a job takes time from doing academic work and thereby retards a student's degree progress. Jamal Abedi and Ellen Benkin (1987, 13) conclude that private means are important: "If doctoral students are adequately supported by their universities, and they do not have to work off campus, this will have a direct impact on the speed with which they complete their degrees." Lisa Gillingham, Joseph Seneca, and Michael Taussig's (1991) research supports the belief that working more hours at a job, as opposed to academic work, has a negative affect on time to degree.

In the case of jobs outside the academic program, a considerable chasm exists between education and the other fields. Students in education work, on average, almost 14.0 hours a week at an unrelated job. This reflects the circumstance that a much larger proportion of students in education are attending part-time, with many working in schools. Humanities and social sciences students reported working an average of almost 6.5 hours a week, while engineering and sciences and mathematics students worked less than 3.0 hours a week at unrelated jobs. Engineering was the only field in which women and men reported a markedly different number of hours working at a job unrelated to their doctoral program, men averaging 3.0 and women 1.4 hours a week.

Overall, the African Americans in our sample worked a larger number of hours on a job not related to their academic program than Asian Americans, whites, and international students. In the social sciences, African Americans averaged 10.5 hours a week, a figure that was significant when compared with both whites and international students. In the field of education, African Americans, Hispanics, and whites averaged significantly more hours worked than international students, and in engineering, Asian Americans and whites worked significantly more hours than international students. In sciences and mathematics, the number of hours worked by whites compared with international students is significant.

CONCLUSION

In addition to providing subsistence, financing is a central component of the experience of doctoral students. The good news is that doctoral students are resourceful and that, at least at the doctoral institutions attended by students in our sample, resources appear to have been abundant for supporting doctoral students through fellowships, research assistantships, and teaching assistantships. The resourcefulness of doctoral students is displayed through their success in cobbling together funding from multiple sources to limit their reliance on both loans and personal resources.

The patterns by field, race, and sex presented in this chapter are addressed further in the relational analyses in chapter 11. Although African Americans have a smaller share of teaching assistantships and research assistantships, and higher rates of borrowing, than their peers, it is important to examine the factors that contribute to these disadvantages before concluding that race or racial discrimination are likely culprits. It is intriguing to us that international students appear to be actively assisted by all forms of support, particularly the teaching and research assistantships, and in most cases do not appear to be less well assisted than their American counterparts. A timely question for the American doctoral enterprise to address in the early years of the twenty-first century is whether it can sustain the same level of productivity if it is forced, in the post-9/11 environment, to rely less on international talent and income.

CHAPTER SEVEN

Socialization

"As I hand in this survey, I feel I should explain something. Shortly before I received your first survey, I decided to abandon my doctoral program, after having my completed dissertation rejected by my committee. Because of this, I no longer consider myself a graduate student." This brief note accompanied a completed survey. We can only imagine the circumstances that led to this disappointing outcome for the student, the department, and the graduate school at the final stage of the program. We suspect the answers lie in what the student did not tell us about his social and academic relationships with graduate faculty, about his relationship with his adviser, whether he had a mentor, and, if so, his relationship with his mentor. These elements are likely to be key in understanding this unfortunate outcome.

Socialization is important at every level of education, but given the restricted range of grades that students receive in doctoral programs and the individual tailoring of doctoral student work, the indexes of socialization in graduate school are especially important gauges of student progress and achievement. The socialization process is important because student socialization contributes to students' performance, satisfaction, and success in doctoral programs. Socialization is also important because the movement to faculty renewal and replacement over the next decade will most likely bring a new focus on issues of faculty recruitment, retention, productivity, and satisfaction. These are all outcomes subsumed in the broad concept of doctoral student socialization—generally, the process by which students acquire the attitudes, beliefs, values, and skills needed to participate effectively in the organized activities of their profession.

Doctoral students should enter their programs with the expectation that the experience, though demanding, will be a positive one in which they benefit both intellectually and socially. Data on enrollment in doctoral programs and production of earned doctorates are routinely monitored by the national government, but the nature and status of socialization of doctoral students for academic and research careers, the reputed hallmarks of doctoral training, have been overlooked. Consequently, the socialization of the growing and diverse population of doctoral students in the United States is a much more nebulous component of graduate education than is suggested by such vital statistics as enrollments and numbers of doctoral degrees awarded. As university graduate program enroll-ments grow and become more racially diverse, the variation in the social-ization of students from different backgrounds who are expected to pro-vide academic and research productivity and leadership in the nation and around the globe becomes increasingly interesting.

For the past four decades, as scholars of graduate education have pro-claimed the importance of socialization, they have at the same time ex-pressed alarm at the limited published evidence about the quality of so-cialization of doctoral students. Rodney Hartnett is one notable scholar who has been astonished by the paucity of research on graduate student socialization. In his words, the "status characteristics in one's professional academic career are often heavily influenced by socialization during grad-uate training. Today's graduate students, after all, are tomorrow's faculty members" (Hartnett 1981, 212).

MODELS OF SOCIALIZATION

Researchers have explored the socialization process in ways that illumi-nate our study. Bernard Rosen and Alan Bates (1967) focus on the Ameri-can graduate school as one agency devoted to training adults to perform professional roles. Defining graduate faculty as agents and graduate stu-dents as neophytes, the authors create an interactive model of socializa-tion that includes such components as student knowledge acquisition, role differentiation, sequential progress, authority models, independent growth, and goal commitment. More recent work has focused on doctoral student interaction with peers as being essential to the student socializa-tion equation (Stein and Weidman 1989b; Weidman, Twale, and Stein 2001). To the notion of faculty as mentors and fellow students as peer sup-porters, Baird (1992) adds the dimension of time, suggesting that social-ization increases as students reach successive stages of their programs. Ac-cording to Baird,

> as students progress through their programs, they are assimilated more and more into the life of their departments and disciplines, thereby gaining greater access to and closer interactions with faculty . . . Those at the beginning of their programs are learning the expectations and demands upon them and are thus somewhat distant from faculty. Those at the dissertation stage, who have served their apprenticeships and are socialized to the norms and methods of their discipline, are expected to work closely with faculty. Likewise, students at the begin-ning of their programs may see other students as unknown quantities or as competitors, in contrast to those at later stages who see other stu-dents as being part of a departmental community.

Having tested his theory in a study of doctoral students at the University of Illinois–Chicago, Baird (1992) reported that more advanced doctoral students spent more time with faculty outside of class and had more mentoring opportunities, as well as more interaction with their fellow graduate students, than beginning or mid-course doctoral students. Baird then developed an integrated model of graduate student socialization in which he incorporated many of the critical elements that had been advanced in prior work. In Baird's (1993b) integrated model, graduate faculty and graduate student peers are seen as important agents of socialization. At the same time students were being socialized to the graduate experience, they were also developing the skills needed for success both in graduate school and in their chosen professions. Baird's model also accounts for the other roles that students play (for example, spouse or partner, parent, employee, a citizen in the community) that may either complement or detract from their roles as graduate students. These additional roles may be different for racial minority and majority students and may also affect the different race-ethnicity groups in different ways. The extent to which minority students are involved in ways that are different from their majority peers is not known, nor are the differences in the effects. Baird (1993b, 8) observes that "in [the integrated] model, attrition is associated with poor social and academic relationships with professors and fellow students, inadequate mastery of the forms of reasoning favored by the discipline, and poor support from spouses, employers and other groups."

John Weidman, Darla J. Twale, and Elizabeth Stein (2001) present the most current thinking about graduate and professional student socialization. The refinements they have made to earlier work (Stein and Weidman 1989b, 1990) can best be characterized as a shift in thinking about socialization as a static linear process to a dynamic nonlinear process.

OVERVIEW OF THE CURRENT STUDY

We incorporated the key components of these socialization models into the current study to represent the quality of student experiences and socialization in doctoral programs. Our measures include doctoral student perceptions of their social and academic interactions with faculty, their relationships with peers, relationships with mentors and advisers, and their career expectations.

Student-Faculty Social Interactions

Our study sought to distinguish the various kinds of interactions involved in the socialization process. We begin where many doctoral students begin the socialization process: faculty social interaction. Our measure of faculty social interaction reflects the general relationships that develop between students and faculty outside of classrooms. The five items that make up the faculty social interaction factor reflect student perceptions of the quality, ease, and satisfaction of their relationships with faculty in their programs. These interactions appear to be highest among engineering, sciences and mathematics, and education doctoral students and relatively low among students in the humanities and the social sciences.

This finding is consistent with Baird's (1990a) observation that academic culture varies from field to field in graduate education and that difference may explain the variations in the quality of student experiences. Baird distinguishes between the collaborative nature of work in the sciences, where graduate students work jointly on projects with faculty members, and the more individualistic atmosphere in the humanities, where students often work alone on their own projects.

In both education and engineering, we observed notable sex differences in student social interaction with faculty. In both fields, male doctoral students perceived social interaction with faculty to be better than their female peers. The gender representation alone of students in these fields appears not to explain this phenomenon, given that women are the dominant sex in the former but men in the latter field. Overall, the higher social interaction among engineering students relative to other fields derives mainly from male doctoral student perceptions of higher social interactions with faculty. In the sciences and mathematics, both sexes perceived identically strong levels of student social interaction with faculty.

Race differences in student social interactions with faculty center on the difference between African Americans and other groups, and mainly in the fields of engineering and sciences and mathematics. The low representation of African Americans in these fields does not appear to help them in terms of social interactions with faculty. African American engineering doctoral students perceived student and faculty interactions to be of lower quality than their Asian American, white, and international counterparts, and they reported the lowest student-faculty social interactions of any race-ethnicity group in any field. Among sciences and mathematics doctoral students, African Americans also perceived student and faculty social interactions to be of lower quality than their white and international student counterparts. In the other fields, no real differences were identified among the race groups regarding student perceptions of the quality of student and faculty social interactions. Given the human capital challenges facing African American engineering and sciences and mathematics students observed in prior chapters, positive student and faculty social interactions would appear to be essential in overcoming other disadvantages. Yet in these two fields of greatest challenge for African Americans, the opposite, negative socialization, is operative. Furthermore, since Hispanics are not showing differences from the other groups, it appears that the faculty social interaction is a particular challenge for African Americans in the fields of engineering and sciences and mathematics rather than minority students generally or even African Americans in every field.

Peer Interactions

Researchers recognize peer interaction as an important component of doctoral student socialization. According to Marjorie Lozoff (1976), one of the functions peer groups serve is to ward off loneliness, and Arlene Daniels (1975) considers peer support to be an important factor in students' motivation to persist in their programs. In a study of students at four North Carolina medical schools, Henry Frierson (1986) concludes that for African American students, having frequent interactions with both African American and white peers was meaningful, but same-race interactions more often elicited favorable feelings. This is one of the few studies that focuses on and finds evidence to support same-race interactions as a factor in student socialization. In their survey of African American graduate and professional students at a large midwestern public university, Emilie Smith and William Davidson (1992) find that peer networking had a positive relationship with attendance at professional conferences and publications. Baird (1990a) underscores the important role that peer groups can play in graduate school.

Our broadly cast peer interaction factor includes five items: the ease of meeting and making friends with other students, participating in informal study groups with other graduate students, participating in sponsored social programs, socializing with graduate students of different racial backgrounds, and socializing informally with other graduate students. A contrast of our findings regarding peer interactions and faculty interactions suggests that the two are indeed different measures of socialization. For example, students in the social sciences and humanities appear to have had positive peer interactions, in contrast with their social interactions with faculty. Sciences and mathematics students also had positive peer interactions. Students of engineering and education reported a low level of peer interactions, but their social interactions with faculty were generally ranked high.

Linda Hite (1985) examines the perception of peer support among men and women and finds that overall there was no gender difference. Our data, in contrast, reveal that in all fields except education, the sexes differed in perceptions of peer interaction, and in each case women experienced higher peer interactions than men. Women in the social sciences, followed closely by women in sciences and mathematics and women in engineering, reported the highest levels of peer interactions. That the peer relations of women in sciences and mathematics and in engineering exceeded those of their male peers in the same field suggests that minority status is not an impediment to peer relations by gender.

In our study, we found that minority-race students were generally not different from white students or each other in social participation with peers across the major fields. Outstanding among the differences in peer interaction by race-ethnicity group was the lower participation of international students compared with each of the race groups in the fields of engineering, sciences and mathematics, and the social sciences. Only in the social sciences was the difference between the social participation of

Hispanics and international students not statistically significant. International students appear to have had comparable peer interactions as their same-field counterparts in the fields in which they were least represented, namely, education and the humanities, and lower peer interactions in the three fields in which they were best represented.

Academic Interactions with Faculty

We define *academic interactions with faculty* to comprise all the aspects that relate to the quality of faculty instruction: faculty availability to meet with students, faculty academic advising, faculty feedback on projects and academic progress, faculty interest in student research and the quality of professional advising, and job placement by faculty. Consistent with their positive social interactions with faculty, engineering and education doctoral students rated their academic interactions with faculty relatively high. Humanities students also gave faculty a positive rating, despite their relatively low social interactions with faculty. On the other hand, our sample's doctoral students in sciences and mathematics and in social sciences rated the quality of their faculty academic interactions relatively low.

Sex differences in the socialization of doctoral students began to appear in the literature in the early 1980s. After acknowledging that women were in the extreme minority in many departments, Hartnett (1981) concludes that in departments with relatively high representations of women, women tended to report more favorable experiences than their female counterparts in programs with small numbers of women. Overall, however, he finds that sex differences in the experiences of doctoral students were small. Our evidence confirms Hartnett's general finding, but we also found evidence to the contrary. Generally, in humanities and in sciences and mathematics we found no difference in women's and men's perceptions of their academic interactions with faculty. On the one hand, in engineering we observed the expected, that women would have lower ratings, corresponding to their lower representation in the field. On the other hand, in education, a predominantly female field, we observed an unexpected sex difference, with women reporting lower ratings of academic relations with faculty than men.

Researchers whose work we have reviewed have delivered a common message about academic interaction with faculty: academic interactions with faculty constitute a major problem for minority students. Beatriz Clewell and Myra Ficklen (1987), Walter Allen, Angela Haddad and Mary Kirkland (1984), and Christine Carrington and William Sedlacek (1976) find that minority graduate students felt alienated and isolated in their graduate schools and typically viewed themselves as being outside the mainstream of their academic departments. In their survey of black graduate students attending eight predominantly white universities, Allen, Haddad, and Kirkland (1984) find that black students tended to rate

African American students' relations with faculty, in general, as being unsatisfactory but rated their own individual relationships with faculty as somewhat better than the overall. These findings confirm those from earlier research by Carrington and Sedlacek (1976) in which black students at the University of Maryland rated the overall black student social life and the racial climate of the institution to be unsatisfactory. Only Nettles (1990b) has found that black and Hispanic students were not different from whites in their perceptions of faculty interactions.

Our study revealed some race differences in student ratings of faculty interactions in engineering and in sciences and mathematics. In the field of engineering, the lower ratings of faculty academic interactions by African Americans resemble their ratings of social interactions with faculty and are statistically different from those of Asian Americans, whites, and international students. Similarly, in sciences and mathematics, African American students' ratings of their interactions with faculty were lower than those of international students, whose ratings in this field and in engineering were the highest. White students rated their interactions with faculty below international students in engineering and in sciences and mathematics. International students' positive academic interactions with faculty are a reminder of their high scores on indexes of preparation and their high likelihood of being teaching and research assistants compared with African Americans. This is yet more evidence that socialization as it pertains to faculty relations is an extraordinary challenge for African Americans both in engineering and in sciences and mathematics. These are, again, the fields that are also in the most desperate need of improving African American representation.

Interactions with Advisers

Every doctoral student in our sample ostensibly had a faculty adviser. Faculty advisers are usually assigned to students at the start of their doctoral programs; and while students or departments may elect to change the faculty adviser during the course of a student's doctoral program, the role is one that is expected to be filled at all times. Given the predetermined form of the student-adviser relationship, it is not surprising that researchers have examined how it influences other aspects of the doctoral student experiences. The overwhelming evidence is that advisers play an important role for students and that the quality of their relationships has consequences. For example, in a study by Penelope Jacks and colleagues (1983), nearly half of students who failed to complete their doctoral programs listed the poor quality of their relationship with advisers as a reason for leaving. Nearly twenty years later, in her study of those who began but did not complete their doctorates, Lovitts (2001, 270) concludes that "a student's relationship with her or his adviser is probably the single most critical factor in determining who stays and who leaves."

Jean Girves and Virginia Wemmerus (1988) have found adviser quality to be associated with student feelings of satisfaction. Pruitt and Isaac (1985) were among the earliest researchers to suggest the importance of mentoring, particularly for minority student success. They find "close ties" between faculty and students to be a common characteristic of the graduate school experience among people who have completed doctoral degrees. This corresponds neatly with our factor representing student perceptions about their interactions with their faculty advisers, which comprises four aspects: student perceptions of the accessibility, quality, and care that faculty display about student careers and the interest of faculty in the personal welfare of students. For each field, race-ethnicity, and sex group, we also examined whether the faculty adviser was the same sex and the same race as the doctoral student.

We distinguished advisers from mentors. In our survey, we defined *faculty or research advisers* as persons "assigned by their department to act in an official capacity in such ways as discussing and approving your coursework, or signing registration forms," and noted that the faculty or research adviser may not be the mentor. Nearly two-thirds (62%) of students reported that their adviser was also their mentor. It is common for academic departments to engage in matchmaking during the admissions process, and therefore it is not surprising to see an extensive dual role for faculty. The only difference we found with respect to students' ratings of interactions with their faculty advisers was that in both engineering and education, men rated their interactions with their advisers as being more positive than did women. This is consistent with our finding regarding faculty social interactions. Otherwise, students across the fields, races, and sexes rated their interactions with advisers much the same.

What is interesting about adviser interactions is the same-sex and same-race match. We found no conclusive evidence in prior research of any advantage to doctoral students of having same-sex or same-race advisers and mentors.[1] One of the impediments faced by researchers who

---

1. Several studies have examined the effect of having a same-sex adviser. Helen Berg and Marianne Ferber (1983) find that students were more comfortable with same-sex faculty in professional relationships. In an exploratory study, Elyse Goldstein (1979) reports that graduate students with same-sex advisers published significantly more research than their peers with opposite-sex advisers. Lucia Gilbert, June Gallessich, and Sherri Evans (1983) find that women as well as men with same-sex role models were more career-oriented and confident and that women with women role models were more satisfied than their male or female peers with male role models. On the other hand, Beril Ulku-Steiner, Beth Kurtz-Costes, and Ryan Kinlaw (2000) conclude that having female faculty in the department and not a same-sex mentor influenced self-confidence, and career commitment, which included leaving the program. The verdict on the extent to which same-race mentoring and advising carries an advantage is still out. Amado Padilla (1994) suggests that for students who want to engage in ethnic research, having a mentor who acknowledges the value of ethnic scholarship may help in instances where there is not an adequate supply of same-race mentors. Given the tendency for underrepresented students to choose advisers of the same sex and race, graduate institutions may experience greater pressure to increase the representation of women and African Americans and Hispanics.

have sought to examine this issue has been the small number and representation of women faculty in some fields (e.g., 8% in engineering) and African American and Hispanic faculty in every field, precluding large-scale examination of the issue. In the field of engineering, for example, the *Digest for Education Statistics 2001* (NCES 2002) notes that in the field of engineering, women overall made up only 10 percent and white women 7 percent of the approximately twenty-five thousand full-time instructional faculty and staff in degree-granting institutions in the United States. By contrast, in the field of education, women represented 58 percent, and white women 46 percent, of the approximately forty thousand full-time instructional faculty and staff. In the same two fields, African Americans represented 2 percent of the faculty in engineering and 9 percent in education, Hispanics 4 percent in engineering and 3 percent in education, Asian–Pacific Islanders 16 percent in engineering and 4 percent in education, and American Indian–Alaskan Natives less than 1 percent of the faculty in both fields.

Nearly 70 percent of the sciences and mathematics students in our study had same-sex advisers, compared with nearly 60 percent in humanities and social sciences and a low of 55 percent of education students. In every field, we found men more likely than women to have same-sex advisers. The differences were most striking in engineering (93% vs. 10%) and in sciences and mathematics (92% vs. 14%). By race, African Americans reported different rates of having same-sex advisers compared with international students in engineering, sciences and mathematics, and social sciences. White students more frequently reported having same-sex advisers than African Americans in sciences and mathematics (67% vs. 47%).

Eighty-one percent of the humanities doctoral students had advisers of the same race, compared with 67 percent of the education and social sciences students, 63 percent of the sciences and mathematics students, and 54 percent of the engineering students. With the exception of the social sciences, women and men were similar in their reports of having advisers of the same race. African Americans and Hispanics reported significantly lower rates of having same-race advisers compared with their white peers in all fields. Having a same-race or same-sex adviser does not necessarily lead to superior socialization, nor are they even necessarily the best matches. But it is clear that whites and males have more opportunities to find such matches than other groups.

Having a Mentor

One of the most talked-about aspects of the doctoral experience is mentoring. People use this term often and seemingly with different meanings. In contrast to solely advising relationships, mentoring relationships between faculty and students are most often unique constructions based upon interests, personalities, and other attributes of the two individuals. At the most basic level, the common interpretation is that a mentor is a faculty person who establishes a working relationship with a student and shepherds her or him through the doctoral process to completion.

Our survey also probed student perceptions about the availability of someone in their department who could be considered a mentor and about whether the mentor also functioned as the student's adviser. In our questionnaire, *mentor* was defined as "someone on the faculty to whom students turned for advice, to review a paper, or for general support and encouragement." Such a definition did not preclude the mentor and faculty adviser being the same individual, but it gave us a chance to examine mentorship, which has been increasingly viewed as critical to doctoral student success. Among others, Hartnett (1976), Blackwell (1987), and Carlos Arce and W. H. Manning (1984) find that graduate students and graduate degree recipients perceived their relationships with faculty and mentors to be the most important factors in successfully completing their degree programs. Robert Bargar and Jane Mayo-Chamberlain (1983) find that students' personal and professional growth as well as their success in search for employment after completing their doctoral programs were related to their relationships with faculty. One contrary finding is Girves and Wemmerus's (1988) conclusion that having a mentor did not predict degree progress, graduate grades, students' involvement in the department, or students' feelings of satisfaction or alienation.

Mentoring experiences appear to have an important effect for women and the different race-ethnicity groups. Shirley Clark and Mary Corcoran's (1986) interviews with 147 faculty from a variety of academic departments at the University of Minnesota–Twin Cities reveal that during the training phase of the careers of faculty women, experiences with advisers and mentors either doubting or encouraging their potential played an important role in their socialization. Faculty women who believed their abilities were doubted during their graduate training were less productive than those who believed they had been encouraged. Access to a mentor is another area of concern. In their study of United Negro College Fund faculty who pursued doctoral degrees, Charles Willie, Michael Grady, and Richard Hope (1991) find that 60 percent of the doctoral students who did not have a mentor reported that they had wanted a mentor but could not find one. Furthermore, Smith and Davidson (1992), assessing students' access to faculty mentoring, find that just over one-third (36%) reported having a mentor and another one-third reported that "no one," meaning faculty or administrators, had helped them significantly while they were in graduate or professional school. The faculty providing help to African American students were 44 percent white and 41 percent African American. Nettles (1990a), however, does not find a difference between white and African American students in their reports of having had mentors at traditionally white graduate schools.

In our study, in each field, both sexes, and all race-ethnicity groups, most students (69%) appear to have found mentors. The range is from 75 percent in the humanities to 64 percent in education, with the other three fields at 71 percent each (see fig. 7.1). In the humanities, sciences and mathematics, and the social sciences, a slightly higher percentage of women than men reported having mentors: 77 percent of women and 72 percent of men in the humanities, and 74 percent of women and 69 percent of men in both sciences and mathematics and the social sciences. Women and men in education and engineering were equally successful at finding mentors. Of the students who had mentors, 70 percent indicated that they found their mentors within the first year, and half of those within the first few months of starting their doctoral program. This suggests that most students enter their doctoral programs seeking mentor. They appear to understand the importance of having one from the very beginning.

Between just over one-half and three-quarters of the doctoral students in each field, of each race group, reported having mentors. In sciences and mathematics, African American and white students reported markedly different rates (57% vs. 76%). In three fields (engineering, sciences and mathematics, and the social sciences), a higher percentage of whites had mentors than international students (76%, 74%, and 74%, respectively, for whites; 68%, 68%, and 67%, respectively, for international students). About 25 percent of the students in our study did not have mentors. This is surprising, given the importance of mentoring in doctoral programs. The extent to which an individual professor combines the roles of adviser and mentor varies by field, race, and sex. "Mentors, unlike advisors, cannot be assigned to specific students. Advisors may be mentors, but many

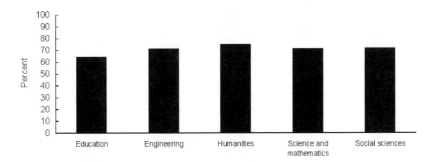

Fig. 7.1. Mentorship, by Field
Source: Survey of Doctoral Student Finances, Experiences, and Achievements.

advisor-advisee associations never evolve to the mentor-protégé relation-ship" (Willie, Grady, and Hope 1991, 72). Most of the students in each field indicated that the adviser and mentor were the same person. By field, 76 percent of engineering students reported that this was the case, compared with 66 percent of science and mathematic students, 57 percent of edu-cation students, 54 percent of social science students, and 52 percent of humanities students. In engineering, a higher percentage of men (78%) than women (66%) reported that their adviser was also their mentor. In other fields, nearly identical percentages of men and women identified their mentors as also their advisers; doctoral students in the humanities reported the smallest percentages (53% women and 51% men). Race-ethnicity was not a factor in determining whether a student's faculty adviser and men-tor were the same person.

Earlier, we examined the tendency for doctoral students to have same-sex advisers among the fields by race and sex of the student. In our sam-ple, men more often than women had same-sex faculty advisers. We ob-served the same pattern for mentors. What is interesting, however, is that while the pattern is similar by sex, the difference is a matter of degree. In every field, women had same-sex mentors to a somewhat larger degree than same-sex advisers. In other words, it appears that when women choose, they are more likely to select female mentors than they are to be assigned female faculty members as advisers. For example, in engineering, the field in which, at 10 percent, women were least likely to have a same-sex adviser, 12 percent choose women to be their mentors. By contrast, 7 percent of male engineering doctoral students were assigned female ad-visers, and 7 percent indicated that women were their mentors. This same pattern of distinction between same-sex advisers and mentors was ob-served by race. Although there is some minor shifting among the race-ethnicity groups, the only pattern of difference worth mentioning was ob-served among Hispanics in engineering, a lower percentage of whom choose same-sex mentors than whites (59% vs. 83%).

Similarly, African American students tend to choose mentors of the same race somewhat more often than they are assigned same-race advis-ers. This was also the case for Hispanics in two of the five fields: engineer-ing and the social sciences. Yet compared with whites, both African Amer-icans and Hispanics in every field reported few instances of having a same-race mentor. The biggest obstacle appears to be the availability of fac-ulty of the same race. In engineering, the field with the least representa-tion of African American faculty, only 18 percent of African American stu-dents were assigned advisers of the same race and 23 percent selected same-race mentors. In education, the field with the largest representation of African American faculty, only 33 percent of African Americans had chosen same-race mentors, compared with 24 percent who reported hav-ing been assigned same-race advisers.

It is somewhat surprising that the majority of African American students in the humanities, but a minority in each of the other fields, had both same-race advisers and same-race mentors. This is further testament that the limited supply of African American faculty is a likely explanation for the low rate at which African Americans have same-race mentors. If humanities is a fair indicator, African American doctoral students, when given the opportunity, most often seek African American mentors. This presents a monumental challenge in the form of a vicious cycle for universities seeking to increase the representation of African American doctorates. It would appear that one of the keys to increasing the supply of African American doctorates is to increase the supply of African American faculty; yet the latter is improbable without the former.

Career Plans

Traditionally, doctoral students have been assumed to be preparing for careers as college and university faculty. Within the past three decades, however, more doctoral students have been training for careers in private industry and in government. Our survey asked students to forecast the type of position they expected to hold immediately after completing their doctorates. Most students in humanities (73%), sciences and mathematics (59%), and the social sciences (55%) expected to become college or university faculty or to seek postdoctoral research or academic appointments (see fig. 7.2). In contrast, only 28 percent of engineering and 38 percent of education doctoral students expected to become college or university faculty or postdoctoral research fellows. Nearly half of all engineering doctoral students (46%) expected to become researchers in the private sector, compared with 17 percent of students in sciences and mathematics, 7 percent in social sciences, 3 percent in education, and 0.8 percent in humanities. Between 11 percent and 13 percent in each of the five fields were

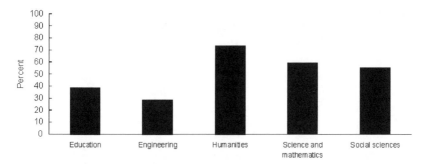

Fig. 7.2. Expectation of First Job upon Doctoral Degree Completion as Faculty or Postdoctoral Research Fellow, by Field
Source: Survey of Doctoral Student Finances, Experiences, and Achievements.

undecided about the type of position they expected to hold after completing their doctoral degrees.

Given the long tradition of doctoral education as the training ground for college and university professors, we thought it important to examine the extent to which this tradition is reflected in the expectations of contemporary doctoral students. Because of the tendency of Ph.D. holders in sciences and mathematics and, to a lesser extent, in engineering, to attain postdoctoral positions as an entry step to faculty positions, thereby extending the training ground into the proving ground, we look at career plans both as combined and as individual tracks. The only sex difference we observed with regard to plans for faculty and postdoctoral positions upon earning their doctoral degree was in the social sciences, where a higher percentage of men (60%) than women (49%) anticipated this career path. When we separated plans for postdoctoral training from plans to pursue a faculty position, however, we found in the social sciences a larger percentage of women (15%) than men (10%) choosing the postdoctoral route as the point of entry. In engineering, a somewhat larger percentage of women (22%) expected to be college and university faculty than men (16%), whereas a larger percentage of men (48%) than women (40%) expected to be researchers in the private sector.

The patterns across race-ethnicity groups in career aspirations appear to be similar, with two exceptions. A smaller percentage of African Americans than other race groups were planning to become college and university faculty or postdoctoral fellows in the field of education. In sciences and mathematics, a smaller percentage of African Americans than other race groups expected to pursue postdoctoral degrees; instead, they planned to go directly into faculty positions. This does not bode well for improving the socialization of African American doctoral students. It would appear that reversing the relatively dismal trend of lower quality of socialization for African Americans in sciences and mathematics and in engineering can only be helped by increasing their representation on university faculty. In the case of sciences and mathematics, this may reflect the high demand for African American faculty who attain the requisite training to qualify for faculty positions and then succeed through the promotion and tenure process at research-intensive universities. This raises the issue of whether postdoctoral training provides a greater opportunity to launch a research agenda without the demands of teaching and its possible impact on prospects for promotion and tenure.

CONCLUSION

In addition to the academic, cognitive, and affective development associated with taking classes, publishing articles, passing qualifying exams, attending to assistantship responsibilities, and writing dissertations, there is also noncognitive and affective development associated with the outside-of-classroom activities in doctoral education. Given that all of the research in the field of education has touted the socialization process for its contribution to career formation and adjustment, we decided that the most important way to examine socialization was in terms of student relationships with peers and student relationships with faculty in their roles as advisers and mentors. Doctoral programs in essence are where students acquire their understanding of the cultural norms of their future professions.

Students experience the socialization process of doctoral education in much the same ways regardless of field, race-ethnicity, or sex. There are important distinctions, however,. That a quarter of the students indicated they did not have mentors may not in and of itself be cause for alarm, but its potential effects on other experiences may make it central to reforms in doctoral education. The relatively low socialization opportunities for African Americans in engineering and in sciences and mathematics are especially disturbing. At this stage, only a long-term solution is apparent—increasing African American faculty in these fields.

CHAPTER EIGHT

Research Productivity

"THE FACULTY GOT JOBS WITH NO PUBLICATIONS, no talks at national conferences. These are people who got appointments to the graduate school with one book to their name. Their students won't get jobs without at least talks, or tenure without that book, nor promotion without two books." As this doctoral student observed, the stakes are rising for entry into the academy as well as for advancement. We would take it one step further and add career choice. The resumes of doctoral students who enter the labor market with doctoral student research accomplishments may well stand out in a pile of applications.

In a devastating critique of publication pressures in the humanities, Harvard University Press executive editor Lindsay Waters (2001, 2) writes, "The rule is getting to be two books for tenure . . . [This] has led to frenzied behavior on the part of graduate students now trying to multiply the number of publications in their [curricula vitae]." While the talk in the humanities is of authoring and editing books, refereed journal articles are the central focus in the social and behavioral sciences, the biological and physical sciences, education, and engineering. As John Creswell (1985) points out, in disciplines in which knowledge is highly codified and individuals agree on important questions and methods (e.g., physics), faculty publish more often in journals (an abbreviated form of communication) than in books (an extended form of communication).

Ever since the University of Chicago's president William Rainey Harper publicly proclaimed in the late nineteenth century that promotion would depend "more largely" on research productivity than on teaching, there has been steadily increasing pressure on faculty to show their stuff, both early and often (cited in Berelson 1960). Therefore, the high status and pressure ascribed to publishing is hardly surprising in academe. What is surprising and somewhat novel is the growing expectation that students publish while they are in the process of pursuing their doctoral degrees. For the past three decades, the typical refrain of the doctoral student experience has been degree completion and time to degree. Because the expectations that doctoral students will produce scholarly work and publish are recent developments, most of the extant research focuses on productivity after degree completion.

As doctoral programs expand and become more diverse, the quality of the training experience is becoming increasingly the focus of doctoral students, graduate faculty, and prospective employers. Publishing before completing a degree may be an indicator of doctoral program quality and student performance as well as student and program marketability. The publication pressures apply especially to doctoral students pursuing academic and research careers. As with other important aspects of doctoral student performance and experience, their personal backgrounds and characteristics influence their prospects for research productivity. Undergraduate preparation, marital status, race-ethnicity, and sex may all be influential. Regardless of the personal backgrounds and characteristics, however, the expectation to demonstrate research productivity as doctoral students is the same for all students.

In the history of research on doctoral education, rarely have researchers focused on the research productivity of students during the doctoral education process (Ethington and Pisani 1993; Feldman 1973; Smith and Davidson 1992). Although students are believed to acquire preparation for lives as scholars and researchers while attending graduate school, evidence of their research productivity during their doctoral student days is not abundant. Evidence of differences by field of study, race, and sex in the research training and productivity during doctoral programs is even sparser. The dissertation—the culminating experience of a doctoral degree program—is the only research product for which there is stable and comprehensive documentation, and analyses of who completes the dissertation or the quality of it are missing from the published research. No standard expectation of research productivity beyond the dissertation and perhaps qualifying and preliminary examinations has emerged in the disciplines or fields of study during the century and a half of doctoral education. Consequently, whatever graduate students produce by way of research appears to be by happenstance or through unofficial or informal networks in academic departments rather than because of formal requirements or stated expectations in the curriculum. Whether student productivity comes from informal networks or elsewhere, a potentially disturbing outcome is the differences in productivity by race and sex.

Much of the research on doctoral student productivity focuses on its contribution to preparing students to become productive faculty members and is most often measured long after doctoral students have joined faculty. Even ratings of graduate training programs have most often been based on the research productivity of graduates after they assume faculty positions rather than while they are doctoral students (Baird 1986; McCormick and Bernick 1982; Morgan and Fitzgerald 1977; Pearson 1985; Robey 1979). Only Hartnett and Willingham develop the argument that publications can be an integral part of the scholarly development process of the doctoral program. In early work, Willingham (1974) presents a three-objective (practitioner, teacher, scholar-scientist) training model for doctoral programs to implement, with an intermediate criterion of publication to meet the scholar-scientist program objective. In a later study, Hartnett and Willingham (1979) promote the idea that publication can be a useful tool for assessing professional development and academic socialization.

By contrast, our interest is in the research productivity of doctoral students while they are pursuing their doctoral degrees. We provide a snapshot of the current level of activity and the students' future potential as researchers. When measuring faculty productivity, researchers appropriately hone in on the singular most prominent indicators for the field of interest. Recognizing, however, that doctoral students are in the apprenticeship phase, we cast a wider net in order to recognize the many ways in which students might demonstrate productivity. In addition to the traditional measures of publishing articles and book chapters and presenting papers at professional conferences, we expanded the list to twenty-two categories to include other measures such as applications for patents and copyrights, publication of textbooks, and development of software. We gave students the opportunity to indicate "five or more" activities in which they had participated in each category. Their responses revealed how naive we had been to expect such breadth and frequency. We learned that though students are achieving research productivity, it is in a narrower range of activities and less frequently than we had anticipated.

A COMPOSITE VIEW
OF RESEARCH PRODUCTIVITY

Since our intention was to examine the major forms in which research productivity is demonstrated—such as conference presentations, journal articles, book chapters, and books—we needed to understand some of the field differences that exist for doctoral students trying to promote themselves. Here, we found it helpful to consider Richard Wanner, Lionel Lewis, and David Gregorio's (1981, 251) caution that "what constitutes an 'article' (or even a 'book') and the difficulty of getting one in print vary across disciplines." Furthermore, as John Creswell and John Bean (1981, 73) note, Anthony Biglan's (1973) "hard-area" faculty produce more journals than books, and "soft-area" faculty produce more books than articles.[1] This finding is also supported by the extensive American Council on Education study that gathered data from 17,399 faculty in the physical and biological sciences, the social sciences, and the humanities with a view to identifying characteristics that contribute to publication activity. The study concludes, "A unitary model of scholarly or scientific productivity cannot be assumed to operate in all academic disciplines" (Wan-

---

1. Biglan's (1973) pure-applied paradigm focuses on whether a department emphasizes pure research or the practical application of subject matter. Chemistry is an example of a pure field ("hard area"), while engineering is an example of an applied field ("soft area").

ner, Lewis, and Gregorio 1981, 250), largely because of differences in how a particular field's characteristics are transformed into scholarly productivity. The larger numbers of articles in a shorter span of time in the sciences, for example, may be a function of the more efficient translation of resources into output in the sciences rather than superior performance by science faculty. Wanner, Lewis, and Gregorio (1981), find that a greater number of articles produced in the sciences was associated with receiving a larger number of grants; the relationship was much weaker for the social sciences.

Our data support much of the foregoing argument. Just over one-half (51%) of the students indicated some type of research productivity (having either presented a research paper at a national conference, published a journal article, published a chapter in an edited book, or published a book). The field with the highest student productivity was engineering (66%), followed by humanities (57%), sciences and mathematics (52%), social sciences (47%), and education (40%).

Beyond field differences, the role of sex has long been considered an important factor in graduate student productivity. Although many researchers have included sex as a variable, only a few have isolated its effects. In surveys of doctoral recipients, William Hamovitch and Richard Morgenstern (1977), Stein and Weidman (1989a), and Herbert Wong and Jimy Sanders (1983) have found that women achieved less scholarly research productivity than men. In our study, as well, women in some fields showed less productivity. Sixty-nine percent of the men in engineering, compared with 51 percent of women, had demonstrated some productivity, and in sciences and mathematics, 54 percent of men compared with 48 percent of women. In all other fields, women and men had achieved comparable levels of overall research productivity.

Race has been generally neglected in the research on doctoral productivity. In a rare instance of this focus, Frank Clemente (1974) examines the comparative research productivity of blacks and nonblacks in the field of sociology. His racial comparisons of the sample of 2,467 members of the American Sociological Association who received Ph.D.s from 1950 to 1966 reveal that nonblacks averaged twice as many published articles and about four times as many published books as blacks. He also finds that nonblacks outperformed blacks on the publication scale developed by Norval Glenn and Wayne Villemez (1970) covering twenty-two journals of sociology and allied fields. However, after controlling for sex, year of Ph.D., quality of department of doctoral training, and age at the time of receiving the Ph.D., Clemente finds the race differences disappeared, leaving him to conclude that when all other preparation factors are equal, nonblacks published no more than blacks. In his study examining correlates of early research productivity for social scientists, physical scientists, and biologists, Pearson (1985) also finds that whites had a slight advantage over blacks in the mean number of articles published before earning a Ph.D. In all three fields, predoctoral publications were highly correlated with publishing articles as well as books.

As noted earlier, more than half of all doctoral students reported having some research productivity. There is little race-ethnicity difference in overall productivity in engineering, humanities, and the social sciences. We are concerned that in the fields of education and sciences and mathematics, however, African Americans appear to be achieving relatively low research productivity. In education, a smaller percentage of African Americans (31%) achieved research productivity than Asian Americans and whites (46% and 41%, respectively). In sciences and mathematics, the gaps are much wider: 28 percent of African Americans demonstrated research productivity, compared with 59 percent of Asian Americans, 52 percent of Hispanics, 56 percent of whites, and 45 percent of international students.

Our research productivity measure provides an overall picture of student engagement. However, it may be more important to deconstruct this measure to appreciate its component parts, each of which is valued differently in the various major disciplines and fields. Whether the focus is on the research productivity of faculty or doctoral students, there is a hierarchy of components. Publishing a textbook or a book in the area of one's expertise is supreme, but in early career stages other forms of productivity are valued differently. In education, the social sciences, and the sciences, for example, publishing an article in a refereed journal carries higher status than presenting a paper at a professional conference; the opposite may be the case. Also, the hierarchy may contain different elements. In some science fields, for example, publishing an article in a refereed journal may be a prerequisite to presenting at a conference. In any case, there is a pecking order in every field, and doctoral students are obliged to learn the rules of their field to gain recognition and employment and to progress up the ladder of success.

Some approach the task of research productivity with great trepidation that can be overcome only through a gradual process of doing research of any type. This may mean starting at the lowest rung and progressing step by step. The first step may involve presenting a conference paper and then progressing through various stages to ultimately publishing an article. In our sample, 60 percent of the students who published an article in a refereed journal presented a conference paper, whereas 49 percent of the people who presented a conference paper also published an article in a refereed journal. Figure 8.1 illustrates the frequency of student research productivity achievement in the four components that make up our measure of overall research productivity. The relative frequency may reflect the level of challenge as well as students' developmental stage in the doctoral program.

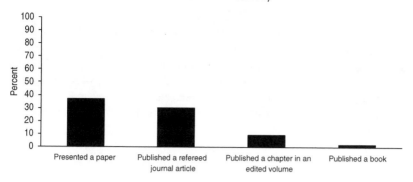

Fig. 8.1. Student Research Productivity
Source: Survey of Doctoral Student Finances, Experiences, and Achievements.

PRESENTING A RESEARCH PAPER
AT A PROFESSIONAL CONFERENCE

One entry-level activity represented in our overall measure of research productivity is the presentation of a research paper (sole or joint authorship) at a professional conference. Overall, 37 percent of doctoral students indicated that they had presented at a professional conference. The range among the fields is considerable, with 56 percent of engineering students, 51 percent of humanities students, 35 percent of social sciences students, 30 percent of education students, and 28 percent of sciences and mathematics students having presented a research paper at a conference. Another entry-level research activity is the presentation of a poster session at a conference. In this arena, students in sciences and mathematics and in engineering are the leaders; more than half of these engineering students reported having contributed to a conference poster session.

While there are no discernable race-ethnicity differences in conference presentation, only in the field of education is there no difference by sex. In sciences and mathematics and in engineering, men had the advantage, whereas in the humanities and social sciences, women had the lead. In sciences and mathematics, 29 percent of the men and 25 percent of the women, and in engineering, 58 percent of the men and 45 percent of the women, had given conference presentations. In the humanities, 54 percent of women and 48 percent of men, and in the social sciences, 37 percent of women and 32 percent of men, gave conference presentations.

PUBLICATION OF A JOURNAL ARTICLE

On one of the more traditional measures of research productivity—publication in a refereed journal—only 30 percent of the doctoral student respondents had seen their names in print in refereed journals, either as sole author or with colleagues and professors. Of these successful writers, half had published one article, and the other half, two or more. Students in engineering and in sciences and mathematics were the most prolific. Forty-seven percent of engineering students and 44 percent of sciences and mathematics students had published articles in refereed journals, compared with 22 percent of social science students, 19 percent of humanities students, and 15 percent of education students. Education students experienced a lower publication rate when contrasted with each of the other fields. In the field of education, publishing an article in a refereed journal is a highly prized accomplishment.

Based on findings in the published literature, we expected to see large race and sex differences in publication of articles in refereed journals, with women trailing men and African Americans trailing the other race-ethnicity groups. In separate studies, Hamovitch and Morgenstern (1977), Stein and Weidman (1989a), and Wong and Sanders (1983) all have found that women trailed men in publishing. Although we found major sex differences regarding publication of a journal article, these differences were dependent on the major field. In education and the social sciences, we found no sex differences. On the other hand, in engineering, humanities, and sciences and mathematics, a larger proportion of men had published articles than women: in engineering, 35 percent of women, compared with 49 percent of men; in humanities, 17 percent of women compared with 22 percent of men; and in sciences and mathematics, 39 percent of women compared with 46 percent of men.

As with sex, our expectation that African Americans would differ from other groups in the rate of article publication comes from the research literature. Smith and Davidson (1992) surveyed 298 African American graduate and professional students attending a large midwestern public university on various aspects of their professional development, including conference attendance and submission of potential journal articles. They find that though the vast majority of the African American students (80%) had attended conferences, only 29 percent had presented a paper at a conference, and far fewer (13%) had submitted a paper for publication in a journal. The faculty providing support (e.g., giving advice on course work, involving students in faculty research, including students in faculty networks) were 44 percent white and 41 percent African American. The authors find that faculty support was consistently related to various types of professional development, including publication opportunities.

African Americans reported lower rates of research article publication than some of their peers in education, sciences and mathematics, and the social sciences (see fig. 8.2). Sciences and mathematics is the field in which African Americans most differed from all their peers: 17 percent of African

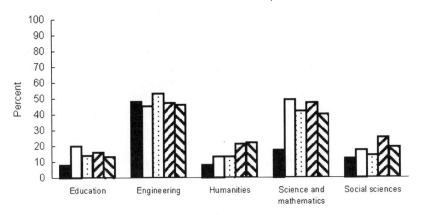

Fig. 8.2. Student Publication of Research Articles, by Race-Ethnicity and Field.
Solid bar, blacks; *open bar,* Asians; *dotted bar,* Hispanics; *ascending hatching,* whites; *descending hatching,* international students.
Source: Survey of Doctoral Student Finances, Experiences, and Achievements.

Americans indicated that they had published a research article, compared with 49 percent of Asian Americans, 42 percent of Hispanics, 47 percent of whites, and 40 percent of international students. Otherwise, our analysis revealed little distinction among race groups within the fields in having published an article.

PUBLISHING BOOK CHAPTERS AND BOOKS

The remaining levels of productivity are publishing a book chapter or a book. Few students reported having published a chapter in an edited volume. Overall, 9 percent had published a book chapter, with the breakdown by field as follows: 13 percent of social science students, 12 percent of humanities students, 10 percent of education students, 7 percent of engineering students, and 5 percent of sciences and mathematics students. Education and humanities doctoral students were most likely to report having published books while still doctoral students. Almost 4 percent of education doctoral students and 3 percent of humanities doctoral students reported having published a book, compared with 1 percent in the social sciences and less than 1 percent each in engineering and in sciences and mathematics.

Only in engineering was there a sex difference in this regard: 3 percent of women, compared with 7 percent of men, had published a chapter in a book. There were no differences by sex in having published whole books in any of the fields. Within each field, doctoral students in each race-ethnicity group had similarly modest experiences publishing chapters in books and whole books.

CONCLUSION

The importance of early demonstrations of research productivity cannot be overstated. In her study of predoctoral activities in chemistry, Barbara Reskin (1979) has found that predoctoral publications foreshadowed greater publication activity during the third through fifth years after the Ph.D. Bean (1982) goes even further, arguing that for students to publish while they are enrolled in graduate school constitutes the initiation of a dichotomy between producing and nonproducing faculty. He writes, "Producers begin early, even in graduate school, and continue to produce at a high level throughout their careers. Non-producers remain nonproductive—they do not improve with age" (Bean 1982, 19).

Other support comes from Wong and Sanders (1983). In their review of the literature on the research and teaching training of men and women, they find research production activities to be determinants of initial placement and career development after the Ph.D. As with the experiences examined in foregoing chapters, African American students face a relative deficit in research productivity, especially in publishing articles in the fields of education, sciences and mathematics, and the social sciences. Their situation is especially severe in the sciences and mathematics, the field in which the largest percentage of students are publishing refereed journal articles while they are enrolled in their doctoral programs. The career stakes associated with research productivity are perhaps the highest among all of the doctoral student experiences examined in our study.

CHAPTER NINE

Satisfaction, Performance, and Progress

I INTEND TO DISCONTINUE my doctoral studies as of May of this year. Why?

1. I cannot find a program that suits my field
2. I could not find a "fit" within an established program/department
3. No money
4. Not clear it would make a significant difference

This doctoral student's summation of the reasons for leaving a doctoral program underscores the relationship between satisfaction and persistence as well as the multiplicity of factors that are associated with decisions to interrupt or permanently leave doctoral studies. In beginning our survey, we assumed, as do most researchers and graduate faculty, that our respondents intended to remain enrolled, progress at a normal rate, and complete their degrees. Consequently, we did not ask our sample whether completing the degree was among their goals, whether they intended to interrupt their studies by taking time off, at what pace they expected to make progress through their degree program, or what level of satisfaction they would require to sustain their goals and effort. Doctoral education is, after all, the end of the formal education pipeline. Although all of postsecondary education is voluntary rather than compulsory, pursuing a doctoral degree is tantamount to electing a lifetime of intellectual engagement and pursuits. Unlike undergraduate education, subscribed to mainly by people at the end of adolescence or in the transition to adulthood, doctoral education is believed to represent nothing less than a commitment by adults to craft their professional lives as scholars, researchers, and leaders within and outside of the academy.

SATISFACTION

In a review of the history of doctoral education in the United States, student satisfaction does not surface as a prominent issue. This may be changing, however, in part because of the emergence of graduate student instructor unions, which now occupy the attention of academic leaders in major U.S. doctorate-granting universities. Although compensation and working conditions are the principal features of the collective bargaining portion of student satisfaction, another part involves the quality of the conditions, experience, and socialization of the experience and the orientation into the profession. It is the latter that concerned us in this research. Our focus is doctoral students' satisfaction with their intellectual development, peer relationships, commitment to their university, collegial relationships with faculty, and the sense of community they felt in their programs and with their overall appreciation for their doctoral experience.

Our survey included several items querying doctoral students on their levels of confidence and satisfaction. First, we inquired about their confidence in their decision to pursue a doctorate; next, we asked them to rate their level of confidence in the particular doctoral program they had chosen and then to indicate their overall satisfaction with their current doctoral program. Each question asked for a response in the form of a 5-point Likert scale, with 1 indicating the lowest rating and 5 indicating the highest.

CONFIDENCE IN CHOOSING
TO PURSUE A DOCTORAL DEGREE

Regarding the broad question of students' confidence in their decision to pursue a doctoral degree, students "agreed" they had made the right decision (mean = 4.07, slightly more than "agree"). Among fields, education students were the most confident with their choice to pursue a doctorate (4.25), while students in the humanities (3.83) were least so. Why doctoral students in education were more confident that they had made the right decision is left to speculation. Education doctoral students are generally older than students in other fields, and more of them are already employed. The doctoral degree is one vehicle for them to use to achieve upward mobility. Humanities doctoral students, on the other hand, face the bleakest employment market among the fields.

We found sex differences regarding students' confidence in electing to pursue a doctoral degree in the fields of education, engineering, and sciences and mathematics. In each case, women were less confident than men that they had made the right decision. For the most part, racial minority students appear to have been comparably certain about their decision to pursue a doctoral degree. Only in four instances did we find differences: In the field of education, Hispanics (4.48) were more confident than both whites (4.21) and Asian Americans (4.20). In the humanities, African Americans (4.30) were more confident than whites (3.74). International students were among the most confident about their decision to pursue a doctoral degree. They expressed more confidence than Asian Americans in sciences and mathematics (4.13 vs. 3.88) and more than white students in engineering (4.22 vs. 3.90), the humanities (4.28 vs. 3.74), and sciences and mathematics (4.13 vs. 3.94).

CONFIDENCE IN CHOICE
OF DOCTORAL PROGRAM

Although students' confidence about pursuing a doctoral degree may reflect their comfort with their field and timing, it does not necessarily reflect their comfort in their chosen academic department. So we also asked about their confidence in having made the right decision in choosing their specific doctoral program. Overall, the students rated their choices high— 3.89, on average, on the 5-point Likert scale; in other words, they are confident. This seems to correspond with Chris Golde and Timothy Dore's (2001) finding that only 15 percent of their sample, if given another opportunity, would choose a different university than the one they were attending. The story is in the subtlety. Although students expressed confidence in their choice of doctoral program—as we expected, given that they are adults pursuing doctoral degrees—the degree of confidence varied among them.

Students in the two professional fields of education and engineering were most confident that they had chosen the correct program, averaging 3.98; students in the social sciences were the least confident, at an average 3.74. Even this difference seems to be splitting hairs. Although education and engineering students reported the highest confidence in their decisions, the responses varied by sex, with men generally reporting higher confidence. In education, women reported a degree of confidence with program choice of 3.92, and men, 4.12; in engineering, women averaged 3.77 on the scale, while men reached 4.02.

Among racial groups, Hispanics were the most confident in their choice of program, averaging 4.07, and African Americans the least confident, averaging 3.85. Even with this difference, on the 5-point scale both groups would have been thought of as being quite confident. In the social sciences and humanities, students expressed equally high levels of confidence that they had chosen the right programs for themselves. Despite an overall high level of confidence, African Americans in sciences and mathematics exhibited less confidence (3.43) with their choice of program than all other race-ethnicity groups. African American engineering students had lower confidence about their program choice than Asian American, white, and international students. Does this suggest a lower level of satisfaction for African American students in engineering and in sciences and mathematics? Hispanics in education reported lower confidence than their Asian Americans counterparts.

There is a distinction between knowing that one is in the right place and being satisfied with that place. It might be hoped that doctoral students would be as satisfied in their doctoral program as they are confident about both their decision to pursue a doctoral degree and their choice of program. After all, the latter two are more distant in time than the former.

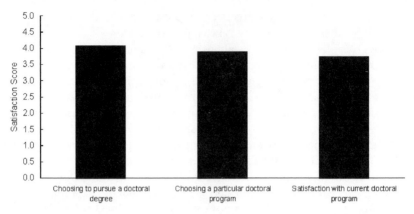

Fig. 9.1. Student Satisfaction on Measures of Doctoral Study (Survey of Doctoral Student Finances, Experiences, and Achievements). Satisfaction was rated on a 5-point Likert scale.
Source: Survey of Doctoral Student Finances, Experiences, and Achievements.

As figure 9.1 illustrates, however, this is not the case. The doctoral students in our sample rated their confidence in their decision to pursue a doctoral degree (4.07) and their choice of graduate program (3.89) higher than their satisfaction with their current doctoral program. Even so, with a rating of 3.73, they are still on the positive side of satisfaction.

Satisfaction
with Current Doctoral Program

At the doctoral level, student satisfaction has been associated with the stages of the doctoral career, more advanced students generally reporting higher satisfaction (Baird 1992). Also, students who are more satisfied with their programs have been found to achieve higher persistence rates (Wilder and Baydar 1991) and to have more positive interactions with peers and faculty (Madden and Carli 1981). The 2000 National Doctoral Program Survey, a large national study of graduate and professional students, concludes that most students (81%) are satisfied with their doctoral program (NAGPS Survey Team 2001). This corresponds with our finding that students in our sample were generally satisfied with their doctoral program.

Although, as noted earlier, education students were most confident that they had made the right decision to pursue their doctoral degrees, engineering students had the highest level of satisfaction with their current doctoral programs (3.80, compared with a mean for all programs of 3.73). Social science students reported the lowest level of satisfaction with their current program (3.59). Sex differences were most notable in education and engineering, women being less satisfied than men in both fields. In education, where they are in the majority (69%), women registered a satisfaction rating of 3.70, compared with 3.90 for men; and in engineering, where they are the minority (15%), women averaged a rating of 3.56, compared with 3.80 for men. In sciences and mathematics, where women tend to be outnumbered by men (32% vs. 68%) though less so than in engineering, the differences were not significant. This raises the question whether, given greater representation of women in engineering, women would be equally satisfied with their programs, as they currently are in sciences and mathematics, or would continue to be less satisfied than men, as they presently are in the field of education.

Although students of all race groups were more satisfied than not, there were differences by race-ethnicity, as there were by sex. In measuring overall doctoral program satisfaction among a sample of four universities, two of which are included in the present study, Nettles (1989) finds no significant differences by race-ethnicity. This is consistent with our finding at the overall level; but in our study, we identified differences by field of study. In engineering and in sciences and mathematics, international and white students reported higher levels of satisfaction than did their African American peers. International, Asian American, and white engineering students each registered 3.80 or higher on the 5-point Likert scale of satisfaction with current program, compared with 3.30 for African American students. Are the fields of sciences and mathematics the other challenging area in satisfaction for African Americans? African American students in our study were less satisfied (3.40) with their doctoral programs than white and international students (3.80 for both groups). The relatively lower satisfaction ratings among African Americans in sciences and mathematics and in engineering give rise to questions concerning the hospitability of these programs to African American students, who represent only 3 percent of each of these two fields in our sample.

Before we get carried away in celebrating the high level of satisfaction among doctoral students, we must point out that our measure of satisfaction captures students' general disposition. We would most likely gain a deeper understanding, and perhaps greater distinctions among student attitudes, if we were able to deconstruct the general into specific elements and focus on critical elements of the doctoral student experience. Such elements might include course-work experience (Baird 1978; Stein and Weidman 1989a) or orientation to scholarship (Stein and Weidman, 1989a). In examining student attrition, Golde (1998) raises other possible influences on student attitudes and satisfaction that might contribute to first-year attrition. These include selecting the wrong department, a relatively strong job market for those without doctoral degrees, and adviser mismatch.

GRADE POINT AVERAGES

One pillar on which student satisfaction has been found to rest is grades (Howard and Maxwell 1980). In doctoral programs, however, student grades are typically taken lightly as objective indicators of the quality of student performance, since most doctoral students earn an A in every course, making it difficult to distinguish between high achievers and average achievers (Girves and Wemmerus 1988; Willingham 1974). For this reason, though we include the grades earned in courses as measures of student performance, we have added other indicators, such as self-perception of performance, research productivity (chap. 8), and rate of progress and degree completion (chap. 10). Nonetheless, grades in courses are as important to doctoral students as grades at other levels, and students devote a great deal of effort to the pursuit of As. That most students receive As in most doctoral courses is not necessarily a sign of grade inflation. An alternative hypothesis is that doctoral programs are structured to ensure high levels of performance among a population of students who are among the most ambitious and elite. To students, grades are probably the best indicator of how well they are performing during the course-work portion of their curriculum, and grades have at least a moderate effect on their satisfaction.

Our sample reported grades that are consistent with general expectations about doctoral student course performance. The average grade point average (GPA) was 3.81 on a 4-point scale, or slightly higher than an A−. Although there are variations by field, the differences are small; the largest difference is only 0.12. Students in sciences and mathematics reported the lowest GPAs (mean of 3.75), while humanities students reported the highest (mean of 3.87). Only in the social sciences and education did we observe a sex difference in GPA, favoring women in both cases. Like the overall differences by field, these differences are miniscule (3.86 for women vs. 3.84 for men in education, 3.82 for women vs. 3.78 for men in social sciences).

We did find a bit of drama in grades. Although doctoral students of each race-ethnicity group reported high grade point averages, African American students in all fields except the humanities reported lower grade point averages than their counterparts in each of the other race groups. The lowest mean GPA reported by African Americans was in sciences and mathematics—3.53 compared with a mean for all sciences and mathematics students of 3.75. Similarly, in engineering, African American students averaged 3.61 compared with a mean for all students of 3.82. This finding is similar to the finding regarding satisfaction, wherein African Americans exhibited a high level of satisfaction but not quite as high as the norm.

STUDENTS' SELF-RATED PERFORMANCE

Even with their high grades, students are often the best judges of their relative performance because they interact with other students in their department and have a sense of how they stand relative to their peers. Students with higher self-concept have been found to experience less stress in doctoral programs (Ulku-Steiner, Kurtz-Costes, and Kinlaw 2000). So we asked students to tell us how they compared with their peers in their programs. They were given four categories of academic performance: in the top 10 percent, in the top 25 percent, in the middle (around 50%), or in the bottom 25 percent. What we observed was a large dose of self-confidence and a middling serving of mutual respect for their fellow students' performance. Approximately 45 percent of all doctoral students rated themselves in the top 10 percent, and another 34 percent situated their performance in the top 25 percent. Education students rated themselves highest of all the field groups, with more than half (57%) placing themselves in the top 10 percent. Around 46 percent of engineering students, 45 percent of humanities students, and 40 percent of social science students rated themselves in the top 10 percent range. Appreciably fewer sciences and mathematics students (35%) rated their performance in this top range. This appears to reflect the actual lower GPAs of sciences and mathematics students cited earlier. Accordingly, the largest single group who self-rated their performance within the bottom 25 percent was sciences and mathematics students, with 2.7 percent compared with a range of 0.6 to 1.8 percent in other fields.

In sum, when women in our sample were in the majority, they tended to rate their academic performance higher than when they were in the minority. This corroborates findings from a study by Beril Ulku-Steiner, Beth Kurtz-Costes, and Ryan Kinlaw (2000) in which a higher percentage of women than men in education rated themselves in the top 10 percent of their class (59% vs. 52%).[1] By contrast, in engineering, 39 percent of women and 48 percent of men, and in sciences and mathematics, 32 percent of women and 36 percent of men, rated themselves in the top 10 percent. In the three remaining fields, women and men had comparable self-ratings of their performance. In education, the humanities, and the social sciences, there were no significant race differences. In engineering and in sciences and mathematics, international students more often rated themselves in the top 10 percent than their U.S. peers.

Stopping Out of a Doctoral Program

Student attrition in its many forms is a common focal point at every level of education from high school onward. Like attrition at other levels, attrition from doctoral education reflects a combination of students' dropping out completely and taking temporary breaks, to continue their studies at some later point. As Hartnett and Willingham (1979, 17) note, "Defining a doctoral-level dropout is not at all simple." In many cases,

---

1. We did not examine whether our data support Sylvia Hurtado's (1994) finding that minority females had lower self-concept than their male counterparts.

dropping out may be not a formal decision on students' parts but rather a consequence of long-term indecision, which at some point becomes a de facto withdrawal. In this case, the official reason given to authorities may not be the true reason for discontinuing enrollment.

The limited research attention that has been devoted to doctoral students who depart before completing (Benkin 1984; Berelson 1960; Bowen and Rudenstine 1992; Clewell 1987; Golde 1998; Lovitts 2001; National Research Council 1996; Nerad and Miller 1996) may have led to an overestimate of the incidence of dropping out from doctoral programs. Only J. A. Creager (1971) has found that 58 percent of graduate students interrupted their studies after they had enrolled, usually to work full-time.

Bowen and Rudenstine (1992) lament the paucity of data on doctoral student attrition. They cite Berelson's 1960 estimates—derived from graduate deans and graduate faculty—that attrition at the doctoral level was running at about 40 percent and themselves estimate 45 to 50 percent depending on major (Bowen and Rudenstine 1992, 124). Berelson suggests that failure to complete the degree did not then preclude an academic or research career. Maresi Nerad and Debra Sands Miller's (1996) more recent estimate of persistence, at 80 percent, resembles the faculty estimates reported by Berelson (1960). Thirty years after Berelson's estimate, the attrition situation appeared to have changed little; in recent times, however, failure to complete the doctorate has more severe career consequences. Bowen and Rudenstine (1992) confess to being troubled not by the early attrition of the approximately 25 percent of entering students at larger programs (10 to 15% in smaller ones) who failed to return for a second year but rather by attrition in later stages of graduate study, ranging from 27 to 30 percent of students who have completed all doctoral work except the dissertation: "The percentage of students who never earn PhDs, in spite of having achieved ABD [all-but-dissertation] status, has risen in both larger and smaller programs, as has the time spent at the dissertation stage by those who completed doctorates. The direction of change is unmistakable, and the absolute numbers are high enough to be grounds for serious concern" (Bowen and Ruden-stine 1992, 253).

In his evaluation of the Ford Foundation Graduate Program, David Breneman (1977) viewed with disdain the doctoral student attrition rates of 50 percent or more in much the way that one would view attrition from professional schools. Doctoral education, however, is a different animal from professional schooling, where students enter as part of a cohort, follow a standard curriculum, complete course work within three or four years, and do not face an expectation for a focus on an independent, original research contribution. Thus estimating and explaining attrition rates in professional schools is much easier than in doctoral programs. Students sometimes take a break from their pursuit of doctoral degrees. Some are dropouts, others are stop-outs.

Dropouts are students who depart and never complete their doctoral degree; stop-outs are students who interrupt their doctoral studies but return and ultimately attain their degrees. Program attrition looms large as an issue among deans of college and university graduate schools because of its obvious economic and human costs. Although some graduate attrition has been linked by previous research to financial pressures, much remains to be learned. Lovitts (2001), for example, muses about how academic dissatisfaction might contribute to the process. Our research design did not permit us to capture the longitudinal dropout numbers, but we were able to explore the related patterns of stop-outs, who may become dropouts. In fact, we are able to report completion rates within the time frame of study.

Doctoral students might temporarily stop working on their degrees at various times and for a variety of reasons. These stop-outs do not include students who were working on preliminary examinations or dissertations and for those particular time periods are not enrolled as full-time students. Again, the few comparisons being drawn are between what was previously reported about attrition and what our present research adds from students' responses about their program withdrawals or other lapses.

We have no number that compares with Berelson's (1960), Bowen and Rudenstine's (1992), Breneman's (1977), or Nerad and Miller's (1996) because we did not ask graduate schools how many students had dropped out of the cohorts included in our study. What we have, instead, are genuine stop-outs, surveyed after they had returned to their programs. Twelve percent of our sample were identified as stop-outs (see fig. 9.2). Nearly 21 percent of students in education, 14 percent in the humanities, 11 percent in the social sciences, 6 percent in engineering, and 5 percent in sciences and mathematics had at some point left their programs to reenter at a later date.

Traditionally, women have been assumed to have higher attrition rates

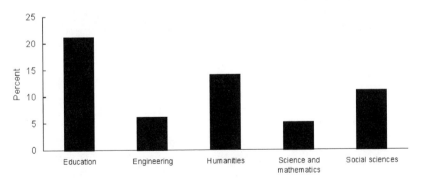

Fig. 9.2. Stopping Out of Doctoral Program, by Field
Source: Survey of Doctoral Student Finances, Experiences, and Achievements.

than men.[2] Our findings support earlier work (Nerad and Miller 1996; Berg and Ferber 1983) that shows differences in attrition rates within certain fields. There were significant sex differences in both engineering and the humanities, but with opposite patterns from those expected. In engineering, fewer female students (3%) stopped out than males (7%), whereas in the humanities, more females (17%) stopped out than males (12%).

The relatively low representation of African American and Hispanic doctoral degree recipients has inspired researchers to examine minority doctoral attrition as one potential contributing factor (Baker 1998; Clewell 1987; Thomas, Clewell, and Pearson 1987). The proportions of African American and Hispanic stop-outs in our sample are comparable with the other U.S. race-ethnicity groups. Differences exist, however, among several U.S. citizen groups and international students. In education, sciences and mathematics, and the social sciences, international students were less likely than other groups to report having stopped out. This could well be because of their need to maintain their student visa status, which is often jeopardized if they fall below full-time enrollment status. In education, a smaller share of international students (11%) reported being stop-outs than African Americans (24%) and whites (22%). In sciences and mathematics, again a smaller share of international students stopped out of their programs (3%) compared with Asian Americans (7%). In the social sciences, the low rate of stopping out among international students (8%) was significant only in comparison with Hispanics (18%).

When Students Stop Out

Researchers have examined the timing of students' departure (Benkin 1984; Bowen and Rudenstine 1992; Girves, Wemmerus, and Rice 1986; Golde 1998; Lovitts 2001; Nerad and Cerny 1991; Nerad and Miller 1996). Whereas Benkin's (1984), Nerad and Cerny's (1991), and Nerad and Miller's (1996) dropouts did not return, the majority of our stop-outs—like theirs—left before advancing to candidacy (70%). Overall, 48 percent left during the course-work stage of their programs, and 22 percent left during the qualifying examination stage. A higher proportion of doctoral students in education (56%) reported having stopped out in the course-work stage than their peers in other fields. Within each of the major fields, men and women and students of different race groups largely reported similar timing of their departure decisions.

Why Students Stop Out

One of the most elusive questions confronting education at all levels is why students fail to complete their degree programs. It is particularly

2. For supporting studies, see Berg and Ferber 1983; Girves, Wemmerus, and Rice 1986; Naylor and Sanford 1982; Ott, Markewich, and Ochsner 1984; Sanford and Naylor 1984; and Solmon 1976. In the 1990s, in a study that controlled for ability and field of study, women had lower completion rates (Baker 1998).

puzzling at the level of doctoral education, since this is an endeavor that adults choose to undertake after completing other levels of postsecondary education and is typically not seen as a prerequisite to professional employment. In trying to explain the causes of attrition, researchers have focused on five broad areas: intellectual ability,[3] financial-economic,[4] personal circumstances,[5] psychosocial impediments,[6] and the doctoral program experience.[7]

In Berelson's (1960) study, graduate deans, graduate faculty, and recent doctoral recipients who reflected on why some of their peers did not earn a degree listed different reasons. Graduate deans attributed attrition to financial limitations (70%). Graduate faculty listed intellectual ability insufficient to do the work (64%). Recent doctoral recipients have stated three reasons: insufficient intellectual ability to do the work (52%), a lack of necessary physical or emotional stamina (49%), and lack of proper motivation (47%). Nineteen years later, in their conversations with graduate deans and faculty members at ten graduate programs (six

3. Student ability has been found to have at best either no relationship or a weak relationship with degree completion (Baker 1998; Ehrenberg and Mavros 1995; Girves and Wemmerus 1988; Pyke and Sheridan 1993; Tucker, Gottlieb, and Pease 1964; Wilson 1965; Zwick and Braun 1988). Only three studies linked higher student academic ability, defined as either grade point average (Hagedorn 1999; Wilder and Baydar 1991) or Graduate Record Examination scores (Attiyeh, 1999; Wilder and Baydar 1991), to either persistence or degree completion.

4. Several studies have examined the effect of types of financial assistance, such as fellowships, research assistantships, teaching assistantships, and, in some cases, the amount of aid, on persistence in the doctoral program (Andrieu and St. John 1993; Bowen and Rudenstine 1992; Cook and Swanson 1978; Dolph 1983; Ehrenberg and Mavros 1995; Girves and Wemmerus 1988; Jacks et al. 1983; Pyke and Sheridan 1993; St. John and Andrieu 1995). Although we do not account for it, the economy has varying influences: In bad times, it can bring students to graduate school because of weak employment opportunities and prompt those in school to stay in for the same reason. In good times the economy can lead people to leave graduate school. Baker (1998) suggests that small differences between the salaries of bachelor of arts and Ph.D. recipients, as well as students' awareness of the difficulty of attaining a faculty job and achieving tenure and the uncertainty of research grant availability, may provide disincentives to completion of Ph.D. degrees.

5. Personal circumstances have also been connected with persistence (Hagedorn and Doyle 1993; Peters and Peterson 1987). The findings are mixed on the influence of marriage as a contributor to persistence (Tucker, Gottlieb, and Pease 1964), a deterrent to persistence (Hagedorn 1999; Pyke and Sheridan 1993), or without effect on persistence (Wilder and Baydar 1991). Having children has been found to have a negative effect on persistence (Wilder and Baydar 1991) as well as no effect at all (Tucker, Gottlieb, and Pease 1964), as has being older (Cook and Swanson 1978; Wilder and Baydar 1991). Full-time enrollment has been positively linked to degree completion (Dolph 1983).

6. Personal relationships with the graduate community have been found to contribute to persistence (Sorenson and Kagan 1967). Peer interactions have also been linked to persistence (Hagedorn 1999; Patterson-Stewart, Ritchie, and Sanders 1997; Tucker, Gottlieb, and Pease 1964; Williams, Gallas, and Quiriconi 1984), and student-faculty interactions also play a role in keeping students engaged in their program (Berg and Ferber 1983; Dolph 1983; Hagedorn 1999; Patterson-Stewart, Ritchie, and Sanders 1997; Tucker, Gottlieb, and Pease 1964; Valentine 1987). Like dropping out or stopping out at other levels of higher education, graduate school attrition has been associated with disappointment (Berelson 1960; Golde 1998; Gregg 1972; Hockey 1994; Lovitts 2001; Tucker, Gottlieb, and Pease 1964; Wright 1964).

7. Once students are actively engaged in their doctoral programs, other obstacles to degree completion may arise, such as a mismatch between the reality of the course-work experience and what they expected (Baird 1978; Bodian 1987); adviser and committee problems (Jacks et al. 1983); dissertation-related problems (Hartnett and Willingham 1979; Jacks et al. 1983; Nerad and Cerny 1991); and department-level characteristics (Baird 1997).

of which were part of the current study), Hartnett and Willingham (1979) learned that graduate deans and faculty viewed students' reasons for leaving as being often personal and not academic. After all, these deans believed that the admissions process had yielded intellectually capable students.

Other researchers have concluded that attrition is probably not owing to a single cause (Jacks et al. 1983; Rudd 1985). As Ernest Rudd (1985, 39) states, "There is a tendency for these groups [qualities of the student, personal and individual problems not related to studies, problems inherent in the research, personal academic problems other than the teaching and supervision, and teaching and supervision] to merge and overlap a little at the edges."

We covered some of this ground in our survey by asking students to choose among eleven reasons why they stopped out. Although we learned much from our respondents, at this stage we did not capture the integration of these various items. The most common reason was to work at a job (33%), followed by financial reasons (28%) and family needs (24%). This general pattern mildly varies across fields, race-ethnicity, and sex. For example, a larger share of men than women in both education and social sciences indicated they had taken time off to work at a job. A smaller share of sciences and mathematics students indicated having left school to work at a job. A much smaller share, fewer than 10 percent, listed lack of social fit, academic difficulties, or lack of academic fit as reasons for their temporary leave.

CONCLUSION

By and large, the doctoral students in our sample remain highly committed to their decisions to pursue doctoral degrees, were confident they had selected the right doctoral program, are satisfied with their doctoral experience, and are achieving at high levels. Although a small percentage are stop-outs, they are illustrations of how students might arrange temporary leaves and later resume a successful track toward the doctoral degree. The subtleties of race and sex differences in education and engineering are matters of concern that could have been overlooked if we had been looking only for different distributions among the highs and lows of satisfaction and performance. That they differ at the highest levels suggests that there is yet much territory to be covered if equality by race and sex in the satisfaction and academic achievement in doctoral programs are to be achieved. The key to attrition, and in our case stopping out, may be found most frequently in the student-reported need to interrupt studies to work at a job, seek additional finances, and tend to family needs. As noted at the outset of this chapter, although the doctoral education population is made up of adults who are deeply committed to fulfilling their educational goals, they also have nonacademic pressures that may be addressed only by leaves of absence. For researchers and administrators who focus on attrition, the lesson may be first to identify the stage when students drop out and then attempt to distinguish, even convert, dropouts into stopouts. There are many questions yet that could be addressed. Are some students silent leavers, departing without saying good-bye?

CHAPTER TEN

Rate of Progress, Completion, and Time to Degree

IN TRUTH I HAD ALREADY STARTED an "unofficial" leave of absence a year ago (or so) to help my parents cope with my father's worsening Parkinson's disease. I managed to finish and obtain approval for my dissertation proposal, and attended to my duties to get manuscripts into print, but that is the extent of my professional activity for the past year. On top of my dad's health concerns, my son's diagnosis (autism) led me to my decision to request an official leave.

Arguably, the decision to take a leave should have been a no-brainer, under the circumstances. For financial reasons, however, it was not. My graduate program requires doctoral students to maintain continuous registration while pursuing a Ph.D. Any break in registration status, including a family leave, will ultimately lead to the assessment of a "degree completion fee" upon finishing—which equals 12 credits (4 semesters) worth of tuition (about $3300). I am extremely close to finishing my degree—the entire front end of the paper has been written and the data have been collected, entered, and scrubbed—which tempted me to try to finish my analyses, perhaps in the wee hours of the morning, when my kids were asleep. Coupled with the expensive therapy bills for my son (which may or may not be covered, depending on the insurance company's whim du jour), I couldn't justify paying [a] $3300 degree completion fee when I could just buckle down and get the darn thing done. In May, I abandoned the "buckle down" approach to juggling career and family. It was a stupid idea, borne of stupid, contextual concerns about "real life" for professional goals. Too many folks in my department seem to have abandoned "real life" for the sake of research and professional advancement; I have no desire to follow that lead, and I certainly will not do so at my son's expense.

The timeliness with which students progress through and complete their doctoral programs has been the focus of frequent study and debate (Hartnett and Willingham 1979; Spurr 1970; Wright 1957). As the least prescriptive of higher education degrees, the doctorate has the unique role of preparing scholars, researchers, and university teachers, and during the early years of the degree, the amount of expected time for candidates to move from baccalaureate to doctoral degree completion was not established.

For the past three decades there has been an increased emphasis on timeliness to completion of the degree. This is, after all, an era of public accountability. In a society where seemingly everything is measured for efficiency, why should the doctoral degree be untouchable? Thus far, however, despite persistent scrutiny (for example, Bowen and Rudenstine 1992; Nerad and Miller 1996), it has managed to remain a bastion of ambiguity and continues to enjoy self-determined efficiency.

The doctoral degree process involves both the art of learning and creating and the science of completing distinctive stages. Assessment tools for measuring what students learn and create during their doctoral programs are not the current focus of graduate faculty, researchers, or policy makers. The prevailing assessments are either graduate faculty evaluations of students' course work and dissertation, peer review of presentations for professional conferences, or editorial board–review of papers for publication in professional journals. The doctoral education process is nonetheless judged for its cost and efficiency in much the same way as other levels of higher education. This explains the fascination of researchers and policy makers with the amount of time students spend working on their doctoral degrees. The notion of time to degree has emerged as a measure of both student success and institutional efficiency. Moody Prior (1962) observes the tension between the desire to prescribe the expected time it takes for students to progress through their doctoral programs and the effort to uphold high expectations in the quality of student work: "The Ph.D. is an open-end degree. Its final requirement is an independent investigation and the presentation of results in an acceptable form; thus although practical considerations can and must act as a check on the duration of this exercise, it cannot be circumscribed by an exact, preordained time limit" (Prior 1962, 284).

Because we could not be certain at the inception of the study that we would ultimately obtain completion data for the sample (and consequently time-to-degree data), we sought an alternative measure of development and progress. The degree completion data presented here are, of necessity, a still photograph snatched from a moving picture. Conceivably, over a longer period, the entire sample might complete their doctorates. All we can document here are the totals, at the six-year benchmark.

RATE OF PROGRESS

As previously noted, research on the amount of time students spend progressing through their doctoral degree programs has focused mainly on the number of years it takes for students to complete their programs and those factors that contribute to time to completion (Bowen and Rudenstine 1992; Ehrenberg and Mavros 1995; Gillingham, Seneca, and Taussig 1991; Tuckman, Coyle, and Bae 1989, 1990; Wilson 1965). While we were waiting in the hopes of achieving completion data for at least some among our sample, we devised an alternative measure to explore students' progress toward their doctorates. This involved examining the time elapsed in relation to the milestones and processes leading up to the degree. Unless the doctoral degree process is divided into stages or milestones, researchers are unable to identify those stages of degree programs that constitute impediments toward completion.

Using Tinto's (1975) theoretical model of undergraduate student retention, Girves and Wemmerus (1988) make a start on this research with the development of a conceptual model showing the contribution of various types of financial support in explaining graduate student degree progress. They observe three steps of doctoral degree progress: completion of courses beyond the master's, completion of the general examination that admits the student to doctoral candidacy, and attainment of the doctoral degree.

As an alternative to examining only degree completion as a measure of degree progress, Nerad and Cerny (1991) describe the doctoral education process as having five stages: taking courses, preparing for and taking the qualifying exam, finding a dissertation topic and an adviser and writing a dissertation prospectus, undertaking the dissertation research and writing (which includes having sufficient funds to cover both the research expenses and the cost of living while writing), and applying for professional employment.

Our rate of progress measure is somewhat more refined in that it includes more milestones, and our estimates of rate are somewhat more complex in that we make field distinctions a prominent dimension. We constructed this rate of progress measure as follows. First, we grouped individuals by their field of study and reported stage of progress. We settled on the following eight stages of progress.

—completed less than half of courses required for a doctoral degree

—completed more than half, but not all, of courses required for a doctoral degree—

—completed all course work required for a doctoral degree

—completed preliminary or general examinations but not yet admitted to doctoral candidacy

—admitted to doctoral candidacy but not yet working on dissertation

—working on dissertation

—completed all degree requirements for a doctoral degree, but degree has not yet been awarded

—doctoral degree has been awarded

With five field groups (education, engineering, the humanities, sciences and mathematics, and the social sciences) and eight possible stages, there are forty possible "field-stage" pairs. First, we calculated the median number of years for each of these forty pairs. Next, we calculated the number of years for each individual person in the sample, based on her or his field and stage. The rate of progress measure was constructed by dividing this field- and stage-specific median value by the time each individual reported being in her or his doctoral program at the time the survey was administered. Specifically, this rate of progress measure takes the form

$$\text{Relative Progress} = (\text{Median Years}_{fs} / \text{Years}_{ifs}),$$

where i = individual, f = field group, and s = stage of progress. Here, values strictly greater than 1 indicate a faster rate of progress relative to the median student in the same stage, values strictly less than 1 indicate slower progress, and values equal to 1 indicate that the student has taken the median number of years to reach her or his particular stage of progress.

This rate-of-progress measure offers perhaps the principal advantage of measuring each student's progress relative to the medians in her or his respective field. Precisely, it measures an individual's progress relative to the median number of years for her or his specific field-stage group. This aspect of the measure allowed us to group individuals at different stages of progress when performing analyses (e.g., conditional means, regression.) on this measure. Compared with an alternative measure we considered (Years_{ifs} − Median Years_{fs}), the ratio we chose avoids the problem of a year's difference meaning something different at the various stages of progress. For example, being a year behind the median at an early stage (for example, when course work has been completed) may be different from being a year behind at the dissertation stage. Our ratio more accurately represents this conceptual difference. Finally, because it relies on the stage- and field-specific median and the individual's own measure of years taken to achieve the present stage, arbitrary assignments are avoided. This measure is z-scored for all analyses.

In our sample, engineering students were making the fastest progress toward their doctoral degrees, followed by students in sciences and mathematics, education, the humanities, and the social sciences. Engineering and sciences and mathematics are the two fields where doctoral training is most like professional schools, with clearly defined curriculums and a priori expectations of time to completion. It is surprising to us that education students are progressing at a faster pace than humanities and social sciences students, given that they are older and more often in school part-time. Doctoral students in the social sciences progressed at a slower pace than students in each of the other fields.

Thirty years ago, Solmon (1976) used multiple national databases to test the common belief that women take longer than men to complete their doctoral degrees. He finds that women and men attending the same graduate institutions and same programs progressed at much the same pace. The fastest completers among doctoral students in Abedi and Benkin's (1987) sample were men. However, we found some major field differences between the sexes. In engineering, women progressed at a faster rate than men, and in the social sciences, men progressed more quickly than women.

Little work appears to have been done examining doctoral progress in terms of students' racial backgrounds coupled with their field of study. Peter Sheridan and Sandra Pyke (1994) include demographic factors in their analysis of time taken to complete doctoral degrees and determine that American citizenship was a contributor to decreasing the time to degree. Abedi and Benkin (1987), however, find a weak relationship between citizenship and field of study with the elapsed time to degree. Our data reveal modest differences among the four U.S. race groups in rate of progress and few between citizens and noncitizens. In education and the social sciences, international students in our sample had a faster rate of progress than students of each of the other race-ethnicity groups. They also had a faster rate of progress than Asian Americans in sciences and mathematics and than Hispanics and whites in engineering and the humanities. The requirement of a visa, regardless of whether F-1 or J-1, imposes a time constraint on international students that is nonexistent for U.S. citizens, which may encourage international students to make faster progress.

COMPLETION RATES

Our research, while mainly cross-sectional, has a longitudinal component. On the one hand, our survey represents a snapshot of doctoral students who had completed at least one year and were enrolled in the fall of 1996. On the other hand, we sought outcome measures of doctoral attainment by tracking our sample of individuals through degree completion. To accomplish this, we relied on dissertation abstracts, the graduation records of the participating universities, and doctoral degree completion information obtained from the Survey of Earned Doctorates (NSF).[1] This process allowed us to compile rates of completion. Doctoral students who transferred and completed their doctoral degree requirements at another university were not included in our group of degree completers. We collected three pieces of information on degree completion: whether a student had completed the degree, the type of doctoral degree attained, and the calendar year in which the degree was conferred.[2]

Researchers have estimated that only half of all doctoral students per-

1. With more than 1.6 million entries, the Dissertation Abstracts database is the single, authoritative source for information about doctoral dissertations and master's theses. The database represents the work of authors from more than a thousand graduate schools and universities.
2. Nearly 87 percent of our sample earned Ph.D.s. An additional 12 percent earned either an Ed.D. (Doctor of Education), DPE (Doctor of Physical Education), DR or Drec (Doctor of Recreation), DHS (Doctor of Hebrew Studies), DME (Doctor of Musical Education), or DRE (Doctor of Religious Education), predominantly from the Harvard Graduate School of Education (22%) and Teachers College, Columbia University (64%). The remaining 1 percent earned the Ph.D. without a dissertation or an Applied Research Doctorate without a dissertation.

sist until graduation (Baird 1993b; Bowen and Rudenstine 1992; Tinto 1993). Overall, nearly 62 percent of the sample completed their doctorates within four years of survey response, from 1997 to 2001, the latest year for which degree completion data are available. The remaining 38 percent may or may not complete their doctoral degrees; the only way their completion rates can be determined would be to continue the search for an indeterminate number of years, using the same three sources.

When we administered our survey in 1997, 44 percent of the students reported that they had completed their preliminary examinations and were in the process of writing a dissertation. Of those who were at the dissertation stage, nearly 80 percent had received a doctoral degree by 2001, four years later. Forty-four percent of the remaining students who in 1997 were at various stages of their doctoral program, from having completed less than half of their course work to having been admitted to candidacy but not yet working on their dissertations, also earned their doctoral degrees by 2001.

As we would expect from the foregoing discussion on rate of progress, among our sample, the fields with the largest share of completers were engineering, and sciences and mathematics, with 75 and 72 percent, respectively, completion rates (see fig. 10.1). The only difference in completion rates between males and females was in education, where 54 percent of the women compared with 49 percent of the men had completed. Among the race-ethnicity groups, the key differences were the lower completion rates of African Americans in contrast to white and international students in engineering, sciences and mathematics, and the social sciences (see fig. 10.2). The only difference between Hispanics and whites was in engineering, with 56 percent of Hispanics completing their degrees compared with 79 percent of whites.

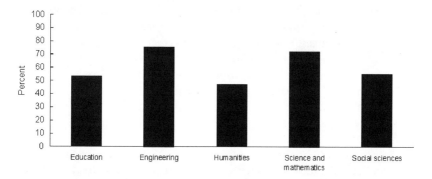

Fig. 10.1. Degree Completion by 2001 among Doctoral Students beyond First Year, by Field
Source: Survey of Doctoral Student Finances, Experiences, and Achievements.

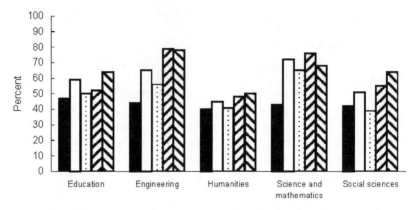

Fig. 10.2. Degree Completion by 2001 among Doctoral Students beyond First Year, by Race-Ethnicity and Field. *Solid bar,* blacks; *open bar,* Asians; *dotted bar,* Hispanics; *ascending hatching,* whites; *descending hatching,* international students. *Source:* Survey of Doctoral Student Finances, Experiences, and Achievements.

Elapsed Time to Degree

Rates of doctoral student progress have typically been measured in three ways: total time to degree, the length of time from completing the bachelor's degree to completing the doctorate; elapsed time to degree, the amount of time from entering a doctoral degree program to completion; and registered time to degree, the amount of time registered in the doctoral program, from starting the program to completion. Bowen and Rudenstine (1992) rely on the first two approaches in their calculations of time to degree: the total time between baccalaureate and doctorate and the elapsed time from entering the doctoral program to receiving a doctoral degree. They report that the gap in time to degree among fields varied depending on which of the measures was used. Students in education, for example, took more time away from school between degrees than did students in the sciences. Using total time to degree, Bowen and Rudenstine find that doctoral students in education took an average 12.4 years, compared with 9.2 for those in humanities, 8.13 in social sciences, 6.9 years in engineering, and 6.1 years in physical sciences. Using elapsed time to degree, education students took 10.3 years, humanities 8.6 years, social sciences 7.4 years, engineering 6.2 years, and physical sciences 5.9 years to complete their doctorates.

Baird's (1990b) analyses of data from the National Research Council indicate that the fastest students were those in chemistry (5.9 years), chemical engineering (5.9), and biochemistry (6.0). The slowest were students in music (10), art history (9.3), French (5.5), and history (5.5). Baird finds that the fields with the narrowest range were the biological and physical sciences and mathematics, and he notes a relatively wide range in the humanities and social sciences, the difference between the fastest and slowest disciplines being four years. He attributes these differences to the "clarity of the central paradigms within disciplines and the degree of agreement about those paradigms" (Baird 1990b, 380). Baird states that the biological and physical sciences have relatively clear and agreed-upon bodies of knowledge and procedures, whereas the humanities and social sciences thrive on differences in definitions, content, and interpretation.[3]

As noted in chapter 5, our results substantially support the Bowen and Rudenstine (1992) observations. Just as other researchers have found time to degree to vary widely by field of study (Baird 1990b; Ehrenberg and Mavros 1995; Tuckman, Coyle, and Bae 1989; Wilson 1965), we found the average time off varied substantially by major field. At slightly more than two years, sciences and mathematics doctoral students reported taking the least amount of time off between receiving their undergraduate degrees and beginning their doctoral degree programs. Education students, on average, took the longest time off by far, at almost 12.0 years. Students enrolled in the remaining three field groups (engineering, the humanities, and the social sciences) each took off an average of between 3.5 to 4.5 years. Note that while the mean for the sample approaches six years, this is largely because of the inclusion of education students.

Our goal was to create a measure of elapsed time to degree. The attendance pattern section of the survey asked students when (by term and year) they had begun their doctoral programs. To calculate an individual's time to degree, we subtracted the year and term the student started her or his doctoral program from the year she or he received the degree. We have degree completion data to 2001. We assumed that all students received their doctoral degrees in the spring, and therefore we added half a year to each degree year. For example, a student who started a doctoral degree program in the fall term 1994 (1994.75) and received the doctoral degree in the early summer of 1999 (1999.50) had a time to degree of 4.75 years. Engineering students were the fastest, at 4.75 years, followed by students in education, sciences and mathematics, and the social sciences, each at 5.75 years; humanities students had the longest median time to degree, 6.75 years (see fig. 10.3).

In addition to median elapsed time to degree, we looked at mean elapsed time to degree (5.97) and continued our analyses to identify dif-

---

3. Based upon his research and review of the research on time to degree, Baird (1990a, 383) gives the following advice to students who would like to "keep their time in graduate school to a minimum: don't take a full-time job; go to graduate school immediately after college; attend full-time; enter the same discipline as your undergraduate major; attend the same college as your undergraduate college; if you can't get a fellowship try to find a job as a research assistant; complete your required coursework and qualifying examinations as soon as possible; find a conscientious adviser; and if you must get married, for goodness sake don't have children."

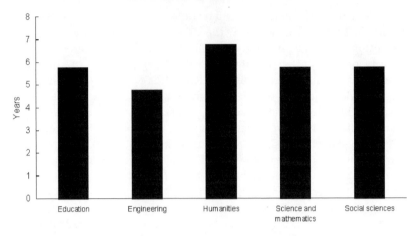

Fig. 10.3. Median Elapsed Time to Degree for Students Completing Doctoral Degree by 2001, by Field
Source: Survey of Doctoral Student Finances, Experiences, and Achievements.

ferences among fields and by race and sex. Overall, engineering students who completed their doctorates within our measurement frame averaged the least time to degree, at 5.23 years. This was faster than the mean for sciences and mathematics (5.71), education (6.28), the social sciences (6.35), and the humanities (7.41). Although students in education were slower than those in two other fields, they showed the largest standard deviation (more than 3 units), indicating the widest variations among its students' completion times.

In general, women in the sample who completed their doctorates within the period of the survey took nearly half of a year longer, on average, than their male peers (6.25 years compared with 5.77 years). This pattern is similar to the pattern that Robert Ibarra (1996) has observed among Latinos, where women had longer elapsed time to degree, which he attributed to their higher part-time attendance. In our study, in the social sciences, male students averaged 6.11 years to the doctorate, while women averaged 6.59 years. With this exception, all fields were remarkably similar.

Pearson's (1985) review of the research, as well as his own research, indicates that while blacks took longer to complete their degrees (bachelor's degree to doctorate), the actual amount of time registered in graduate school was similar for blacks and whites (Blackwell 1981; National Board on Graduate Education 1976). Smith and Tang's (1994) analyses of the data from the 1990 Survey of Earned Doctorates concurs with Pearson's findings: African Americans had the longest time to degree (bachelor's degree to doctorate) in the doctoral population.

As might be expected, given their faster rate of progress, international students who earned a doctoral degree were significantly ahead of all other groups on time to degree. They averaged 5.32 years compared with 5.99 years for Asian Americans, 6.21 for whites, 6.26 for African Americans, and 6.34 for Hispanics. Examining these differences by field, we found that international students in education (5.17) were ahead of both whites (6.50) and African Americans (6.27). In engineering, international students led at 4.89 years, compared with whites at 5.50 and Hispanics at 6.00. In sciences and mathematics, international students averaged 5.47 years, compared with whites at 5.76 years and Asian Americans at 6.02 years. In the social sciences, international students averaged 5.81 years to completion, compared with 6.46 for whites, 7.21 for Asian Americans, and 7.49 for Hispanics.

Several researchers have considered why time to degree might be protracted. It is not surprising that the reasons suggested for prolonging doctoral study are similar to the those for failure to complete degrees. The type of financial support can hasten or lengthen time to degree (Abedi and Benkin 1987; Bowen and Rudenstine 1992; Ehrenberg and Mavros 1995; Gillingham, Seneca, and Taussig 1991; Hauptman 1986; National Research Council 1996; Nerad and Cerny 1991; Wilson 1965). Navigating the dissertation stage can also influence the time it takes to complete a degree (Council of Graduate Schools 1990; Isaac et al. 1989; Nerad and Cerny 1991; Rudd 1986).

CONCLUSION

The pressures of efficiency and accountability in doctoral education cannot be ignored. Questions of time to degree, rate of progress, and completion rates will become as common as they are at the undergraduate level and will rival questions of publication rates, grant funding, and student qualifications for the attention of graduate faculty. We have introduced a new measure of efficiency that we call rate of progress, which we believe to be a reasonable barometer of time to degree, allowing both faculty and students to assess students' accomplishments and progress. Graduate faculty may eventually wish to set standards and expectations that can be conveyed to students about expected rates of progress and time to completion. We might then expect differences in the rates across disciplines to dissipate—or at least to be explained by differing requirements in different disciplines and fields.

CHAPTER ELEVEN

Predicting Experiences and Performance

UP TO THIS POINT, we have noted many similarities as well as differences among doctoral students by field, race-ethnicity, and sex in the way they experience doctoral education and in the ways they perform. Now we turn our attention to elements that contribute to student experiences and outcomes. One might look at our relational analyses as identifying the attributes of doctoral students that are most valued in doctoral programs. Our goal throughout this process of statistical deconstruction is to display the character of the Ph.D. experience. On the one hand, we are searching for explanations for many of the field, race-ethnicity, and sex differences observed in earlier chapters of this book; on the other hand, we are exploring whether those differences are sustained when the characteristics, backgrounds, and other experiences of people within these groups are held constant.

In a sense, these relational analyses allow us to identify tangible and fluid elements beyond the commonly immutable characteristics of field, race-ethnicity, and sex. This process can be beneficial to present and prospective students as well as to university faculty and administrators in knowing what to expect as they chart paths through the doctoral education process. It may also be useful to graduate institutions that are interested in knowing how different types of students experience doctoral programs.

Using the statistical tools of logistic and linear regression, we are able to identify significant predictors in our major areas of emphasis: financial support, socialization, research productivity, satisfaction, stopping out, rate of progress, degree completion, and elapsed time to degree.[1] We examined eleven elements both as predictors and as outcomes of doctoral student experiences:

---

1. Logistic regression is used for predicting the likelihood that an event, such as receiving a fellowship, will occur. The results of the logistic regressions are presented as odds ratios for the likelihood of an event occurring. Odds ratios greater than 1 mean that the odds an event will occur are increased; odds ratios less than 1 mean that the odds of an event occurring are decreased. When the odds ratio is 1, the odds are unchanged (Menard 1995). Inverse odds ratios are presented for values less than 1 and signify lower odds. Linear regression was used for predicting a continuous outcome, such as time to degree. In the time-to-degree example, positive coefficients indicate that the variable in question is associated with a longer time to degree, and negative coefficients indicate a shorter time to degree.

—ever having a fellowship

—ever having a teaching assistantship

—ever having a research assistantship

—incurring educational debt as a doctoral student

—peer interactions

—having a mentor

—student-faculty social interactions

—academic interactions with faculty

—interactions with faculty adviser

—having some research productivity

—overall satisfaction with doctoral program

As our conceptual model suggests, we expected each of these elements to be prominent features of doctoral student experiences and likely contributors to outcomes. We attempted first to identify the extent to which each of these elements was important and then to address the crucial question of how one might isolate the elements that have the most positive consequences. How strong is the influence of each of these attributes on a student's success, and which students are least and most challenged in acquiring these attributes? For example, if we find that having a fellowship contributes favorably to student experiences in completing a doctoral degree, then the question remains, what student attributes enhance their chances of receiving fellowships?

In our preliminary analyses, we discovered that major field was a feature that typically distinguished student characteristics, experiences, and outcomes. Consequently, instead of conducting analyses for all fields combined, we performed separate regression analyses for each of the five fields. Our exploratory analyses also involved investigating which variables should be included in each regression analysis and which should be eliminated either because of collinearity between and among the variables or because they contributed little to explaining the particular student experience or outcome. Appendix F presents the individual regression tables (F.1 to F.20), as well as a summary table (F.21), that illustrate the variables included in the final model, as well as those that we considered but elected not to include.[2] The regression tables in this chapter present the statisti-

---

2. In appendix F, the bottom rows of the logistic regression tables contain two pieces of statistical information: a likelihood ratio test statistic that compares the full model with the null model, and an R^2 statistic that is commonly used in logistic regression. The statistic used is sometimes termed the McFadden (1973) pseudo R^2. It corresponds to Henry Theil's (1970) uncertainty coefficient. The pseudo R^2 is a measure of proportional reduction of error, so that the possible values are between 0 and 1, with larger values corresponding to stronger predictions. In general, the pseudo R^2 measures the improvement in prediction of the dependent

cally significant predictors of the twenty measures of the doctoral study experience, with positive (+) denoting predictors that contributed to students' experience and negative (−) denoting aspects that detracted from students' experience. Because of our interest in differences by race, citizenship, and sex (discussed in earlier chapters), we included these variables in all the relational analyses.

We limit our discussion to variables that proved to be significant, and thus any given variable may appear in one section but not in another, based on its value in explaining a given experience or outcome that we are measuring. We also included in our analyses of each field any single variable that was significant in at least one field. Consequently, some variables are presented that emerged as significant in a single field. While some relationships at the end of each section may appear to have a negligible effect on the student experience for large numbers of doctoral students, some of these minor relationships have meaningful consequences in the lives of doctoral students, and understanding some of the nuances may help illustrate the experience.

In this chapter we present the findings with respect to the various relationships in each of these key areas, and in chapters 12 and 13 we interpret these findings, seeking meaningfulness for student experiences during their doctoral education. This chapter is designed in such a way that readers have the option to go directly to topics of particular interest, to see the significant correlates that we found, or to read successively through each of the critical topics, to build a comprehensive picture. In either case, it should be borne in mind that all types of outcomes that we examine—financial support, socialization, research productivity, satisfaction, stopping out, rate of progress, degree completion, and elapsed time to degree—are determined by a variety of societal, institutional, faculty, and student conditions and factors, any one of which is difficult to isolate from the others. For example, the shape and condition of the economy, institutional endowments, the labor market, and the competitiveness of student applicant pools are all important factors in determining the types and amounts of aid students receive. Ronald Lindahl, Martin Rosenzweig, and Warren Willingham (1974) point out that many models fail to capture student motivation and students' responses to program demands, per-

---

variable that results from use of the linear logistic model in which the listed predicting variables have been used (Haberman 1982). The measure of predictive accuracy is the logarithmic penalty function, so that, if the logistic model is correct, then the pseudo R^2 compares the unconditional entropy of the dependent variable with the conditional entropy of the dependent variable, given the predicting variables. Sampling properties of the pseudo R^2 are described in Haberman (1982). Like the R^2 statistic in regression analysis, the pseudo R^2 measures association rather than goodness of fit, for the logistic model may fit perfectly but the pseudo R^2 is small, and the logistic model may not fit correctly and the pseudo R^2 is large. This issue is addressed by Zvi Gilula and Shelby Haberman (2001). In examining pseudo R^2 statistics, it should be noted that the cited references provide a number of examples from the social sciences and that these cited pseudo R^2 statistics generally are less than 0.2.

sonal problems, and changes in market forces. We focus on many of the student characteristics and experiences that can be affected by policy. Our primary interest is to identify tangible matters that might be addressed by students and graduate institutions through policy and practice to enhance student experiences and throughput.

FINANCIAL SUPPORT

How students finance their doctoral programs is a continuous focal point for both students and institutions from the beginning of the application process through the time degrees are conferred. Students use a variety of strategies to finance their doctoral education, including fellowships and positions as teaching assistants (TAs) or research assistants (RAs). The following analyses display the predictors for each of these types of financial support, both at the beginning of students' doctoral enrollment and during their program. We also examine students' acquisition of debt during their doctoral program.

Fellowship Offer on Entry to Program

Initial fellowship offers, either for a single year or for multiple years, appear to be a tool that graduate schools use to compete for talented, underrepresented, or full-time students. We asked students in our sample to indicate whether they had been offered a fellowship for any of the first five years of their doctoral programs. Their responses were aggregated into a dichotomous measure. Although several elements contribute to receiving a fellowship offer at the time of admission, three appear to tell the big story across the fields. Having relatively high Graduate Record Examination (GRE) verbal scores, being a member of an underrepresented race group, and being initially enrolled as a full-time student all appear to enhance student prospects of being offered a fellowship when they are admitted into their doctoral programs (see table 11.1).[3]

Of the three parts of the GRE General Test, only the verbal score is a significant predictor in every field of whether students receive a fellowship offer upon entering their doctoral programs.[4] A 100-point increase in GRE verbal scores increased the likelihood of such an offer, by a factor of nearly 1.6 in humanities and the social sciences, 1.2 in engineering, and 1.3 in sciences and mathematics and in education. By contrast, GRE quantitative scores were predictors of such fellowship offers only in humanities and in sciences and mathematics, where higher scores increased the odds by 1.3 and 1.2, respectively. GRE analytical scores were not found

---

3. For a discussion of the use of GRE scores in the regression analyses, see appendix G.
4. We included all three parts of the GRE General Test in the regressions for predicting fellowship offers, teaching assistant offers, and research assistantship offers at admission since the GRE General Test, regardless of each part's significance, is a critical part of the admissions process.

Table 11.1
Predictors of Receiving a Fellowship Offer (Single Year or Multiyear) on Entry to Doctoral Program, by Field

Independent Variable[a]	Education	Engineering	Humanities	Sciences and Mathematics	Social Sciences
GRE verbal (100s of points)	+	+	+	+	+
GRE quantitative (100s of points)			+	+	
GRE analytical (100s of points)					
Male				−	
African American[b]	+	+	+	+	+
Hispanic	+		+	+	+
Asian American	+		+		+
International		−	+	−	
Age at start of doctoral program (1 yr.)	−		−	−	−
Master's upon entry	−	−			
Selective undergraduate institution	+				
Private graduate school	+		+		+
Full-time student when first enrolled	+	+	+		+
n (unweighted)	1,504	797	1,171	1,635	2,187

Source: Survey of Doctoral Student Finances, Experiences, and Achievements.
[a]Parents' SES was not a significant predictor in any field and was dropped from the models.
[b]All racial groups and international students are compared with whites.

to be a predictor of being offered a fellowship at the time of admissions in any field.

Fueling the prominence of market forces in offers of fellowships at the time of admission is the pressure on academic departments to achieve diversity. African Americans and Hispanic doctoral students are in short supply in every field, and Asian Americans are scarce in education, humanities, and the social sciences. Fellowships may be one tool used by graduate schools to address this supply problem. In every field, African Americans had a higher likelihood than whites of receiving a fellowship offer at admissions. A similar pattern emerged for Hispanics in education, humanities, sciences and mathematics, and the social sciences. In all fields except engineering and sciences and mathematics, Asian Americans had an advantage over whites in the probability of receiving an initial fellowship offer. For international students, the effect was pronounced only in humanities, where international students were more likely to receive offers than whites; but in engineering and the social sciences, international students were less likely than whites to receive a fellowship offer.

The relationship between full-time attendance and fellowship receipt presents a chicken-and-egg conundrum. We cannot be certain whether students received fellowship offers because they applied to attend full-time or, rather, their full-time attendance was facilitated by the fellowship offer. We found full-time attendance when first enrolled to be a factor in receiving fellowship offers in education (nearly 8 times more likely), humanities (7 times more likely), the social sciences (5 times more likely), and engineering (3.5 times more likely). It may be that fellowship offers more often enabled or even required full-time attendance.

On top of our main story—which centers on GRE verbal performance, race-ethnicity, and full-time status—several background characteristics contributed to the odds of students' receiving fellowship offers upon entering doctoral programs. Younger students in engineering, sciences and mathematics, and the social sciences appeared to have a slight advantage over older students. For instance, a twenty-five-year-old entering doctoral student in engineering was 2.1 times more likely to receive a fellowship than a thirty-five-year-old entering student. This finding is significant for students in sciences and mathematics and the social sciences, as well, where a twenty-five-year-old is 1.6 and 1.9 times more likely, respectively, to be awarded a fellowship than a thirty-five-year-old student. The probability of receiving a fellowship is further enhanced when we compare age differences of twenty years—such as a twenty-five-year-old and a forty-five-year-old. Doctoral students entering programs in engineering, sciences and mathematics, and the social sciences at the age of twenty-five are 4.3, 2.4, and 3.5 more likely, respectively, to receive fellowships upon entry than students who entered any of those fields at the age of forty-five. There were no statistical differences by age in education or the humanities.

Sex played a seemingly minor role in these initial offers, with only women entering sciences and mathematics programs being somewhat more likely to benefit than men. Perhaps this slight advantage for women reflects a combination of the supply-and-demand market forces and national policy. Women are relatively underrepresented in sciences and mathematics, and the National Science Foundation and other governmental sponsors of academic research have been supporting the policy of increasing the representation of women in these fields. Based on that argument we might also have expected the same in engineering, where women are in even shorter supply. However, sex was not a predictor of early offers in engineering. This difference between sciences and mathematics and engineering may be a function of the greater availability of fellowships in sciences and mathematics.

Several admissions attributes and criteria predicted receipt of fellowships. Education students who attended selective undergraduate institutions were 1.5 times more likely to receive early fellowship offers. Having already earned a master's degree came into play only in engineering, humanities, and the social sciences, where it was negatively associated with the likelihood of a fellowship offer. Students attending private graduate schools in the fields of humanities, the social sciences, and education were more likely than their public school–educated colleagues to receive fellowships (3.2 times more likely in humanities, 1.8 times in the social sciences, 1.7 times in education).

Teaching Assistantship Offer on Entry to Program

Two common elements of teaching assistantship offers upon entry are full-time status and age (see table 11.2). Students enrolled full-time at the

Table 11.2
Predictors of Receiving a Teaching Assistantship Offer (Single Year or Multiyear) on Entry to Doctoral Program, by Field

Independent Variable[a]	Education	Engineering	Humanities	Sciences and Mathematics	Social Sciences
GRE verbal (100s of points)			+		+
GRE quantitative (100s of points)					+
GRE analytical (100s of points)					
Male				−	+·
African American[b]		−		+	−
Hispanic		−		+	
Asian American					
International	−	−			
Age at start of doctoral program (1 yr.)	−	−	−	−	−
Private graduate school		−			−
Full-time student when first enrolled	+	+	+	+	+
n (unweighted)	1,550	815	1,199	1,693	2,241

Source: Survey of Doctoral Student Finances, Experiences, and Achievements.
[a]Parents' SES, selective undergraduate institution, and master's upon entry were nonsignificant predictors in all fields and were dropped from the models.
[b]All racial groups and international students are compared with whites.

start of their doctoral programs in the social sciences were more than 6.2 times as likely to receive teaching assistantship offers, and those enrolled full-time in education more than 5.0 times as likely, to receive such offers as their part-time peers. In engineering, humanities, and sciences and mathematics, the effect was not as strong: 2.7 in engineering, 3.3 in humanities, and 2.5 in sciences and mathematics. This is probably a reflection of both the requirement of full-time attendance in return for offers of significant financial support and the enhanced possibility of full-time enrollment because of the offered financial support.

In every field, older students were less likely to receive teaching assistantship bids. A one-year increase in age was associated with students being 1.1 times less likely to be offered teaching assistantships in education, engineering, the humanities, sciences and mathematics, and the social sciences. The relationship between age and receiving a teaching assistantship is more pronounced when we compare age differences of ten and twenty years. For example, a thirty-five-year-old enrolled in a doctoral program in education was 1.3 times less likely to receive a teaching assistantship than an otherwise comparable twenty-five-year-old. Similar differences were found across the four remaining fields—a twenty-five-year-old was 1.7, 1.4, 1.7, and 1.9 times more likely, respectively, to receive a teaching assistantship than a thirty-five-year-old in engineering, humanities, sciences and mathematics, and the social sciences. The gap in the likelihood of receiving a teaching assistantship is even more pronounced as the age difference grows: twenty-five-year-olds were 1.8, 2.8, 2.0, 3.0, and 3.6 times more likely, respectively, to receive teaching assistantships than forty-five-year-olds in education, engineering, humanities, sciences and mathematics, and the social sciences.

Teaching assistantship offers seem to be more prevalent in public universities. In engineering and the social sciences, students attending private graduate schools were less likely to receive early offers of teaching assistantships. In the fields of education, humanities, and sciences and mathematics, however, there was no difference between public and private institutions in the prevalence of teaching assistantship offers at the time of enrollment. Perhaps this funding pattern reflects the combination of smaller undergraduate enrollments and class size in private universities and the lower reliance on entering doctoral students in the instructional process in private universities. Our sample also includes some large public universities where faculty benefit from the involvement of graduate student instructors who provide substantive support with undergraduate teaching.

Student background characteristics played a spotty role in determining who received a teaching assistantship upon entering a doctoral program. Sex played a role only in the humanities and in sciences and mathematics, with men being somewhat less likely to be TAs in humanities (1.5 times) but somewhat more likely than women in sciences and mathematics (1.4 times). In sciences and mathematics, the opposite sex effect was observed for fellowship offers, where women were more likely to receive the offers (see table 11.1).

We also found differences among the race groups, with African Americans being less likely than whites to receive teaching assistantships in sciences and mathematics and in engineering. Conversely, African Americans were more likely than whites to receive teaching assistantship offers in the humanities. Hispanics were less likely than whites to receive offers at admissions in engineering but more likely in humanities. International students were less likely than their white classmates to be offered teaching assistantships at the point of entry in education and engineering.

For offers of teaching assistantships, in contrast to fellowships, the GRE General Test played a minor role in predicting who received a teaching assistantship upon entry. Only in humanities and the social sciences was higher performance on the GRE verbal test associated with an increased likelihood of being offered a teaching assistantship (by a factor of 1.3).

Research Assistantship Offer on Entry to a Doctoral Program

The pattern that emerged for fellowship recipients with respect to age and enrollment status at the start of their doctoral program also applied to those who received research assistantships (see table 11.3). With the exception of humanities, being younger increased students' odds of receiving research assistantships. Each additional year decreased a student's chance of receiving a research assistantship by 1.04 in education, 1.09 in engineering, 1.08 in sciences and mathematics, and 1.06 in the social sciences. Furthermore, an increase of ten years in age diminished students'

Table 11.3
Predictors of Receiving a Research Assistantship Offer (Single Year or Multiyear) on Entry to Doctoral Program, by Field

Independent Variable[a]	Education	Engineering	Humanities[b]	Sciences and Mathematics	Social Sciences
GRE verbal (100s of points)		+			
GRE quantitative (100s of points)		+		−	+
GRE analytical (100s of points)		−			
Male					
African American[c]		−		−	
Hispanic					
Asian American					
International	−	−			−
Age at start of doctoral program (1 yr.)	−	−		−	−
Selective undergraduate institution		−			
Full-time student when first enrolled	+	+		+	+
n (unweighted)	1,513	797	1,177	1,641	2,197

Source: Survey of Doctoral Student Finances, Experiences, and Achievements.
[a]Parents' SES, private graduate school, and master's upon entry were nonsignificant predictors in all fields and were dropped from the models.
[b]The model is not statistically significantly different from the null model. This suggests that there is no relationship between the predictors and receiving a research assistantship.
[c]All racial groups and international students are compared with whites.

likelihood of receiving research assistantships by 1.5 in education, 2.3 in engineering, 2.1 in sciences and mathematics, and 1.7 in the social sciences. These numbers grew larger for age differences of twenty years. Full-time enrollment increased students' odds of receiving research assistantships in education, engineering, sciences and mathematics, and the social sciences.

Of the three parts of the GRE General Test, the quantitative portion appeared to have an effect on initial offers of research assistantships in engineering, sciences and mathematics, and the social sciences. In engineering and the social sciences, each 100-point gain resulted in an increased likelihood of being offered a research assistantship (1.3 each). On the other hand, in sciences and mathematics, higher scores reduced the likelihood (by 1.3) of initial research assistantship offers. This is the opposite effect observed in fellowships in sciences and mathematics, where relatively high GRE quantitative scores contributed to the likelihood of receiving a fellowship. These two sets of relationships may be related: the competition may compel sciences and mathematics graduate faculty to offer fellowships to students with relatively high GRE quantitative scores, thus leaving the research assistantships for students with relatively low quantitative scores. Only in engineering did student performance on the verbal and analytical sections of the GRE General Test govern research assistantship offers. Higher verbal scores increased student odds of receiving a research assistantship in engineering by 1.2, while higher analytical scores decreased the odds by the same factor. We also found that for engineering students, having attended selective undergraduate institutions decreased by 1.4 the odds of receiving research assistantship offers at the time of admissions.

We observed no sex effects for research assistantship offers at the point of admissions, but we did observe race-ethnicity effects. Among the race groups, whites in engineering were 2.7 times more likely than African Americans to receive offers of research assistantships, and in sciences and mathematics, 4.0 times more likely. Given that African Americans were favored in offers of fellowships, it is understandable that, compared with whites, they were not favored in offers of research assistantships in engineering and in sciences and mathematics. It is surprising, however, that this did not hold for Hispanics. International students in education, engineering, and the social sciences were also somewhat less-likely recipients.

Fellowship over the Course of Doctoral Study

Two-thirds of the students in our sample entered their doctoral programs with offers of financial support, but financing doctoral programs is a continuous process that involves applications and offers throughout. We looked at our sample to see whether, over the course of their experience, they had ever been fellowship recipients (see table 11.4). Students' race-ethnicity was a prominent predictor of ever receiving fellowships, as it was in receiving offers of fellowships at the time of admission, and the GRE General Test also continued to play an important role. Although age played a limited role at the point of entering a doctoral program, it was much more prominent after students matriculated. A few of the doctoral program experiences, namely, being an RA, amount of time in program, and postdegree career expectations, were all found to be factors in pre-

Table 11.4
Predictors of Receiving a Fellowship over the Course of Doctoral Study, by Field

Independent Variable[a]	Education	Engineering	Humanities	Sciences and Mathematics	Social Sciences
Male			—	—	
African American[b]	+	+	+	+	+
Hispanic	+	+	+	+	+
Asian American	+				
International	—			—	+
Parents' SES[c]				+	
Household income ($1,000s)	—				—
Age at start of doctoral program (1 yr.)	—		—	—	—
GRE verbal (100s of points)	+			+	+
GRE quantitative (100s of points)					
GRE analytical (100s of points)					+
Master's upon entry			—		—
Selective undergraduate institution	+	+			
Private graduate school	+		+		+
Always full-time doctoral student	+			+	
Ever was a teaching assistant	+			—	
Ever was a research assistant	+	—	+	—	
Time in doctoral program (yrs.)		+	+	+	+
Expect first job to be faculty or postdoctorate position	—	+		+	+
n (unweighted)	1,435	774	1,113	1,590	2,071

Source: Survey of Doctoral Student Finances, Experiences, and Achievements.
[a]Married or domestic partner and children under eighteen were nonsignificant predictors in all fields and were dropped from the models.
[b]All racial groups and international students are compared with whites.
[c]Parents' SES is a composite of educational attainment and occupational prestige.

dicting who received fellowships over the course of their doctoral program experiences.

In every field we found the probability of African Americans and Hispanics receiving fellowships during their doctoral studies to be higher than for their white peers. In education, where they are not as well represented as in the other fields, Asian Americans were more likely to receive fellowships than whites. International students in engineering and in sciences and mathematics were less likely than whites to receive fellowship support, whereas in the social sciences, international students were more likely to receive such support.

The GRE General Test played a much more restricted role in predicting receiving a fellowship over the course of doctoral study than in predicting receiving a fellowship at the point of admission. Higher GRE verbal scores had a significantly positive effect on the award of fellowships over the course of the doctoral experience, but only in the fields of education, sciences and mathematics, and the social sciences. Conversely, though GRE quantitative scores were a significant predictor of fellowships at the time of admissions in humanities and in sciences and mathematics, they did not predict fellowship receipt over the course of the doctoral program. Also, unlike fellowships at the point of admissions, where GRE analytical scores were not significant in any field, higher GRE analytical scores increased the odds of receiving a fellowship over the course of doctoral study in the social sciences.

In four fields, other characteristics—age at the start of the doctoral program, career expectations of having a faculty or postdoctoral research position upon competing the degree, amount of time enrolled in a doctoral program, and having been a research assistant—were predictors of ever receiving a fellowship. In every field except the humanities, fellowships were awarded to younger students at higher rates than to their older peers. The older students were when entering their doctoral programs, the lower were their chances of receiving fellowships. Student career expectations were also a predictor of receiving fellowships over the course of doctoral study, and the field of education was different from the others. In engineering, sciences and mathematics, and the social sciences, students anticipating a faculty or postdoctoral position upon degree completion were more likely to receive fellowships; in education, students who held such expectations were less likely to receive a fellowship; and in humanities, career aspirations to become a faculty member had no effect. Having been in their doctoral programs longer slightly improved students' odds of receiving fellowships in engineering, humanities, sciences and mathematics, and the social sciences.

As illustrated in chapter 7, doctoral students typically rely on multiple types of funding awards during the course of their doctoral programs. What is not shown is the extent to which receiving one type of award contributed to receiving other types. Our regression analyses reveal that students appear to have received their financial support from different sources in combinations at the same time and at different times during the course of their doctoral studies and that the extent to which various sources of support complemented one another varied across fields. This suggests that recipients of one type of award may be attractive candidates for multiple other types of financial support. Students who received research assistantships in engineering and in sciences and mathematics were 2.0 times less likely than their peers to be awarded fellowships. On the other hand, in education and the humanities, students who received research assistantships were more than twice as likely to also be awarded fellowships. In the humanities, in which the availability of research assistantships is more limited, students needed to rely more on fellowships. Similar to the pattern observed with research assistantships, students in the field of education who were TAs were nearly twice as likely as those without teaching assistantships to also receive fellowships, whereas in sciences and mathematics, TAs were 1.5 times less likely than their peers to win fellowships. This situation may also be related to the scarcity of teaching assistantships in the field of education, making fellowships a more essential component of student support.

Admissions criteria also affected who received fellowships over the course of their doctoral studies. Doctoral students who began their programs already having earned master's degrees were slightly less likely to receive fellowships in engineering, the humanities, and the social sciences. Education and engineering students who had attended selective U.S. undergraduate institutions had an edge (1.6 times and 1.4 times, respectively) in fellowship receipt. In a possible reflection of both the larger endowments and the higher price of private universities, students attending private graduate schools in the fields of education, humanities, and the social sciences were more than twice as likely as their peers at public institutions in these fields to receive fellowships. Having been a full-time student throughout the course of doctoral study was positively associated with receiving a fellowship in the fields of education and sciences and mathematics.

Several student demographic characteristics were found to be associated with receiving a fellowship over the course of a student's doctoral experiences. Men were less likely than women to receive fellowships in engineering and in sciences and mathematics. In sciences and mathematics, this mirrors the pattern seen in the award of a fellowship offer at admissions, in engineering, however, we did not see an advantage for women in the offer of fellowship at admissions. Parental socioeconomic status (SES), defined here in terms of educational attainment and occupational prestige, had a slightly beneficial effect on students' receipt of fellowships in sciences and mathematics. Education and social sciences students with lower student household incomes were more likely to receive fellowships; in these fields, the odds of receiving a fellowship during doctoral study were 10 percent and 20 percent higher for students with household incomes of $20,000 than for students with household incomes of $40,000 and $60,000, respectively.

Teaching Assistantship over the Course of Doctoral Study

Just as engineering and social science students attending public graduate schools were more likely to receive offers of teaching assistantships when they were admitted, being enrolled at a public graduate school was a predictor of receiving a teaching assistantship over the course of the doctoral program in these same two fields (see table 11.5). In fact, only in the field of education did attending a doctoral program at a public university not make a significant contribution to being a teaching assistant over the course of a student's doctoral experience. Attending a private graduate school was associated with a decrease in the odds of being a teaching assistant by 1.3 in engineering, sciences and mathematics, and the social sciences and by nearly 2.5 in humanities. This finding raises the possibility, at least, that public universities find it easier, politically and economically, to involve doctoral students in undergraduate instruction than private universities.

Although the GRE verbal test was found to be a predictor of receiving a teaching assistantship in two fields (humanities and the social sciences) at the time of admissions, over the long haul the influence of verbal test scores was more prevalent. GRE verbal scores predicted who received a

Table 11.5
Predictors of Being a Teaching Assistant over the Course of Doctoral Study, by Field

Independent Variable[a]	Education	Engineering	Humanities	Sciences and Mathematics	Social Sciences
Male	—				
African American[b]		—			
Hispanic	—	—			
Asian American			—		
International	—	—		—	+
Married or domestic partner	+				
Household income ($1,000s)	—	—			—
Age at start of doctoral program (1 yr.)	—	—	—	—	—
Always full-time doctoral student	+		+		+
GRE verbal (100s of points)	+	+	+		+
GRE quantitative (100s of points)				+	
GRE analytical (100s of points)					+
Master's upon entry					—
Private graduate school		—	—	—	—
Ever received a fellowship	+				—
Ever was a research assistant	+		+	+	+
Time in doctoral program (yrs.)	+	+	+		+
Expect first job to be faculty or postdoctoral position	+	+			+
n (unweighted)	1,509	806	1,167	1,673	2,193

Source: Survey of Doctoral Student Finances, Experiences, and Achievements.
[a]Parents' SES, children under eighteen, and selective undergraduate institution were nonsignificant predictors in all fields and were dropped from the models.
[b]All racial groups and international students are compared with whites.

teaching assistantship during doctoral programs in four fields. For every 100-point increase in GRE verbal score, the likelihood of receiving a teaching assistantship award increased by 1.2 in education, engineering, and the social sciences and by 1.4 in humanities. Higher GRE quantitative scores had the same effect (1.3 times) in only sciences and mathematics, and higher GRE analytical scores proved to be a predictor (1.2 times) only in the social sciences.

Given the relative advantage of African Americans and Hispanics in receiving fellowship awards, it is somewhat surprising to see only limited disadvantage for these students in receipt of teaching assistantships. The African Americans in our sample were disadvantaged only in the field of engineering, and Hispanics, only in engineering and education. African Americans were nearly 4.0 times, Hispanics nearly 3.0 times, and Asian Americans nearly 2.0 times less likely than white students to be awarded teaching assistantships in engineering. In education, Hispanics were 1.7 times less likely than whites to receive TA positions. International students' chances of being teaching assistants compared with their white peers were either positive or negative depending on the field. International students were 1.7 times more likely than whites to attain a TA position in the social sciences but 2.2 times less likely in education, 2.0 times less likely in engineering, and 1.5 times less likely in sciences and mathematics.

Student age upon starting the doctoral program, sex, marital status, and household income all predicted being a teaching assistant.[5] In every field, younger students were more likely than older ones to receive teaching assistantships at some point during their doctoral studies. Only in the field of engineering did sex prove to be an important predictor, women being favored over men by a factor of 1.5. Married and partnered students in the field of education proved to have an advantage (1.7 times) in acquiring teaching assistantships.

In education, engineering, and the social sciences, students with lower household incomes were slightly more likely to be teaching assistants. A student in education or engineering with a household income of $20,000 was 1.2 times more likely to be a TA during her or his doctoral program than a student with a household income of $40,000. The odds of being a TA increased as the gap in household income widened: students with household incomes of $20,000 in education and engineering were 1.5 and 1.4 times more likely, respectively, to be TAs than students with household incomes of $60,000. The relationship between household income and the likelihood of being a TA in the social sciences was slightly weaker: the probability that students with household incomes of $20,000 were offered teaching assistantships was 13 percent higher than for students with

5. "Married" includes students living in domestic partnerships.

household incomes of $40,000 and 27 percent higher than for students with household incomes of $60,000.

Beyond GRE scores, race, and public versus private sector status of doctoral institution, a variety of other elements appear to have played a role in determining who received teaching assistantships over the course of doctoral programs in each field. In the social sciences, students who held master's degrees upon entering their doctoral programs were less likely than others to be teaching assistants. Continuously enrolled full-time students in education, humanities, and the social sciences had a greater likelihood of obtaining teaching assistantships—2.1 times more likely in education and humanities and 1.7 times more likely in the social sciences. Similarly, students in education, engineering, humanities, and the social sciences who had spent a longer time in their programs were more likely eventually to receive teaching assistantships.

In the field of education, students who received fellowships were 1.7 times more likely to also be awarded teaching assistantships. In sciences and mathematics, the effect was reversed, with fellowship recipients being slightly less likely to receive TA posts. With the exception of engineering, however, recipients of research assistantships were more likely to receive teaching assistantships over the course of their doctoral programs (nearly twice as likely in education and the social sciences). Since teaching assistantships provide opportunities for training in a critical element of faculty roles, it is not surprising that in education and the social sciences, students who expected their first job after receiving their doctorates to be either as faculty or postdoctoral research fellows were about twice as likely as others to receive teaching assistantships. In engineering, the effect was similar but weaker (1.4).

Research Assistantship over the Course of Doctoral Study

The award of research assistantships shows some similarities to awards of teaching assistantships (see table 11.6). Type of graduate school (public vs. private) played a role, as it did in receipt of teaching assistantships, but far less so. It appears that while teaching assistants are more important to public universities, research assistants are vital to both public and private doctoral programs. The one exception appears to be in the social sciences. As was also true of teaching assistantships, social sciences doctoral students attending public graduate schools were more likely to receive RA positions than their private university counterparts. Given that 64 percent of social sciences students were engaged as teaching assistants and 49 percent as research assistants over the course of their doctoral programs (as reported in chap. 7), the choice between public and private doctoral programs may be an important consideration for the type of training experience of social sciences doctoral students. In the field of education, attending a public university appears to enhance a student's chance of

Table 11.6
Predictors of Being a Research Assistant over the Course of Doctoral Study, by Field

Independent Variable[a]	Education	Engineering	Humanities	Sciences and Mathematics	Social Sciences
Male					−
African American[b]	−	−		−	
Hispanic	−				
Asian American					
International	−	−			−
Married or domestic partner		+			
Household income ($1,000s)		−		−	
Children under 18		−			
Age at start of doctoral program (1 yr.)	−	−		−	−
Always full-time doctoral student	+			+	
GRE quantitative (100s of points)					+
Master's upon entry		−			
Private graduate school	−				−
Ever received a fellowship	+	−	+	−	
Ever was a teaching assistant	+		+	+	+
Time in doctoral program (yrs.)	+	+		+	+
Expect first job to be faculty or postdoctoral position				−	+
n (unweighted)	1,509	783	1,121	1,640	2,148

Source: Survey of Doctoral Student Finances, Experiences, and Achievements.
[a]Parents' SES, GRE verbal, GRE analytical, and selective undergraduate institution were nonsignificant predictors in all fields and were dropped from the models.
[b]All racial groups and international students are compared with whites.

becoming a research assistant over the course of her or his doctoral program, whereas with respect to teaching assistantships, institution sector was inconsequential.

At the time of entering their doctoral programs, international students in education and the social sciences, African American and international students in engineering, and African Americans in sciences and mathematics were disadvantaged, compared with their white peers, in receipt of research assistantship offers. The African Americans' and international students' disadvantage was more severe after they had enrolled in their doctoral programs than when they were first admitted. African Americans were nearly 4.5 times less likely than whites to be RAs over the course of their doctoral programs in engineering, 3.4 times less likely in sciences and mathematics, and 2.2 times less likely in education. Similarly, international students in education and engineering were nearly 2.0 times less likely, and in the social sciences slightly less likely (1.4), than whites to receive this form of support over the course of their doctoral program. In addition, Hispanics, who did not appear to be at a disadvantage at the time of admission, appear to have been disadvantaged in the long term in the field of education.

In chapter 6 we questioned whether the higher rates at which African Americans and Hispanics received fellowships might have reduced their opportunities to compete for research assistantships. Our analyses show that receiving a fellowship reduced these students' prospects of becoming research assistants in engineering and sciences and mathematics but increased them in the fields of education and humanities. Therefore, the higher rates at which African Americans and Hispanics received fellowships might have placed them at a disadvantage with respect to research assistantships in engineering and sciences and mathematics but not in education and the humanities. African Americans' lower probability of having been RAs in engineering and in sciences and mathematics and the lower probability of both African Americans and Hispanics in the field of education seem to be have been a function of race. International students faced similar types of challenges in education, engineering, and the social sciences.

Students in all fields relied on multiple sources of funding throughout their doctoral programs, but less so, it appears, in engineering and in sciences and mathematics than in other fields. In education and humanities, students who received fellowships during their doctoral programs were twice as likely to also receive research assistantships as those who did not receive fellowships. In engineering and in sciences and mathematics, however, the effect was reversed: fellowship recipients were more than 2 times less likely to receive RA positions than those who did not receive fellowships. Teaching assistants were more likely to receive research assistantships in education, the social sciences, and the humanities, and sciences and mathematics. In engineering, however, being a TA conferred no apparent advantage in becoming an RA.

Other characteristics appear to determine who becomes a research assistant over the course of a doctoral program, but they are less pervasive than race-ethnicity, the public or private status of the graduate school, and type of funding. Men were moderately disadvantaged (1.3 times) in receiving RA positions in the social sciences. Younger students had an edge over older ones in all fields except the humanities. Married and partnered students in engineering were nearly twice as likely to receive research assistantships as unmarried students. Engineering students who did not have children under the age of eighteen appear to have been more likely to receive such support. Students with household incomes of $20,000 in engineering and in sciences and mathematics had a higher probability of being RAs than students with household incomes of $40,000 (30% higher in engineering and 20% higher in sciences and mathematics). Those probabilities grew with the gap in income: the probability of students with household incomes of $20,000 and $60,000 becoming RAs was 69 percent and 44 percent higher, respectively, than for students with household incomes of $60,000 in engineering and sciences and mathematics, respectively.

Continuing full-time student status proved to be a strong predictor of being an RA in education (2.6 times more likely) and sciences and mathematics (2.0 times more likely). Analogous to receiving an RA position at admissions, GRE quantitative scores had a weak association with a research assistantship award over the course of students' studies. In the social sciences, a 100-point increase in the GRE quantitative score was associated with higher chances of receiving an RA position at the time of enrollment (1.3) and over the course of doctoral studies (1.2). In engineering, students with master's degrees were 2.0 times less likely to receive research assistantships. In all but humanities, students who spent a longer time in their programs were slightly more likely to receive research assistantships. Students who aspired to become faculty or to pursue postdoctoral research after graduating were more likely to receive RA positions in the social sciences but less likely to do so in sciences and mathematics.

Education Debt Incurred during the Doctoral Program

We examined the educational debts accumulated by students at various stages of their educational process, including debt accumulated during undergraduate education, amount of debt owed at the start of doctoral programs, and amount of debt accumulated during the doctoral program. Given our focus on doctoral students' experiences, the most important of these is whether students took on debt during their doctoral programs. As reported in chapter 6, around 30 percent of students incurred debt during their doctoral programs. This is similar in size to the proportion of students who reported having debt at the start of their doctoral program. Our objective here is to isolate the characteristics and attributes that distinguish students who accumulated debt during doctoral programs from those who did not.

Across all programs, several predictors of incurring debt during a doctoral program can be highlighted (see table 11.7). Because of visa requirements, which generally require international students to demonstrate that they have funding sufficient to support them through their studies, it is not surprising that in all fields they were less likely than whites to accumulate educational debt during their doctoral studies. Among U.S. race-ethnicity groups, African American students in education were nearly twice as likely as white students to accumulate educational debt; conversely, Asian Americans in education were 1.8 times less likely than whites to be carrying debt. In sciences and mathematics, Asian Americans were nearly three times less likely than whites to be carrying educational debt.

Up to this point, we have seen limited influence of socioeconomic status on the type of financial assistance students received at the doctoral level. The only instance thus far has been the singular relationship of parental SES to the probability of sciences and mathematics doctoral students' receiving fellowships over the course of their programs. This simply suggests that, unlike undergraduate education, offers of student aid at the doctoral level are largely based on merit rather than need. Regarding debt acquisition during doctoral programs, however, parental SES is an im-

Table 11.7
Predictors of Incurring Education Debt over the Course of Doctoral Study, by Field

Independent Variable[a]	Education	Engineering	Humanities	Sciences and Mathematics	Social Sciences
Male					
African American[b]	+				
Hispanic					
Asian American	−				−
International	−	−	−	−	−
Parents' SES[c]		−	−	−	−
Household income ($1,000s)	−	−	−	−	−
Age at start of doctoral program (1 yr.)	−				
Married or domestic partner		+		+	
Children under 18		+			
GRE quantitative (100s of points)	−	−		−	−
GRE analytical (100s of points)		+		−	
Selective undergraduate institution				−	−
Private graduate school	+		−	−	+
Ever received a fellowship	+	−	−		
Ever was a research assistant		+			
Ever was a teaching assistant	+	+		+	
Time in doctoral program (yrs.)				+	+
n (unweighted)	1,213	673	979	1,450	1,875

Source: Survey of Doctoral Student Finances, Experiences, and Achievements.
[a]Master's upon entry, GRE verbal, and always being full-time were nonsignificant predictors in all fields and were dropped from the models.
[b]All racial groups and international students are compared with whites.
[c]Parents' SES is a composite of educational attainment and occupational prestige.

portant factor in every field except education. In the other fields, students from lower-SES backgrounds were more likely to incur debt. In addition, in all fields students with lower household incomes during their doctoral program were more likely to acquire debt. Even though doctoral programs reputedly do not award financial assistance on the basis of need, clearly 30 percent of doctoral students exhibited a financial need for aid. Their source of aid appears to be loans.

The good news is that awards of fellowships and both types of assistantships appear not to discriminate against low SES students. On the other hand, low SES students accumulated debt burdens that their high SES counterparts did not. That education students appeared to be immune to the parental SES relationship to debt is understandable, given that they were, on average, nearly twelve years older upon entering their doctoral programs than students in the other fields and therefore much further removed from the influence of their parents' SES. The decision by education doctoral students to accumulate debt appears to be influenced only by their own household incomes, and, as is true for students in other fields, the higher the household income, the less likely is their dependence on debt.

An assortment of other student demographics was also found to relate to educational debt and in various directions. Older students in education were slightly less likely to be carrying educational debt. Married and partnered students in engineering were nearly three times as likely to have debt as their unmarried and unpartnered peers, and married and partnered students in sciences and mathematics nearly twice as likely to report debt. Engineering students who were parenting children under the age of eighteen also were more than twice as likely to report education debt.

There are also relationships between GRE scores and education debt in all fields except the humanities. Higher GRE quantitative scores were associated with a slightly lower likelihood of incurring debt in education (1.3), engineering (2.1), sciences and mathematics (1.3), and the social sciences (1.4). For engineering students, the odds of having debt were positively associated with a 100-point increase in GRE analytical scores. Students in education attending private graduate schools were twice as likely to have education debt, and students in the social sciences who attended private graduate schools were 1.3 times as likely. In contrast, in sciences and mathematics and in humanities, studying at a private graduate school was associated with being less likely to take on debt (1.8 times and 1.5 times, respectively).

In education, students who received fellowships during their programs were 1.4 times more likely to have educational debt, but in engineering and humanities, fellowship recipients were nearly 2.0 times less likely to have debt. In engineering, students who were research assistants were 4.4 times more likely to be carrying debt. In engineering and in sciences and mathematics, students who worked as teaching assistants were more than twice as likely to have educational debt, and TAs in education were 1.4 times more likely. Students who spent more time in their programs in humanities, sciences and mathematics, and the social sciences were all more likely to report having educational debt.

Socialization

Every day, doctoral students interact with many people from different parts of their universities who perform various roles. These people include fellow doctoral students, the faculty in their departments, support staff in their departments, academic administrators, and service people at their institutions. We chose to focus on student experiences with the two groups that are reputed by scholars to have the most influence on student experiences: peers and faculty. We found that different student characteristics and experiences predicted peer interactions and faculty interactions and, therefore, concluded that peer interaction and student-faculty social interaction do indeed represent different dimensions of doctoral student socialization, so we examine them here separately.

Peer Interaction

Peer interaction refers to students' informal involvement with peers. In humanities, sciences and mathematics, and the social sciences, women reported greater social interactions with their peers than men (see table 11.8). Men's scores were .09 of a standard deviation (SD) lower than

Table 11.8
Predictors of Having Peer Interaction, by Field

Independent Variable[a]	Education	Engineering	Humanities	Sciences and Mathematics	Social Sciences
Male	+		−	−	−
African American[b]					
Hispanic			+		
Asian American					
International		−		−	
Parents' SES[c]		+			
Household income ($1,000s)				−	
Married or domestic partner					−
Age at start of doctoral program (1 yr.)		−		−	−
Children under 18	−				
GRE verbal (100s of points)					+
GRE quantitative (100s of points)	−			−	−
GRE analytical (100s of points)					+
Master's upon entry	−				
Private graduate school	+			+	+
Always full-time doctoral student	+				+
Expect first job to be faculty or postdoctoral position	−		+		
Ever received a fellowship	+	+		+	+
Ever was a research assistant		+		+	
Ever was a teaching assistant	+		+	+	+
Time in doctoral program (yrs.)					−
n (unweighted)	2,504	883	1,323	1,850	2,461

Source: Survey of Doctoral Student Finances, Experiences, and Achievements.
[a]Selective undergraduate institution was not a significant predictor in any field and was dropped from the models.
[b]All racial groups and international students are compared with whites.
[c]Parents' SES is a composite of educational attainment and occupational prestige.

women's in engineering, .24 SD lower in humanities, .13 SD lower in sciences and mathematics, and .13 SD lower in the social sciences.[6] Conversely, in education, men had more positive social interactions with peers (.12 SD). In engineering, there was no difference. In humanities, being Hispanic was associated with positive social interactions with peers, while being an international student both in engineering and in sciences and mathematics was negatively associated with peer interactions, relative to being white.

It should not be surprising that funding over the course of one's doctoral experience may contribute to peer interaction. In all fields except engineering, being a teaching assistant contributed favorably to students' social participation. Similarly, in engineering and in sciences and mathematics, being a research assistant contributed favorably to students' social participation. A common belief is that a by-product of student participation as teaching or research assistants is a greater connection to their departments because students are likely to have office space and be required to conduct their assistantship assignments in their department offices. By contrast, fellowships have typically been viewed as funding vehicles that may require limited social engagement of students with their departments, since students may not receive office space or be required to spend

6. See appendix D for a discussion of z-scores.

time in department offices. Hence we were surprised to see that in all fields except humanities, having a fellowship contributed favorably to development of students' social interactions with peers. It could be that the reduced workload of fellowship recipients relative to research and teaching assistants offers students more flexible schedules, allowing them to establish peer connections, and perhaps even a greater sense of belonging in their academic programs.

There is no consistent pattern of the influence of student background characteristics upon developing relations with peers. Engineering students with higher parental SES showed stronger peer interactions. In sciences and mathematics, students with lower household incomes reported weaker social relationships with peers. Married and partnered students in the social sciences and education students with children under the age of eighteen reported weaker social relations with peers. In engineering, sciences and mathematics, and the social sciences, older students were less positive than younger ones about social relationships with their fellow students.

A similar sporadic pattern of influence is seen for admissions characteristics. In the social sciences, higher GRE verbal and analytical scores were weakly associated with positive peer interactions, whereas higher GRE quantitative scores appear to be associated with weak social interactions with peers for students in education, sciences and mathematics, and the social sciences. In engineering, possession of a previous master's degree made positive social interactions with peers less likely. Attendance at a private university for graduate school in education, sciences and mathematics, and the social sciences was positively related to good social relationships with peers. In both education and the social sciences, continuing enrollment as a full-time student was a predictor of strong peer relationships.

Expecting to have a career as a college or university professor or in a postdoctoral position had a positive effect on social participation in the humanities but a negative effect in education. Social science students who had spent a longer time in their programs perceived their social relations with peers to be less positive.

Having a Mentor

Most students in each field had mentors—proof, perhaps, of the importance to doctoral students of securing someone to guide them through their apprenticeship and usher them into their chosen profession. Seventy percent of students who had mentors identified their mentors during their first year of doctoral study, and 50 percent found their mentors within a few months of entering their doctoral programs (as reported in chap. 7). Owing to the relative speed with which students identified their mentors, we focused on student demographic characteristics and their admissions attributes. The following analyses examine the attributes that help to predict whether a student will be successful in acquiring a mentor.

There were no standout predictors across all fields that distinguished students who found mentors from those who did not (see table 11.9). Taken together with findings from our earlier analyses on finances and socialization and analyses later in this chapter, the relationships we observed for mentoring are likely to provide insights into the doctoral student experience. For example, engineering, sciences and mathematics, and social sciences students with higher parental SES appear to have had a significantly greater likelihood of having a mentor. Given the importance of having a mentor, the social-class barriers that emerge in these three fields could be an important matter.

Up to this point, Asian Americans have been rarely mentioned in our discussion of the doctoral student experiences. Anecdotal evidence suggests that Asians tend to blend in with whites and exhibit few outstanding differences. Mentoring is one area in which Asian Americans appear to be noticeably different from whites. The Asian American engineering students in our sample were 2.0 times less likely than whites to have mentors. In a similar vein, international students in engineering were 1.6 times less likely, and international students in education 1.5 times less likely, to have mentors. African Americans in sciences and mathematics were 2.6 times less likely than whites to find mentors, another layer of mounting evidence that the doctoral experience is particularly challenging for this group.

There were no sex differences across the fields for mentoring. Another illustration of the limited influence of GRE scores in predicting doctoral student experiences once students matriculate is mentoring. None of the three sections of the test had a strong relationship on mentoring, and when a relationship existed, it was the opposite of what might be ex-

Table 11.9
Predictors of Having a Mentor, by Field

Independent Variable[a]	Education	Engineering	Humanities[b]	Sciences and Mathematics	Social Sciences
Male					
African American[c]				−	
Hispanic					
Asian American		−			
International	−	−			
Parents' SES[d]		+		+	+
GRE verbal (100s of points)		−			
GRE quantitative (100s of points)				−	
Private graduate school	−			−	
n (unweighted)	1,617	815	1,190	1,676	2,204

Source: Survey of Doctoral Student Finances, Experiences, and Achievements.
[a]Age at start of doctoral program, selective undergraduate institution, GRE analytical, master's upon entry, and first or only choice of doctoral program were nonsignificant predictors in all fields and were dropped from the models.
[b]The model is not statistically significantly different from the null model. This suggests that there is no relationship between the predictors and having a faculty mentor.
[c]All racial groups and international students are compared with whites.
[d]Parents' SES is a composite of educational attainment and occupational prestige.

pected. Lower GRE verbal scores in engineering and lower GRE quantitative scores in sciences and mathematics were associated with increased odds of having a mentor. This is yet another sign that while students with lower GRE scores appear to be at a disadvantage regarding the types of financial awards they receive, they do not appear to be disadvantaged in the doctoral education socialization process. Finally, the likelihood of finding a mentor was 1.2 times less for students attending private graduate schools in education and in sciences and mathematics.

Student-Faculty Social Interactions

Student-faculty social interaction is a measure of the relationships that develop between students and faculty outside of classrooms. The four items that constitute the measure reflect student perceptions about the quality and ease of their social relationships with faculty. A variety of characteristics and experiences are related to positive student-faculty social interactions, the most prominent being students having mentors, being enrolled at their first or only choice of doctoral program, and spending relatively little time pursuing their doctoral degrees (see table 11.10).

In all fields, students with mentors reported strong student-faculty social interactions. In fact, having a mentor may be the key to positive student-faculty social interactions. The size of the increases in student-faculty interactions by virtue of having a mentor were larger than increases based on any other attribute we studied. Students with faculty mentors, relative

Table 11.10
Predictors of Student-Faculty Social Interactions, by Field

Independent Variable[a]	Education	Engineering	Humanities	Sciences and Mathematics	Social Sciences
Male	+	+			+
African American[b]				−	
Hispanic					
Asian American					
International		+			
Married or domestic partner					−
Age at start of doctoral program (1 yr.)				+	
Household income ($1,000s)	+		+		
GRE verbal (100s of points)	−	−		−	
GRE quantitative (100s of points)		+			
GRE analytical (100s of points)				+	
Private graduate school			−	−	−
Always full-time doctoral student	−	+			
Time in doctoral program (yrs.)		−	−	−	−
First or only choice of doctoral program	+	+	+		+
Ever received a fellowship				+	
Ever was a teaching assistant			−	−	
Has a mentor	+	+	+	+	+
Expect first job to be faculty or postdoctoral position	+		+	+	
n (unweighted)	2,469	884	1,317	1,834	2,444

Source: Survey of Doctoral Student Finances, Experiences, and Achievements.
[a]Parents' SES, children under eighteen, selective undergraduate institution, master's upon entry, and ever was a research assistant were nonsignificant predictors in all fields and were dropped from the models.
[b]All racial groups and international students are compared with whites.

to those without mentors, reported an increase in student-faculty social interactions ranging from a .44 SD increase in sciences and mathematics to as high as .63 SD increase in education.

In all fields except sciences and mathematics, attending one's first or only choice of doctoral program contributed favorably to social interactions with faculty, .30 SD in education, .20 SD in engineering, .16 SD in humanities, and .31 SD in the social sciences. Students who expected to be college or university faculty or postdoctoral researchers also had more favorable views of student-faculty social interactions in education, the humanities, and sciences and mathematics compared with students with alternative career plans.

With the exception of the field of education, students experienced increasingly negative perceptions of student-faculty social interaction with each passing year of enrollment. For every year longer that students remained in their doctoral programs, their student-faculty social interaction score declined, from .04 SD (in engineering and humanities) to .06 SD (in sciences and mathematics and the social sciences). Perhaps education doctoral students have acquired a level of maturity that is not captured by their age or length of time in program. Education doctoral students, in contrast to their counterparts in other fields, appear to have had a higher tolerance for social interactions with their professors, even after being enrolled for a lengthy period of time.

It is a common belief that having a teaching or research assistantship gives students an opportunity to develop relationships with faculty. Surprisingly, fellowships and teaching assistantships were of little consequence to doctoral student interactions with faculty. Having a fellowship in the humanities had a positive effect on student-faculty social interactions, whereas being a teaching assistant in humanities and in sciences and mathematics had a small negative effect. Research assistantships had no predictive value for students' ratings of their relationships with faculty.

We find a negative relationship between GRE verbal scores and student-faculty social interactions. One might expect relatively high GRE verbal scores to be associated with high student-faculty social interactions, but among our sample, this was not the case. Students with relatively high GRE verbal scores actually experienced *lower* social interactions with faculty than their counterparts with lower GRE verbal scores. For every 100-point increase in GRE verbal scores, we observed a decline in the student-faculty social interaction score in education, engineering, and sciences and mathematics. The relationship was strongest in education, where a 100-point increase in GRE verbal was associated with a decline of .11 SD in student-faculty social interactions. Conversely, GRE quantitative scores had a positive relationship with student-faculty social interactions in engineering, and GRE analytical scores had a positive relationship in sciences and mathematics.

The demographic characteristics of doctoral students appear to have a limited affect on the quality of doctoral students' social interactions with faculty. African Americans rated student-faculty interactions lower than whites in sciences and mathematics, whereas international students in engineering rated them higher. This is yet another indication of the extraordinary challenge that African American doctoral students are facing in sciences and mathematics and the positive experience that international students seem to be having in engineering. The lower student-faculty social interactions among African Americans in sciences and mathematics is likely to be related to factors that are not examined in this research. Unlike engineering, it seems not to be related to their lower GRE scores, having a mentor, or attending a first-choice doctoral program. Because the regressions include many tangible variables that are plausible predictors of student interactions with faculty, it is possible that racial prejudice or bias against African Americans is more pervasive in sciences and mathematics than in other fields.

Men reported higher ratings of student-faculty social interactions than women in education, engineering, and the social sciences. As with African Americans in sciences and mathematics, bias against women in education and engineering seems also plausible. The sex composition of doctoral students in the two fields, however, is opposite. Women make up the majority (69%) of our education student sample and the minority (15%) of our engineering student sample.

Sciences and mathematics students who were relatively older when they were admitted into their doctoral programs had a significantly more positive view of student-faculty social interactions than their younger counterparts. Students in education and humanities who had higher household incomes showed slightly stronger social interactions with faculty, whereas married students in the social sciences had less favorable social interactions with faculty.

In the field of education, being a full-time student resulted in reduced social interactions with faculty, while in engineering, it had the opposite effect. In humanities, sciences and mathematics, and the social sciences, doctoral students attending public graduate schools had more positive views of their interaction with faculty than their private university counterparts.

Student-Faculty Academic Interactions

The two previous measures focus on social relationships of doctoral students. Our first measure of academic relationships, faculty academic interactions, measures students' opinions about the overall quality and performance of their faculty in teaching, research, and advising and how accessible faculty are to students. Although this measure relates to students' academic relations with faculty, the most important correlates appear to be the same as the ones identified in connection with their social interaction with faculty. As with the social interaction with faculty, having positive faculty academic interactions was associated with having a mentor, attending one's first or only choice of doctoral program, expecting to achieve a faculty or postdoctoral research position upon completing a degree, and spending less time progressing through the degree program (see table 11.11). The similarity between the correlates of faculty social interaction and academic interaction leads us to reason that student-faculty interactions have a halo effect. No matter how much we work to establish unique measures of student relationships with faculty, we have not succeeded in isolating clear and distinctive relationships. Perhaps they do not exist and, consequently, student social relations with faculty carry over to their academic relations, and vice versa.

Having a mentor seems to be the key predictor of students' feelings about their academic interactions with faculty. In all five fields, having a faculty mentor resulted in increases of .45 to .73 SD in the academic interaction with faculty index. Similarly, in all fields, students attending their first-choice doctoral program gave higher ratings to their academic interactions with faculty (an increase of roughly .2 SD). In all fields, aspiring to careers as college or university faculty or in postdoctoral positions was also positively related to student ratings of their academic interactions with faculty. In contrast to the positive predictors of students'

Table 11.11
Predictors of Student-Faculty Academic Interactions, by Field

Independent Variable[a]	Education	Engineering	Humanities	Sciences and Mathematics	Social Sciences
Male	+	+			
African American[b]					
Hispanic					
Asian American	−	+			
International				+	
Parents' SES[c]		+			
Household income ($1,000s)	+		+		
Married or domestic partner		+			−
GRE verbal (100s of points)	−	−		−	
GRE quantitative (100s of points)		+			
GRE analytical (100s of points)				+	
Selective undergraduate institution	−	−			
Private graduate school		+			−
Always full-time doctoral student		+			
First or only choice of doctoral program	+	+	+	+	+
Has a mentor	+	+	+	+	+
Ever was a research assistant					+
Ever received a fellowship		+		+	
Ever was a teaching assistant	−				
Time in doctoral program (yrs.)	−	−	−	−	−
Expect first job to be faculty or postdoctoral position	+	+	+	+	+
n (unweighted)	2,415	875	1,296	1,814	2,393

Source: Survey of Doctoral Student Finances, Experiences, and Achievements.
[a]Children under eighteen and age at start of doctoral program were nonsignificant predictors in all fields and were dropped from the models.
[b]All racial groups and international students are compared with whites.
[c]Parents' SES is a composite of educational attainment and occupational prestige.

ratings of their academic interaction with faculty, in all fields except education, being enrolled in the doctoral program for a longer period of time was negatively related to student ratings of faculty academic interactions.

Also like student-faculty social interactions, higher GRE verbal scores were related to *lower* student ratings of their academic interaction with faculty in education, engineering, and sciences and mathematics. Higher GRE quantitative scores were associated with higher student ratings of academic interactions with faculty only in the field of engineering. This seems reasonable, given that engineering can be a highly quantitative field. High GRE analytical scores were associated with higher student ratings of faculty academic interactions in sciences and mathematics.

As mentioned earlier, the common wisdom is that research and teaching assistantships connect doctoral students with graduate faculty, giving them greater appreciation of their social interactions. Our data provide no support for such an assertion. Research and teaching assistants did not, in general, have a more favorable view of their academic interactions with faculty. Only in the social sciences did serving as a research assistant seem to enhance a student's view of faculty academic interactions. Engineering students who were teaching assistants held negative views of faculty academic interactions, whereas those with fellowships were relatively happy with their faculty academic interactions. Sciences and mathematics fellowship recipients were positive about faculty academic interactions.

Illustrative of the relative challenge for women in engineering and education, men gave faculty academic interactions higher ratings than did women. Asian American students had negative academic interactions with faculty in education but positive experiences in engineering. International students in sciences and mathematics had positive ratings of their academic interactions with faculty.

Interactions with Faculty Advisers

Interactions with faculty advisers measure students' perceptions about the accessibility, care, and interest that faculty display about their advisees' welfare, progress, and careers. With the exception of education, students who have the same person serving as both adviser and mentor were happier with their doctoral experience (see table 11.12). In the other four fields, students scored from .65 SD to .90 SD higher on our faculty adviser interaction index. Similarly, students in all five fields who aspired to either faculty or postdoctoral researcher positions on graduation generally rated their interactions with their faculty advisers positively.

With the exception of engineering and humanities, students' funding experiences contributed to their positive perceptions of their interactions with their faculty advisers. Research assistants in the social sciences had more positive perceptions of their faculty adviser interactions than their peers who were not RAs. In education and in sciences and mathematics,

Table 11.12
Predictors of Student Interactions with Faculty Adviser, by Field

Independent Variable[a]	Education	Engineering	Humanities	Sciences and Mathematics	Social Sciences
Male					
African American[b]					
Hispanic					
Asian American					
International					
Parents' SES[c]		+		+	
Household income ($1,000s)		+			
GRE verbal (100s of points)	−		−	−	
Private graduate school	−				
First or only choice of doctoral program	+				+
Time in doctoral program (yrs.)				−	−
Always full-time doctoral student			+		
Ever received a fellowship	+			+	
Ever was a research assistant					+
Expect first job to be faculty or postdoctoral position	+	+	+	+	+
Adviser as mentor		+	+	+	+
n (unweighted)	2,370	844	1,136	1,645	2,168

Source: Survey of Doctoral Student Finances, Experiences, and Achievements.
[a]Married or domestic partner, children under eighteen, age at start of doctoral program, GRE quantitative, GRE analytical, selective undergraduate institution, and ever was a teaching assistant were nonsignificant predictors in all fields and were dropped from the models.
[b]All racial groups and international students are compared with whites.
[c]Parents' SES is a composite of educational attainment and occupational prestige.

fellowship recipients also had higher ratings of their faculty academic interactions.

The good news is that sex, race-ethnicity, and citizenship were not predictors of students' interactions with their advisers. Moreover, parental SES in engineering and sciences and mathematics and student household income in engineering had a limited effect on student interactions with their faculty advisers.

Students attending their first-choice graduate schools had higher ratings of faculty academic interactions in education and the social sciences. Two patterns that we saw in student-faculty interactions and academic interactions with faculty continue. First, students who were enrolled in their programs longer were less positive in sciences and mathematics and the social sciences, and students with higher GRE verbal scores reported lower ratings of their academic interactions with faculty in education, humanities, and sciences and mathematics.

RESEARCH PRODUCTIVITY

Given the restriction in the range of doctoral students' grades and the lack of prescribed length of curriculum, perhaps the best indicator of doctoral student performance is research productivity. Few people matriculating in doctoral programs are ever awarded grades other than As or Bs, and most are hard pressed to estimate how long it will take them to complete their degrees. Regardless of field, student scholarship and research are valuable achievements in doctoral programs. Because half of the doctoral students in our sample achieved some research productivity (as reported in chap. 8), research productivity seems to be one of the most discriminating aspects of the doctoral student performance and experience.

Included among our survey's twenty-two measures of research productivity were presentations of research papers at national conferences, publication of research articles in refereed journals, and publication of book chapters or entire books. Because so few students published either a chapter or a book, our analyses here consider the predictors for only three areas: whether a student had overall productivity (a variable that represents a composite of the aforementioned forms of productivity), whether a student published an article, and whether a student presented a paper at a national conference.

Three elements of doctoral programs are prevalent in relation to overall student research productivity. Students who achieve productivity were more likely to be enrolled in their programs for a longer time; they were more likely to have mentors; and they were more likely to have assistantships. With the exception of humanities, where teaching assistantships were favored, research assistantships were preferable (see table 11.13).

Given the expectation that research skills will be learned during the doctoral curriculum, it is not surprising to find that in all fields the longer students were enrolled in their doctoral programs, the more likely they were to produce all forms of research productivity. Because the initial focus of any doctoral program curriculum is course work, and the expectation of independent scholarship and the like is preserved for the latter stages of the curriculum, it is reasonable to expect research productivity to

Table 11.13
Predictors of Overall Student Research Productivity, by Field

Independent Variable[a]	Education	Engineering	Humanities	Sciences and Mathematics	Social Sciences
Male		+		+	
African American[b]				−	−
Hispanic					
Asian American					
International					
Children under 18	−				
Master's upon entry			+		
GRE quantitative (100s of points)					−
Selective undergraduate institution	−				
Private graduate school		+			
Ever received a fellowship	+			+	+
Ever was a research assistant	+	+		+	+
Ever was a teaching assistant			+	−	
Has a mentor	+	+	+	+	+
Time in doctoral program (yrs.)	+	+	+	+	+
Expect first job to be faculty or postdoctoral position	+				+
n (unweighted)	1,502	774	1,118	1,591	2,131

Source: Survey of Doctoral Student Finances, Experiences, and Achievements.
[a]Parents' SES, married or domestic status, age at start of doctoral program, household income, GRE verbal, and GRE analytical were nonsignificant predictors in all fields and were dropped from the models.
[b]All racial groups and international students are compared with whites.

be a function of longevity as much as it is the acquisition of skills. Thus our measures of research productivity represent a tacit benchmark of student achievement and perhaps a common goal of every doctoral program, just as important as grades and degree completion.

To the extent that research productivity is important in doctoral programs, the 30 percent in our sample who were without mentors may have been at a disadvantage. Mentoring made a clear positive contribution to research productivity across all five fields, increasing the likelihood of productivity 1.4 times in sciences and mathematics and in education, 1.7 times in engineering, 2.1 times in humanities, and 2.2 times in the social sciences.

Type of funding also had consequences for research productivity. Research assistantships in all fields except humanities, and teaching assistantships in the humanities, contributed favorably to overall research productivity. Research assistantships made at least as big a contribution as mentoring to overall research productivity, making education students twice as likely, engineering students 1.8 times as likely, sciences and mathematics students 2.7 times as likely, and social sciences students 1.8 times as likely to demonstrate research productivity. Teaching assistants in the humanities were twice as likely to show productivity as non-TAs, but in sciences and mathematics, they were 1.5 times less likely. Fellowships contributed to research productivity in education, sciences and mathematics, and the social sciences. Fellowship recipients were about 1.5 times more likely than other students to display some form of productivity.

Although student personal background characteristics played only a spotty role in overall research productivity, it showed up in important places. Men in engineering were 2.3 times as likely as women, and men in sciences and mathematics 1.3 times as likely, to show some research productivity. African Americans were nearly 2.5 times less likely than whites to exhibit research productivity in sciences and mathematics and 1.7 times less likely in the social sciences. There were no other general effects among the race-ethnicity groups.

Perhaps it is encouraging that any perceived deficiencies that students exhibited upon entering doctoral programs, such as relatively low GRE scores and type of undergraduate institution, were overcome by perseverance, mentoring, and assistantships. Although higher GRE quantitative scores had a negative effect on productivity for social sciences students, performance on the GRE, in general, was not significant as long as these other attributes of student experience were in place.

The attributes of individuals at the time of admissions played a sporadic role in predicting which students would produce research. Only in engineering were students attending selective undergraduate institutions less likely to show research productivity. Humanities students who had already achieved master's degrees upon entry to their doctoral programs were 1.6 times more likely to produce research. Career expectations had a modest role in determining student research productivity. Education and social sciences students who expected to have faculty jobs or postdoctoral research posts after degree completion were 1.6 times and 1.9 times, respectively, more likely to exhibit research productivity.

Type of university played a minor role in distinguishing the likely producers of research from the nonproducers. This is a testament to the universality of research in doctoral education. Attending a private graduate school was positively associated with research productivity for students in engineering.

Recognizing that the composite measure captures overall productivity, can we gain a better sense of the development of research productivity in each field by looking at each of the parts? Peter Syverson, the vice president for research at the Council of Graduate Schools, reacted to our composite measure of research productivity by asking how one gets started. Although we do not present the details of each of these measures here, tables 11.14 and 11.15 illustrate predictors of presenting papers (sole or joint authorship) and publishing research articles (sole or joint authorship), two of the components of our composite measure. The story of overall research productivity prevails on the component measures: in our sample, mentoring, time to degree, and assistantships were the keys to relatively high productivity. Gender and race were also associated with research productivity in its component parts. Men in engineering and in sciences and mathematics were at an advantage in both presenting a paper at a national

Table 11.14
Predictors of Presenting a Paper at a National Conference (Sole or Joint Authorship), by Field

Independent Variable[a]	Education	Engineering	Humanities	Sciences and Mathematics	Social Sciences
Male			+	+	
African American[b]					
Hispanic			−		
Asian American					
International			−		
Married or domestic partner				+	
Children under 18		−			
GRE verbal (100s of points)	+				−
GRE quantitative (100s of points)					−
GRE analytical (100s of points)		+			
Selective undergraduate institution		−			
Private graduate school	−	+		−	−
Ever received a fellowship	+			+	
Ever was a research assistant	+	+		+	+
Ever was a teaching assistant				+	−
Has a mentor	+	+	+		+
Always full-time doctoral student	−				
Time in doctoral program (yrs.)	+	+	+	+	+
Expect first job to be faculty or postdoctoral position	+	+			+
n (unweighted)	1,451	769	1,110	1,585	2,119

Source: Survey of Doctoral Student Finances, Experiences, and Achievements.
[a]Parents' SES, household income, age at start of doctoral program, and master's upon entry were nonsignificant predictors in all fields and were dropped from the models.
[b]All racial groups and international students are compared with whites.

Table 11.15
Predictors of Publishing a Research Article (Sole or Joint Authorship), by Field

Independent Variable[a]	Education	Engineering	Humanities	Sciences and Mathematics	Social Sciences
Male		+		+	
African American[b]	−			−	−
Hispanic					−
Asian American					
International					
Age at start of doctoral program (1 yr.)			−		
Selective undergraduate institution	−				
Private graduate school	−			+	
Ever received a fellowship				+	
Ever was a research assistant	+	+		+	+
Ever was a teaching assistant	+		+	−	
Has a mentor	+	+		+	+
Time in doctoral program (yrs.)	+	+	+	+	+
Expect first job to be faculty or postdoctoral position	+				+
n (unweighted)	2,303	844	1,260	1,733	2,330

Source: Survey of Doctoral Student Finances, Experiences, and Achievements.
[a]Parents' SES, married or domestic partner, children under eighteen, household income, GRE verbal, GRE analytical, GRE quantitative, master's upon entry, and always being full-time were nonsignificant predictors in all fields and were dropped from the models.
[b]All racial groups and international students are compared with whites.

conference and publishing a research article. The experience of African Americans in presenting papers at national conferences was comparable to that of their white peers, though they had different opportunities to publish research articles from those of their white peers in education, sciences and mathematics, and the social sciences. Hispanic doctoral students were 2.9 times less likely than white students to present at national conferences in sciences and mathematics and 2.1 times less likely to publish articles in the social sciences. In the humanities, international students were 2.5 times less likely to present papers than white students.

SATISFACTION WITH DOCTORAL PROGRAM

Now that we have a better understanding of student finances, socialization, and productivity, our next interest is students' satisfaction with their doctoral programs. Interactions with people have the greatest effect on student satisfaction. Consistently, across all five fields of study, students with relatively high perceived academic interactions with faculty were more satisfied with their doctoral programs. Another important predictor of overall satisfaction was student-faculty social interactions. An increase in student perceptions of student-faculty social interactions was associated with higher overall satisfaction in every field. Adviser interactions were important for students in sciences and mathematics, engineering, and the social sciences. An increase in perceptions of peer interactions was also positively associated with students' satisfaction with their doctoral programs in all five fields.

Keeping in mind that, as reported in chapter 9, doctoral students, overall and across demographic groups, appeared to be satisfied with their doc-

Table 11.16
Predictors of Overall Satisfaction with Doctoral Program, by Field

Independent Variable[a]	Education	Engineering	Humanities	Sciences and Mathematics	Social Sciences
Male			+		
African American[b]					
Hispanic					
Asian American				−	
International				−	
Married or domestic partner		+		+	
GRE verbal (100s of points)				−	
Private graduate school	−				
Always full-time doctoral student				+	
Time in doctoral program (yrs.)	−	−			−
First or only choice of doctoral program	+			+	+
Expect first job to be faculty or postdoctoral position		+	+	+	+
Ever was a teaching assistant					−
Incurred education debt as doctoral student				−	
Peer interaction	+	+	+	+	+
Student-faculty social interactions	+	+	+	+	+
Interactions with faculty adviser		+	+	+	+
Academic interactions with faculty	+	+	+	+	+
n (unweighted)	2,501	886	1,323	1,850	2,161

Source: Survey of Doctoral Student Finances, Experiences, and Achievements.
[a]Parents' SES, age at start of doctoral program, children under eighteen, household income, selective undergraduate institution, GRE quantitative, GRE analytical, master's upon entry, ever received a fellowship, ever was a research assistant, and has a mentor were nonsignificant predictors in all fields and were dropped from the models.
[b]All racial groups and international students are compared with whites.

toral programs, we still observed some sex and race-ethnicity differences. Our relational analyses suggest that in all but two fields, demographic characteristics played an unimportant role in determining doctoral student satisfaction (see table 11.16). The lower satisfaction of women in engineering (observed in chap. 9) persisted, even after controlling for the quality of experiences in their interactions with faculty. On the other hand, the lower satisfaction observed for women in education and for African Americans in engineering and in sciences and mathematics disappeared once we adjusted for the quality of their program experiences and other background characteristics. The only other demographic effects observed were in sciences and mathematics, where Asian Americans and international students were less satisfied than whites.

With the exception of the social sciences, it appears that finances, in the form of either debt incurred during the doctoral program or award of teaching assistantships, exerted a minor but significant influence on student satisfaction. Teaching assistants in the social sciences were less positive about their program experiences, as were students in sciences and mathematics who had incurred debt, while students who anticipated a faculty or postdoctoral research position as their first job expressed greater satisfaction with their programs in engineering, humanities, sciences and mathematics, and the social sciences.

Admission to one's first-choice doctoral program made for a higher level of satisfaction in education, sciences and mathematics, and the social sciences, but being enrolled for a longer time had a negative effect on student satisfaction in education, engineering, and the social sciences. Continuous enrollment as a full-time student was a plus for program satisfaction in sciences and mathematics. In engineering only, enrollment in a private graduate school predicted lower satisfaction with the doctoral program, and in sciences and mathematics, higher GRE verbal scores were associated with lower satisfaction.

STOPPING OUT OF A DOCTORAL PROGRAM

Occasionally, for various reasons, students temporarily stop working on their doctorates. These stop-outs do not include students who were working on preliminary examinations or dissertations or attending part-time. In our study, about 12 percent of the respondents stopped out; the range was from 20 percent in education to 5 percent in sciences and mathematics. Owing to the small numbers of students who stopped out of their doctoral programs in general and by field, we did not conduct separate analyses by field of study. Rather, we ran a single regression and included field as a predictor of stopping out (see table 11.17). Field of study played a role in determining which students stopped out of their doctoral programs. Compared with education students, students in sciences and mathematics were 2.6 times less likely, social science students 1.4 times less likely, and engineering students 2.1 times less likely, to have stopped out.

Household income was a contributor to students' stopping out. A higher household income was associated with stopping out. It is likely that the higher incomes are the result, rather than the cause, of stopping out. Students from families with higher parental SES were less likely to stop out of their doctoral program.

Table 11.17
Predictors of Stopping Out of a Doctoral Program

Independent Variable[a]	Fields Combined
Sciences and mathematics[b]	−
Social sciences	−
Humanities	
Engineering	−
Parents' SES[c]	−
Household income ($1,000s)	+
Married or domestic partner	−
Children under 18	+
First or only choice of doctoral program	+
Ever was a research assistant	−
Peer interaction	−
Overall satisfaction with doctoral program	−
n (unweighted)	8,235

Source: Survey of Doctoral Student Finances, Experiences, and Achievements.
[a]Sex, race-ethnicity, age at start of doctoral program, masters' upon entry, GRE quantitative, GRE verbal, GRE analytical, selective undergraduate institution, private graduate school, ever was a teaching assistant, ever received a fellowship, student-faculty social interaction, student-faculty academic interaction, interaction with faculty adviser, has a mentor, incurred education debt as a doctoral student, and expect first job to be faculty or postdoctoral position were nonsignificant predictors in all fields and were dropped from the models.
[b]All fields are compared with education.
[c]Parents' SES is a composite of educational attainment and occupational prestige.

Among the demographic characteristics, sex, race-ethnicity, and age at the start of doctoral program did not predict who would stop out of their doctoral programs. Marital status (including domestic partnership) and having children under the age of eighteen were associated with stopping out but in opposite directions. Being married was associated with persistence, while having children was associated with stopping out. Single students were 1.5 times less likely to stop out than their married or partnered peers. Students with children were 1.6 times more likely to stop out.

Socialization also appears to influence stopping-out behavior. Students who gave higher ratings to peer interactions were more likely to persist, as were students with higher levels of satisfaction with their doctoral programs. Being at one's first or only choice of doctoral program appears to contribute to persistence. Students who were research assistants had a higher probability of persisting.

Other measures that were not predictors of stopping out of a doctoral program are worthy of note. Our analyses did not find stopping out to be significant in relation to either GRE test scores (on any of the three parts) or financial debt acquired during doctoral programs. Many aspects of student experiences other than those we measured could also be associated with stopping out, such as changes in personal life beyond marriage and having children or other academic or personal events.

RATE OF PROGRESS

Rate of progress is our measure of students' median time through eight stages of their doctoral programs. This measure allows us to take a continuous snapshot of the factors that are important for students across the five fields of study. It is not surprising that, for all students in the sample, the largest predictor of steady progress in every field was continuous full-time enrollment (see table 11.18). As well, for students in education, engineering, and humanities, having a mentor made a considerably positive difference in accelerating progress. Older students in education, engineering, humanities, and sciences and mathematics appear to have made faster progress than younger students, and in humanities and the social sciences, international students progressed faster than their white peers. In engineering, men made slower progress than women. In the social sciences and in sciences and mathematics students with children under the age of eighteen also made slower progress. For students in education and the social sciences, higher parental SES was associated with faster progress; students in engineering and in sciences and mathematics with lower household incomes appear to have been slowed in their progress.

Counter to what one might expect, students with higher GRE verbal scores made slower progress in education, engineering, sciences and mathematics, and the social sciences. Students with higher GRE analytical scores made faster progress in education, sciences and mathematics, and

Table 11.18
Predictors of Rate of Progress in Doctoral Program, by Field

Independent Variable[a]	Education	Engineering	Humanities	Sciences and Mathematics	Social Sciences
Male		−			
African American[b]					
Hispanic					
Asian American					
International			+		+
Parents' SES[c]	+				+
Household income ($1,000s)			−	−	
Children under 18			−	−	−
Age at start of doctoral program (1 yr.)	+	+	+	+	
GRE verbal (100s of points)	−	−		−	
GRE analytical (100s of points)	+			+	+
Master's upon entry					+
Private graduate school	+			+	+
Always full-time doctoral student	+	+	+	+	+
Ever received a fellowship		−		+	
Ever was a teaching assistant	−				
Had some research productivity				−	
Incurred education debt as doctoral student					−
Has a mentor	+	+	+		
n (unweighted)	2,419	861	1,309	1,806	2,426

Source: Survey of Doctoral Student Finances, Experiences, and Achievements.
Note: A plus sign (+) indicates a relatively faster rate of progress while a minus sign (−) indicates a relatively slower rate of progress.
[a]Married or domestic partner, selective undergraduate institution, GRE quantitative, ever was a research assistant, and academic interactions with faculty were nonsignificant predictors in all fields and were dropped from the models.
[b]All racial groups and international students are compared with whites.
[c]Parents' SES is a composite of educational attainment and occupational prestige.

the social sciences. Social sciences students who entered their programs having already earned master's degrees also made faster progress, as did those studying education, sciences and mathematics, and the social sciences at private graduate schools. Fellowship recipients in the field of engineering had a slower rate of progress, while those in sciences and mathematics progressed relatively faster, compared with nonrecipients. Students who held teaching assistantships in education, as well as students in sciences and mathematics who demonstrated some research productivity, appear to have made slower progress. Student debt burdens appear to be an impediment to progress only for students in the social sciences.

DOCTORAL DEGREE COMPLETION

For our analyses of doctoral degree completion, only those students (nearly 62% of the sample) who had completed their degrees by 2001 were categorized as completers. Conceivably, as more respondents complete their degrees, some of the variables could increase in importance and others decrease, but for the moment, this glimpse of what has been happening is more extensive than any previous research. By analyzing the data for students who completed their degrees, we are able, at least, to provide a fresh look at the elements that contributed to their success.

Research productivity proved to be an important predictor of doctoral degree completion in all five fields (see table 11.19). Students in sciences

Table 11.19
Predictors of Doctoral Degree Completion by 2001 for Students beyond the First Year, by Field

Independent Variable[a]	Education	Engineering	Humanities	Sciences and Mathematics	Social Sciences
Male					
African American[b]		−			
Hispanic		−			−
Asian American		−		−	
International					+
Age at start of doctoral program (1 yr.)		−			
Married or domestic partner	+	+		+	
Children under 18	−				
GRE verbal (100s of points)	−	−			−
GRE analytical (100s of points)					+
Master's upon entry	+				
Private graduate school				+	
Selective undergraduate institution				+	
First or only choice of doctoral program		+		+	
Always full-time doctoral student	+		+	+	+
Time in doctoral program (yrs.)	+	+	+	+	+
Ever received a fellowship	+				
Ever was a research assistant				+	
Ever was a teaching assistant	+		+		
Has a mentor	+	+			+
Expect first job to be faculty or postdoctoral position	+			+	+
Had some research productivity	+	+	+	+	+
n (unweighted)	1,436	769	1,107	1,581	2,105

Source: Survey of Doctoral Student Finances, Experiences, and Achievements.
[a]Parents' SES, household income, GRE quantitative, and incurred educational debt as a doctoral student were nonsignificant predictors in all fields and were dropped from the models.
[b]All racial groups and international students are compared with whites.

and mathematics with research productivity were 3.9 times more likely to complete their doctorates than those without. In the other four fields, the effect was similar, although not as large: humanities, 3.0 times; engineering 2.7 times; education, 1.8 times; and the social sciences, the lowest, 1.6 times. With the exception of engineering, another key predictor of degree completion was maintaining full-time enrollment. In sciences and mathematics, students who maintained full-time enrollment were 4.0 times more likely than their part-time peers to complete their degree programs: for humanities, 2.8 times more likely; for the social sciences, 1.9 times; and for education, 1.6 times. Students who had spent more time in the program were slightly more likely to complete their degrees in every field except education. Education is also by far the field with the longest time to degree.

Having a mentor made a small but significant contribution toward degree completion in the fields of engineering (1.7), the social sciences (1.5), and education (1.4). Students in the fields of education, sciences and mathematics, and the social sciences who expected their first postdoctoral job to be as college faculty or postdoctoral researcher were also slightly more likely to complete their programs ahead of their peers with other career intentions.

Various funding options played a limited role in predicting degree completion. Being a teaching assistant somewhat improved a student's chances of completion in both education and humanities. Research assistantships made a slight contribution in sciences and mathematics. Holding a fellowship was significant only for students in education.

What role did admissions criteria play in predicting degree completion? Attending one's first choice of doctoral program made a small but significant contribution toward completion in engineering and in sciences and mathematics. Students in education, engineering, and the social sciences who achieved higher GRE verbal scores were less likely to complete their doctorates than their peers with lower scores. Students in social sciences with higher GRE analytical scores were also less likely to finish their degrees.

Gender did not influence degree completion in any field. In engineering, African Americans were 6.7 times less likely, Hispanics 2.5 times less likely, and Asian Americans 1.8 times less likely than whites to complete their degrees. Compared with those of their white peers, the odds of completing their degrees were also lower for Hispanics in the social sciences and for Asian Americans in sciences and mathematics. In engineering, older students were less likely than younger ones to finish their degrees. However, engineering students who were married or had domestic partners were twice as likely to finish their doctorates, as were married students in education and in sciences and mathematics, although the effect was less strong. The presence in the household of children under the age of eighteen appears to have been an impediment to completion only in the field of education.

TIME TO DEGREE

For the nearly 62 percent of the sample who completed their degrees over the four years of the study, we have been able to calculate time to degree by matching the individuals with the dates at which they started their programs. Aside from continuing full-time enrollment, which as we might expect was a significant predictor of faster progress in all five fields, the other significant predictors vary by field (see table 11.20).

Among the demographic characteristics found to be related to time to degree were a few race-ethnicity matters and socioeconomic status effects. Hispanics in engineering took three-quarters of a year longer, and Asian Americans a third of a year longer in sciences and mathematics and nearly a year longer in the social sciences, than whites to complete their programs. In the fields of engineering and the social sciences, the higher a students' parental socioeconomic status, the less time it took them to earn their degrees. Engineering students with relatively high student household incomes took more time to achieve their degrees, as did students in sciences and mathematics.

It appears that having a mentor in the humanities and the social sci-

Table 11.20
Predictors of Elapsed Time to Degree for Doctoral Degree Completers by 2001, by Field

Independent Variable[a]	Education	Engineering	Humanities	Sciences and Mathematics	Social Sciences
Male					
African American[b]					
Hispanic		+			
Asian American				+	+
International					
Parents' SES[c]	−				−
Household income ($1,000s)		+		+	
Married or domestic partner		−	−	−	
Children under 18		+	+		+
Age at start of doctoral program (yrs.)	−				
GRE verbal (100s of points)	+	+		+	+
GRE analytical (100s of points)	−			−	−
Selective undergraduate institution		+			
Private graduate school		+		−	+
Master's upon entry	−	−			
Always full-time doctoral student	−	−	−	−	−
Has a mentor			−		−
Incurred education debt as doctoral student					−
n (unweighted)	1,304	650	610	1,299	1,281

Source: Survey of Doctoral Student Finances, Experiences, and Achievements.
Note: A minus sign (−) indicates a relatively shorter elapsed time to degree completion.
[a]GRE quantitative scores, ever was a research assistant, ever received a fellowship, ever was a teaching assistant, and had some research productivity were nonsignificant predictors in all fields and were dropped from the models.
[b]All racial groups and international students are compared with whites.
[c]Parents' SES is a composite of educational attainment and occupational prestige.

ences is associated with shorter time to degree. This is another example of how mentoring positively influences student experiences, but interestingly not in every field, as it did with research productivity. How students financed their doctoral degrees played a limited role in determining time to degree. None of the three major forms of student support—fellowships, teaching assistantships, or research assistantships—predicted time to degree. Only in the social sciences was debt incurred as a doctoral student a factor in lengthening time to degree.

Students with higher GRE verbal scores took significantly longer to finish their degrees in the fields of education, engineering, sciences and mathematics, and the social sciences. Conversely, higher GRE analytical scores predicted shorter time to degree in education, sciences and mathematics, and the social sciences. Prior attendance at a selective undergraduate institution predicted longer time to degree for engineering students, as did attendance at a private graduate school for both engineering and social sciences students. However, attendance at a private graduate school was associated with a shorter time to degree for sciences and mathematics students. Earning a master's degree before entering a doctoral program also promoted a shorter time to degree in both education and engineering. While the presence in the household of a spouse or partner was a stronger predictor of a shorter time to degree for students in engineering, humanities, and sciences and mathematics, the presence in the household of children under eighteen was a strong predictor of longer time to degree for students in engineering, humanities, and the social sciences. Age was a factor only for students in education, reducing the time to degree.

CONCLUSION

Several points should be borne in mind as we conclude our presentation of the results of our regression analyses. First, although we have generally seen commonalities across fields for each of the outcome measures, we have also seen that for each dependent measure no two fields have the exact same set of attributes. This is evidence that research on doctoral students should examine each field separately. Tables 11.21 to 11.25 summarize the regression findings by field.

Second, even when we adjust for other aspects of the doctoral student experience, we still observe that for some outcomes, women and students of specific race-ethnicities have varied experiences. In our view, this is evidence that while discrimination by race and gender are not the dominating story of student doctoral education experience, it is pervasive enough to raise concerns for doctorate-granting institutions.

Third, admissions criteria exert limited power in predicting student experiences in doctoral programs. The present research supports the rationale for the existing criteria in their relationship to some of the early experiences we examined, such as type of finances and assistantships students are awarded, but much less with respect to the long-term experiences, performance, and achievements.

Fourth, having a mentor and being a research assistant are stable predictors of several positive doctoral program outcomes. Our findings on research productivity are especially revealing about the importance of doctoral students' having a mentor.

Finally, bearing in mind what we have learned, we must not forget that some important aspects of the doctoral student experience are not covered by these analyses. These include the factors that predict who is admitted to a doctoral program, the early first-year experiences of doctoral students, the acquisition of critical teaching skills, passing a qualifying examination, the quality or haste of a dissertation, and what predicts the transition from being a doctoral student to being a professional.

Table 11.21

Significant Predictors in the Education Regression Models

Predictor Variable	(1)	(2)	(3)	(4)	(5)	(6)	(7)	(8)	(9)	(10)	(11)	(12)	(13)	(14)	(15)	(16)	(17)[a]	(18)	(19)	(20)
Male								+		+	+									
African American[b]	+			+		−	+									−				
Hispanic	+			+		−	−													
Asian American	+			+			−					−								
International		−			−	−	−		−											
Parents' SES																		+		
Age at start of doctoral program (1 yr.)		−			−	−	−	−	−									+		−
Married or domestic partner				+														+		
Children under 18								−										−		
Household income ($1,000s)				−		−		−		+	+									
GRE verbal (100s of points)	+			+	+					−	−	−		+				−	−	+
GRE quantitative (100s of points)						−	−													
GRE analytical (100s of points)																		+	−	
Selective undergraduate institution	+			+						−								+		
Master's upon entry																		+	−	
First or only choice of doctoral program										+	+	+			+					
Full-time when first enrolled	+	+	+																	
Private graduate school	+			+		−	+	+	−			−		−	−			+		
Ever received a fellowship					+	+	+	+				+	+	+				+		
Ever was a teaching assistant				+		+	+	+								+		−		+
Ever was a research assistant				+	+								+	+	+					
Incurred education debt as doctoral student																				
Always full-time doctoral student					+	+	+		+		−							+	+	−
Time in doctoral program (yrs.)						+	+						+	+	+	−			+	
Peer interaction															+					
Has a mentor										+	+		+	+	+			+	+	
Student-faculty social interactions															+					
Adviser as mentor																				
Academic interactions with faculty															+					
Interactions with faculty adviser																				
Had some research productivity																		+		
Overall satisfaction with doctoral program																				
Expect first job to be faculty or post-doctoral position	−	+					−			+	+	+	+	+	+			+		

Source: Survey of Doctoral Student Finances, Experiences, and Achievements.
Note: A plus sign (+) indicates a statistically significant positive predictor on student experience. A minus sign (−) indicates a statistically significant negative influence on student experience. Column heads are as follows: (1) fellowship at entry; (2) teacher assistantship at entry; (3) research assistantship at entry; (4) ever received a fellowship; (5) ever received a teaching assistantship; (6) ever received a research assistantship; (7) incurred education debt while a doctoral student; (8) peer interaction; (9) had a mentor; (10) student-faculty social interaction; (11) academic interaction with faculty; (12) interaction with faculty adviser; (13) research productivity; (14) presented paper at national conference; (15) published research article; (16) satisfaction with doctoral program; (17) stopped out of doctoral program; (18) rate of progress; (19) completed doctoral degree; (20) time to degree.
[a]Separate field regressions were not run for stopping out of a doctoral program.
[b]All racial groups and international students are compared with whites.

Table 11.22
Significant Predictors in the Engineering Regression Models

Predictor Variable	(1)	(2)	(3)	(4)	(5)	(6)	(7)	(8)	(9)	(10)	(11)	(12)	(13)	(14)	(15)	(16)	(17)[a]	(18)	(19)	(20)
Male				−	−					+	+		+	+	+	+	−			
African American[b]	+	−	−	+	−	−												−		
Hispanic		−		+	−													−		+
Asian American				−				−				+						−		
International	−	−	−	−	−	−	−	−	−	+										
Parents' SES						−	+	+			+	+								−
Age at start of doctoral program (1 yr.)	−	−	−	−	−	−		−							−			+	−	
Married or domestic partner					+	+					+					+		+	+	−
Children under 18					−	+							−	−				−		+
Household income ($1,000s)				−	−	−						+						−		+
GRE verbal (100s of points)	+		+		+					−		−						−	−	+
GRE quantitative (100s of points)			+				−			+	+									
GRE analytical (100s of points)			−				+							+						
Selective undergraduate institution			−	+									−	−	−					+
Master's upon entry	−			−		−			−											−
First or only choice of doctoral program										+	+								+	
Full-time when first enrolled	+	+	+																	
Private graduate school		−			−						+		+	+		−				+
Ever received a fellowship						−	−	+			+					−				
Ever was a teaching assistant							+				−									
Ever was a research assistant					−		+	+					+	+	+					
Incurred education debt as doctoral student																				
Always full-time doctoral student										+	+	+		−				+		−
Time in doctoral program (yrs.)		+	+	+						−	−		+	+	+	−			+	
Peer interaction															+					
Has a mentor										+	+		+	+	+			+	+	
Student-faculty social interactions															+					
Adviser as mentor												+								
Academic interactions with faculty															+					
Interactions with faculty advisor															+					
Had some research productivity																			+	
Overall satisfaction with doctoral program																				
Expect first job to be faculty or postdoctoral position			+	+						+	+		+		+					

Source: Survey of Doctoral Student Finances, Experiences, and Achievements.
Note: A plus sign (+) indicates a statistically significant positive predictor of student experience. A minus sign (−) indicates a statistically significant negative influence on student experience. Column heads are as follows: (1) fellowship at entry; (2) teacher assistantship at entry; (3) research assistantship at entry; (4) ever received a fellowship; (5) ever received a teaching assistantship; (6) ever received a research assistantship; (7) incurred education debt while a doctoral student; (8) peer interaction; (9) had a mentor; (10) student-faculty social interaction; (11) academic interaction with faculty; (12) interaction with faculty adviser; (13) research productivity; (14) presented paper at national conference; (15) published research article; (16) satisfaction with doctoral program; (17) stopped out of doctoral program; (18) rate of progress; (19) completed doctoral degree; (20) time to degree.
[a]Separate field regressions were not run for stopping out of a doctoral program.
[b]All racial groups and international students are compared with whites.

Table 11.23
Significant Predictors in the Humanities Regression Models

Predictor Variable	(1)	(2)	(3)[a]	(4)	(5)	(6)	(7)	(8)	(9)[b]	(10)	(11)	(12)	(13)	(14)	(15)	(16)	(17)[c]	(18)	(19)	(20)
Male		−						−												
African American[d]	+	+		+																
Hispanic	+	+		+			+													
Asian American	+																			
International	+							−						−				+		
Parents' SES						−														
Age at start of doctoral program (1 yr.)		−			−													+		
Married or domestic partner																				−
Children under 18																				+
Household income ($1,000s)							−			+	+									
GRE verbal (100s of points)	+	+		+								−								
GRE quantitative (100s of points)	+																			
GRE analytical (100s of points)																				
Selective undergraduate institution																				
Master's upon entry	−			−									+							
First or only choice of doctoral program										+	+									
Full-time when first enrolled	+	+																		
Private graduate school	+			+	−		−	−												
Ever received a fellowship						+	−													
Ever was a teaching assistant							+	+			−		+	+	+			+		
Ever was a research assistant				+	+															
Incurred education debt as doctoral student																				
Always full-time doctoral student					+													+	+	−
Time in doctoral program (yrs.)				+	+		+			−	−		+	+	+			+		
Peer interaction																+				
Has a mentor							+	+					+	+				+		−
Student-faculty social interactions																+				
Adviser as mentor												+								
Academic interactions with faculty																+				
Interactions with faculty adviser																				
Had some research productivity																		+		
Overall satisfaction with doctoral program																				
Expect first job to be faculty or postdoctoral position								+			+	+	+			+				

Source: Survey of Doctoral Student Finances, Experiences, and Achievements.
Note: A plus sign (+) indicates a statistically significant positive predictor of student experience. A minus sign (−) indicates a statistically significant negative influence on student experience. Column heads are as follows: (1) fellowship at entry; (2) teacher assistantship at entry; (3) research assistantship at entry; (4) ever received a fellowship; (5) ever received a teaching assistantship; (6) ever received a research assistantship; (7) incurred education debt while a doctoral student; (8) peer interaction; (9) had a mentor; (10) student-faculty social interaction; (11) academic interaction with faculty; (12) interaction with faculty adviser; (13) research productivity; (14) presented paper at national conference; (15) published research article; (16) satisfaction with doctoral program; (17) stopped out of doctoral program; (18) rate of progress; (19) completed doctoral degree; (20) time to degree.
[a]The model is not statistically significantly different from the null model. This suggests that there is no relationship among the predictors and receiving a research assistantship.
[b]The model is not statistically significantly different from the null model. This suggests that there is no relationship among the predictors and having a faculty mentor.
[c]Separate field regressions were not run for stopping out of a doctoral degree.
[d]All racial groups and international students are compared with whites.

Table 11.24
Significant Predictors in the Sciences and Mathematics Regression Models

Predictor Variable	(1)	(2)	(3)	(4)	(5)	(6)	(7)	(8)	(9)	(10)	(11)	(12)	(13)	(14)	(15)	(16)	(17)[a]	(18)	(19)	(20)
Male	−	+		−					−				+	+	+					
African American[b]	+	−	−	+	−			+	−							−		−		
Hispanic	+			+									−							
Asian American									−							−			−	+
International	−			−	−		−	−			+					−				
Parents' SES				+				−		+		+								
Age at start of doctoral program (1 yr.)	−	−	−	−	−				−	+								+		
Married or domestic partner						+								+		+			+	−
Children under 18																−				
Household income ($1,000s)						−	−	−										−		+
GRE verbal (100s of points)	+			+					−	−	−		−					−		+
GRE quantitative (100s of points)	+	−		+					−	−	−									
GRE analytical (100s of points)									−		+	+						+		
Selective undergraduate institution									−										+	
Master's upon entry																				
First or only choice of doctoral program											+					+		+		
Full-time when first enrolled		+	+																	
Private graduate school					−		−	+		−					−	+		+	+	−
Ever received a fellowship						−	−		+	+	+	+	+	+	+	+				
Ever was a teaching assistant					−		+	+	+		−		−	−	−					
Ever was a research assistant					−	+			+				+	+	+			+		
Incurred education debt as doctoral student																−				
Always full-time doctoral student				+		+										+		+	+	−
Time in doctoral program (yrs.)				+		+			−	−	−		+	+	+			+		
Peer interaction																+				
Has a mentor									+	+			+		+					
Student-faculty social interactions																+				
Adviser as mentor												+								
Academic interactions with faculty																+				
Interactions with faculty adviser																+				
Had some research productivity																		−	+	
Overall satisfaction with doctoral program																				
Expect first job to be faculty or postdoctoral position				+		−			+	+	+					+		+		

Source: Survey of Doctoral Student Finances, Experiences, and Achievements.
Note: A plus sign (+) indicates a statistically significant positive predictor of student experience. A minus sign (−) indicates a statistically significant negative influence on student experience. Column heads are as follows: (1) fellowship at entry; (2) teacher assistantship at entry; (3) research assistantship at entry; (4) ever received a fellowship; (5) ever received a teaching assistantship; (6) ever received a research assistantship; (7) incurred education debt while a doctoral student; (8) peer interaction; (9) had a mentor; (10) student-faculty social interaction; (11) academic interaction with faculty; (12) interaction with faculty adviser; (13) research productivity; (14) presented paper at national conference; (15) published research article; (16) satisfaction with doctoral program; (17) stopped out of doctoral program; (18) rate of progress; (19) completed doctoral degree; (20) time to degree.
[a]Separate field regressions were not run for stopping out of a doctoral degree.
[b]All racial groups and international students are compared with whites.

180

Table 11.25
Significant Predictors in the Social Sciences Regression Models

Predictor Variable	(1)	(2)	(3)	(4)	(5)	(6)	(7)	(8)	(9)	(10)	(11)	(12)	(13)	(14)	(15)	(16)	(17)[a]	(18)	(19)	(20)
Male						−		−		+										
African American[b]	+			+									−		−					
Hispanic	+			+									−						−	
Asian American	+																			+
International			−	+	+	−	−											+	+	
Parents' SES							−		+									+		−
Age at start of doctoral program (1 yr.)	−	−	−	−	−	−			−											
Married or domestic partner							−		−		−									
Children under 18																		−		+
Household income ($1,000s)				−	−		−													
GRE verbal (100s of points)	+	+		+	+				+									−	−	+
GRE quantitative (100s of points)		+	+			+		−	−				−	−						
GRE analytical (100s of points)				+	+				+									+	+	−
Selective undergraduate institution					−															
Master's upon entry	−			−	−													+		
First or only choice of doctoral program										+	+	+				+				
Full-time when first enrolled	+	+	+																	
Private graduate school	+	−		+		−	−	+	+		−	−			−			+		+
Ever received a fellowship									+				+							
Ever was a teaching assistant						+		+							−					
Ever was a research assistant				+						+	+	+	+	+						
Incurred educational debt as doctoral student																		−		−
Always full-time doctoral student					+				+									+	+	−
Time in doctoral program (yrs.)			+	+	+	+	−			−	−	−	+	+	+	−			+	
Peer interaction																+				
Has a mentor										+	+		+	+	+				+	−
Student-faculty social interactions																+				
Adviser as mentor												+								
Academic interactions with faculty																+				
Interactions with faculty adviser																+				
Had some research productivity																			+	
Overall satisfaction with doctoral program																				
Expect first job to be faculty or postdoctoral position				+	+	+				+	+	+	+	+	+				+	

Source: Survey of Doctoral Student Finances, Experiences, and Achievements.
Note: A plus sign (+) indicates a statistically significant positive predictor on student experience. A minus sign (−) indicates a statistically significant negative influence on student experience. Column heads are as follows: (1) fellowship at entry; (2) teacher assistantship at entry; (3) research assistantship at entry; (4) ever received a fellowship; (5) ever received a teaching assistantship; (6) ever received a research assistantship; (7) incurred education debt while a doctoral student; (8) peer interaction; (9) had a mentor; (10) student-faculty social interaction; (11) academic interaction with faculty; (12) interaction with faculty adviser; (13) research productivity; (14) presented paper at national conference; (15) published research article; (16) satisfaction with doctoral program; (17) stopped out of doctoral program; (18) rate of progress; (19) completed doctoral degree; (20) time to degree.
[a]Separate field regressions were not run for stopping out of a doctoral program.
[b]All racial groups and international students are compared with whites.

CHAPTER TWELVE

Interpreting Field Differences

WE BEGAN THIS STUDY quietly congratulating ourselves on having found the rare opportunity to explore how, hovering on the edge of the twenty-first century, an increasingly diverse doctoral student population experienced doctoral programs. There is unprecedented diversity in doctoral education in the United States today, and diversity by race-ethnicity and sex, we thought, were key to understanding the variety in student experiences. We expected to observe at the doctoral level the kind of demographic distinctions among student experiences and performance that we typically find both at earlier levels of education and in postbaccalaureate professional schools.

Our descriptive and regression analyses confirmed yet another area of diversity, namely, field of study. Our conceptual framework guided us through an exploration and eventual discovery of the similarities and differences in experience and performance of students across these demographic and field categories and helped us identify possible reasons for the differences. Our exploration has permitted us to corroborate some prevailing axioms, refute others, create new conceptions of the preparation of students for doctoral programs, assess the quality of doctoral students' experiences and performance, and identify the varying challenges across the fields.

While the degree is still labeled the doctorate, across the length and breadth of academe it increasingly means different things to different schools, disciplines, and people. We selected eight characteristics for understanding how doctoral students are different across fields of study: Graduate Record Examination (GRE) scores, financial support, mentoring, student interactions with faculty, research productivity, rate of progress, degree completion and time to degree, and career expectations. Within these variations lie some of the standards by which the degree is pursued and acquired, the conditions under which students operate, and the customs to which they become acculturated. As Lovitts (2001) has pointed out, the departments differ in culture, socialization processes, academic rigor, dissertation requirements, and in other ways. These differences were reflected in student responses to our survey. Through its history, the doctoral degree has gone from elitist study for the leisure class to academic union card to cutting-edge business and industry credential. Its mutability may have ensured its survival, but as the differences among the five fields infiltrate other areas of student life, any vestigial commonality seems diminished. As should become clear when we attempt to interpret our findings and reach conclusions, the Ph.D. is grand and desirable packaging, but the enclosed goods may be highly variable.

Doctorate-granting institutions and departments may come to recognize in the following discussion the practices that promote student success, and they may, as a consequence, reexamine their practices in areas that students have identified as being deficient. Our concern is for balance. To some of us, the Ph.D. was mythic even before we acquired one. Indeed those who succeed through the process are game for the adventure and may even carry a retrospective reverence for the process. But without clearer and more widely communicated uniform structures and standards, *mythic* may take on a more negative connotation, especially for the broader pool of degree prospects. Our personal stake in the matter aside, the United States needs this degree, but the degree needs at least to be more transparent, both generally and across the various fields. The eight topics we have selected give a greater sense of the variety of images, allowing us to uncover the mystique among the major fields.

GRADUATE RECORD EXAMINATION SCORES

We mark the beginning of the doctoral education experience at the points of student application and admissions. At this stage, students have accumulated a variety of assets, and they begin the process in a variety of ways. In our model, these attributes are measured by the selectivity of their undergraduate institutions, performance on admissions examinations, admissions to their choice of doctoral programs, prior graduate degrees, whether they are attending private or public institutions, and whether they are attending as full-time or part-time students. As we have pointed out, each of these factors exerts an influence on various aspects of outcomes, but the most intriguing of these is the admissions tests, mainly because they display the greatest distinctions among the demographic and field diversity of our subjects.

For sixty years, the GRE General Test has been used as an admissions tool, along with other information (letters of recommendation, college transcripts, personal statements, graduate application forms, and, in some fields, GRE subject tests), in screening potential doctoral students. Although test scores, like birth certificates, are permanent records, once students progress beyond the first year of graduate school, their scores become immaterial. This raises several questions about both the GRE General Test as an instrument and the policies of the graduate schools that use it in the admissions process. Could the GRE General Test be reconstructed to add more value as a tool to help graduate institutions identify student capacities to establish mentoring relationships, achieve research productivity, advance at a reasonable rate of progress, and complete the degree? While some may argue this to be too much of a burden to place on a single admissions instrument, we would argue, based on our findings—especially in the cases of minority students—that to adequately forecast student success in doctoral programs, selection judgments must go beyond the present GRE General Test framework. For the additional information, doctoral admissions committees rely on letters of recommendation, personal statements written by applicants, and transcripts of prior academic performance. None of these alternative sources of information, however, is expected to carry the objectivity and precision of the GRE. For admissions committees and prospective students to improve their forecasting of student experience and success beyond the first year, more precision may need to be applied to these additional streams of information.

For the immediate rewards it offers, the GRE General Test is a valuable device in the current environment of doctoral education. Overall, GRE General Test scores offer institutions and departments a handy tool for assigning value to students in the form of the type of financial support they are offered. Each component has unique strengths. Any student hoping for an offer of a fellowship should pay attention to the verbal section of the GRE. In every field, students with high verbal scores are more likely to receive fellowships. In receiving teaching and research assistantships on initial enrollment, performance on the GRE General Test is also important.

Our findings raise questions about the strength of the GRE General Test alone and the possible need to standardize other admissions information that graduate programs review from such sources as letters of recommendation, personal statements, and application forms. Although various parts of the test are reasonable predictors of financial support at the start and during a student's program, further applicability is limited and erratic. Our finding about the episodic relationship of the GRE General Test to outcomes concurs with findings from prior research on the relationship of GRE scores to graduate grade point averages (Morrison and Morrison 1995; Sternberg and William 1997) and degree completion (Graduate Record Examination Board 1972; National Research Council 1995). In some fields, such as engineering, higher scores on the GRE quantitative section appear to predict more positive faculty interactions on academic matters; in others, such as education, higher GRE verbal scores signify a higher probability of presenting a paper at a conference.

For the most part, however, higher GRE scores, in the limited ways in which they have predictive value, edge in the negative direction. The best example of this comes from the analysis on doctoral program completion. With one exception, any of the three sets of scores that proved significant in the analysis suggested that students with higher GRE scores were *less* likely to complete their degree than those with lower scores. This gives credence to Bowen and Rudenstine's (1992, 182n. 10) finding (though not statistically significant) that students with lower GRE verbal scores completed their degrees in slightly higher proportions than students with higher GRE scores. Furthermore, we found that some GRE scores were even predictive of a longer time to degree. Of course, the GRE General Test is designed not for forecasting the outer reaches of doctoral programs but rather for facilitating entry screening decisions; therefore, it is not surprising that as students grow narrower in their intellectual focus, prior performance on the General Test becomes less relevant, as do other antecedent attributes. These findings suggest that, in addition to greater standardization of complimentary information such as transcripts, letters of recommendation, and applications, including personal statements, perhaps future research on field differences in doctoral education should explore the predictive value of GRE subject tests for forecasting such outcomes as degree completion or time to degree.

The GRE General Test appears to have great value in assisting faculty in making entry decisions but somewhat less stable value in predicting long-term success. Since the GRE General Test scores appear to have little systematic relationship to such important outcomes as rate of progress, student-faculty social interaction, student-faculty academic interaction, research productivity, and degree completion, it is perhaps appropriate to search for other information and criteria, either as part of the GRE General Test or in addition to it, that might carry more predictive value of doctoral students' experiences. Quite simply, faculty and high-scoring students themselves may have unrealistic expectations of the value of high GRE General Test scores. Higher scorers may be expected to achieve greater productivity, have a faster rate of progress, have an easier time connecting with faculty, and have a higher completion rate. Our data suggest the opposite. These outcomes may, in part, be affected by the effort, desire, and determination to achieve and succeed on the part of lower-scoring students.

It is also possible that the GRE as presently constructed fails to either identify or reward those lower-scoring applicants who may have the capacity to achieve productivity, to make faster progress, to relate to faculty, and to complete at a higher rate. Departments that rely heavily on GRE scores to predict student outcomes may be unintentionally creating halo effects, whereby scores influence faculty perceptions about students' general abilities and, in turn, influence their expectations about other outcomes such as mentoring relationships and research collaborations. After all, who would not want to be associated with a student who has been pronounced brilliant by the entire department? All these assumptions based on the present use of GRE scores by admissions committees may underestimate the capacity of lower scorers to achieve productivity, make rapid progress, relate to faculty, and complete their degrees. One possible serendipitous effect of the GRE General Test may be that it alerts lower-scoring students to the need to develop compensatory strategies and work habits to ensure their success.

This raises several questions about the value of background characteristics of students. We have elected to raise these questions most pointedly about the GRE General Test, simply because it is the only standardized measure and, despite its limitations in forecasting long-term student success in doctoral programs, it exerts a stronger relationship to outcomes than other attributes observed during the admissions process. Also, among the admissions information, the GRE reveals the greatest degree of difference among students across demographic and major field categories. Three questions in particular need to be addressed about the GRE General Test as an instrument and about its role in the admissions process:

—Could the GRE General Test be reconstructed to incorporate features that better distinguish the qualities that have been found essential to doctoral study?

—Could the GRE General Test be expanded to capture in a more systematic fashion the valuable information that comes through personal statements and letters of recommendation that presently are not standardized? For example, could such an assessment help graduate institutions identify student strengths and weaknesses in establishing mentor relationships?

—Could the GRE General Test rate students' conceptualization, research, and writing skills with a view to exploring potential productivity?

The factors that seem to count in degree completion—qualities like peer and faculty relationship building, self-direction, work ethic, and so on—are mostly unknown when a student is admitted into a doctoral program. Several researchers (Baird 1985; Enright and Gitomer 1989; Hartnett and Willingham 1979) have explored the potential for taking into consideration additional qualities. Although such explorations could be useful improvements to the admissions process, such scrutiny, however delicate and well intended, may be too heavy a burden to place on a single admissions instrument. This would be especially problematic if what we are observing in student accomplishments in the latter stages of the doctoral curriculum is the transformation they undergo as a consequence of their doctoral experience rather than the human capital attributes they present at the time of admissions. In effect, maybe it should be the goal of doctoral curriculums and proscribed experiences to cancel out any influence that the GRE General Test may have over the course of student progress through to completion.

Nevertheless, for prospective students, the knowledge that GRE General Test scores are likely to have mixed influence on their experiences after the first year should not reduce their efforts to gain high ratings. Achieving high scores continues to be in students' best interest for gaining access to graduate programs and perhaps for financial support. By contrast, students who score low on the GRE General Test can take heart that the prospects of their success in achieving research productivity, making timely progress, and completing degrees are potentially no less than those of higher-scoring students within the same fields. As we have shown, other important variables, such as mentoring, bear at least equally on these experiences.

FINANCIAL SUPPORT

Experts of the student experience rightfully place a premium on type of funding as a key element. Personal socioeconomic status of students is also important. We have explored both. Beyond meeting admissions criteria, funding is the next important consideration of faculty and students in the pursuit of doctoral degrees.

Our data suggest that doctoral students generally hail from comfortable financial circumstances, students from low parental educational and occupational backgrounds being only weakly represented. However, family background apparently does not translate into doctoral students' own household incomes. With the exception of the field of education, most students can anticipate earning a low income of their own while they are doctoral students. The field of education is different because students are often established in their professions before beginning their doctorates and are earning relatively high incomes compared with their peers in other graduate fields. This generally widespread lack of external income puts pressure on students to gain academic financial support in the form of fellowships or assistantships. The principal issue involves the distribution of financial support across race groups and, to a lesser extent, across fields of study. Students in fields such as engineering and sciences and mathematics tend to be liberally supported with research assistantships during their doctoral work, while humanities and education students receive relatively few such opportunities. Conversely, nearly three-quarters of the students in the humanities and sciences and mathematics and two-thirds of students in the social sciences received teaching assistantships.

In addition to the types and amounts of financial support students are offered and receive, there are three aspects of finances that we found compelling. The first is the attributes of students that enable them to acquire different types of funding. The second is how various types of financial support help students to achieve the numerous milestones in the process of earning degrees. The third is the chicken-and-egg conundrum of which comes first, the funding or the milestones. The last of these questions is the most difficult to address. Funding leads to milestones and milestones lead to funding in many ways at different times, making it difficult to isolate the occurrence and the effects. We examined the attributes that lead to funding and to how types of funding affect experiences. We left the chicken-and-egg conundrum on the table for future research.

Like Girves and Wemmerus (1988), we learned that teaching and research assistantships contribute in different ways to the quality of student experiences. For students of education, the humanities, sciences and mathematics, and the social sciences, teaching assistantships increased the prospect of valuable peer interactions, with the accompanying benefits of socioemotional support and departmental orientation. For students who acquire research assistantships, primarily in engineering and in sciences and math, the same phenomenon is observed: a higher level of peer interaction and corresponding support systems. A slightly different story emerges with respect to interactions with faculty: TAs gave lower ratings of social interactions with faculty in sciences and mathematics and lower ratings of academic interactions with faculty in engineering. In the social sciences, being an RA contributed positively to student perceptions of their academic interactions with faculty.

The benefits from assistantships, however, go beyond better peer connections or faculty interactions to include research productivity. For students in education and the humanities, serving as a teaching assistant may lead to opportunities to publish research articles during the course of the doctoral program. In contrast, TAs in sciences and mathematics may have fewer opportunities to publish. This field-dependent conclusion about the value of teaching assistantships is somewhat novel, primarily because until now researchers have not been able to break apart the fields. For example, the relationship that we observe between teaching assistantships and research productivity for students of sciences and mathematics is somewhat consistent with the conclusion reached by Ethington and Pisani (1993) that being a TA is an impediment to the acquisition of research skills. On the other hand, our opposite finding in education and the humanities is not consistent with that conclusion. By the same token, Ethington and Pisani conclude that having either a teaching or a research assistantship contributed to students' scholarly productivity and that students who participated in both types of funding produced even more. Our difference with their findings as it pertains to education and the humanities may be a result of our capacity to analyze the data by field rather than being limited to the aggregation of all doctoral students together.

Regarding research assistantships, in keeping with Ethington and Pisani's general conclusion, we found research assistants in every field except the humanities to be more likely to have had their names appear in print. While it is easy to say that their assistantships contributed to the production of publishable material, one might expect the process to be considerably more complex. Publications do not just happen; generally, publishing implies a level of faculty collaboration that is only hinted at here. Nevertheless, we feel justified in concluding that the benefits students derive from assistantships in general and the particular types of assistantships in their chosen field go a long way toward launching their scholarly careers.

Fellowships are often useful for helping universities compete for the hottest prospects from applicant pools. Curiously, fellowships appear to have little affect in any field with regard to overall program satisfaction. Similarly, fellowships did not make students less likely to stop out of their programs, although research assistantships had this positive effect. These outcomes run somewhat counter to Ronald Ehrenberg and Panagiotis Mavros's (1995) Cornell study, which finds that lack of financial support played a major role in dropout rates in the fields of economics, physics, and mathematics but not in the humanities. One of our respondents looked beyond the financial stability that these support mechanisms provide to the additional way they contribute to student satisfaction: "Surely [financial support] affects the experiences of students . . . not only in terms of their financial stability and scholastic achievements, but also with regard to the dignity and professional respect they are able to claim."

The message for prospective students seems apparent: research assistantships have a reputation for providing important academic advantages. We are hesitant, however, to confirm a status hierarchy among the various types of financial support that applies equally to all aspects of the doctoral experience. Although we can point to a connection between research assistantships and research productivity, we did not survey for a potentially equal gain in teaching outcomes among students holding teaching assistantships.[1] Without this measure, we suggest, both kinds of assistantships are prestigious and carry with them unique rewards.

We found fewer contraindications for teaching assistantships than did previous studies. The main contradiction in our findings with prior research is that teaching assistantships did not seem to lead to a slower rate of progress in any field of study, and for the 62 percent of our sample who completed their doctoral degrees, being a teaching assistant was not associated with a prolonged time to degree. The latter finding runs counter to Bowen and Rudenstine's (1992) finding that being a TA lengthened time to degree. They suspect that the additional time required to prepare to teach might have detracted from students' own work in pursuing completion.

Research assistantships had a positive effect on degree completion only for sciences and mathematics students, and fellowships were a strong predictor only for education students. Fellowships, teaching assistantships, and research assistantships did not predict elapsed time to degree in any field, and only in the social sciences did students who incurred debt take

1. Marsh and Hattie (2002) found that teaching effectiveness and research productivity are nearly uncorrelated.

a longer time to complete their degrees. Ideally, the equal-handed provision by institutions of both kinds of assistantships across the range of fields might be a worthy goal, since the two appear to help produce different outcomes at strategic points in the process. The rewards likely to be seen include increased departmental prestige through early publication by doctoral students and the focusing of some attention on teacher preparation, a matter that doctoral programs are accused of neglecting.

MENTORING

One sunny day a young student-rabbit came out of her hole and was promptly caught by a fox. "I am going to eat you for lunch," said the fox.

"Wait!" said the rabbit. "I am almost finished writing my Ph.D. dissertation."

"That's a stupid excuse," said the fox. "What is the title of this masterpiece?"

"My dissertation is called 'The Superiority of Rabbits over Foxes and Wolves.'"

"You're crazy," said the fox. "Everyone knows a fox will always win over a rabbit."

So the rabbit invited the fox to come to her hole and read it for himself. "If you're not convinced, then you can go ahead and have me for lunch."

Since the fox had nothing to lose, he went with the rabbit into her hole. The fox never came out.

A few days later the rabbit was taking another break from writing when a wolf captured her. Again, the rabbit postponed death by intriguing the wolf with her implausible title, "The Superiority of Rabbits over Foxes and Wolves." Again, her captor agreed to visit the rabbit's hole to view this dissertation and, again, never came out.

Eventually, the rabbit finished writing her dissertation and was out celebrating when she encountered an old rabbit-friend.

"What's up?" asked the friend.

"I just finished writing my dissertation about the superiority of rabbits over foxes and wolves," said the student-rabbit.

"That doesn't sound right," commented her friend.

"Oh, yes," said the student-rabbit. "You should come over and read it for yourself."

So they went together to the rabbit's hole, and there the friend saw the controversial dissertation in one corner, piles of fox and wolf bones in two other corners, and in the middle a LION!

And the moral is: Your dissertation theme doesn't really matter—as long as you have the right dissertation adviser.[2]

---

2. This "fable" in a slightly different version was first published in Devine and Cohen (1992), *Absolute Zero Gravity: Science Jokes, Quotes, and Anecdotes.*

Our book has demonstrated the solid statistical basis of this fable. Mentoring, however, is a missing element in the leading research on doctoral education. Berelson (1960) and Bowen and Rudenstine (1992) do not account for mentoring in their analyses of doctoral student experiences and outcomes, and yet it appears to be a prominent element in the process. In case studies and personal interviews of doctoral students, Golde (2000) and Lovitts (2001) identify the consequential role of advisers, but they do not distinguish advisers from mentors.

Mentoring and advising appear to make a difference in several areas. In the area of socialization—the training and assimilation of behaviors and thought patterns of academic life—students with mentors felt more positive about their relationships with faculty both outside and inside the classroom. Similarly, we found that having a faculty member who served as both adviser and mentor resulted in higher ratings of student interactions with their faculty adviser. While we lack the qualitative data to reinforce these ideas, it appears that making one solid faculty connection paves the way for a more favorable outlook on a student's other faculty interactions. By meshing successfully with one part of the department, students achieve a higher level of integration across the department. We suspect that few faculty members have considered their mentoring efforts as a sort of ambassadorship on behalf of their counterparts, and yet clearly by boosting one student's confidence they set in motion a wave of good feelings beneficial to all parties.

Contribution to Retention and Progress

These findings about the importance of mentoring have further consequences that have not emerged from previous work. While Girves and Wemmerus (1988) do not find a relationship between having a mentor and completing a doctoral degree, our regressions show that in the fields of education, engineering, and the social sciences, having a mentor is positively related to degree completion and to faster time to degree in the humanities and social sciences. With the growing concerns about doctoral noncompleters and the time it takes students to earn degrees, the lesson for both students and their departments seems clear. For students, the notion is that mentoring acts like an umbrella, fending off the isolation of academic pursuits and sheltering the vulnerable enterprise beneath. For departments, the lesson is more prosaic: mentoring is an investment in student success, and the return on investment comes initially in the form of student retention and, later, alumni respect and goodwill.

Contribution to Productivity

While these consequences of mentoring or its lack rate high in importance, they were not the only notable outcomes. We found a great deal of rhetoric, and despite hearing many speeches and conversations about the importance of mentoring, we found few examples (Girves and Wem-merus 1988; Cronan-Hillix et al. 1986) of research that either employed it or measured it and assessed its effect on student performance and experi-ences. We turned our attention to this void in the research. Faculty men-tors also have some bearing on research productivity, increasing the like-lihood as much as two times for humanities and social sciences students. Individuals with mentors in all fields except sciences and mathematics were more likely to present papers at national conferences than peers with-out one. Having a mentor was also positively associated with publishing articles for students in the social sciences, education, engineering, and sci-ences and mathematics. Overall, our findings were unambiguous. If dem-onstrations of research productivity are among a department's avowed mission, then mentoring to the greatest extent possible offers a guarantee of success. How mentors foster research productivity is the next logical question. What supportive, nurturing behaviors do mentors exhibit that promote productivity among their protégés?

The importance of research productivity is two-pronged. First, for suc-cessful doctoral candidates, it gives their curricula vitae a necessary boost as they go job hunting. Second, as Bean (1982) and others have noted, there are clear connections between graduate school and postdoctoral pro-ductivity. Mentors serve an additional role in helping students make this connection between research productivity and postdoctoral success, espe-cially students seeking academic careers. Institutionally, then, colleges and universities are likely to be well served by promoting and supporting qual-ity mentors in all fields, thus ensuring the supply of productive candidates for employment, career advancement, and mobility. The higher research productivity associated with mentoring will enhance students' job oppor-tunities.

Student Expectations

While statistically the importance of high-quality advisers and men-tors is undeniable, in practice the mentor's value appears to have a great deal to do with the student's experiences in her or his program. As this un-solicited communication from one of our survey respondents makes clear, doctoral students expect not only course work and dissertation support from their advisers but also professional advancement. It seems in this par-ticular institution students had to find their own advisers: "I don't really consider the relationship that of a mentor. That is, of a patron. Indeed, I have to ask for information and help. It isn't forthcoming. In a conversa-tion he mentioned that a friend was working on a guide to Tolstoy and was looking for contributors. I said, 'Did you mention my name?'" It hadn't occurred to him, despite [his] knowing I taught a seminar on the subject, hearing papers I've given at national conferences, and having dis-cussed Tolstoy with me. I signed a [book] contract last month."

This anecdote raises the broader issue of what exactly is encompassed in the concept of mentorship. Does it imply simply morale-building chats, or more active promotion of the student's interests on all fronts, be they publication, introductions, or job opportunities? This is the sort of professorial mindfulness that a department can hardly legislate, but without a doubt, some such expectation or hope resides in the minds of most advisees, and some seem to be disappointed. From our data, for instance, the interactions with a mentor overflowed into the emotional realm, with students in engineering, sciences and mathematics, and the social sciences who had a positive relationship with their advisers (in this case, not mentors) more likely to report higher levels of satisfaction with their doctoral program. This concurs with Nettles's (1989) finding that support and encouragement from a mentor and increased interaction with faculty raised student satisfaction.

Meeting student expectations for mentoring or quality advising poses a dilemma for administrators. Although it seems likely that many students chose their institutions with the hope of some sort of patronage by important figures in their discipline, the students, on their part, need to recognize that the department cannot mandate the intimate, personal connections that are subsumed under the general label of mentorship. Indeed, one has to question how this sort of mentoring-advising is structured on the faculty side. What are the responsibilities, and what are the rewards?

With the variability of faculty duties and responsibilities across fields and institutions, it is difficult to generalize about advising and mentoring issues. In light of much vagueness about what a doctoral student can expect, it is easy to see why students feel they occasionally sink to the bottom of their professors' minds. One survey respondent added the following note: "Overall, I do not believe that dissertation research and writing is considered an important part of the life of [this] university. Professors and graduate students tend not to collaborate; instead, each tends to do their own things. Advisors receive no compensation for their advising, nor is dissertation advising mandatory (to my knowledge). Of my close friends working on dissertations, one decided to transfer to another university even though it meant redoing course work and general exams, while another found that her topic had become obsolete and her advisor retired so that she was advised to develop a new topic."

Another student noted that at one institution, the professor-adviser had sixty or so dissertation students. While this student found the professor friendly and helpful within the range of his expertise, "his ability to discuss alternative approaches which he himself had found useful was distinctly limited. At our rare meetings, he could primarily only encourage my persevering with the project. Also, I did not believe he could provide me with employment connections in my field." Another professor had more expertise in the student's area, but "unfortunately, he generally was not interested in advising dissertation students . . . Receiving comments from the latter advisor was always a matter of several months, and when they came they tended to be of little help. Perhaps a different system of advising would have allowed me to direct my energies more effectively toward the completion of an acceptable dissertation."

Clearly, some faculty take their responsibility to graduate students more seriously than others, but the duty itself is neither well recognized nor celebrated. Imagine how different the foregoing scenario with the Tolstoy specialist might have been if the professor had been granted departmental credit for his advisees' publications and job placements. From our data and similar comments, it seems there is a whole piece of the support puzzle that has yet to be solved, and only the institutions can take action to remedy the lack.

STUDENT INTERACTIONS WITH FACULTY

Mentoring captures the interpersonal relationship a student has with one special faculty person. The association that students have with the entire faculty in their academic departments is also valuable for their satisfaction with their doctoral programs. Our measure of student interactions with faculty is two-dimensional, involving their perceptions of their academic interactions and their social interactions with faculty. Student perceptions of their interactions with faculty would be more a curiosity than cause for concern if our data did not show that that these views spilled over into other areas of their doctoral experience. We examined how each of these two dimensions contributed to a variety of student experiences and found that students with higher ratings of student and faculty interactions on each dimension and in every field were more satisfied with their doctoral programs. Although we would like to think that student interactions with faculty precedes satisfaction, Margaret Madden and Linda Carli (1981), examining the reverse effect, find that more satisfied students experienced greater interactions with their faculty. We suppose it is just impossible to know which comes first, satisfaction or faculty interactions. For doctoral programs in any field in which satisfaction is an issue of concern, positive academic and social interactions may be the key.

Contribution to Positive Views of Student-Faculty Interactions

What should doctoral programs focus on to achieve positive social and academic interactions with faculty? These two dimensions share several common predictors: career interests, amount of time in program, choice of doctoral program, and mentoring. Students who aspired to faculty positions as their first job after completing their doctoral programs had been enrolled in their programs for a relatively short time, were attending the doctoral programs of their first choice, and had mentors tended to achieve relatively high levels of academic and social interaction with faculty.

While Baird (1992) finds that the longer students are enrolled, the more access and interactions they appear to have with faculty, we found that students became less enchanted in both academic and social interactions with faculty the longer they were enrolled.

Some of the contributors to academic and social interactions with faculty offer some clarity. For example, it seems logical that a student who attends her or his first choice of program is predisposed to having a more positive view of interactions with faculty than one who does not. Very likely, the students have carefully examined their chosen institutions, the departments, and the individual faculty members with a view to determining both quality and personal fit. At the same time, once the student is enrolled, widely acknowledged departmental prestige can produce a halo effect for all its members. Similarly, students with mentors tended to be more charitable in their assessments of faculty interactions. In all five fields, having a faculty mentor resulted in a much more positive view of faculty. This, again, may be the halo effect, meaning that a strong positive connection with a single faculty member makes a doctoral student well disposed or even well connected to the rest of the department. Generally, an expectation that one's first postdoctoral job will be as faculty or a postdoctoral researcher is a strong predictor that students will achieve positive academic and social interactions with their faculty. It stands to reason that some sort of modeling or understanding of the faculty role would develop among students inclined in this direction.

Although in our study GRE General Test scores were not associated with major differences in the quality of student experience, they had a small impact, both positive and negative, on how students assessed their faculty interactions. In education, engineering, and sciences and mathematics, higher GRE verbal scores were related to lower student perceptions of academic and social interactions with faculty. Are we possibly seeing students who command a superior level of oral and written language feeling that they are not being adequately recognized by their faculty for those strengths, or rather some idealized notion of faculty discourse that is not being fulfilled? Conversely, higher GRE quantitative scores were associated with higher student perceptions of faculty academic and social interactions in engineering. Higher GRE analytical scores were associated with higher student perceptions of faculty academic and social interactions in sciences and mathematics. One might speculate that just the opposite is happening here: the better equipped students are with quantitative or analytic skills, the more likely they are to respect faculty who routinely demonstrate these abilities.

As walking a mile in another's shoes contributes to understanding the other person, one might expect that conducting faculty-type work as either a research assistant or a teaching assistant would have a uniform positive effect on student assessments of faculty academic and social interactions. Not so. Research assistantships were only weak predictors of better ratings of academic interactions with faculty in the social sciences and were not predictive of social interactions. Serving as a teaching assistant predicted a negative rating of academic interactions with faculty in engineering and a negative rating of social interactions with faculty in the humanities and in sciences and mathematics. While students in some fields who served as teaching assistants were less impressed by faculty with whom they shared the undergraduate instructional load, there is at least one other possible interpretation for assistantships' lack of impact. Although researchers in the past have stressed the social and professional connections that assistantships help students create, it might be that these connections are relatively narrow and, even if they are congenial and stimulating, do not extend to the rest of the department.

Convergent Views of Social and Academic Interactions

The two dimensions of student interactions vary by field of study, and within a field student academic interactions may be different from their social interactions with faculty. Students in engineering, education, and humanities held generally positive views about their academic interactions with faculty, while those in sciences and mathematics and the social sciences had relatively low opinions. When these findings on academic interactions with faculty are compared with the findings on student-faculty social interactions, students in the social sciences again had the lowest perceptions of their social interactions with faculty. Despite having positive views about their academic interactions with faculty, students in the humanities were nearly as negative as social sciences students about their faculty social relationships.

We offer several possible explanations from analyses of our own data and other issues that should perhaps be examined. It is possible that faculty in both humanities and the social sciences may not be strong on empathy and personal support or that students in these fields are tougher raters of these types of interactions with faculty. Another possible explanation is that faculty in these fields may be too stretched by their roles to adequately accommodate all those who want a little part of their attention. Alternatively, the findings may suggest that students, particularly in the humanities, who rate faculty quality high remain in awe of their faculty and are hesitant to initiate social contacts.

Other explanations suggest themselves. Among our five fields, a larger share of both humanities and social sciences students saw their future employment direction as faculty in a college or university. It is possible that while students in other fields were relating or not relating to their faculty, students in the humanities and social sciences were both judging and rejecting them as role models for their intended academic careers. George Kuh (2001), in a recent book on issues in higher education, raises another possibility. After an analysis of the ways in which traditional faculty think and value, Kuh suggests that these can be very different from the techniques and purposes of students, resulting in both anxiety and confusion on students' part. Obviously, without individual interviews we can offer no definitive explanation of these field differences, we can only offer starting points for future study.

Still looking at apparent anomalies, we found that students in sciences and mathematics gave the highest ratings to their faculty social interactions (which would be consistent with lab-based teamwork and casual daily contact) but rated academic interactions low. A number of issues may underlie these opinions. One suggestion might be the shelf life of knowledge in these fields, generally rated at no more than five years. Some faculty may be perceived as seriously out of date. Another complex issue, since many of these students have clearly identified their interest in working outside academe, may be their desire for job contacts beyond the institution, which less current or less well connected faculty are unable to supply. At the same time, students may well have been resisting and resenting faculty pressures to become professors. As well, individual responses to the questions about instruction, advising, feedback, job placement, and research support contribute to both the positive and negative viewpoints. Sorting these out of the generalized overview would help us to understand these puzzles.

Enlarging our window on their experiences with faculty, various respondents communicated personal difficulties with aspects of the faculty relationship in short notes accompanying their surveys. One of the worst-case scenarios that a doctoral student at the candidacy stage can imagine is the departure from the scene of her or his dissertation chair. One student described this dilemma: "My advisor announced that he is retiring at the end of the year. He is the only professor in the department with whom I would consider doing doctoral work . . . I have considered changing to a different field, but I have not yet made a decision." Another student expressed a similar sense of difficulty with establishing relationships with faculty beyond the mentor: "I have been extremely disappointed in my doctoral program, especially recently. My advisor (who had also acted as chair of my dissertation) left our university for another. It was never mentioned among the faculty that were left that students who had this faculty member should find a new advisor. I have pretty much felt deserted. I am still looking for a chair for my dissertation. Faculty are extremely unhelpful."

A humanities respondent pointed to the clay feet beneath the academic gowns and trappings of faculty and expressed some discontent with faculty relationships: "I am appalled by how badly read the students, and some of the professors, are. As theory continues to hold sway in the graduate English departments, I know students who do not understand references to Greek mythology or the Bible or to Shakespeare, but who blithely 'deconstruct' the social meanings of the text—and with no knowledge of the times in which they were written. They seem to think Elizabeth Bennet [the protagonist in Jane Austen's *Pride and Prejudice*] should have gotten a job. The professors have only praise for such performances in public. In private it is sometimes another matter. I find the intellectual claims of the academy suspect."

These student views represent a relatively recent development in higher education that is worth noting: students' sense of entitlement. The consumer model of today's society has infiltrated higher education to the point at which students' expectations for personal support, prioritized access, and clear directions may run beyond any department's supply chain. Quite simply, students may be demanding services that no department can deliver. We wonder . . . and worry.

Insensitivity constitutes another issue about which students complain regarding their faculty interactions: A student wrote compellingly about a group of graduate students at the Modern Language Association convention bemoaning the competition ranging from four hundred to fifteen hundred applicants for every job. "We were, obviously, rather down. Two of the professors wandered over, one my adviser, and began regaling us with stories about their original job searches when they were offered more than one job on the spot at the MLA. After listening for some time I interrupted, 'Is this supposed to encourage us? To make us feel better?' They apologized and went away. The other students were stunned I would dare to be so rude. They were fearful about those letters of recommendation, about the power of these men—who as far as I'm concerned were the ones being rude."

As tenure and tenure-track positions become increasingly rare and prized, faculty smugness of this sort can be expected to draw resentment. Academe happens to be one of the last workplaces where the young are made to stand aside until their elders decide to take themselves off the scene. The resistance on one side and the impatience on the other are bound to make for uncomfortable situations in fields such as the humanities and social sciences, where teaching careers are most likely to be the students' goal. It seems entirely reasonable that tensions will develop between the students' passion to study and the reduced expectations in the marketplace that are unique to some fields.

Finally, recognizing that students who aspire to academic positions tend to have more positive interactions with their faculty, this is not an association that should be taken for granted. At least some students in our sample felt strongly that they were owed stronger faculty support than they were getting, as this writer indicated: "The professors, in general, have no clue about the reality of today's job market—despite the fact that they sit on search committees and see the numbers of applications and read in professional journals and the national magazines about the problem. I have heard more than one of the faculty at the Graduate Center say, 'Oh well. The really good ones will get jobs.' This from people charged with helping us."

RESEARCH PRODUCTIVITY

In contrast to mentoring, research productivity has drawn far less attention from researchers, and obviously from students, if our 51 percent overall participation rate accurately represents students' activities in this area. This suggests that research productivity is not an established standard and expectation of doctoral programs—at least not on a par with writing a dissertation, a requirement of all who receive a doctoral degree. As the survey shows, we subscribe to a multidimensional definition of research productivity, one that includes twenty-two different ways students could recognize and report on their activities. Among these were presentations at professional conferences, publishing books, book chapters, and book reviews, developing software, submitting articles for publication, publishing articles, writing grant proposals, and submitting copyrights or patents. We did not, however, capture the extent to which student productivity was either individualized or collaborative with professors or other students. This may be particularly important to the 40 percent of students who indicated an interest in faculty careers.

Although our study makes explicit our own assumption that research productivity is a desired outcome of the doctoral process, we are obliged to ask why students present such a minimal showing in this area. One reason may lie in the disinclination of students in certain fields to pursue research-based careers. Students may perceive the time required for research productivity as impeding their progress toward the degree. Our data show, however, that research productivity has the opposite effect. In all fields, students with research productivity were more likely to complete their degrees, and research productivity did not impede the progress of those who earned their doctoral degrees. The degree completion outcome goes a long way toward justifying the emphasis we have been giving to research productivity. When we look across all five fields for a universal predictor of degree completion, the one we find is "some research productivity." As a by-product of research productivity, students may benefit in related areas such as writing their dissertation proposals, carrying out dissertation research and analysis, and writing their dissertations. There appears to be nothing more important as a predictor in any of the fields (except perhaps full-time attendance) that promotes development of the skills eventually needed to write and successfully defend one's dissertation. Research productivity does not detract from timely degree completion. Even students who do not intend an academic career should take heed: research practice ultimately pays off when it matters most.

Two additional clues to the lack of productivity lie in the close relationships we have found between mentoring and research productivity, on the one hand, and research assistantships and research productivity, on the other. Quite possibly many of the students did not understand the short- and long-term benefits of authoring and presenting papers and similar activities. That having a mentor and a research assistantship are so highly predictive of research productivity across disciplines and demographic groups suggests that this should become a departmental benchmark for creating optimal doctoral student experiences. For students aiming at academic or research careers, it is likely that research productivity may come to be viewed as an indicator of success in doctoral programs to rival degree completion and time to degree.

It is not clear to what extent students with research productivity gain an advantage in the labor market, but productivity is a clear sign of students' professional development and socialization in their discipline or field of study. Consistent with pressures on departments to increase the emphasis on public demonstrations of research productivity, we note the shrinking outlets for such work. Conference proposals face growing competition as more students vie for places; conferences themselves are limited in number and frequency; scholarly journals grapple with cost problems and cutbacks. In such an environment, students' engagement in research productivity requires solid and ongoing disciplinary support to prosper beyond its current limitations.

RATE OF PROGRESS

As we have observed, variability in the rate of progress is high, both across fields of study and across race-ethnicity groups. Only the international students, who appear to march to a different drummer (see chap. 13), stand out as having achieved rapid progress. Yet when we examine the factors that contribute to the rate of progress, we find little support for a view that financial hardship is slowing some respondents. Household income was only a weak predictor of slower progress in engineering and in sciences and mathematics, and only in the social sciences were students with educational debt progressing at a relatively slower pace. In the same vein, we found the ability to remain a full-time graduate student an obvious condition of speedier progress. Working on a doctorate part-time seems to be a recipe for prolonging the process.

These variations in the rate-of-progress findings suggest that departments could be doing more to set out the desired milestones for course work, comprehensive examination, dissertation proposal, and the rest and then monitor more closely student progress toward them. In other words, impose a structure and schedule for the doctoral process where seemingly none exists. Some of our respondents seem to have considered this possibility, and one even pointed to the very real problem that schedules entail for both students and faculty. As one student added in a cryptic note about how academics are not much driven by timetables, "It strikes me as typical of my experiences with the academy . . . Deadlines are guidelines that are not necessarily meaningful." In addition, we can anticipate that not all students will appreciate institutions' efforts to set in place monitoring and support policies. One respondent who had reached candidacy complained, "One of the biggest barriers to completing my degree is my department's attitude that students are not sacrificing enough to deserve a degree from this institution (i.e., I have been asked to quit my job, I have been asked to be present in the dept. 2–2½ days/week) at this late date in my doctoral program."

Another doctoral student responded to the Survey of Doctoral Student Finances, Experiences, and Achievements with a veritable catalogue of problems that can impede progress. While some of these issues are not susceptible to research or institutional intervention, they illustrate well the personal and idiosyncratic nature of the process.

> Among other issues one could cite that bear directly upon a student's progress in his/her degree . . . are the following: (1) the student's financial obligations to both his/her immediate and extended families—before, during, and immediately after the completion of doctorate; (2) the impact of the loss of an academic advisor, or of one or more dissertation reader(s) on the protraction of one's studies; (3) various unexpected technical difficulties that result in the loss of the major portions of one's research (as, for example, irreparable damage to one's field notes, or computer malfunctions); (4) exigent personal circumstances (such as divorce, ill-health faced by oneself or a significant family member, or the death of a beloved friend or family member); and (5) the rhythm of marriage and family life, which imposes its owns set of constraints upon a student's ability to commit him/herself single-heartedly to the tasks imposed by the degree program. Furthermore, carrying extensive debt can itself significantly affect a student's sense of confidence and esteem as s/he proceeds through the doctorate, and influence the results s/he may obtain; it can also proscribe his/her ultimate career choice.

Extrapolating a plan of action from these findings is far from easy. It appears, however, that many students may not have a notion of the various milestones and the pace they should be setting. A faculty mandate to spell these out clearly might speed the dawdlers and enable whole cohorts to reach the dissertation stage more evenly. Golde and Dore (2001) similarly suggest annual formal evaluations of student progress among a list of mechanisms for achieving the connection that departments owe students. At the same time, a more lock-step approach for students at the beginning of the degree might permit more emphasis to be placed on faculty contact time and efforts during the dissertation process—a commentator in Bowen and Rudenstine's *In Pursuit of the Ph.D.* (1992, 260) described it as a "black hole," where obstacles and deadlines seem to multiply.

DEGREE COMPLETION
AND TIME TO DEGREE

In contrast to published findings of completion rates hovering around 50 percent (Baird 1993b; Bowen and Rudenstine 1992; Tinto 1993), 62 percent of our sample had completed the doctoral degree by 2001. Our metric is a bit different from others in that we included in our sample only students who had already completed one year of doctoral study rather than all students who entered, some of whom would have dropped out during the first year. We have not attempted to follow up with the remaining 38 percent. Therefore, we are not aware of whether they have discontinued their pursuit or are continuing to make progress. For those who completed, the median elapsed time to degree was 5.75 years for the entire sample and, specifically, 5.75 for students in education, sciences and mathematics, and the social sciences, 4.75 for engineering students, and 6.75 for students in the humanities. Our rates are faster than those found by other researchers, but as more people complete, the average time to degree will increase. The differences among the fields are consistent with findings reached in prior research (Baird 1990b; Bowen and Rudenstine 1992; Ehrenberg and Mavros 1995; Tuckman, Coyle, and Bae 1989; Wilson 1965).

That Bowen and Rudenstine (1992), a decade ago, presented time to degree as a crisis in doctoral education may have prompted universities to address the problem, and so the rates we observe in our study may represent the fruits of their efforts. But when we consider that more than half of our sample had already begun their dissertations in 1996 when we selected our sample, and 62 percent of the sample had completed their degrees by 2001, we get a fairly discouraging picture of the dragged-out process the doctoral experience has become for at least a good portion of the students. For those who did not reach their degree goal in this time frame, it continues to be a process with an unknown ending. As such, the process seems inefficient.

If students are arriving at institutions capable of doctorate-level work (and no one seems to be questioning the general qualifications of these cohorts), one has to ask why, with effective course work, support, and counseling, they are not progressing in a steady movement toward completion. We have identified some of the facilitating factors such as the developmental roles of mentors. In fact, student research productivity, which we thought in the beginning might be an impediment, seems to have had a positive influence on completion. We also conjectured that students' financial burdens would impede degree completion and time to degree, but we found that only in the social sciences did financial burden lengthen the time to degree. We have not found severe roadblocks that would account for the apparent difficulties and prolongation of the degree process. The only impediment appears to be part-time status. We can hypothesize that by reverting to part-time status while they are completing their degrees, students are effectively loosening their ties with their departments, putting themselves at risk of seeing their professors become less engaged, move on, or retire. This is where institutional intervention could play a major role by ensuring support and monitoring through the dissertation process.

Doctoral programs, particularly in their later stages, are characterized by highly personalized relationships involving high stakes, at least for the student participant. The most treacherous period occurs at the end of the process, after students have invested enormous time, energy, and resources toward completing a degree. This is when they appear to develop the greatest amount of dissatisfaction with their professors. The extent to which these relationships break down contribute to the ABD (all-but-dissertation) status is unknown, but even for the broader population of doctoral students this would appear to be something that universities should address. The longer students work on their degrees, the less satisfied they appear to become with their doctoral program. We do not know whether this is a short-term dissatisfaction or whether these students carry these dispositions with them into the ranks of alumni or their professional careers. We wonder, however, whether such feelings, coming at the end of such a monumental trail, might not endure for some time.

Even when the research is accomplished, writing may not be a natural activity for many doctoral students. Even the most self-directed may hesitate when confronted with a blank screen. At the same time, we suspect that few departments offer the coaching facilities that would help students focus and produce a steady flow of chapters for critique by their dissertation committees. Somewhere in the loneliness of the dissertation process, students are going astray. Among the myriad challenges for graduate institutions, reducing attrition at this point of the process should become a priority.

CAREER EXPECTATIONS

One way in which our study breaks new ground is its demonstration of the significance of field differences in students' career expectations. In 1999 less than half the students granted doctorates had faculty career plans (see chap. 2). We found differences by field in which an even smaller percentage of engineering (28%) and education (38%) students expected to obtain faculty or postdoctoral positions after completing the degree compared with nearly three-quarters of humanities students and more than half of the students in the social sciences and sciences and mathematics who had such career expectations. This is consistent with Golde and Dore's (2001, 6) statement that "most doctoral students in the traditional arts and sciences are primarily interested in a faculty career."

There are a couple of possible explanations for why students are turning away from academic careers. One is the greater market demand for people with Ph.D.s, and another is students' declining interest in emulating the professional careers of their mentors and faculty. We are concerned, however, that graduate faculty fully make the adjustment to accommodate the broader interest of students, given the lower ratings of academic and social interactions with faculty reported by students who are not pursuing faculty careers. In part, the disinterest in academic careers is an undercurrent of dissatisfaction with academic life. As one respondent reported, "I am thoroughly disillusioned with the system of higher education in this country. Even if I could get a job, highly unlikely in today's market, I would not. As I said to a friend who is a professor of political science, 'Don't take this wrong, but I don't want to become one of you people.' I find the life of the university narrow without having a compensating dimension of depth. Especially as the market becomes tighter, the pursuit of 'profession' rather than thought becomes dominant." The writer, self-identified as a humanities student, went on to berate the cultural divide: "Before I went to graduate school, I used to pooh-pooh the idea of the ivory tower. Professors pay taxes, have mortgages, have children, I would say. The university is necessarily part of the 'real world.' Not so, I find . . . There is, indeed, a feeling of the elect and the goats, of the washed and unwashed, and of the clergy and the lay population."

Much remains to be learned about why students in fields like sciences and math are turning away from academic positions and why the overall decline has been steady for the past two decades. While employment opportunities obviously have an impact on student thinking, the previously cited responses suggest that other factors, like academic antipathy, may also be operating.

This lack of interest in faculty careers in some fields rubs off on other parts of the students' experiences. Students who do want to become faculty or postdoctoral researchers appear to have the advantage in many desirable outcomes. Such aspirations contribute to a more positive appreciation of student-faculty social interactions among education, humanities, and sciences and mathematics students, to greater peer interaction among humanities students, and to a higher assessment of faculty academic interactions among students in every field. As well, in every field the desire for careers in academe made it more likely that doctoral students would interact positively with their faculty advisers. Faculty aspirations also contributed strongly to the likelihood that education, engineering, and social sciences students would present papers at conferences and to overall research productivity for education and social science students.

As one might expect, there was a clear connection between teaching aspirations and teaching assistantships, with students who wanted to be faculty more likely to have been teaching assistants in education, engineering, and the social sciences. For social sciences students, the connection between faculty aspirations and research assistantships was strong. Another area in which faculty aspirations had a broad impact involved students' overall satisfaction with their doctoral program. Here, students in engineering, the humanities, sciences and mathematics, and the social sciences who expected to become faculty or postdoctoral researchers were more likely to be satisfied with their doctoral programs than were their contemporaries who intended to work elsewhere. Finally, and logically, faculty aspirations were a moderate predictor of degree completion for education, sciences and mathematics, and social sciences students, since without completion they most likely would be overlooked for academic positions.

Although some disciplines (for example, computer sciences) are competing with industry to retain the best and brightest of their Ph.D. graduates for the professoriate, by and large employment prospects for the multitude of doctoral students have not brightened appreciably. To their credit, universities are increasingly supporting seminars and counseling on alternatives to academic employment for their Ph.D. graduates. Nevertheless, the dark at the end of the tunnel remains a fearsome prospect for some students, and possibly one more cause of the ABD phenomenon.

CONCLUSION

At the opening of this chapter, we expressed our hope that our analyses would be useful to prospective students, current students, and other stakeholders like faculty and administrators and that fellow researchers might be persuaded that our conceptual models—our ways of defining, measuring, and analyzing doctoral student experiences—will yield insight into the quality of student experiences and performance. Doctoral education in its numerous components is complex, and no one set of characteristics and attributes is likely to produce an explanation of experiences and outcomes, even if we exclude consideration of field, race-ethnicity, and gender differences. At the same time, we have arrived at some useful findings for the various stakeholders that address some common questions about the doctoral education process. Key among these are findings relating to the value of the GRE, the role of finances and mentoring, and the rate of progress in doctoral programs.

We began with one of the traditional features of graduate admissions and indeed one of the mystical elements in terms of its predictive validity. The overwhelming majority of students who enter doctoral programs take the GRE beforehand, yet they seem to know little about its value beyond admissions. No doubt it is a valuable and valued tool for graduate admissions committees in deciding which applicants to admit and which to offer various types of finance to. Our conclusion is that prospective students and researchers are wise to focus on the GRE and its relationships to student admissions, finances, and performance in the beginning. Our analyses suggest, however, that beyond that initial stage, GRE scores might as well be forgotten, because they tend to lose their association with much that matters in the process, such as research productivity and mentoring relationship. Given that the GRE was not intended for these longer-term purposes, the weak relationship is not completely surprising, and the search for predictors of continuing term achievement and success like persistence and graduation continues to be the topic of graduate admissions committees and leaders of graduate education. What remains mystifying about the GRE and its predictive value is its weak longevity. Future research could explore whether faculty actions are addressing the distinctions or whether the variability of experiences are reduced over time.

Finances are on par with GRE scores in their mystical character. We found funding and type of funding, unlike GRE scores, to have strong long-term associations with doctoral student experiences and outcomes. As more students enter their doctoral programs with the expectation of achieving research productivity and completing their degrees in a more timely fashion, a more refined understanding of the relationship of timing and sequencing of fellowships and various types of assistantships should lead to further demystification about how finances contribute to student productivity and completion in the various fields of study. Our findings provide the opening hypothesis that with the exception of the humanities, research assistants have an edge in research productivity. A second hypothesis with which to begin further exploration of finances is that electing to be a teaching assistant does not retard one's progress. Testing the timing and sequencing of types of financial assistance will be the more challenging enterprise for researchers to undertake.

Another set of valuable lessons resides in the power of mentoring for student socialization, research productivity, and degree completion. We found, unequivocally, that students with mentors benefit on all three counts. The concept of mentoring is one that is widely used in rhetoric but seldom measured, even in the most legendary studies of doctoral education. This seems counterintuitive, given the apprenticeship nature that has characterized doctoral education throughout its history. Although some have found mentoring to provide a rather weak contribution to student outcomes, we found it to be among the strongest. We found value in distinguishing mentors from advisers, and yet we also found that students benefited from both roles' being played by a single faculty person. As with other vital features of doctoral education, we have advanced the measurement of mentoring yet have left much still to be explored. One example is how we measured mentoring. Rather than measuring the nature and intensity of mentoring relationships, we simply noted whether or not a student had a mentor. We discovered enough strength in the relationship of mentoring to outcomes to fuel both the rhetoric and further more focused investigations.

Part of what we have accomplished in this research has been to generate new measures like research productivity and rate of progress and to contrast their contribution to experiences and outcomes with more conventional measures like time to degree and degree completion. This is also instructive for both students and researchers seeking to understand more about the nuances of doctoral education. For the former, it reveals that indeed there are many targets of success to pursue and measure in addition to the conventional factors of course grades, degree completion, and time to degree. For students, rate of progress broken down into milestones, as we measured it, provides a way of monitoring progress in smaller increments. While we elected to examine the average rate of completion across eight milestones, we have defined each one and thereby opened the prospect of identifying the variety of attributes required for achieving each one. As expected, major field differences emerged; the surprise was the distinction of international students, who outpaced all the other categories of student.

CHAPTER THIRTEEN

Group-Specific Implications

THE GENERAL IMPLICATIONS of our findings are described in the preceding chapter, with some emphasis on field distinctions. In this chapter we try to tease out from the findings the experiences of students within specific groups. Here, we explore the differences among the race-ethnicity groups on central elements of the study (such as the single principal difference evidenced by international students—their rate of progress), the relatively few areas of difference between the sexes, and findings related to other student characteristics such as age, marital status, child rearing, household income, and parental background.

RACE DIFFERENCES
Admissions and Financial Assistance

Because of their lower Graduate Record Examination (GRE) scores, African Americans and Hispanics have different experiences in their doctoral programs from those of their white counterparts. In our sample, being African American or Hispanic was related to a greater likelihood of receiving a fellowship, despite these lower scores. While this may seem counterintuitive, given our finding (reported in chap. 12) that fellowships were usually associated with higher scores, this has been a common finding over the past three decades (Baird 1976; Malaney 1987). The distribution of financial support reflects market forces of both supply and demand, specifically, the need for diversity in graduate school enrollments and among researchers and faculty. Fellowships are awarded to two not necessarily discrete groups. On the one hand, the most qualified students of all races, defined largely on the basis of high GRE scores, received monetary awards with no strings attached, allowing universities to compete for the best students. On the other, the best qualified among the least represented students, generally African Americans and Hispanics, received fellowships, also allowing universities to compete to achieve greater diversity. Assistantships of both kinds (teaching and research) appear to be reserved for the most highly qualified doctoral students, again based on GRE scores—which, without special efforts, excludes many minorities from consideration. Stated in those terms, it is not difficult to imagine the agonies institutions and departmental committees endure as they attempt both to compete for the most promising students and to achieve racial diversity.

For African Americans and Hispanics at the doctoral level, assistantships might represent higher status and greater academic opportunities than fellowships. For African Americans, the lower prospect of attaining an assistantship has been observed since the late 1980s (Brazziel and Brazziel 1987; Nettles 1989). While fellowships are an important and necessary means of support, they may not ensure the research apprenticeship experience that is vital for careers as scholars and researchers. Our analyses indicate that for doctoral students in sciences and mathematics, in particular, being African American is a good predictor of not having a mentor. The quality of the mentor may be important, as well. African Americans' and Hispanics' scores, combined with the lower rates of having assistantships, may also be associated with a lack of opportunity to recruit the most productive faculty as mentors. From our perspective, productive faculty publish, teach, secure grant funding, and perform public service. This creates double jeopardy because the most productive faculty, we suspect, are also the most likely to engage in sponsored research, with assistantships to allocate. The same faculty are also likely to seek students with the highest admissions credentials (GRE scores and grade point averages), and the lower GRE scores of African American students may thereby place them at a disadvantage. Presently, there are two options for providing greater access to assistantships for African American students: either African American graduate students achieve higher GRE scores, in order to be selected by productive faculty for their research-intensive assistantships, or faculty give African American graduate students with lower scores an opportunity to demonstrate their talents.

Fellowships

We are emphasizing here the ways in which the different funding mechanisms influence the rest of a student's doctoral experience. Fellowship recipients in engineering and the humanities, for example, are less likely to run up education debt. So there may be clear benefits to having a fellowship. Fellowship recipients in every field except the humanities tended to have better social interactions with their peers than nonrecipients. Fellowship recipients both in engineering and in sciences and mathematics felt more positive about their academic interactions with their faculty. As well, fellowship awards in education, sciences and mathematics, and the social sciences were moderate predictors of research productivity. (The only caveat here is that both research and teaching assistantships, depending on the field, are also associated with the various research activities.) Fellowships make only a tiny contribution to sciences and mathematics students' rates of progress, and only in education are fellowship holders slightly more likely than others to complete their degrees. On the whole, then, while fellowships do enable minorities to participate in doctoral studies, this form of aid is by no means as far-reaching in its effects as either kind of assistantship.

Assistantships

An important factor in the low publication rates by African Americans in some fields is their lower rates of participation in research assistantships. Research assistants in all fields except the humanities (where teaching assistantships somewhat filled the same role) had a greater likelihood of presenting at conferences and publishing articles. Students in sciences and mathematics who were research assistants were more than 2.5 times more likely to publish articles or present papers (with corresponding advantages in other fields). With these data in view, we begin to recognize the disadvantages visited on African Americans, who are least likely overall to hold research assistantships. In the field of education, for example, 19 percent of African Americans received research assistantships, compared with 29 percent of whites and 37 percent of Asian Americans. In sciences and mathematics, only 38 percent of African Americans in sciences and mathematics were research assistants, compared with 72 percent of Asian Americans, 67 percent of Hispanics, 71 percent of whites, and 65 percent of international students. For all departments, increasing the number of African American research assistants is likely to yield a higher percentage of African American doctoral students who publish articles in refereed journals and present conference papers.

As we have seen, instead of these research assistantships, with their beneficial spin-offs, African Americans and Hispanics tend to be awarded fellowships, which separate them from both research obligations and opportunities. One result of these institutional and departmental policy decisions appears to be the widespread disparity in productivity just documented. Although clearly minority students should be actively seeking out research assistantships, this may be a suggestion ahead of its time. Faculty these days may fear accusations of political incorrectness in rejecting more diversity in their classrooms. At the same time, however, they may be far more anxious about working with underrepresented students, who may have relatively low GRE scores and low undergraduate grade point averages and who may have attended less prestigious undergraduate colleges. This may be especially the case when faculty with sponsored research projects and tight deadlines have students with higher GRE scores and grade point averages competing against minority students for research assistantships.

While graduate programs seek ways of spreading research and teaching assistantships to include more underrepresented minorities, they also need to review the effect of how minority fellowships have been delivered. Are they achieving the desired outcome for students in their institutions, and are they structured in such a fashion that they are defensible against attacks from both within and outside the academy? The actions of the leadership at the Horace H. Rackham Graduate School at the University of Michigan–Ann Arbor provide one example of broadening teaching and research opportunities. Over the past decade, a succession of progressive deans led a reinvention of its targeted awards to include opportunities for fellowship recipients to engage in the practice of teaching and research with faculty. Graduate schools are also faced with addressing pockets of resentment, fending off opponents of affirmative action who are not persuaded that the targeted fellowships are an appropriate vehicle for achieving diversity. Some might argue that the division between fellowship recipients and teaching and research assistants determines who interacts with whom, potentially alienating groups from one another into the future. For many doctoral students, their future professional colleagues are their graduate school classmates. This could be another structure among many that drive wedges between the nation's future scholars.

THE MENTORING CHALLENGE

Many scholars advocate the importance of mentoring for success in doctoral programs (Arce and Manning 1984; Bargar and Mayo-Chamberlain 1983; Blackwell 1987; Hartnett 1976). Our findings affirm the research about the importance of mentoring toward student social and academic interactions with faculty, research productivity, and degree completion. Although 70 percent of the doctoral students in our sample, overall, reported having a faculty mentor, more African American students (36%) than whites (29%) did not have access to a mentor. This is the result of the high rate of African American sciences and mathematics majors—43 percent—lacking mentors. In fact, sciences and mathematics may be the best illustration of the power of mentoring. Compared with their white colleagues, African Americans in the field of sciences and mathematics had lower perceptions of student-faculty social interactions, were less likely to publish articles, and were less likely to have overall research productivity. In no other field did we observe differences between African Americans and whites in having a mentor or in social and academic interactions with faculty. We conclude that mentoring was the difference, at least for African American students in sciences and mathematics.

Asian American and international students' experiences suggest that mentoring might have a different influence on students of diverse cultural backgrounds. Asian Americans in engineering, for example, did not report lower social and academic interactions, nor were they less productive, than their white counterparts, yet they were less likely to have mentors. The same is true for international students in engineering and education.

SOCIALIZATION

Among the strengths of this study is its reliance on student judgments made after completing the first year as doctoral students. While judgments about faculty quality normally involve issues such as publication, prestige of the university attended, faculty rank and tenure status, and faculty-sponsored research, here doctoral students are rating faculty on how well they interact on a regular basis as students progress through the apprenticeship process. In our view, doctoral student perceptions of their academic interactions with faculty—their teaching, availability, advising, and interest in students—are paramount. Just as faculty seek the respect of their academic disciplines and their peers, they should also value how their students view them.

The overall alarming differences by race relating to students' perceptions of their academic interactions with faculty in engineering appear to be corrected when such elements as GRE performance, mentoring, funding, and job expectations are addressed. The bad news is that engineering schools appear to be troubling places in need of improvement for the success of many of their African American students. The good news is that we have identified tangible elements such as mentoring, funding, and full-time enrollment as targets for engineering schools to focus on in attempting to correct the racial differences in experiences.

Bob Suzuki (1989) refers to Asian Americans as the "model minority." By this, Suzuki means that in their experiences and performance, Asian Americans largely mimic their white counterparts. Our data often corroborate Suzuki's notion, but not always. Academic interactions with faculty are one place where there appear to be some differences. In our study, Suzuki's theory holds firm in engineering, with Asian Americans tending to rate faculty relationships positively. By contrast, Asian Americans in education viewed their academic interactions with faculty less favorably. The remedies for African Americans in engineering do not appear to apply as well to Asian Americans in education. Schools and colleges of education need to search for explanations beyond those included in this study.

Effects on Productivity

Smith and Davidson (1992) have found that publishing an article was less common among African Americans than among other doctoral students. In general, we found that African Americans in engineering and humanities were not different from their white peers in publishing articles. We have concerns, however, with their publishing experience in education, sciences and mathematics, and the social sciences. Another sign of African Americans' struggle in sciences and mathematics is their lower rate of research article publication. Our regression analyses show that in sciences and mathematics African Americans were more than three times less likely than whites to publish. African Americans were also less likely to have published articles than whites in education and the social sciences. No other race-ethnicity group faced comparable challenges, although Hispanics in the social sciences were less likely to publish than whites. Hispanics were also handicapped in another area of research productivity. According to our analysis, Hispanics in sciences and mathematics were nearly three times less likely than white students to present papers at conferences. As our regressions indicate, other factors such as time in program contribute to publication and presentation productivity, but for many of the fields, mentoring is the key.

The research record of sciences and mathematics doctoral students is important in light of their immediate career expectations. In sciences and mathematics, a common career path is to hold a postdoctoral position before taking a faculty position. When we combine expectations to hold a faculty position and a postdoctoral position as one measure, African Americans are comparable with their U.S. citizen peers. When we disaggregate the two career pursuits, African Americans reported a lower expectation of becoming postdoctoral researchers compared with white doctoral students. The combination of lower publication rates and expectations of forgoing postdoctoral training should concern faculty and administrators. This suggests the need for sciences and mathematics faculty to accelerate the research productivity of African American students or address the higher expectation of entering faculty ranks without the additional training that is associated with postdoctoral fellowships.

Departmental structures, including workshops, tutorials, and editing sessions, could conceivably assist all students in their presentation and publication work. Support activities like the workshops need not become an additional faculty load but could be assigned to senior graduate students who have achieved some success in these areas. To teach is to learn again, and teaching activities of this sort could increase the number of producers and reinforce the strengths of those who are already producing.

The burden is not solely on the shoulders of students. Faculty may also need to expand the canons of scholarship. Pruitt and Isaac (1985) voice concern about the academic environment that minority students face and the unenthusiastic reception that scholarship related to minority issues receives from white faculty. Amado Padilla (1994) suggests that two potential obstacles to minority scholars' publishing may be the lack of interest by traditional professional journals in featuring topics devoted to ethnicity and race and the limited support or academic recognition of "ethnic" journals such as the *Journal of Black Psychology* and the *Hispanic Journal of Behavioral Sciences*. Doctoral students voiced their concern about the acceptance of their ethnic scholarship in interviews conducted by Ibarra (1996).

Effects on Student Satisfaction

In an era of customer service, when universities are concerned about satisfying their fee-paying "clients," doctoral students may be the least of their concerns. Nevertheless, pernicious hints of discomfort, even misery, among minorities should concern administrators and faculty. Our research provides some plausible clues to correcting much of the discomfort.

As we observe in chapter 9, African Americans, for example, were less satisfied in their doctoral programs than white students in engineering and sciences and mathematics. When their experiences and backgrounds are comparable, however, their lower satisfaction disappears. Until they achieve equity in background and experience, African American doctoral students will not reap the full benefits of their programs.

While better black representation in all fields has smoothed the way beyond the hardships endured by Edward Bouchet (the first black doctoral recipient) and W. E. B. DuBois, African American students continue to be unacknowledged pioneers in some areas of learning. In the economically critical areas of engineering and sciences and mathematics, African Americans in our sample total barely one hundred, a tiny representation among the more than twenty-seven hundred students in our sample who were studying in these two fields. The effect may be cyclical: not enough African American students are entering these fields to attract departmental attention to their mentoring and other support needs, and, as one result, recruiters of African American youth have fewer success stories with which to bolster their efforts.

It is also part of the popular rhetoric that doctoral students' satisfaction is among the lesser concerns of doctoral faculty. This element of student experiences may become more important as universities work to ensure their doctoral alumni are actively engaged and contributing to their alma maters. In turn, more positive doctoral experiences among the future generation of faculty will shape how they interact with their students down the line.

Effects on Degree Completion

The sample for this study was selected in 1996, and at that point more than half of the students had completed their preliminary examinations and were in the process of writing a dissertation. Six years later, in 2001, 62 percent of the sample had completed their doctoral degrees. Of the remaining 38 percent, it appears that many were minority students. African Americans were significantly less likely to complete their doctoral degrees compared with whites in engineering, sciences and mathematics, and the social sciences (see chap. 10). Like social interactions with faculty and satisfaction, background characteristics and experiences, when equal for African Americans and whites, tend to correct the difference in completion, with the exception of the field of engineering. This cannot be explained by the old bugbears, research productivity and mentoring, given that African Americans in engineering are not faltering. Hispanics had lower completion rates in engineering than whites. We remain concerned that in no field does the percentage of African Americans who successfully completed their doctoral degree approach 50 percent. Only in the humanities and social sciences did fewer than 50 percent of Hispanics complete their doctoral degrees.

When it comes to degree completion, we uncovered another racial difference. Asian Americans in engineering were less likely than their white peers to have mentors, but they felt more positive about their academic interactions with faculty. This is another of the few cases in which Asian Americans differed from their white counterparts.

INTERNATIONAL STUDENTS

The experience of the international students in our sample diverged from that of U.S. students in several ways: faster rate of progress, lower acquisition of debt, and lower peer interactions. Most international students were found in two fields: engineering and sciences and mathematics. This suggests an emphasis in their native countries on building scientific infrastructure and technology and perhaps indicates something about the U.S. cultural component of the three other fields in U.S. universities.

The principal difference between international students and their peers was their rate of progress, which may well have its roots in the visa requirements. Even in two of the slower fields for degree completion, education and the social sciences, international students were moving at a faster pace than their American peers in each of the other race-ethnicity groups. In speculating on some of the possible reasons for this speed, one must consider that their visa requirements for continuous enrollment, their interactions with faculty, and their financial circumstances played critical roles.

To obtain student visas, international students must verify adequate funding for the anticipated length of their doctorate programs. This can create pressure to complete in one of two ways. If this funding is institutionally guaranteed, students may expect it to be term limited or even variable. From our data, it appears that international students do very well with respect to departmental support. Collectively, 57 percent of noncitizens received teaching assistantships during the course of their doctoral programs, on a par with the leading groups—Asian Americans (59%) and whites (57%). As for research assistantships, noncitizens nearly tied with Asian Americans (61% vs. 62%) as the leading recipients. Only for fellowships were international students less often recipients, with 45 percent reporting this source of assistance, compared with 81 percent of Hispanics, the leading group.

The relative ease with which international students attain assistantships is most likely a reflection of their relatively high skill and preparation. When we adjusted for other factors, we found international students less likely to be recipients of teaching assistantships in education, engineering, and sciences and mathematics but more likely in the social sciences. When we adjusted for other factors, they were less likely to be awarded research assistantships in education, engineering, and the social sciences. Unlike U.S. nationals, international students may be far less likely to be able to borrow if their funding does not stretch to completion, thus possibly creating an extra incentive toward speeding up their studies. Finally, when international students and their families are faced with making up any deficiency in a currency likely weaker than the U.S. dollar, there may be another incentive toward swift completion. Reducing this drain on family resources could well prompt foreign students to push through their programs.

On peer interactions, our respondents tended to support the idea that international students pursued their doctoral studies with a sense of efficient timeliness. International students in engineering and sciences and in mathematics were less likely than their white peers to participate in extracurricular and even cocurricular activities, conceivably allowing for a greater focus on the dissertation tasks. We may be seeing a reflection of this among international sciences and mathematics students, who express lower overall satisfaction with their doctoral programs than white students. Language and culture differences are plausible reasons for the lower level of social interaction and satisfaction.

According to the National Science Foundation's *Science and Engineering Indicators* 2002 report (National Science Board 2002), which tracks trends in research spending, fewer foreign students are currently flowing into science and engineering programs in the United States (Southwick 2002). The number of foreign students earning Ph.D.s in science and engineering declined from 13,381 in 1996 to 11,368 in 1999, after a decade of steady growth. Given the high representation of international students in these fields, doctoral programs may notice some changes in the demographic makeup of their programs, which may have consequences for student experiences. First, international students have played a substantial role in the teaching and research assistantship functions. If their enrollments continue to decline as we have observed over the past ten years, then graduate schools will be faced with the need to compensate for the loss of graduate student labor. Second, the lower levels of social interaction and satisfaction among international students in some fields should not be dismissed as trivial. In the face of growing competition from European, Asian, and Australian doctoral programs, focusing on hospitable academic environments may become increasingly important for U.S. institutions if they wish to remain competitive. Finally, U.S. graduate schools should perhaps take a look at the funding arrangements of international students, particularly their lower likelihood of assuming debt, as a possible model for supporting more American doctoral students, especially to the extent that it contributes to full-time continuous enrollment. It would appear that economic incentives could be manipulated to encourage students toward speedier completion.

SEX DIFFERENCES

One surprising aspect of our findings involves the relatively few sex differences that emerged. The research literature on the experiences of women doctoral students is sparse. Therefore, we had limited precedent for the sex differences we examined. It appears on the surface that women have achieved sufficient critical mass in most fields to enable them to progress without handicap. Support for this opinion comes from women's own views of their doctoral performance. When we asked students to rate their performance, women doctoral students more often than men rated themselves in the top 10 percent of their class (48% for women vs. 43% for men).

Degree completion has been a popular subject of research on doctoral students. Researchers are not the only ones worried about degree completion. Many doctoral students are concerned with completing their degrees and also with completing in a timely fashion. While researchers (e.g., Zwick 1991) have found women to have lower completion rates than men, we found, with minor exceptions, women and men to be comparable on both rate of completion and timeliness of completion. For the completers, when all other things are the same, elapsed time to degree was comparable for women and men. Men's slight advantage in the social sciences disappeared when such things as martial status, age, GRE General Test scores, having a mentor, and always being full-time were equal.

Degree completion is not everything, and there are some small problem areas in other aspects of doctoral education where sex is the central divider. As Hartnett (1981) reminds us, it is important to examine women and men's experiences at the graduate level by discipline. By looking at the discipline level, we begin to locate pockets of difference across the graduate experience. Reviewing some of these differences will help point up the critical areas in which women may face obstacles and others where they have an advantage.

An area of concern for women is research productivity in engineering and in sciences and mathematics. Adjusting for several background and experience factors, men showed a significant advantage in paper presentations, publishing research articles, and, consequently, overall research productivity. The most consistent contributors to these productivity measures were having a mentor and being a research assistant during the course of one's studies. Our findings indicate that women are not deficient in either measure in these two fields: therefore we are not able with our data to explain the lower productivity of women. There is further evidence that funding mechanisms in these two fields are not prohibiting women from achieving productivity. Women in engineering and in sciences and mathematics did better than men in receiving fellowships, and fellowships were contributors to productivity. Women in engineering were more likely to land teaching assistantships, which contributed to productivity, but women in sciences and mathematics were less likely, which detracted from productivity. In our analysis, neither funding nor mentoring eliminated the male advantage; therefore, conventional indicators of departmental efforts to support women in their studies are not appropriate targets for improving research productivity.

The significance of women's lower productivity, however, is important enough that it deserves closer scrutiny, because productivity is a source of human capital development and ultimately contributes to upward mobility in these fields. One hint of a problem comes from a retrospective study by Clark and Corcoran (1986) in which women faculty recalled that during their graduate training, faculty had raised concern about their potential and about the unlikelihood that they, as women, would have careers that would include research productivity. Perhaps in the casual conversations of graduate students and faculty, we might trace the roots of male-female differences in this area of research productivity.

A second area of concern is the sex difference in interactions with peers and faculty. The women in our sample reported superior peer interactions in the humanities, sciences and mathematics, and the social sciences, whereas men appeared to have the advantage in education; there was no difference in engineering. In education, engineering, and the social sciences, men experienced higher levels of social interaction with faculty. This male advantage in education and engineering persisted in their academic interactions with faculty, where men rated their faculty more favorably than did women. This may correspond directly to the lower ratings women in these fields gave to their social interactions with faculty and may be connected with the predominance of male faculty, at least in engineering and possibly in some schools of education, reminding us that not all fields have achieved a balance of sexes in their faculty mix. These findings are reminiscent of the conclusions drawn by earlier researchers (Bargar and Mayo-Chamberlain 1983; Feldman 1974; Hite 1985; Holmstrom and Holmstrom 1974; Kaplan 1982; Sandler 1991), who find that women were disadvantaged in their relationships with faculty. Another indication of this imbalance is that men in all fields reported having a greater opportunity to have a same-sex adviser. This was particularly striking in engineering and in sciences and mathematics. Yolanda Moses (1989), bell hooks (2000), and Sarah Nieves-Squires (1991) call attention to the added challenge that African American and Hispanic women face in navigating the student-faculty graduate school terrain, a challenge that we do not account for in these analyses.

Overall, the finding that men rated student-faculty social interactions higher than women is the most troubling observation, because it implies the continuing existence of the "old boys club" and possible sex discrimination. Even women's reported higher levels of social contact with their peers may fall short of the advantages their male colleagues possess in their interactions with faculty, especially in engineering and education. After all, in all fields except the social sciences, women are as likely as men to plan to hold faculty or postdoctoral positions upon completing their doctoral degrees; and student aspirations to faculty or postdoctoral fellow positions are a stable predictor of student-faculty academic interaction in every field.

The growth of representation of women among graduate students (58%) and doctoral degree recipients (44%) shows a semblance of parity. Beyond mere numerical balance, the question still lingers whether academic women can have it all—marriage, children, and professional life (Lynch 2002). Although we have not answered this practical question, we have seen that women students in education and the humanities appeared less often to be married, and women in sciences and mathematics, more often. Women in education, engineering, and sciences and mathematics less often had children under the age of eighteen. Pushing beyond the numbers, the more important issue may be related to the problem of role congruence that is normally associated with women. The question is whether the progress of women is hampered by their spousal-partner or parent role compared with their male counterparts. This question is beyond the scope of our present analyses but is one that we plan to address in subsequent analyses.

Older Students

The adage that the would-be scholar should "be a monk and start early" may have taken root in financial aid offices. Certainly, based on previous research (Baird 1976; Malaney 1987; Wilder and Baydar 1991), our finding that older students were less likely to receive fellowships, research assistantships, and teaching assistantships during the course of their studies did not surprise us. This situation held true for all fields.

While older students' social participation with faculty or peers varied depending on the field of study, higher age proved a good predictor of rate of progress. In the current study, for the fields of education, engineering, the humanities, and sciences and mathematics, when we adjusted for other factors, older students progressed at a faster pace. Only in engineering were older students less likely to complete their degrees, and only in education was age a weak predictor of taking less time to complete the degree. The comparable or shorter time to degree for older students is counter to findings by Tuckman, Coyle, and Bae (1990) that the age of doctoral students was the most stable predictor, contributing to a longer time to degree in all fields examined.

One might ask whether institutions and departments are unreasonably cutting themselves off from the benefits of these older students' previous experience in ignoring them as recipients of the various forms of financial support. It appears that neither party is benefiting to the extent possible. The older students are still finishing their degrees in reasonable times and at reasonable rates, but they are not being given opportunities to contribute to their departments at the frequency of their younger peers; consequently, the potential impact on department research production and sociability may be understated.

MARRIED AND PARTNERED STUDENTS

Given that students in doctoral and first professional programs are the most mature of all students in our educational system, it is not surprising that many are married or in domestic partnerships and even have children. The marital commitment can be expected to affect student experiences (Baird 1990a; Feldman 1973; Girves and Wemmerus 1988; Hawley 1993). Overall, nearly 54 percent of the sample were married or in domestic partnerships. More education students than those in any other field reported being married or having partners. This had a few implications for the students' other experiences, depending on their field of study. For example, married and partnered engineering students were nearly twice as likely to receive research assistantships, and married and partnered education students were somewhat more likely to receive teaching assistantships. Marriage or a domestic partnership was also a reasonably strong predictor of higher education debt for students in engineering and in sciences and mathematics. On our measures of peer interactions and social and academic interactions with the faculty in the department, married and partnered students in the social sciences were less positive about these interactions. Yet they reported no difference in their perceptions of their academic interactions with their faculty advisers.

With one exception, marital status did not contribute to predicting student research productivity. One could say that this is a contemporary perspective on Feldman's (1973) finding that married men were the most productive, making more presentations and publishing more articles. Married status appears to contribute to degree completion and the timeliness of completion. Married students were less likely to stop out than their unmarried counterparts. Similarly, in education, engineering, and sciences and mathematics, being married or in a partnership proved to be a good predictor (twice as likely in engineering) of completing one's degree. Married and partnered students also had a shorter elapsed time to degree compared with their single peers in engineering, the humanities, and sciences and mathematics.

CHILDREN IN THE HOUSEHOLD

Having children under the age of eighteen is the enemy of speedy time to degree. The good news is that by and large doctoral students with children in the household had experiences similar to those of their peers without children. They report similar social interactions with peers and similar social and academic interactions with faculty, as well as similar levels of research productivity. Perhaps not surprisingly, students with children were more likely to stop out of their programs. Our findings that among students with children under eighteen, those in engineering, the humanities, and the social sciences who completed their degrees took longer to do so corroborates the findings of other researchers (Abedi and Benkin 1987; Nerad and Cerny 1993; Tuckman, Coyle, and Bae 1990; Wilson 1965). We found only two instances where funding might contribute to a prolonged time to degree. Engineering doctoral students with children under eighteen were two times less likely than their peers to be awarded research assistantships and were more than twice as likely to be carrying education debt.

We caution doctoral students, graduate faculty, and administrators to be careful consumers of the findings of a lack of difference between students with children and those without. Our analyses do not shed light on how students with children navigate the demands of a doctoral program while raising a family or how having children may differentially influence the doctoral experience for women and men. Simply allowing more time for students with children to complete their degrees may not suffice. For example, our conversations with doctoral students revealed the need for affordable, convenient child care.

STUDENT HOUSEHOLD INCOME

Because doctoral students are further removed from their parents than are undergraduate students, their own household incomes become an important measure of their class status. In our sample, the higher the household income was, the higher students' perceptions of their social as well as academic interactions with faculty in education and the humanities. In engineering, higher household income contributed to higher ratings of students' interactions with their faculty advisers. Students with higher household incomes were more likely, however, to stop out of their doctoral programs. In engineering and in sciences and mathematics, doctoral students with higher household incomes showed slower rates of progress and, for those who earned their degrees, a longer time to degree completion.

PARENTAL SOCIOECONOMIC STATUS

Parental education and occupation does not weigh heavily on students' doctoral experiences. One might suppose that students from more comfortable family circumstances may be able to draw on family resources for financial support. This may, in fact, be true, given that in all fields but education, doctoral students from higher socioeconomic (SES) backgrounds accumulated less education debt than their peers. Moreover, parental SES emerged as a moderate predictor of students' rates of progress in both education and the social sciences, and it proved to be a moderate predictor of a shorter time to degree for engineering and social sciences students.

Here again, we can only speculate, but it is a reasonable conjecture that students from higher SES families may supplement their graduate school fellowships or assistantships with family financial support.

Aside from the financial aspects, parental SES and social capital contributed to student interactions with peers and faculty. Parental SES plays a varied role in students' experiences. For example, engineering students from higher SES backgrounds were more likely to report positive social interactions with their peers, as well as more positive academic interactions with faculty in their department and their academic adviser, than their less privileged peers. In sciences and mathematics, students from higher SES backgrounds reported more positively on their interactions with their faculty advisers. In engineering, sciences and mathematics, and the social sciences, students from higher SES families were more likely than their peers to find that all-important mentor.

We suspect, but obviously cannot prove without corresponding qualitative evidence, that the aforementioned outcomes reflect family exchanges of various sorts. Aspiring doctoral students from more affluent backgrounds may be given parental assistance in the application and financial aid processes; they may have been coached from birth about appropriate interactions with their "superiors" and peers; they may have had influential role models and relationships before the Ph.D. process; and the higher SES of their parents may provide for a level of ongoing financial and emotional support as they proceed through their programs. While it is only a hypothesis, most doctoral students can identify the persons in their program who made it all look easy because of who they were and the affluent circumstances from which they came.

CONCLUSION

The catalogue of challenges to institution and departmental policy makers is extensive, as the foregoing sections demonstrate. Yet these are challenges that doctoral programs will be compelled to address as students demand more equity. The questions raised by the growing diversity within the student body include the following: What will be the result of African Americans' and Hispanics' achieving greater access to research and teaching assistantships? How will women become increasingly integrated into both the social and academic interactions within their departments? What changes will ensue as international students are encouraged to contribute more broadly to the academic community? What will cause administrators to recognize and respond to the growing trend to second and even third careers and treat older students more even-handedly? How will institutions make ongoing provisions for family life among their doctoral students? All of these directions promise rewards to both institutions and students in measures of satisfaction, fulfillment of aspirations, and enhanced reputation and prestige.

CHAPTER FOURTEEN

The Doctoral Student Experience

New Answers and New Questions

WE BEGAN THIS RESEARCH seeking to understand how students experience doctoral education. As we prepare to lay down our survey for the time being, we have acquired a rich understanding of the variety of backgrounds, experiences, and performance of doctoral students and improvements that are needed. The two questions with which we conclude this work are variants of the two that we raised at the beginning. Then we asked, What do we need to understand, and how might we improve the experience of doctoral students? Now we articulate both our understanding of the experience and the process toward improvement.

THE NEW UNDERSTANDINGS

The major challenge for doctoral faculty arises from the diversity of the students. While doctoral students share many common characteristics, they differ in their origins, their interactions, and their aspirations from students of a half century ago. The worst fear of earlier educational historians (James 1971; Veysey 1978)—doctorates for the masses—seem to have been realized, with the growing interest of all sectors of the population in earning this terminal degree. As we have seen, however, doctoral students' purposes for this degree differ markedly from those of students sixty years ago—a fact that may be reshaping the degree itself.

When most participants in William James's time were aiming at academic or parallel research careers, faculty had an easier time matching students to the mold. Today's students, by way of contrast, pursue very individual paths. They may be more or less interested in teaching, in research, or in accumulating publications as students, depending on their long-term goals. On the other hand, students looking to roles in government, business, and industry, where publications and conference presentations may not be so highly valued, may well be forging ahead without attention to traditional academic pursuits. Students also expect faculty, and particularly their advisers, to bring to the table a worldly outlook, not a strictly academic one, in terms of job prospects and disciplinary hot topics. As a result, students appear to be calling on faculty advisers and mentors to adapt themselves, and ultimately the doctoral degree, to their multiple interests. In fact, we may be witnessing the transformation of the degree from its traditional role as the ultimate certificate of focused learning to a more modish credential signifying particular abilities. None of this can be making it easy for faculty to respond to all their students' needs, both expressed and unexpressed. Yet it may be that nothing is more vital to degree completion than students' relationship with the faculty.

Our focus on research productivity outcomes of various kinds implies a bias in that direction as opposed to the advantages that can be gained by doctoral students who develop their teaching skills. We know how teaching and research assistantships relate to research productivity; but we did not assess the association and, therefore, do not know how teaching and research assistantships relate to doctoral students' becoming effective teachers. Since just slightly less than a majority indicated an interest in pursuing faculty careers, we still have much to learn about the training and rewards associated with teaching assistantships, such as how to develop an effective syllabus; the value of various approaches to developing, rehearsing, and delivering lectures; the reinforcement of one's own knowledge, accomplished by making it accessible to undergraduates; and the excitement of gaining new adherents to one's chosen discipline. Longitudinal studies are also needed to measure the relationship of doctoral students' teaching apprenticeships to the quality of teaching among faculty. Just as research productivity enhances the attractiveness of newly minted doctorates in the research and professorial marketplace, teaching experience among recent doctoral recipients must also have market value.

If there is a moral to be drawn from our earlier parable about the rabbit, fox, wolf, and lion, it is simply that the doctoral student must find her or his own "lion." Herein lies the mystery, the way that mentoring bridges the gap between students' personal and professional identities. There are a number of aspects of mentoring that we believe deserve further investigation. First, we need to know much more about how these relationships are established. Rabbits and lions, after all, are not natural allies. How much of the relationship derives from altruism on the part of the professor, and how much depends on the student's early demonstration of skills or other intellectual qualities? We need to understand the communications processes that render these arrangements functional. While we have seen the critical role that mentoring plays in doctoral student progress, we need to know how goal setting occurs. What time commitments are required by both parties to make the mentoring arrangement viable and productive?

Knowing how mentors in various fields go about expanding the horizons of their protégés would be illuminating for all prospective doctoral students but especially for the 30 percent whom our survey identified as prospects for failing to secure such relationships. What combination of professional contacts, resources, and similar factors do they provide or suggest that would help students along their way? We have noted the tendency for a dissertation period slump, which some students survive and some do not. What sorts of interventions do mentors make that spur their students forward, and how far do these interventions extend into the personal realm? We would like to examine the nature of these mentoring relationships—in particular, to measure the extent of mentor leadership and guidance or full-blown collaboration. Finally, to secure the importance of these arrangements in all departments, institutions need to know the benefits to their organizations of successful mentoring. Our data demonstrate that mentored students are more successful. The payoffs to the institution are not hard to imagine.

Our research has not addressed the anxiety students may experience when thinking about how to pay for graduate school or how valuable a partial award from a university may be toward achieving various outcomes. We have no cost-benefit ratio to contribute to the student financing discussion. What we do know is that having funding is better than not, that the type of funding has consequences, and that the type of award is related most often to students' demographic characteristics. We do not know the various approaches students take to secure their finances or the criteria universities use in awarding funding.

As well, our findings about financial support mechanisms suggest other ways to measure both adequacy and outcomes beyond what we accomplished, ways that could contribute much more to understanding the quality of student experiences. For example, while we measured the amount of money students received, we did not know the length of time they received these amounts or the patterns and combinations of awards at various stages of their program. It could be valuable toward improving doctoral student experiences to learn whether starting with a fellowship and then moving on to a research or teaching assistantship is more helpful than an early assistantship followed by fellowships and how each of these combinations contributes to optimizing student success. It would also be useful to know whether the combination of teaching and research assistantships develops a more complete and productive individual than only one of these support mechanisms.

For the past five decades scholars have been interested in the speed and efficiency with which doctoral students complete their degrees. Doctoral programs may be the most loosely structured and individually tailored of all higher education degrees. While departments publish curriculums and requirements for qualifying examinations and dissertations, students are often encouraged to pursue their individual interests, no matter how narrow or esoteric. Consequently, time to degree and rate of progress are not determined solely by course completion in the discipline but rather are associated with a combination of courses and academic work that students choose to undertake. The question remains whether students need better guidance on where their pursuits may lead and how long this may take; even some experienced faculty may be unable to provide a proximate estimate. While we have noted that students grow increasingly disgruntled in the latter stages of their programs, we cannot say how much of this disaffection can be attributed to self-designed dissertation topics that have proved unwieldy and complex. Mark this up as one more area in which faculty should provide both cautions and examples of ill-fated ventures.

Other concerns about the time factor abound. Faculty should be concerned that the average dissertation is taking well over four years; precisely how much longer than four years depends on field of study. Why is it taking students so long to write their dissertations? Are they unsure of the topic when they complete their course work and preliminary examinations? Are they having difficulty interacting with faculty over the focus and approach to writing their dissertations? Are they experiencing difficulty recruiting and convening the dissertation committee? Are they choosing topics that require multiple years of investigation? Are they running out of funding? These issues were not of interest to us at the outset of this research. But given that over the six years of our study 62 percent of our sample completed their degrees, a deeper examination than we were able to accommodate in this study is warranted.

The vignettes of doctoral student life that accompany some of our survey responses bring a different kind of understanding. While we elected to use one type of investigation for our survey, we recognize that student interviews might be a good complement to the survey responses. How might case studies that include faculty and administrator perspectives, as well as those of students, contribute to even greater understanding of doctoral student experiences? Among the compelling questions are the following:

—What are the individual experiences of the women and African Americans in engineering, and how does being in such an extreme minority affect them?

—How do the one-third of students without mentors feel about their connection to their fields and their progress through doctoral programs?

—How can students achieve more research productivity in the face of curriculum demands?

—How can doctoral programs be structured so that students gain both the teaching and research preparation necessary for today's faculty and other career requirements?

Several years ago, Donald Kennedy (1997, vii) described universities as "societies without rule." "They nevertheless perform rather well," he continued, "but much of what goes on behind the walls is deeply mysterious to those outside." One can extend Kennedy's imagery of cabalistic procedures to the doctoral process, which sometimes seems mysterious even to those most intimately involved. Some students, like our following respondent, seem to resent the arcane nature of the process: "Like many naïfs before me, I thought education, even higher education, was about intellectual questioning. Instead I found its heart of darkness—it is about obeying the rules to advance through a (meaningless) hierarchy so ye can judge others as ye have been judged."

This book has been about laying bare that "heart of darkness," exposing the experiences of current doctoral students to the light in hopes of smoothing and speeding their passage. Golde and Dore (2001) and Lovitts (2001) have identified lack of information as a critical factor for people who are progressing through the doctoral programs. For institutions, this information deficit has major consequences for doctoral student retention and ultimate completion of the degree.

As one student wrote plaintively, "Part of the lack of help I felt . . . has to do with my being an 'older' student—older than what? I ask. There seemed to be an assumption that I knew what I was doing and what was going on. In some ways I did, but the professional mysteries were, inevitably, that. Each profession has its folkways. Since I got jobs for myself and was competent in many ways, some social, I was assumed to know that which I didn't. I asked, but some don't." As this student reflects, some students learn to use these channels better than others, and indeed age does not appear to make the channels more accessible. While this may be assumed to be part of the socialization process, doctoral study was not intended to approximate a scavenger hunt, with students piecing together the process. At the moment, questions about curriculum requirements, dissertation parameters, and qualifying examinations are left to the faculty to decide. Institutions and departments need work, lots of work, on their communication strategies. As for doctoral students themselves, unless they are able to examine the nature, process, and issues of the doctoral enterprise, they will continue to be enablers of their own dependencies.

THE IMPROVEMENT PROCESS

The process for improvement involves both macro- and micro-level restructuring of doctoral education in U.S. universities and rethinking policies and practices pertaining to admissions, curriculum expectations, and types of student support. At the macro level for the large producers of doctoral degrees, the process of improvement includes increasing the emphasis on student research productivity as an expectation in doctoral education that is equal in importance to degree completion and time to degree. Presently, research productivity is not universal and appears to happen as much by chance as by design.

Another macro-level improvement would require institutions to determine a relationship between admissions criteria—like the Graduate Record Examination (GRE)—and doctoral program outcomes. The GRE appears to be universally applied in the admissions process, yet its usefulness in predicting other outcomes—such as research productivity, rate of progress, and time to degree—is highly variable. Does the GRE serve its entire purpose in the screening process, or should we not expect such a universally applied standard to provide a forecast of student productivity, relationships with faculty, rate of progress, and degree completion? Because GRE scores have a strong influence on admissions decisions, and in some cases financial support decisions, it is imperative that institutional leaders refine their expectations and application of the GRE in decision making. Considering the resources students invest in preparing for and taking the GRE, and those institutions invest in reviewing student GRE test performance, it would be economical to try to maximize the test's usefulness beyond its primary purpose.

A third macro-level issue for graduate education leaders requires a broad agreement on what constitutes an appropriate time frame for completion of the latter stages of the degree process. While the course requirements are reasonably well articulated by most graduate programs and are more similar than different across institutions, the process of completing dissertations is inconsistent across institutions and across disciplines and is ambiguous in its standards. In some cases, only doctoral faculty and actual degree recipients have comprehended it successfully. Such standards as we are suggesting do not require that specific parameters be spelled out, such as the number of months in which to write a dissertation proposal, to collect or analyze data, or to write the dissertation draft. Rather, we envision a series of benchmarks to which both students and advisers are expected to adhere. The result would be a more attentive process with general guidelines. Meanwhile, increased oversight of student progress might lead to higher completion rates as well as a reduction in time to degree.

At the micro level, the improvements center on human interaction—namely, the interaction between faculty and students. Our survey of students underscores the importance students place on their experiences with faculty. Whether they are reporting on mentoring, research productivity, program satisfaction, or degree completion, the common element is human interaction. Students with mentors are more productive and successful than those without. Therefore, an indicator of the quality of the doctoral program should include the degree to which students have mentors. Of our overall sample, 70 percent indicated having a mentor. Faculty should be acknowledged for their roles as mentors to the same extent as for their scholarship, teaching, and service. At a micro level, academic departments also have to identify strategies and mechanisms that ensure the mentoring relationships are productive in establishing students in their chosen fields.

Doctoral programs are notorious for awarding fellowships to attract highly prized students for merit or diversity, or both, as they compete with comparable programs in other universities. We have worked with students who have all types of funding, ranging from one-year fellowships through five-year fellowships that see their recipients through the entire process. The quality of their experiences vary, and the consequences of this practice are mixed. Some students who receive fellowships that lack terms of engagement in either research or teaching are isolated from the professional development activities that constitute social and cultural capital acquisition. Others use this funding opportunity to construct their individual experiences with faculty who share their intellectual interests. There may be no optimum pattern; rather, the effectiveness of fellowships may lie in their timing. Fellowships may be most important at the early stage, to help students begin and adjust to the process of doctoral education, and during the latter stages of dissertation completion. During the middle of the process, the active engagement with faculty on research and teaching assignments that is generally achieved through assistantships has no substitute as a vehicle for preparing students for their postdoctoral careers.

The other micro-level improvement that is needed relates specifically to the level of satisfaction that doctoral students experience during the latter stages of their doctoral programs. As we have seen, the longer students are enrolled in their program, the less enamored they are of their faculty and the less satisfied with their program overall. We know that faculty devote a great deal of attention to students during the course work and qualifying examinations, but it seems these attentions fade the longer students persist in their programs. Each department has to conduct self-examinations to discover ways to improve the level of satisfaction and involvement of doctoral students during the dissertation process. While this appears to be applicable in the broad scheme, it can be addressed only one department at a time. And only after such self-examination on the part of departments can we determine any contribution that improved satisfaction makes to degree completion, time to degree, and success in one's chosen career.

CONCLUSION

In the past century and a half, doctoral education has established itself as a permanent and essential part of the American educational landscape. Despite its growth, it continues to remain small and elite; therefore, it is not often a central focus of higher education, and its importance is often overlooked. We would argue that doctoral programs should be one of the first places that one turns for answers to problems in education. For example, in looking for the causes of the severe underrepresentation of African Americans, Hispanics, and Native Americans in the nation's university faculty and in scientific professions or women faculty in science, technology, engineering, or mathematics fields, the first place to look should be doctoral programs. Similarly, in searching for explanations for low rates of university faculty research productivity, the first place to look should be the quality of their preparation and experiences in doctoral programs.

Periodically examining the doctoral process, as James (1971), Berelson (1960), and Bowen and Rudenstine (1992) have done in the past, will contribute to its development and refinement. Doctoral programs are highly productive centers of education that are populated with many of the nation's, and indeed the world's, most talented people. The doctoral education process, however, is multidimensional and complex. Students and faculty should devote more attention, just as we have, to enhancing the doctoral student experience. Both parties should consider the role of funding and more active mutual engagement both academically and socially, while making sure that such engagement contributes to advancing students toward such valued outcomes as scholarship production and degree completion. The major field, we have learned, affects each of these areas, and depending on the major field, people of both sexes and diverse races experience doctoral programs differently. This study represents student perspectives about their experiences. We are grateful to the more than nine thousand students who provided the content of our knowledge about their lives as they experience doctoral education. Despite the diversity of the participants' experiences, their aims and pursuits are common. They all seek to earn the three magic letters: Ph.D.

WHEN I WALKED INTO MICHAEL NETTLES'S office in the spring of 1995, I could not have imagined the academic journey that lay ahead of me or the time it would take to see our work into publication. At that time, five years to the degree was a daunting proposition. Equally daunting was my gamble that a faculty member whom I barely knew would solve my immediate funding problem and also help me work through an academic research topic that is important to me: the experience of doctoral students. My gamble produced a multitude of wins for me. First and foremost, I earned my Ph.D. in a timely four and a half years. Along the way, I made an unexpected decision. I chose not to use the data that Michael and I were collecting for this study in writing my doctoral dissertation. Instead, I examined the influence of undergraduate debt on doctoral degree aspirants' decisions to apply to and enroll in graduate or first professional school immediately after earning their bachelor's degrees. I analyzed the Baccalaureate and Beyond database from the National Center for Education Statistics. This choice has served me well. I have a research issue that is my own, as well as one that I share with Michael.

Gaining a mentor was my second big win. As our data show, having a mentor can make a world of difference in a doctoral student's life. As my mentor, Michael exemplifies good academic habits, promotes me in professional pursuits, pushes me to spread my wings in new directions, and supports me when my progress is slow or difficult.

Having a solid research experience while earning my doctoral degree was the third win. A series of different organizations funded my research assistantships, and I never had a funding dry spell. The research assistantships benefited me in the ways our data show: I gave conference papers and published while a doctoral student. I rate highly the quality of my interactions with faculty in my program. I was given the opportunity to be a daily presence in my academic department and to have regular non-classroom contact with my peers. After finishing course work, I started a Women's Research Group. I invited the women of my cohort to meet on a regular basis to talk about the research each of us was conducting. It was a regular opportunity to vet new ideas, questions for qualifying examinations, dissertation hypotheses and questions, and conference papers. I benefited from a strong community of graduate student peers.

At the University of Michigan, I found an entrepreneurial faculty for whom support and collaboration with doctoral students was more the norm than the exception. This is not incidental: the university, through the Horace H. Rackham Graduate School, has a long history of supporting doctoral students and faculty. And while Rackham gives, we have learned that it also listens to its students and alumni. This typifies the graduate community. We have experienced this firsthand through the Council of Graduate Schools' annual conferences, where we have had standing-room-only audiences of graduate school deans as we were thinking aloud about our findings and absorbing insights from deans and graduate faculty from our institutions and others. The lessons we have taken from our research have established a friendly and interested audience that we are confident will now provide leadership in the areas of research productivity, rate of progress, and student satisfaction. The challenge ahead will be to connect with yet another important audience for this research: current and prospective doctoral students. It is their experiences that we are interested in continuously improving.

—Catherine M. Millett

CRITERIA AND BROAD MAJOR FIELDS
USED IN THIS STUDY

Table A.1
Criteria Used to Select Institutions to Participate in the Study

Institution	Geographic Location[a]	Carnegie Classification	Ranking by Degrees Conferred[b]	Ranking by Fund Revenue[b]	Minority Ph.D.s Conferred, 1989–1993[c]				
					Asians	Hispanics	Blacks	Native Americans	Total
City University of New York Graduate Center	Mid-Atlantic	Doctoral I	42	101	n.a.	57	n.a.	n.a.	57
Clark Atlanta University	South Atlantic	Doctoral I			n.a.	n.a.	156	n.a.	156
Columbia University	Mid-Atlantic	Research I	4	14	n.a.	n.a.	n.a.	n.a.	n.a.
Harvard University	New England	Research I	13	17	79	63	52	n.a.	194
Howard University	South Atlantic	Research I		24	n.a.	n.a.	164	n.a.	164
Indiana University	East North Central	Research I	24	94	n.a.	n.a.	n.a.	10	10
New York University	Mid-Atlantic	Research I	20	43	n.a.	68	n.a.	n.a.	68
Ohio State University	East North Central	Research I	6	35	n.a.	n.a.	108	n.a.	108
Princeton University	Mid-Atlantic	Research I	46	27	n.a.	n.a.	n.a.	n.a.	n.a.
Rutgers University	Mid-Atlantic	Research I	25	69	n.a.	n.a.	n.a.	n.a.	n.a.
Stanford University	Pacific	Research I	9	5	151	54	n.a.	10	215
Teachers College[b]	Mid-Atlantic	Research I	4	14	n.a.	47	130	n.a.	177
Temple University	Mid-Atlantic	Research I	39		n.a.	n.a.	79	n.a.	79
University of California–Berkeley	Pacific	Research I	1	26	201	97	57	10	365
University of California–Los Angeles	Pacific	Research I	10	13	185	103	n.a.	8	96
University of Maryland–College Park	South Atlantic	Research I	16	56	50	n.a.	121	n.a.	171
University of Michigan	East North Central	Research I	5	9	63	66	77	n.a.	206
University of North Carolina–Chapel Hill	South Atlantic	Research I	32	31	n.a.	n.a.	69	9	78
University of Texas–Austin	West South Central	Research I	7	32	48	112	53	8	221
University of Wisconsin–Madison	East North Central	Research I	2	11	n.a.	58	n.a.	10	68
Vanderbilt University	East South Central	Research I	49	45	n.a.	n.a.	n.a.	n.a.	n.a.

Source: For ranking of doctoral degrees conferred by 60 large institutions from 1982–83 to 1991–92, and for ranking of current fund revenues received from the federal government by the 120 institutions of higher education receiving the largest amounts, see NCES (1994). For ranking of producers of minority Ph.D.s from 1989 to 1993, see NRC (1995).
[a]Geographical regions are New England, Mid-Atlantic, South Atlantic, East North Central, East South Central, West North Central, West South Central, Mountain, and Pacific.
[b]Columbia University main division and Teachers College are combined in this column.
[c]Institutions marked n.a. are not among the leading producers of minority Ph.D.s for these racial-ethnic groups, though they may have awarded Ph.D.s to minorities.

Table A.2
Ranking of Institutions in the Study, by Field, 1995

Institution	Biological Sciences	Economics	Education	Engineering	English	History	Mathematics	Physics	Political Science	Psychology	Sociology
City University of New York Graduate Center					24	25					
Clark Atlanta University											
Columbia University and Teachers College[a]	20	12	4	23	11	7	8	10	17	24	13
Harvard University	2	1	1	22	3	7	1	2	1	6	6
Howard University											
Indiana University			13		16	17			17	13	10
New York University		25	40				13				
Ohio State University			9		18			23	17	24	25
Princeton University	9	1	n.a.[b]		19	7	1	1	2	6	9	15
Rutgers University			49		38	17	21	16	23		
Stanford University	1	1	2	4	3	4	5	2	3	1	8
Temple University			33								
University of California–Berkeley	2	6	3	2	1	3	1	2	3	2	3
University of California–Los Angeles	20	12	10	16	13	7	8	15	9	6	6
University of Maryland–College Park		23	21	25			22	13			
University of Michigan	16	10	22	8	13	6	8	13	2	2	3
University of North Carolina–Chapel Hill	24		32		17	13			16	13	5
University of Texas–Austin			27	8	17	18	19	12	22	16	13
University of Wisconsin–Madison	9	12	5	12	17	10	13	15	9	9	1
Vanderbilt University			6								

Source: America's Best Graduate Schools (1995).
[a]Columbia University and Teachers College are combined in this table.
[b]Education is not offered at Princeton University.

SOCIAL AND ACADEMIC OUTCOMES
OF DOCTORAL STUDENTS IN THE
BIOLOGICAL AND PHYSICAL SCIENCES

At the 2002 "Coming Up a Winner: Students and the Ph.D. Gamble" invitational conference at the University of Michigan–Ann Arbor, several attendees expressed concern over the inclusion of students in the biological and physical sciences in the same broad analytic category (sciences and mathematics). They questioned whether the backgrounds and experiences of the students were similar enough to justify grouping them together in a single major field. In response to their concerns, we performed several analyses to investigate the validity of our decision to combine them into our broad category of sciences and mathematics. We examined several dichotomous and continuous outcomes.

The six continuous outcomes in these analyses include interactions with advisers, peer relations, student-faculty social interactions, academic interactions with faculty, overall satisfaction with doctoral program, and time to degree. The means of each these outcomes do not differ between the biological and physical sciences ($p < .05$), although differences in time to degree were marginally significant ($p = .06$). As such, in terms of these outcomes, the experiences of doctoral students in these two fields do not differ. It is important to stress that considerable variation exists within the biological and the physical sciences, not just between them.

Despite the lack of overall difference between the biological and physical sciences in the continuous outcomes, the relationship between sex and these outcomes could differ between fields, as could the relationship between race and these continuous outcomes. For example, women could be at a disadvantage on a particular outcome in the biological but not in the physical sciences. Using two-way analysis of variance, we explored this possibility. We found that the relationship between sex and these outcomes and between race and these outcomes is the same in both the biological and the physical sciences. Although women and minority doctoral students may have different experiences from males and nonminority students, these experiences are unrelated to field of study.

The analytic results with the dichotomous outcomes are less clear. We explored four dichotomous outcomes: incurred education debt as a doctoral student, presented a paper at a national conference, published a journal article, and had some research productivity. Unlike the continuous outcomes, differences do exist between the biological and the physical sciences on certain of the dichotomous outcomes. Doctoral students in the physical sciences were more likely than students in the biological sciences to have presented a paper, to have published an article, and to have some research productivity. A potential explanation is the different number of males and females in each field; half of biological sciences doctoral students in the sample are female, while almost three-quarters of physical sciences students are male. Perhaps the differences in these aspects of research productivity derive not from the field distribution by sex but from the disproportionate number of males in the physical sciences. This is, however, not the case. Even after controlling for sex (through logistic regression), students in the physical sciences were still more likely to have presented a paper, to have published an article, and to have some research productivity.

Again, in contrast with the continuous outcomes, the relationship between sex and several dichotomous outcomes differs. For example, 8.1 percent more males than females in the biological sciences published an article, whereas 6.5 percent more males than females did so in the physical sciences. In terms of publishing chapters in edited volumes, there were no differences by sex in the physical sciences, but more than twice as many men in the biological sciences published a chapter in an edited book. In substantive terms, however, this difference is misleading, in that only fifteen females and thirty-one males published a chapter. Indeed, the proportions are quite different (more than double), but they mask the fact that few students actually accomplish publication of a chapter in an edited book. In terms of overall productivity, there were no differences by sex in the biological sciences, whereas slightly more males (62.5%) than females (55.0%) had some research productivity in the physical sciences. In sum, the relationship between sex and individual outcomes does appear to differ slightly in certain aspects of research productivity between the biological and physical sciences. These differences, however, are marginally significant and substantively immaterial.

The situation is quite similar with differences by race-ethnicity within the biological and physical sciences. In general, white and Asian students were more likely to have research productivity, and this advantage is constant between the biological and physical sciences. For example, although students in one field may be more likely to have some form of productivity, racial differences are maintained, as all groups show an increase in similar proportions. As with sex, however, the relationship between race and these productivity outcomes differs slightly in some isolated instances. For example, Asian students in the physical sciences (14.2%) were almost twice as likely as Asian students in the biological sciences (7.4%) to have incurred educational debt during doctoral study. Hispanic students in the physical sciences (66.0%) were more likely to have some research productivity than Hispanics in the biological sciences (50.0%).

SURVEY OF DOCTORAL STUDENT FINANCES, EXPERIENCES, AND ACHIEVEMENTS

SURVEY OF DOCTORAL STUDENT FINANCES,

EXPERIENCES, AND ACHIEVEMENTS

CONDUCTED BY

MICHAEL T. NETTLES

AND

CATHERINE M. MILLETT

THE CENTER FOR THE STUDY OF HIGHER AND POSTSECONDARY EDUCATION

UNIVERSITY OF MICHIGAN

Thank you for participating in this research on doctoral students. You are one of a carefully selected sample of doctoral students from twenty leading universities and eleven disciplines who were chosen to participate in the research. Your participation is critical for the success of this study, and to inform policy makers about ways to improve support of graduate education.

Michael Nettles and Catherine Millett are researchers at the Center for the Study of Higher and Postsecondary Education at the University of Michigan and are collaborating with the leaders of your graduate school to conduct this research. The main purpose of this study is to learn more about the financing and other experiences of today's doctoral students so that public policy makers and university leaders will have contemporary information to use in their efforts to improve funding and other aspects of graduate education.

This Survey of Doctoral Student Finances, Experiences, and Achievements asks you to respond to questions about *your* progress, performance and experiences in your current doctoral program. We estimate that the survey will take around 30 minutes to complete. The survey contains 88 questions, many of which have several parts. Your responses will be combined with those of other participants and will be reported as group averages. Your individual responses will be kept confidential, identified only by number, and never connected with your name in any report. No student will be individually identified in any of the analyses or reports.

Our funding is not sufficient to compensate everyone. But, as a token of our appreciation for your participation in the study, we will enter your name into a random selection for the following cash payments as soon as we receive your completed survey

- a $500 cash payment,
- a $400 cash payment,
- a $300 cash payment, and
- ten $100 cash payments.

We anticipate that the random selection will be held around May 1997. In addition, we will produce a report of our findings and make the report available to your institution. Thank you very much for your cooperation.

INSTRUCTIONS FOR COMPLETING THE SURVEY OF DOCTORAL STUDENT FINANCES, EXPERIENCES, AND ACHIEVEMENTS

Most of the questions in the survey ask you to either check a response or write a number in a space provided. Please do not circle the response itself. If a question asks you to fill in information, please write the information in the space provided.

In some cases, your answer to a particular question will determine whether you continue on to the next question or skip a question or several questions. You will know the appropriate questions to skip by the directions to the right of your response to the question.

The survey has the following seven parts:

A). Your application and enrollment process   E). Your future plans
B). Your current doctoral program experience   F). Your undergraduate experiences
C). Your attendance patterns   G). Your background
D). Financing your doctoral education

Mailing instructions for returning the completed survey are on page 28.

GLOSSARY

Academic Year - the period of the regular session, generally extending from September to June, usually equated to two semesters or trimesters, three quarters, or the period covered by a 4-1-4 plan, but not including the summer.

Administrative Assistantship - monies (tuition/fees and/or a stipend) given to students with the expectation of administrative services to be rendered.

Faculty or Research Advisor - a person assigned by your department/program to act in an official capacity in such ways as discussing and approving your coursework, or signing registration forms.

Full-time/Part-time Attendance - universities have different definitions of full-time students. For example, at the University of Michigan, students enrolled for 6 or more semester credits, or students who are actively involved in thesis or dissertation preparation are considered full-time. For this survey, we would like you to use your own university's definitions of full-time and part-time attendance.

Grants/Scholarships/Fellowships - monies and/or tuition/fee waivers given to students with no expectation of repayment or of services to be rendered.

Mentor - a faculty member to whom you turn for advice, to review a paper, or for general support and encouragement. This person may or may not be your faculty advisor. If you have more than one mentor, please comment on the mentor with whom you work most closely.

Research Assistantship - monies (tuition/fees and/or a stipend) given to students with the expectation of research services to be rendered.

Teaching Assistantship - monies (tuition/fees and/or a stipend) given to students with the expectation of teaching services to be rendered.

Tuition/Fee Waiver - monies given only for tuition/fees to students with no expectation of repayment or of services to be rendered.

University Loans - monies given to students with the expectation that the amount will be repaid, usually with some interest, to the university.

A. YOUR APPLICATION AND ENROLLMENT PROCESS

This section is concerned with your process of applying to your doctoral program.

A-1. At what point in your formal educational experience did you first decide you wanted to earn a doctoral degree? (Check one response.)

_____ 1. Elementary school

_____ 2. High school

_____ 3. Undergraduate college

_____ 4. Immediately after completing college

_____ 5. After completing college and while working

_____ 6. During master's program

_____ 7. After completing master's degree and while working

A-2. About how old were you when you decided you wanted to earn a doctoral degree? _____

A-3. Do you have a master's degree? (Check one response.)

_____ 1. Yes

_____ 2. No   (If 'NO,' **GO TO** A-8)

A-4. In what year did you receive your master's degree? If you have more than one master's degree, please indicate the year you received each one.

1. First master's degree   19 _____

2. Second master's degree   19 _____

A-5. Did you earn a master's degree at the same institution where you are earning your doctoral degree? (Check one response.)

_____ 1. Yes, my only master's degree   (If 'YES,' **GO TO** A-7)

_____ 2. Yes, one of my master's degrees

_____ 3. No

A-6. Write the name and the city and state of the institution (s) where you received your Master's degree(s).

1. First Master's degree: _____

2. Second Master's degree: _____

A-7. Did you have a Master's degree when you applied to your current doctoral program? (Check one response.)

_____ 1. Yes

_____ 2. No

A-8. When you first enrolled in your current graduate program, what was the highest degree you planned to pursue? (Check one response and indicate your major field of study.)

_____ 1. Doctorate degree, field of study _____

_____ 2. Master's degree, field of study _____

_____ 3. Master's as first step to doctorate, field of study _____
_____

A-9. How many years elapsed between the time that you completed your baccalaureate degree and officially entered graduate school to work on each of the following graduate degrees? (Check one response for each degree.)

From Completion of Baccalaureate Degree	To Beginning of First Master's Program	To Beginning of Second Master's Program	To Beginning of Doctoral Program
Less than one year	____ 1	____ 1	____ 1
1 - 4 years	____ 2	____ 2	____ 2
5 - 9 years	____ 3	____ 3	____ 3
10 - 14 years	____ 4	____ 4	____ 4
15 - 19 years	____ 5	____ 5	____ 5
20 - 24 years	____ 6	____ 6	____ 6
25 years or more	____ 7	____ 7	____ 7
Not applicable	____ 8	____ 8	____ 8

A-10. Please rank order the three most important reasons you took time off between completing your baccalaureate (B.A. or B.S.) degree and entering your doctoral program, with "1" being the most important and "3" being the least important of the three reasons.

If you did not take time off between completing your baccalaureate degree and entering your doctoral program (please do not include summers)   GO TO A-11

____ 1. Needed a break from school.

____ 2. Wanted to gain work experience.

____ 3. Didn't know that I was going to pursue my doctoral degree.

____ 4. Spouse was enrolled in school.

____ 5. Started a family.

____ 6. Wanted to save money to enter graduate school.

____ 7. Wanted to reduce the outstanding balance on my undergraduate loans.

____ 8. Other _____

A-11. Please rank order the three most important reasons you decided to apply to a doctoral program, with "1" being the most important and "3" being the least important of the three reasons.

____ 1. I needed a doctorate to advance in my field of study.

____ 2. I needed a doctorate for an entry-level position in my field of study.

____ 3. I wanted to change my field of study.

____ 4. I could not find a job, so I decided to go back to school.

____ 5. A faculty member recommended that I pursue my doctorate.

____ 6. I wanted to increase my knowledge in my field of study.

____ 7. I wanted to pursue personal interests.

____ 8. I wanted to earn more money, and expect my earnings will increase with a doctorate.

____ 9. Other (specify)   _____

A-12. Please indicate your scores within the following score ranges on each of the three general test sections of the Graduate Record Examination (GRE). (Check one response per column.)

GRE Score Ranges	Verbal Score	Quantitative Score	Analytical Score
Less than 400	____ 1	____ 1	____ 1
401 - 450	____ 2	____ 2	____ 2
451-500	____ 3	____ 3	____ 3
501-550	____ 4	____ 4	____ 4
551-600	____ 5	____ 5	____ 5
601-650	____ 6	____ 6	____ 6
651-700	____ 7	____ 7	____ 7
701-750	____ 8	____ 8	____ 8
751-800	____ 9	____ 9	____ 9
Did not take the GRE	____ 10	____ 10	____ 10

A-13. At the time that you applied to doctoral programs, what choice was the institution where you are currently enrolled? (Check one response.)

____ 1. Only choice
____ 2. First choice of several institutions
____ 3. Second choice of several institutions
____ 4. Third choice of several institutions
____ 5. Not one of my top three choices

A-14. Please rank order the three most important reasons you chose your current doctoral department/program, with "1" being the most important and "3" being the least important of the three reasons.

____ 1. Quality of the program or department
____ 2. Prestige of the institution
____ 3. I needed/wanted to study with a particular professor at this institution
____ 4. Financial support offered
____ 5. Recommendations of faculty from my undergraduate institution
____ 6. Recommendations of faculty from my master's institution
____ 7. It was the only program that accepted me
____ 8. Recommendations of family
____ 9. Recommendations of friends
____ 10. Location
____ 11. I could attend part-time
____ 12. I received tuition/fees assistance
____ 13. Other (specify) _____

241

A-15. Did the institution where you decided to enroll offer you financial support at the time you were first admitted?

    ____ 1. Yes

    ____ 2. No   (If 'NO,' **GO TO** A-18)

A-16. At the time that you first enrolled in your doctoral program, what type of financial support were you offered and for which years were you offered support? (Check all that apply.)

Type of Financial Support	First Year	Second Year	Third year	Fourth year	Fifth year
1. Fellowship	____ 1	____ 1	____ 1	____ 1	____ 1
2. Research Assistantship	____ 2	____ 2	____ 2	____ 2	____ 2
3. Teaching Assistantship	____ 3	____ 3	____ 3	____ 3	____ 3
4. Administrative Assistantship	____ 4	____ 4	____ 4	____ 4	____ 4
5. Tuition/Fees Waiver	____ 5	____ 5	____ 5	____ 5	____ 5
6. Loans	____ 6	____ 6	____ 6	____ 6	____ 6

A-17. Was the offer of financial support that you received in writing at the time of admission to your current doctoral program the same as the financial support that you actually received when you enrolled?

    ____ 1. Yes

    ____ 2. No

A-18. Did you win a competitive fellowship for your doctoral studies that allowed you to take your fellowship to any institution that accepted you and that you chose to attend?

    ____ 1. Yes, (Name of fellowship) _____

    ____ 2. No

A-19. When you first enrolled in your current doctoral program were you enrolled full-time?

    ____ 1. Yes

    ____ 2. No

B. YOUR CURRENT DOCTORAL PROGRAM EXPERIENCE

This section of the survey is about your experiences in your current doctoral program. Questions B-1 through B-15 are about your attitudes and behaviors related to various aspects of your current doctoral program.

B-1. Which of the following letter grades or grade point equivalents best describe your cumulative grade point average <u>during your doctoral study?</u> (Check one response.)

____	A or A+ (4.0)	____	C+ (2.75 to 2.99)
____	A- (3.75 to 3.99)	____	C (2.50 to 2.74)
____	B+ (3.50 to 3.74)	____	C- (2.25 to 2.49)
____	B (3.25 to 3.49)	____	D+ or less (less than 2.25)
____	B- (3.00 to 3.24)	____	Did not receive grades

B-2.   Compared with other students in your program, how would you rate your academic performance? (Check one response.)

_____   1.   I am in the top 10 percent

_____   2.   I am in the top 25 percent

_____   3.   I am in the middle (around 50 percent)

_____   4.   I am in the bottom 25 percent

B-3.   Check the one response on each line below that best reflects your agreement or disagreement with each of the following statements. (Check one response on each line)

	Strongly Disagree	Disagree	Neither Agree nor Disagree	Agree	Strongly Agree
1. At least one faculty member in my program has had a strong impact on my intellectual development.	____ 1	____ 2	____ 3	____ 4	____ 5
2. It has been easy for me to meet and make friends with other students in my program.	____ 1	____ 2	____ 3	____ 4	____ 5
3. I am confident that I made the right decision in choosing to pursue my doctoral degree.	____ 1	____ 2	____ 3	____ 4	____ 5
4. I am confident that I made the right decision in choosing this doctoral program.	____ 1	____ 2	____ 3	____ 4	____ 5
5. It is easy to develop personal relationships with faculty members in this program.	____ 1	____ 2	____ 3	____ 4	____ 5
6. There is a great deal of contact between professors and students in my program outside the classroom.	____ 1	____ 2	____ 3	____ 4	____ 5
7. I am satisfied with the level and types of student organizations and committees in my program.	____ 1	____ 2	____ 3	____ 4	____ 5
8. There is a strong sense of community, a feeling of shared interest and purpose in this program.	____ 1	____ 2	____ 3	____ 4	____ 5
9. Overall, I am satisfied with the doctoral program in which I am currently enrolled.	____ 1	____ 2	____ 3	____ 4	____ 5

B-4.   Indicate your level of satisfaction with each of the following by checking the appropriate response on each line. (Check one response on each line)

	Very Dissatisfied	Dissatisfied	Neither Satisfied nor Dissatisfied	Satisfied	Very Satisfied
1. Quality of faculty instruction	___ 1	___ 2	___ 3	___ 4	___ 5
2. Fairness of my program in providing financial support	___ 1	___ 2	___ 3	___ 4	___ 5
3. Fairness by professors in my program in grading	___ 1	___ 2	___ 3	___ 4	___ 5
4. Collegial atmosphere between the faculty and students	___ 1	___ 2	___ 3	___ 4	___ 5
5. Communication between faculty and students	___ 1	___ 2	___ 3	___ 4	___ 5
6. Availability of the faculty to meet with students	___ 1	___ 2	___ 3	___ 4	___ 5
7. Quality of overall faculty-student relations	___ 1	___ 2	___ 3	___ 4	___ 5
8. Quality of academic advising provided by faculty	___ 1	___ 2	___ 3	___ 4	___ 5
9. Quality of feedback on scholarly projects or academic progress	___ 1	___ 2	___ 3	___ 4	___ 5
10. Quality of professional advising and job placement	___ 1	___ 2	___ 3	___ 4	___ 5
11. Class scheduling	___ 1	___ 2	___ 3	___ 4	___ 5
12. Faculty interest in my research	___ 1	___ 2	___ 3	___ 4	___ 5

B-5.   How would you describe the work space that your graduate department provides for you? This includes research assistantship or teaching assistantship space, or space allocated for other reasons. (Check one response)

_____   1.   I have no work space in my department.

_____   2.   I have a cubicle.

_____   3.   I have a desk.

_____   4.   I have my own office.

_____   5.   I share an office with one person.

_____   6.   I share an office with two people.

_____   7.   I share an office with three or more people.

244

Survey: Doctoral Student Finances, Experiences, Achievements

B-6. A faculty or research advisor is a person assigned by your department/program to act in an official capacity in such ways as discussing and approving your coursework, or signing registration forms. Please note that your faculty or research advisor may not be your mentor. Do you have a faculty member who serves as your advisor?

   _____ 1. Yes

   _____ 2. No   (If 'NO,' **GO TO** B-9)

B-7. Please check one response on each line regarding <u>your faculty or research advisor.</u>

	Yes	No
1. Is your faculty/research advisor the same sex as you?	___ 1	___ 2
2. Is your faculty/research advisor the same race as you?	___ 1	___ 2

B-8. Below is a list of statements that might describe your <u>faculty/research advisor</u> at the current time. Check the one response on each line that best characterizes your view of your advisor.

My faculty /research advisor	Strongly Disagree	Disagree	Neither Agree nor Disagree	Agree	Strongly Agree
1. Is accessible for consultation	___ 1	___ 2	___ 3	___ 4	___ 5
2. Offers useful criticisms of my work	___ 1	___ 2	___ 3	___ 4	___ 5
3. Has concern for my professional development	___ 1	___ 2	___ 3	___ 4	___ 5
4. Is interested in my personal welfare	___ 1	___ 2	___ 3	___ 4	___ 5

B-9. Many doctoral students have someone on the faculty to whom they turn for advice, to review a paper, or for general support and encouragement. This person may be thought of as a mentor. If you have more than one mentor, please comment on the one with whom you work most closely. Do you have a faculty member who serves as your <u>mentor</u>?

   _____ 1. Yes

   _____ 2. No   (If 'NO,' **GO TO** B-13)

B-10. Is your mentor the same person as your faculty advisor?

   _____ 1. Yes   (If 'YES,' **GO TO** B-12)

   _____ 2. No

B-11. Please check one response on each line regarding <u>your mentor.</u>

	Yes	No
1. Is your mentor the same sex as you?	___ 1	___ 2
2. Is your mentor the same race as you?	___ 1	___ 2

B-12. How long did it take you to locate <u>your mentor</u>? (Please check one response.)

   _____ 1. I located a mentor within a month of entering the program.

   _____ 2. I located a mentor within the first term of my doctoral study.

   _____ 3. I located a mentor within the first year of my doctoral study.

   _____ 4. I located a mentor within the first two years of my doctoral study.

   _____ 5. It took me longer than two years to locate someone to serve as a mentor.

B-13.　Please indicate the approximate number of hours per week you are currently spending engaged in each of the following activities.

1. Reading and preparing for classes in your doctoral program　　___hours per week

2. Conducting research and writing papers for classes　　___hours per week

3. Conducting research in your field outside of regular classwork　　___hours per week

4. Writing a dissertation　　___hours per week

5. Writing grant proposals　　___hours per week

6. Teaching classes (including teaching, grading papers, preparing courses, advising students)　　___hours per week

7. Working at a job related to your academic program (this includes research and administrative assistantships)　　___hours per week

8. Working at a job not related to your academic program　　___hours per week

9. Other (specify) _____　　___hours per week

B-14.　Approximately how many times have you done the following activities since enrolling in your doctoral program? (Check one response on each line.)

Activities	Zero	One	Two	Three	Four	Five or More
1. Participated in an independent study	___ 0	___ 1	___ 2	___ 3	___ 4	___ 5
2. Served as a teaching assistant for a class	___ 0	___ 1	___ 2	___ 3	___ 4	___ 5
3. Taught a class	___ 0	___ 1	___ 2	___ 3	___ 4	___ 5
4. Attended professional or scholarly meetings	___ 0	___ 1	___ 2	___ 3	___ 4	___ 5
5. Presented at a poster session	___ 0	___ 1	___ 2	___ 3	___ 4	___ 5
6. Presented a research paper at a national conference	___ 0	___ 1	___ 2	___ 3	___ 4	___ 5
7. Submitted a research article for publication	___ 0	___ 1	___ 2	___ 3	___ 4	___ 5
8. Published a research article in a refereed professional or trade journal	___ 0	___ 1	___ 2	___ 3	___ 4	___ 5
9. Published a research article in a non-refereed professional or trade journal	___ 0	___ 1	___ 2	___ 3	___ 4	___ 5
10. Published reviews of books, articles, or creative works	___ 0	___ 1	___ 2	___ 3	___ 4	___ 5
11. Published chapters in edited volumes	___ 0	___ 1	___ 2	___ 3	___ 4	___ 5
12. Published a textbook	___ 0	___ 1	___ 2	___ 3	___ 4	___ 5

B-14. (continued) Approximately how many times have you done the following activities since enrolling in your doctoral program? (Check one response on each line.)

Activities	Zero	One	Two	Three	Four	Five or More
13. Published other books	____ 0	____ 1	____ 2	____ 3	____ 4	____ 5
14. Published a monograph	____ 0	____ 1	____ 2	____ 3	____ 4	____ 5
15. Applied for patents or copyrights	____ 0	____ 1	____ 2	____ 3	____ 4	____ 5
16. Sold computer software that you developed	____ 0	____ 1	____ 2	____ 3	____ 4	____ 5
17. Received an award or honor	____ 0	____ 1	____ 2	____ 3	____ 4	____ 5
18. Received an internal research grant on your own	____ 0	____ 1	____ 2	____ 3	____ 4	____ 5
19 Worked with a faculty member on a research or consulting project separate from a class project	____ 0	____ 1	____ 2	____ 3	____ 4	____ 5
20. Applied for an external research grant with a faculty member	____ 0	____ 1	____ 2	____ 3	____ 4	____ 5
21. Received an external research grant with a faculty member	____ 0	____ 1	____ 2	____ 3	____ 4	____ 5
22. Other marks of professional recognition (specify)	____ 0	____ 1	____ 2	____ 3	____ 4	____ 5

_____

B-15. How often have you done each of the following? (Check one response on each line.)

Activity	Never	Seldom	Sometimes	Often	Very Often
1. Participated in an informal study group with other graduate students	____ 1	____ 2	____ 3	____ 4	____ 5
2. Participated in school or program sponsored social activities with other graduate students	____ 1	____ 2	____ 3	____ 4	____ 5
3. Discussed academic issues outside the classroom with faculty members	____ 1	____ 2	____ 3	____ 4	____ 5
4. Received some type of feedback about your academic progress (in addition to grades in courses) from faculty	____ 1	____ 2	____ 3	____ 4	____ 5
5. Socialized with graduate students of different racial/ethnic backgrounds	____ 1	____ 2	____ 3	____ 4	____ 5

B-15. (continued) How often have you done each of the following? (Check one response on each line.)

Activity	Never	Seldom	Sometimes	Often	Very Often
6. Socialized informally with a faculty member.	____ 1	____ 2	____ 3	____ 4	____ 5
7. Discussed your career plans and ambitions with a faculty member.	____ 1	____ 2	____ 3	____ 4	____ 5
8. Discussed personal problems or concerns with a faculty member.	____ 1	____ 2	____ 3	____ 4	____ 5
9. Socialized informally with other graduate students.	____ 1	____ 2	____ 3	____ 4	____ 5
10. Participated in some campus activity (e.g., chorus, clubs).	____ 1	____ 2	____ 3	____ 4	____ 5

C. YOUR ATTENDANCE PATTERNS

This section pertains to your attendance patterns in your current doctoral program.

C-1. When did you first enroll in this doctoral program? (Check one response for the term and then fill in the year.)

_____ 1. Fall   19 _____   _____ 3. Spring   19 _____

_____ 2. Winter   19 _____   _____ 4. Summer 19 _____

C-2. Are you currently pursuing your doctoral degree full-time? Please use your institution's definition of full-time attendance and include, if applicable, involvement in thesis or dissertation preparation that is considered full-time by your institution. (Check one response.)

_____   1.   Yes

_____   2.   No

C-3. Which of the following best describes your current status in your doctoral program? (Check one response only.)

_____   1.   Completed less than half of courses required for a doctoral degree

_____   2.   Completed more than half, but not all of courses required for a doctoral degree

_____   3.   Completed all course work required for a doctoral degree

_____   4.   Completed preliminary/general examinations but not yet admitted to doctoral candidacy

_____   5.   Admitted to doctoral candidacy but not yet working on dissertation

_____   6.   Working on dissertation

_____   7.   Completed all requirements for a doctoral degree, but doctoral degree has not yet been awarded

_____   8.   Doctoral degree has been awarded

C-4.   When do you expect to complete your doctoral degree?
(Check one response and fill in the year.)

	Term	Year	Year
_____	1. Fall	19 ___	20 ___
_____	2. Winter	19 ___	20 ___
_____	3. Spring	19 ___	20 ___
_____	4. Summer	19 ___	20 ___

C-5.   Have you ever pursued your degree on a part-time basis while in your present doctoral program? (Include the present term but do not count summers.) (Check one response.)

    _____   1.   Yes

    _____   2.   No   (If 'NO,' **GO TO** C-7)

C-6.   Why did you/are you pursuing your doctoral degree on a part-time basis? (Check all that apply.)

    ____   1.   Financial reasons

    ____   2.   Family needs

    ____   3.   Health reasons

    ____   4.   Worked at a job

    ____   5.   Traveled

    ____   6.   Got married

    ____   7.   Started a family

    ____   8.   Academic difficulties

    ____   9.   Lack of academic fit with my program

    ____   10.   Lack of social fit with my program

    ____   11.   Other reasons (specify) _____

C-7.   Have you ever stopped out of school for a semester or quarter since you first started this doctoral program? (Do not count summers and exclude nonregistration for dissertation research purposes.) (Check one response.)

    _____   1.   Yes

    _____   2.   No   (If 'NO,' **GO TO** D-1)

C-8.   At what point during your doctoral program have you interrupted your program for at least a semester or quarter? If you have interrupted your program more than once, please check all that apply.

    _____   1.   After the first semester or quarter

    _____   2.   After the first academic year but before completing coursework

    _____   3.   At the end of my course work but prior to completing my written qualifying exam

    _____   4.   At the end of my course work but prior to completing my oral qualifying exam

    _____   5.   After completing my qualifying exam

C-9.   Why did you stay out of school for a semester or quarter? If more than once, please check the reasons for the first time and the most recent time that you interrupted your program for a semester or quarter. (Check all that apply.)

Reasons	First Time	Most Recent Time
Lack of social fit with my program	____ 1	____ 1
Financial reasons	____ 2	____ 2
Family needs	____ 3	____ 3
Health reasons	____ 4	____ 4
Worked at a job	____ 5	____ 5
Changed occupational priorities	____ 6	____ 6
Traveled	____ 7	____ 7
Got married	____ 8	____ 8
Started a family	____ 9	____ 9
Academic difficulties	____ 10	____ 10
Lack of academic fit with my program	____ 11	____ 11
Other reasons (specify)	____ 12	____ 12

C-10. For how long did you stay out of your doctoral program before reentering? Do not count summers. Please refer to the first time if you have interrupted your program more than once. (Fill in the number on the appropriate line.)

____   semesters

____   quarters

D.   FINANCING YOUR DOCTORAL EDUCATION

This section of the survey asks about how you finance your doctoral program.

D-1.   Which of the following best describes your overall student/work status since you entered your doctoral program? Note: assistantships, fellowships, and summer employment are not defined as employment in this question. (Check one response.)

____   1.   Full-time student with no employment

____   2.   Full-time student with full or part-time employment

____   3.   Part-time student with no employment

____   4.   Part-time student with full or part-time employment

____   5.   Alternating periods of any of the above

(please write the numbers) _____

Survey: Doctoral Student Finances, Experiences, Achievements

D-2. Please indicate each of the following sources of support that you received this year, previous years, summers, or never. (You may check more than one response per column, if appropriate.)

Doctoral Program Sources of Support	This Academic Year	Previous Academic Year (s)	Summer(s)	Never
1. Fellowships/grants/scholarships	____ 1	____ 1	____ 1	____ 1
2. Research assistantship	____ 2	____ 2	____ 2	____ 2
3. Teaching assistantship	____ 3	____ 3	____ 3	____ 3
4. Administrative assistantship	____ 4	____ 4	____ 4	____ 4
5. Residence hall or program assistantship	____ 5	____ 5	____ 5	____ 5
6. Travel grant	____ 6	____ 6	____ 6	____ 6
7. Dissertation grant	____ 7	____ 7	____ 7	____ 7
8. University research grant	____ 8	____ 8	____ 8	____ 8
9. Research grant from a private foundation	____ 9	____ 9	____ 9	____ 9
10. Loans (federal or university sponsored)	____ 10	____ 10	____ 10	____ 10
11. Tuition/fee waiver only	____ 11	____ 11	____ 11	____ 11
12. Employer Tuition Assistance Plan	____ 12	____ 12	____ 12	____ 12
13. Other (specify) _____	____ 13	____ 13	____ 13	____ 13

D-3. Have you received fellowships/grants/scholarships or research assistantships from any of the nonuniversity sources?

Nonuniversity Source of Support	This Academic Year	Previous Academic Year (s)	Summers	Never
1. Nationally competitive fellowships (e.g. from such foundations as Ford, Mellon, Rockefeller, Spencer)	____ 1	____ 1	____ 1	____ 1
2. Federal support (e.g. NIH Traineeship or Fellowship, NSF Fellowship, Patricia Roberts Harris Fellowship, USDA Fellowship, Fulbright, FLAS, Javitts Fellowship)[1]	____ 2	____ 2	____ 2	____ 2
3. Federal research assistantships (e.g. NIH, NSF, USDA, Department of Education)	____ 3	____ 3	____ 3	____ 3

D-4. Have you received financial assistance of any type (fellowship, assistantship, tuition/fee waiver, etc.) targeted for the following groups? (Check all that apply)

____   1.   Members of your race or ethnic group
____   2.   Members of your sex
____   3.   Members your age group
____   4.   I have not received funding based on my membership in a group
____   5.   Uncertain if I have received targeted funding

---

[1] Abbreviations: NIH, National Institute of Health; NSF, National Science Foundation; USDA, U.S. Department of Agriculture; FLAS, Foreign Language Area Studies Fellowship.

D-5. Indicate the approximate proportion of your tuition and fees for academic year 1996-97 that is provided by each of the following sources. (Check one response on each line).

Source of Support	None	Less than 50%	About 50%	More than 50% but not all	All
1. Personal sources (self, parents, relatives, friends, spouse's/partner's income)	___ 1	___ 2	___ 3	___ 4	___ 5
2. Assistantship (research, teaching, or administrative)	___ 1	___ 2	___ 3	___ 4	___ 5
3. Grant or fellowships	___ 1	___ 2	___ 3	___ 4	___ 5
4. Other employment related to your doctoral study	___ 1	___ 2	___ 3	___ 4	___ 5
5. Other employment not related to your doctoral study	___ 1	___ 2	___ 3	___ 4	___ 5
6. Loans	___ 1	___ 2	___ 3	___ 4	___ 5
7. Employer's Tuition Assistance Plan	___ 1	___ 2	___ 3	___ 4	___ 5
8. Other (please specify)_____	___ 1	___ 2	___ 3	___ 4	___ 5

D-6. Approximately how much financial support are you receiving for tuition and fees for 1996-97 from each of the following sources? (In estimating the dollar amount, please round to the nearest $100.)

Source of Support	Dollar Amount (round to nearest $100)
1. Personal sources (self, parents, relatives, friends, spouse's/partner's income)	$_____
2. Assistantship (research, teaching or administrative)	$_____
3. Grant or fellowship	$_____
4. Other employment related to your doctoral study	$_____
5. Other employment not related to your doctoral study	$_____
6. Loans	$_____
7. Employer's Tuition Assistance Plan	$_____
8. Other (please specify)_____	$_____

D-7. If you received a grant or fellowship please indicate the source of funding:

_____ 1. Did not receive grants or fellowships

_____ 2. My own university

_____ 3. External funders (please specify) _____

_____ 4. Uncertain of funding source

D-8.   In 1996-97, which of the following benefits do you receive from your university as part of your financial support? (Check all that apply)

    ____   1.   Do not receive benefits

    ____   2.   Health insurance or health care

    ____   3.   Dental insurance or dental care

    ____   4.   Life insurance

    ____   5.   Wellness program

    ____   6.   Child care

    ____   7.   Graduate student housing

    ____   8.   Meals

    ____   9.   Pension fund

    ____   10.   Professional development funds for students to present papers at conferences

    ____   11.   Other (specify) _____

D-9.   Estimate the annual cost of your school related expenses for the current year (September 1, 1996 - August 31, 1997) for yourself and your spouse/partner, if you have one who is a student.

	Your Own (Round to nearest $100)	Your Spouse's/Partner's (Round to nearest $100)
1. Tuition and fees	$_____	$_____
2. Books	$_____	$_____
3. Dissertation expenses	$_____	$_____
4. Other education expenses	$_____	$_____

D-10.   Estimate the annual living expenses (excluding school-related expenses that you provided in D-9) for the current year that you and/or your spouse/partner incur for (1) your immediate family and (2) your extended family.

Living expenses include room and board if living on campus, or rent or mortgage and food, if you live off-campus. In addition, living expenses include such expenses as insurance, utilities, dependent care, personal expenses, repayment of loans, transportation, and any other living expenses.

1. Immediate family/individual living expenses $_____
(include spouse/partner and family)

2. Extended family living expenses (e.g., parents) $_____

D-11.   How many children do you have whose educational expenses you are paying?

    ____   1.   No children   (If 'NO CHILDREN,' **GO TO** D-13)

    ____   2.   One child

    ____   3.   Two children

    ____   4.   Three children

    ____   5.   Four children or more children

D-12. What is the total amount of your children's educational expenses (tuition, books, supplies, and uniforms) that you will pay this current year (September 1, 1996 to August 31, 1997)? (Check one response in each column)

Educational Expenses	Daycare	Elementary School	High School	College
Not applicable	____ 1	____ 1	____ 1	____ 1
Up to $4,999	____ 2	____ 2	____ 2	____ 2
$5,000 - $9,999	____ 3	____ 3	____ 3	____ 3
$10,000 - $14,999	____ 4	____ 4	____ 4	____ 4
$15,000 - $19,999	____ 5	____ 5	____ 5	____ 5
$20,000 - $24,999	____ 6	____ 6	____ 6	____ 6
$25,000 - $29,999	____ 7	____ 7	____ 7	____ 7
$30,000 - $34,999	____ 8	____ 8	____ 8	____ 8
$35,000 - $39,999	____ 9	____ 9	____ 9	____ 9
$40,000 - $44,999	____ 10	____ 10	____ 10	____ 10
$45,000 - $49,999	____ 11	____ 11	____ 11	____ 11
$50,000 or more	____ 12	____ 12	____ 12	____ 12

D-13. In 1996-97, do you pay for eldercare for your parents and/or your spouse/partner's parents? (Check one response.)

____ 1. Yes, please specify the annual cost $_____

____ 2. No

D-14. In 1996-97, does the financial support that you receive from your university cover all your graduate school costs and living expenses? (Check one response.)

____ 1. Yes   (If 'YES,' **GO TO** D-17)

____ 2. No

D-15. In 1996-97, approximately how much is the gap between your own annual school costs and living expenses (including your graduate school expenses: tuition and fees, books, equipment) and the funding you receive from your institution? Please round to the nearest $100.

Funding gap $_____

D-16. How do you finance the gap between your expenses and the funding you received from your institution? (Check all that apply.)

____ 1. My own outside employment

____ 2. Loans

____ 3. Credit card debt

____ 4. Spouse or partner's support

____ 5. Personal savings

____ 6. Other family support

____ 7. Other _____

D-17. Approximately how much do you currently owe for your <u>education</u> (include both undergraduate and graduate debt) and <u>other types of indebtedness</u> now? (Check one response in each column.)

Dollar Amount	Education Credit Card Debt	Education Loan Debt	Noneducation Credit Card Debt	Noneducation Loan Debt
None	___ 1	___ 1	___ 1	___ 1
Up to $4,999	___ 2	___ 2	___ 2	___ 2
$5,000 - $9,999	___ 3	___ 3	___ 3	___ 3
$10,000 - $14,999	___ 4	___ 4	___ 4	___ 4
$15,000 - $19,999	___ 5	___ 5	___ 5	___ 5
$20,000 - $24,999	___ 6	___ 6	___ 6	___ 6
$25,000 - $29,999	___ 7	___ 7	___ 7	___ 7
$30,000 - $34,999	___ 8	___ 8	___ 8	___ 8
$35,000 - $39,999	___ 9	___ 9	___ 9	___ 9
$40,000 - $44,999	___ 10	___ 10	___ 10	___ 10
$45,000- $49,999	___ 11	___ 11	___ 11	___ 11
$50,000 or more	___ 12	___ 12	___ 12	___ 12

E. YOUR FUTURE PLANS

This section of the survey asks about the plans you are making for when you receive your doctoral degree.

E-1. What type of position do you expect to hold <u>immediately</u> after completing your doctoral degree? (Check one response).

____	1.	Faculty at a college or university
____	2.	Faculty at an elementary or secondary school
____	3.	Administrator or manager in the private sector
____	4.	Researcher in the private sector
____	5.	Administrator or manager in government
____	6.	Researcher in government
____	7.	Professional in a clinic, agency or hospital
____	8.	Self-employed or private practice
____	9.	Homemaker
____	10.	I will continue graduate or professional education
____	11.	I will hold a postdoctoral research or traineeship
____	12.	Administrator in a college or university
____	13.	Administrator in elementary or secondary school
____	14.	I am undecided about what I want to do after completing this doctoral program
____	15.	Other (specify) _____

F. YOUR UNDERGRADUATE EXPERIENCES

This section of the survey asks about your undergraduate experiences and preparation for your doctoral program.

F-1. Did you earn your baccalaureate degree at the same institution where you are earning your doctoral degree? (Check one response.)

　　____　1.　Yes　　　　　　　　　　　　　　(If 'YES,' **GO TO** F-3)

　　____　2.　No

F-2. Write the name of the institution and the city and state where you received your baccalaureate degree.

_____

Name of Institution

_____

City　　　　　　　　　　　　　　　State

F-3. In what year did you receive your baccalaureate degree?　　　19____

F-4. Into which of the following general categories do your undergraduate major, Master's degree(s) and current doctoral studies fall? (Check <u>one response in each</u> column.)

Field of Study	Undergraduate	First Master's	Second Master's	Doctoral
1. Biological sciences (e.g. biochemistry, biophysics, biology, molecular biology)	___ 1	___ 1	___ 1	___ 1
2. Economics	___ 2	___ 2	___ 2	___ 2
3. Education	___ 3	___ 3	___ 3	___ 3
4. Engineering	___ 4	___ 4	___ 4	___ 4
(specify)_____				
5. English	___ 5	___ 5	___ 5	___ 5
6. History	___ 6	___ 6	___ 6	___ 6
7. Mathematics, statistics	___ 7	___ 7	___ 7	___ 7
8. Physical sciences (e.g., chemistry, physics)	___ 8	___ 8	___ 8	___ 8
9. Political science	___ 9	___ 9	___ 9	___ 9
10. Psychology	___ 10	___ 10	___ 10	___ 10
11. Sociology	___ 11	___ 11	___ 11	___ 11
12. Other (specify)	___ 12	___ 12	___ 12	___ 12
_____				
13. Not applicable	___ 13	___ 13	___ 13	___ 13

F-5. If your undergraduate grade point average were converted to a letter grade or grade point equivalent, what would it be?

_____	A or A+ (4.0)	_____	C+ (2.75 to 2.99)
_____	A- (3.75 to 3.99)	_____	C (2.50 to 2.74)
_____	B+ (3.50 to 3.74)	_____	C- (2.25 to 2.49)
_____	B (3.25 to 3.49)	_____	D+ or less (less than 2.25)
_____	B- (3.00 to 3.24)	_____	Did not receive grades

F-6. For each of the following sources of financial support for your underbgraduate education, indicate whether it was a major source, a minor source, or not a source of financial support. (Check one response on each line.)

Undergraduate Education Source of Support	Major Source	Minor Source	Not a Source
1. Personal sources (self, parents, relatives, friends, spouse's/partner's income)	_____ 1	_____ 2	_____ 3
2. Government educational grants (Pell, SEOG)	_____ 1	_____ 2	_____ 3
3. University or college grants or scholarships	_____ 1	_____ 2	_____ 3
4. Other private grants or scholarships	_____ 1	_____ 2	_____ 3
5. On-campus employment during the school year (include college work-study)	_____ 1	_____ 2	_____ 3
6. Off-campus employment during the school year	_____ 1	_____ 2	_____ 3
7. Off-campus employment during the summer	_____ 1	_____ 2	_____ 3
8. Loans	_____ 1	_____ 2	_____ 3
9. Other	_____ 1	_____ 2	_____ 3

(please specify)_____

F-7. About how much money did you owe on the cost of your underbgraduate education when you received your undergraduate degree? (Check one response.)

_____	1.	None
_____	2.	Up to $4,999
_____	3.	$5,000 - $9,999
_____	4.	$10,000 - $14,999
_____	5.	$15,000 - $19,999
_____	6.	$20,000 - $24,999
_____	7.	$25,000 - $29,999
_____	8.	$30,000 - $34,999
_____	9.	$35,000 - $39,999
_____	10.	$40,000 - $44,999
_____	11.	$45,000 - $49,999
_____	12.	$50,000 - or more

F-8. About how much money did you owe on the cost of your <u>undergraduate education</u> and <u>other types of indebtedness</u> when you started your doctoral program?

(Check one response in each column.)

Dollar Amount	Education Credit Card Debt	Education Loan Debt	Noneducation Credit Card Debt	Noneducation Loan Debt
None	___ 1	___ 1	___ 1	___ 1
Up to $4,999	___ 2	___ 2	___ 2	___ 2
$5,000 - $9,999	___ 3	___ 3	___ 3	___ 3
$10,000 - $14,999	___ 4	___ 4	___ 4	___ 4
$15,000 - $19,999	___ 5	___ 5	___ 5	___ 5
$20,000 - $24,999	___ 6	___ 6	___ 6	___ 6
$25,000 - $29,999	___ 7	___ 7	___ 7	___ 7
$30,000 - $34,999	___ 8	___ 8	___ 8	___ 8
$35,000 - $39,999	___ 9	___ 9	___ 9	___ 9
$40,000 - $44,999	___ 10	___ 10	___ 10	___ 10
$45,000- $49,999	___ 11	___ 11	___ 11	___ 11
$50,000 or more	___ 12	___ 12	___ 12	___ 12

G. YOUR BACKGROUND

This section of the survey pertains to your family background and your current marital and economic status.

G-1. What is your sex? (Check one response.)

___ 1. Male

___ 2. Female

G-2. When were you born? (i.e., 07/04/76)

_____   _____   _____

Month   Day   Year

G-3. Where were you born?

_____

City   (State)   Country

G-4. Citizenship status (check one response).

___ 1. U.S. citizen or U.S. National   (**GO TO** G- 7)

___ 2. U.S. permanent resident visa, granted 19 _____

___ 3. Temporary visa (F-1, J-1, etc.)

G-5.   If you have a U.S. permanent resident visa or temporary visa (F-1, J-1, etc.), please name your country of citizenship:

_____

G.6.   Do you intend to return to your home country when you receive your doctoral degree?

____   1.   Yes

____   2.   No

G-7.   Please mark the <u>one</u> race or ethnicity which you think applies to you best?

____   1.   Hispanic

        ____   a.   Mexican, Mexican American, Chicano

        ____   b.   Cuban, Cubano

        ____   c.   Puerto Rican, Puertorriqueno, or Bouricuan

        ____   d.   Latino

        ____   e.   Other Hispanic (please specify) _____

____   2.   African American/Black, not of Hispanic origin

____   3.   Asian or Pacific Islander (specify)

        ____   a.   Chinese

        ____   b.   Filipino

        ____   c.   Japanese

        ____   d.   Korean

        ____   e.   Vietnamese

        ____   f.   Southeast Asian (Laotian, Cambodian/Kampuchean, etc.)

        ____   g.   Pacific Islander

        ____   h.   East Indian/Pakistani

        ____   i.   Other Asian (please specify) _____

____   4.   Middle Eastern (please specify) _____

____   5.   American Indian/Native American/Alaskan Native

        Tribe: _____

____   6.   White, not of Hispanic origin

____   7.   Mixed-race or mixed-ethnicity

        Please specify _____

____   8.   Race Not Included Above, please specify   _____

G-8. Following are several broad groupings of occupations. Select the one grouping that most closely represents the occupation of your father or male guardian and your mother or female guardian. If either or both are deceased, retired, or unemployed please select the most recent job they held. (Check one response in each <u>column.</u>)

Occupation	Father or Male Guardian	Mother or Female Guardian
Doctor, lawyer, college professor, high-ranking business executive, etc.	____ 1	____ 1
Teacher, mid-level business executive, accountant, pharmacist, nurse, etc.	____ 2	____ 2
Small business owner, farmer, foreman, supervisor, store manager, etc.	____ 3	____ 3
Electrician, plumber, secretary, dental assistant, butcher, etc.	____ 4	____ 4
Truck driver, mail carrier, nurses' aide, sales clerk, receptionist, etc.	____ 5	____ 5
Laborer, custodian, farm worker, waiter, waitress, etc.	____ 6	____ 6
Homemaker	____ 7	____ 7

G-9. What is the highest level of education completed by your father or male guardian and your mother or female guardian? (Check one response in each <u>column.</u>)

Level of Education Completed	Father or Male Guardian	Mother or Female Guardian
Elementary school or less	____ 1	____ 1
Some high school	____ 2	____ 2
High school diploma or equivalent	____ 3	____ 3
Some college, business or trade school	____ 4	____ 4
Associate degree	____ 5	____ 5
Bachelor's degree	____ 6	____ 6
Some graduate or professional school	____ 7	____ 7
Master's degree	____ 8	____ 8
All but dissertation (ABD)	____ 9	____ 9
Doctoral degree (Ph.D., Ed.D., D.A.)	____ 10	____ 10
Professional degree (J.D., M.D.)	____ 11	____ 11

G-10. Has your marital or domestic partnership status changed <u>during</u> your enrollment in your doctoral program? (Check one response.)

    ____   1.   No

    ____   2.   Yes, I have married.   **(GO TO** G-12)

    ____   3.   Yes, I have entered a domestic partnership.   **(GO TO** G-12)

    ____   4.   Yes, I have divorced.   **(GO TO** G-16)

    ____   5.   Yes, I have ended a domestic partnership.   **(GO TO** G-16)

    ____   6.   Yes, I have been widowed.   **(GO TO** G-16)

    ____   7.   Yes, my domestic partner passed away.   **(GO TO** G-16)

G-11. What is your current marital or domestic partnership status? (Check one response.)

    ____   1.   Married

    ____   2.   Single and living with a partner of the same sex

    ____   3.   Single and living with a partner of the opposite sex

    ____   4.   Single and living with a roommate(s)   **(GO TO** G-16)
                who is/are not a partner(s)

    ____   5.   Single and living alone   **(GO TO** G-16)

    ____   6.   Divorced   **(GO TO** G-16)

    ____   7.   Widowed   **(GO TO** G-16)

G-12. What is the highest level of education completed by your spouse or partner? (Check one response.)

    ____   1.   Elementary school or less

    ____   2.   Some high school

    ____   3.   High school diploma or equivalent

    ____   4.   Some college, business or trade school

    ____   5.   Associate's degree

    ____   6.   Bachelor's degree

    ____   7.   Some graduate or professional school

    ____   8.   Master's degree

    ____   9.   All but dissertation (ABD)

    ____   10.   Doctoral degree (Ph.D., Ed.D., D.A.)

    ____   11.   Professional degree (J.D., M.D.)

G-13. Is your spouse or partner a student? (Check one response)

    ____   1.   Yes

    ____   2.   No   (If 'NO,' **GO TO** G-15)

G-14. What is your spouse's/partner's enrollment status? (Check one response.)

_____ 1. Part-time undergraduate

_____ 2. Full-time undergraduate

_____ 3. Part-time graduate student

_____ 4. Full-time graduate student

G-15. What is your spouse's or partner's employment status? (Check one response.)

_____ 1. Not employed

_____ 2. Retired

_____ 3. Employed full-time

_____ 4. Employed part-time

G-16. How many children do you have in each of the following age groups?
(Check one response on each line.)

			Number of Children			
Age Range	Zero	One	Two	Three	Four	Five or more
Under 5 years	___ 0	___ 1	___ 2	___ 3	___ 4	___ 5
5 - 13	___ 0	___ 1	___ 2	___ 3	___ 4	___ 5
14 - 18	___ 0	___ 1	___ 2	___ 3	___ 4	___ 5
19 - 24	___ 0	___ 1	___ 2	___ 3	___ 4	___ 5
25 and over	___ 0	___ 1	___ 2	___ 3	___ 4	___ 5

G-17. How many dependents do you claim on your federal tax returns? This should be the same
response that you report on line 4 of your federal income tax return. Note: you should include
yourself as a dependent. (Check one response.)

_____ 1. None

_____ 2. One

_____ 3. Two

_____ 4. Three

_____ 5. Four

_____ 6. Five or more

_____ 7. Nonapplicable

Survey: Doctoral Student Finances, Experiences, Achievements

G-18. What is your best estimate of your annual gross (before taxes) income from earnings this year (1996)? This should include stipends, assistantships, and tuition/fees waivers if they are considered taxable income in the state where you live. If you are married or live with a partner give the gross income of your spouse/partner separately. (Check one response.)

Income Ranges	Your Income	Spouse or Partner's Income
Less than $9,999	____ 1	____ 1
$10,000 - $19,999	____ 2	____ 2
$20,000 - $29,999	____ 3	____ 3
$30,000 - $39,999	____ 4	____ 4
$40,000 - $49,999	____ 5	____ 5
$50,000 - $59,999	____ 6	____ 6
$60,000 - $69,999	____ 7	____ 7
$70,000 - $79,999	____ 8	____ 8
$80,000 - $89,999	____ 9	____ 9
$90,000 - $99,999	____ 10	____ 10
$100,000 or more	____ 11	____ 11

FOLLOW-UP SURVEYS (VOLUNTARY)

Please give us the names, permanent addresses, and phone numbers of two people who will know your whereabouts in future years (2 years, 5 years, and 7 years). This is important in case we need to conduct a follow-up study of the participants in this research to learn about their continuing degree progress and achievements. This information will not be listed in any report.

Your First Name	**Middle Name**	**Last Name**

Name of First Person

Street Address

City	State	Zip code

Phone Number (please include area code)

Name of Second Person

Street Address

City	State	Zip code

Phone Number (please include area code)

GRADUATE RECORD EXAMINATION SCORES:

To carry out this study, we want to include Graduate Record Examination (GRE) scores along with the data you supply in your survey responses. Our experience has been that students are often unable to recall their GRE scores. Therefore we are requesting permission to obtain your scores from the GRE files. Your scores, like your individual responses, will be kept confidential and used solely for research purposes. These scores will not be associated with your survey response but will be used to provide an average and range of scores for all respondents in any report. Consent is voluntary. You may return the completed survey without authorizing the release of your GRE scores.

Thank you for your cooperation.

I authorize the release of my Graduate Record Examination (GRE) scores from Educational Testing Service (ETS) for research purposes related to the "Survey of Doctoral Student Finances, Experiences, and Achievements."

_____

Print: First Name   Middle Initial   Last Name

_____

Signature

_____

Street Address

_____

City   State   Zip code

Approximate date that you most recently took the GREs: _____

Name that you used the <u>most recent time</u> you took the GREs (e.g., maiden name)

_____

Print: First Name   Middle Initial   Last Name

Social Security Number (voluntary): _____

RETURNING COMPLETED SURVEY:

Thank you for your cooperation. Please return the survey in the postage-paid envelope provided to:

Michael T. Nettles and Catherine M. Millett

University of Michigan

Center for the Study of Higher and Postsecondary Education

610 E. University Ave., 2002 SEB

Ann Arbor, MI 48109-1259

Tel: (313) 764-9499

264

METHODOLOGY

The Survey of Doctoral Student Finances, Experiences, and Achievements database includes more than eight hundred variables. We have used approximately forty variables in the analyses. A description of the variables follows. Depending on the individual analyses, a variable may be either the predictor of an outcome or an outcome measure.

Academic Interactions with Faculty Index: This index is the result of an exploratory factor analysis on questions related to faculty instruction and faculty willingness and ability to provide professional and academic counseling.

Adviser Is Mentor: A dichotomous variable that equals 1 if the respondent's faculty adviser was the same person as her or his mentor. A faculty adviser was defined as a faculty or research adviser assigned by the department or program to act in an official capacity in such ways as discussing and approving course work or signing registration forms. Students were instructed that their mentor may be someone other than their faculty or research adviser. This is a dichotomous variable coded 1 if the person who was the student's faculty adviser was also her or his mentor; coded 0 otherwise.

Age at Start of Doctoral Program: This is constructed by subtracting birth year from year of entrance into doctoral program.

Always Full-time Doctoral Student: Respondents indicated their overall student and work status since entering their doctoral program, based on their own institution's definition of full-time status. Assistantships, fellowships, and summer employment were not defined as employment in this question. The definitions for full- and part-time status are more ambiguous at the graduate school level than at the undergraduate level. At the undergraduate level, the number of courses more frequently determines status or credit hours students take in a given term. In graduate programs, credit hours can be the sole determinant of status, but most often a combination of time spent working on a graduate teaching or research assistantship plus credit hours, rather than courses or credit hours alone, determines whether one is a full-time or part-time student. While institutional policies vary in the number of course credits and assistantship work hours that determine full- or part-time status, they are sufficiently similar to justify asking students to make a judgment based on their knowledge of their own institution's policies. This is a dichotomous variable coded 1 if the respondent reported an overall student-work status as a full-time student with no employment; coded 0 otherwise.

Children under Eighteen: A dichotomous variable coded 1 if the respondent had a child under the age of eighteen; coded 0 otherwise.

Doctoral Degree Completion: A dichotomous variable coded 1 if the respondent had earned a doctoral degree as of June 2001; coded 0 otherwise.

Ever Received a Graduate Fellowship: A dichotomous variable coded 1 if the respondent had received a graduate fellowship at any time during the doctoral program; coded 0 otherwise.

Ever Was a Research Assistant: A dichotomous variable coded 1 if the respondent was a research assistant at any time during the doctoral program; coded 0 otherwise.

Ever Was a Teaching Assistant: A dichotomous variable coded 1 if the respondent was a teaching assistant at any time during the doctoral program; coded 0 otherwise.

Expects First Job to Be Faculty or Postdoctoral Fellow: A dichotomous variable coded 1 if the respondent stated that she or he expected to hold a faculty position at a college or university or a postdoctoral research position immediately after completing the doctoral degree; coded 0 otherwise.

Field of Study in Doctoral Program: This variable uses the following five categories: education, engineering, the humanities, sciences and mathematics, and the social sciences. In relational models, field is used to split the regressions into five separate models.

First or Only Choice of Doctoral Program: A dichotomous variable coded 1 if the respondent was enrolled in her or his only or first choice of doctoral program; coded 0 otherwise.

Full-time When First Enrolled in Doctoral Program: A dichotomous variable coded 1 if the respondent enrolled full-time at the start of her or his doctoral program; coded 0 otherwise.

GRE Verbal Score, GRE Quantitative Score, GRE Analytical Score: Respondents were asked to provide their Graduate Record Examination (GRE) scores for each of the three parts of the GRE General Test: verbal, quantitative, and analytical. Respondents were also asked to give the researchers permission to obtain their scores from the Graduate Record Examination Board. This was particularly important for respondents who could not recall their scores. GRE Board scores were used if available; otherwise, the midpoints of the respondent's self-reported scores were used. In the relational analyses, scores are reported with 100-point intervals.

Have a Mentor: Respondents were asked on the survey to indicate whether they had a faculty member who served as a mentor. Mentor was defined as a faculty member to whom they turn for advice, to review a paper, or for general support and encouragement. This is a dichotomous variable coded 1 if the respondent had a mentor; coded 0 otherwise.

Have Research Productivity: A dichotomous variable coded 1 if the respondent reported having participated in any of four research activities (presenting a paper, publishing a chapter, publishing an article, publishing a book); coded 0 otherwise.

Household Income: This variable measures self-reported income of the respondent and, if applicable, the respondent's spouse or partner by taking the midpoints of the income ranges from survey question G-18.

Incurred Education Debt as a Doctoral Student: A dichotomous variable coded 1 if the value was greater than one when the respondent's undergraduate debt at the start of their doctoral program was subtracted from their response to a question about total undergraduate and graduate school debt at the time of the survey; coded 0 otherwise.

Interaction with Faculty Adviser Index: This index derives from exploratory factor analysis on questions related to respondents' perceptions of their advisers' concern for their professional and personal well-being.

Male: A dichotomous variable coded 1 if the respondent was male; coded 0 otherwise.

Married or Partnered: A dichotomous variable coded 1 if the respondent reported being married or having a domestic partner; coded 0 otherwise.

Master's Degree on Entry: A dichotomous variable coded 1 if the respondent obtained a master's degree before enrolling in current doctoral program; coded 0 otherwise.

Overall Satisfaction with Doctoral Program: A 5-point Likert-scale question that asked respondents their agreement with the statement, "Overall, I am satisfied with the doctoral program in which I am currently enrolled."

Parent Socioeconomic Status: This is a composite score consisting of the following four items: mother's occupation, father's occupation, mother's education, and father's education. In all analyses, this measure has been standardized (z-scored; mean = 0, SD = 1) to facilitate the interpretation of results.

Peer Interaction Index: This index is the result of an exploratory factor analysis on questions related to the extent to which respondents participated in student-oriented campus activities.

Presented a Paper: A dichotomous variable coded 1 if the respondent had presented a paper at a national conference during graduate study; coded 0 otherwise.

Private Graduate School: A dichotomous variable coded 1 if the respondent was enrolled in a doctoral program in a private university; coded 0 otherwise.

Published an Article: A dichotomous variable coded 1 if the respondent published one or more articles (sole authored or jointly) during their graduate study; coded 0 otherwise.

Race-Ethnicity: This variable uses the following five categories: African American, Hispanic American, Asian American, white or other, and non-

U.S. citizen. In relational models, race is characterized as four separate dichotomous variables (African American, Hispanic, Asian American, and non-U.S. citizen), with the white students serving as the reference group.

Rate of Progress: A continuous variable that measures the pace at which a respondent progressed through her or his doctoral program relative to other respondents in the same field.

Received a Graduate Fellowship Offer at Entry: A dichotomous variable coded 1 if the respondent received a fellowship offer at the time of admission to the doctoral program for any year during the first five years of doctoral study; coded 0 otherwise.

Received a Research Assistantship Offer at Entry: A dichotomous variable coded 1 if the respondent received a research assistantship offer at the time of admission to the doctoral program for any year during the first five years of doctoral study; coded 0 otherwise.

Received a Teaching Assistantship Offer at Entry: A dichotomous variable coded 1 if the respondent received a research assistantship offer at the time of admission to the doctoral program for any year during the first five years of doctoral study; coded 0 otherwise.

Selectivity of the Undergraduate Institution: A dichotomous variable coded 1 if the respondent earned a bachelor's degree from a most competitive, highly competitive +, or highly competitive institution, based on the *Barron's Profiles of American Colleges and Universities* (1999) rankings, and 0 if the bachelor's degree was earned from a lower-ranked U.S. institution or from a non-U.S. institution.

Stopping Out of Doctoral Program: A dichotomous variable coded 1 if the respondent reported that she or he had stopped out of the doctoral program for a semester or quarter since first starting the doctoral program (excluding summers or nonregistration for dissertation research purposes); coded 0 otherwise.

Student-Faculty Social Interaction Index: This index is the result of an exploratory factor analysis on questions related to respondents' perceptions of student-faculty relations.

Time in Doctoral Program: Indicates the amount of time (in years) the respondent had been enrolled in a doctoral program at the time the survey was completed.

Time to Degree (Elapsed): Indicates the amount of time from the respondent's first enrollment in the doctoral program until the year (up to 2001) the doctorate was conferred.

SPECIALLY CONSTRUCTED VARIABLES

Rate of Progress

The rate of progress measure was constructed as follows: First, respondents were grouped by their field of study and reported stage of progress. The following eight stages of progress were used:

—Respondent has completed less than half the course work required for doctoral degree

—Respondent has completed more than half, but not all, of the course work required for doctoral degree

—Respondent has completed all course work required for doctoral degree

—Respondent has completed preliminary and general examinations but has not yet been admitted to doctoral candidacy

—Respondent has been admitted to doctoral candidacy but is not yet working on dissertation

—Respondent is working on dissertation

—Respondent has completed all degree requirements for doctoral degree, but degree has not yet been awarded

—Doctoral degree has been awarded

Since there are five field groups (education, engineering, the humanities, sciences and mathematics, and the social sciences) and eight possible stages, there are possible field-stage pairs to which respondents could be assigned. Next, we computed the median number of years that respondents had been in their doctoral programs for each of these forty pairs. After the assignment of a median number of years to each eligible person in the sample (based on their field and stage), a rate of progress measure was constructed by dividing this field- and stage-specific median value by the time the respondent reported having been in her or his doctoral program at the time the survey was given. More specifically, this rate of progress measure takes the form

$$\text{Relative Progress} = (\text{Median Years}_{fs} \, / \, \text{Years}_{ifs}),$$

where i = individual, f = field group, and s = stage of progress. Here, values strictly greater than 1 indicate a faster rate of progress relative to the median student in stage s, values strictly less than 1 indicate slower progress, and values equal to 1 imply that the student has taken the median number of years to reach her or his particular stage of progress.

This rate of progress measure offers perhaps the principal advantage of measuring students relative to their respective medians. More precisely, it measures individual progress relative to the median number of years for a respondent's specific field-stage group. This aspect of the measure allows us to group respondents at different stages of progress when performing analyses (e.g., conditional means, regression, etc.) on this measure. Compared with an alternative measure we considered (i.e., $\text{Years}_{ifs} - \text{Median Years}_{fs}$), the ratio avoids the problem of a year's difference meaning something different at the various stages of progress. For example, being a year behind the median at an early stage (e.g., completed course work) may be different from being a year behind at the dissertation stage. The ratio more accurately represents this conceptual difference. Finally, since it relies on the stage- and field-specific median and the respondent's own measure of years taken to achieve the present stage, arbitrary assignments are avoided. This measure is z-scored for all analyses.

Creating Factors

A further operation was needed to reduce the data collected by Section B of the survey instrument. The items in Section B, subtitled "Your Current Doctoral Program Experience," were intended to gather information on students' opinions about their doctoral programs as well as their relevant experiences within these programs. By the nature of the questions, a natural and conceptual separation of the variables resulted, allowing factor analyses to condense some of the information (see table D.1). For example, the four items from Section B-8 all relate to interactions with a faculty adviser. A correlation matrix for these produced values of .3 or higher, allowing us to proceed to extract factors from these and the other three sets of items.

Table D.1
Factor Analysis of the Survey of Doctoral Student Finances, Experiences, and Achievements

Factor and Survey Item	Factor Loading	Internal Consistency (alpha)
Peer interaction (z-scored)		.731
B-3.2 It has been easy for me to meet and make friends with other students in my program.	.642	
B-15.1 [I have] participated in an informal study group with other graduate students.	.637	
B-15.2 [I have] participated in school- or program-sponsored social activities with other graduate students.	.701	
B-15.5 [I have] socialized with graduate students of different racial-ethnic backgrounds.	.706	
B-15.9 [I have] socialized informally with other graduate students.	.789	
Student-faculty social interactions (z-scored)		.916
B-3.5 It is easy to develop personal relationships with faculty members in this program.	.845	
B-3.6 There is a great deal of contact between professors and students in program outside the classroom.	.800	
B-4.4 [I am satisfied with the] collegial atmosphere between the faculty and students.	.886	
B-4.5 [I am satisfied with the] communication between faculty and students.	.904	
B-4.7 [I am satisfied with the] quality of overall faculty-student relations.	.900	
Academic interactions with faculty (z-scored)		.853
B-4.1 [I am satisfied with the] quality of faculty instruction.	.643	
B-4.6 [I am satisfied with the] availability of the faculty to meet with students.	.742	
B-4.8 [I am satisfied with the] quality of academic advising provided by faculty.	.840	
B-4.9 [I am satisfied with the] quality of feedback on scholarly projects or academic progress.	.840	
B-4.10 [I am satisfied with the] quality of professional advising and job placement.	.703	
B-4.12 [I am satisfied with the] faculty interest in my research.	.765	
Interactions with faculty adviser (z-scored)		.873
B-8.1 [My] adviser is accessible for consultation.	.797	
B-8.2 [My] adviser offers useful criticisms of my work.	.843	
B-8.3 [My] adviser has concern for my professional development.	.911	
B-8.4 [My] adviser is interested in my personal welfare.	.852	

Extraction was performed through principal components analysis. Following common practice (Kim and Mueller 1978; Long 1983), four factors with Eigenvalues greater than 1.0 were extracted and retained. To simplify the factor structure, a Varimax rotation was employed, and the rotated component matrix was sorted by the size of the loadings within the particular factor. A total of four factors emerged, which have been standardized (z-scored). The four factors are as follows:

Peer Interaction Index: This index is the result of an exploratory factor analysis on questions related to the extent to which respondents participated in student-oriented campus activities.

Student-Faculty Social Interaction Index: This index is the result of an exploratory factor analysis on questions related to respondents' perceptions of student-faculty relations.

Academic Interactions with Faculty Index: This index is the result of an exploratory factor analysis on questions related to respondents' perceptions of faculty instruction and faculty willingness and ability to provide professional and academic counseling.

Interactions with Faculty Adviser Index: This index derives from exploratory factor analysis on questions related to respondents' perceptions of their advisers' concern for their professional and personal well-being.

Independent Variables and z-scores

The independent variables include both individual and institutional characteristics that may plausibly affect the experiences of doctoral students. To enable clear comparisons, some of these variables such as socioeconomic status (SES) had to be standardized through the use of z-scores. Effectively, the mean of the variable is 0, and the standard deviation is 1. For example, the histogram in figure D.1 is the distribution of so-

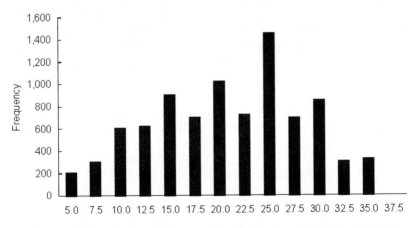

Fig. D.1. Student Socioeconomic Status. SD = 7.47, mean = 21.0, N = 8,756.35.
Source: Survey of Doctoral Student Finances, Experiences, and Achievements.

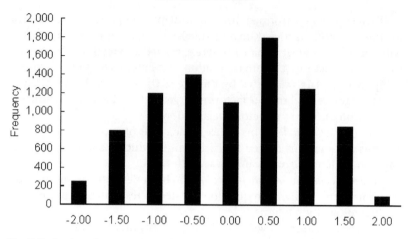

Fig. D.2. Student Socioeconomic Status (z-scored). SD = .99, mean = 0, N = 8.765.35.
Source: Survey of Doctoral Student Finances, Experiences, and Achievements.

cioeconomic status before being z-scored. A score of 21 on this metric (the mean) obviously has little meaning to the reader. The histogram in figure D.2 illustrates the distribution of socioeconomic after it has been standardized. In this z-scored metric, 0 is the mean, and every unit represents one standard deviation; moving from 0 to 1.5 represents an increase of 1.5 standard deviations.

WEIGHTING THE DATA

The purpose of the weights is to correct for an oversampling of minority students in the survey sample. As the standard against which the representativeness of our sample is judged, we chose the graduate student enrollment (master's and doctoral students) in 1996 in the fields represented in the sample. If this proved impossible, data from other years were obtained. Weights are referenced to this 1996 group, since it should be more representative of the true population of doctoral students than is our sample.

The actual weighting formula is such that it tries to match our sample's distribution exactly to that of the base. Thus the formula is as follows:

$$W = \frac{\text{Total enrolled within race \& field (institution population)}}{\text{Total enrolled within race \& field (sample)}} * \frac{\text{Total enrolled (sample)}}{\text{Total enrolled (institution population)}}$$

This will match every proportion in our sample to that of the base and will eliminate any problem with oversampling of minority students.

The oversampling of minorities was intended to produce a sample of these respondents that was large enough for analysis. Since this was not an issue with respect to sex, females were not oversampled. As such, the weight variable does not account for sex. This may be problematic if the proportion of females in our survey differs dramatically from that in our target population. However, there seems to be little empirical difference in the proportion of females in our survey and the proportion of females enrolled in graduate programs in 1996, our reference group for weight construction.

Table D.2
Weighting the Survey Database

	Black	Asian	Hispanic	White	International	Total	% of Total
1996 Graduate student enrollment							
Biological and physical sciences, mathematics and statistics	408	1,486	349	8,796	4,828	15,867	25.90
Economics, political science, psychology, and sociology	925	575	446	6,306	2,684	10,936	17.85
English and history	350	318	270	4,474	406	5,818	9.50
Education	1,894	974	1,014	12,482	1,486	17,850	29.14
Engineering	284	1,227	276	4,625	4,371	10,783	17.60
Total	3,861	4,580	2,355	36,683	13,775	61,254	100.00
% of total	6.30	7.48	3.84	59.89	22.49	100.00	
Survey sample[a]							
Biological and physical sciences, mathematics and statistics	80	223	71	958	521	1,853	20.51
Economics, political science, psychology, and sociology	342	166	193	1,431	332	2,464	27.27
English and history	133	88	102	931	72	1,326	14.67
Education	354	138	213	1,594	208	2,507	27.74
Engineering	34	158	23	342	329	886	9.81
Total	943	773	602	5,256	1,462	9,036	100.00
% of total	10.44	8.55	6.66	58.17	16.18	100.00	
Actual weights by Total method, using Graduate Student Enrollment database							
Biological and physical sciences, mathematics and statistics	0.75234	0.98300	0.72512	1.35445	1.36701		
Economics, political science, psychology, and sociology	0.39899	0.51098	0.34089	0.65006	1.19258		
English and history	0.38820	0.53307	0.39049	0.70891	0.83183		
Education	0.78926	1.04117	0.70226	1.15515	1.05389		
Engineering	1.23220	1.14559	1.77020	1.99493	1.95987		

Sources: IPEDS Enrollment survey (1996) data from the U.S. Department of Education, National Center for Education Statistics database system, http://nces.ed.gov/ipeds/ (August 2000); NSF-NIH Survey of Graduate Students and Postdoctorates in S&E (1996) data from the National Science Foundation's WebCASPAR database system, http://webcaspar.nsf.gov/ (August 2000). We also consulted the websites of twenty institutions for the humanities data in August 2000.
[a]Preweighted sample of 9,036 cases (those not missing race or field data).

DIFFERENTIAL EFFECTS OF ATTENDANCE AT HISTORICALLY BLACK COLLEGES AND UNIVERSITIES

It is important to keep in mind that the number of students in the sample attending historically black colleges and universities (HBCUs) is relatively small (n = 195, unweighted; n = 143, weighted). For example, only 16 percent of the African American students in the sample attended HBCU institutions. Hence, the extent to which HBCU students might influence our African American multivariate regression coefficients is somewhat limited. Furthermore (and somewhat surprisingly), only three-quarters of students in the sample who attend Howard and Clark Atlanta Universities are in fact African American (only 62% weighted). Hence "HBCU student" is not synonymous with "African American." Of the remaining HBCU students, 13 percent are international students (24% weighted), and 9 percent are white (12% weighted).

The proportion of HBCU students varies considerably by field. Almost 40 percent are in the social sciences (28% weighted), while fewer than 11 percent are in engineering and the humanities combined (weighted or unweighted). Students at historically black colleges and universities have substantially lower incoming Graduate Record Examination (GRE) scores, with a roughly 200-point gap on each GRE test separating them from students at other colleges. This advantage for non-HBCU students holds true even when comparing only African Americans at HBCU and non-HBCU institutions, although the gaps are considerably smaller (since the comparison is within the African American population). On average, non-HBCU African American doctoral students enter graduate study with a 100-point advantage over their HBCU peers (weighted results). These entering academic differences are also evident in the fact that although almost 40 percent of non-HBCU African American doctoral students in the social sciences attended selective undergraduate institutions, only one HBCU African American student in the social sciences did so.

DIFFERENTIAL EXPERIENCES AMONG HBCU AND NON-HBCU AFRICAN AMERICANS

Based on simple *t*-tests, it does appear that HBCU and non-HBCU students in some domains in certain fields are having different experiences. (These associations are unadjusted. The adjusted relationships are discussed with the multivariate analyses and may provide different results than the simple descriptives.) African American HBCU students in education and in sciences and mathematics reported more positive student-faculty social interactions and more positive views of academic interactions with faculty. No statistically significant differences existed in engineering or the humanities, but this may be because of the small number of African American HBCU students in these fields. However, across all fields, African American students in HBCU and non-HBCU programs reported statistically similar levels of overall satisfaction.

In the field of education, more than three times as many non-HBCU African Americans as HBCU African Americans had "some research productivity." No statistically significant differences existed within the other fields. African American students at HBCU and non-HBCU institutions were equally likely to have mentors. In all fields but engineering, non-HBCU African American students were more likely to have received fellowships at some point during their doctoral studies. No differences existed in having had a research assistantship. However, non-HBCU African American students in education were five times more likely to have served as teaching assistants. In sum, although African Americans in certain fields and in certain psychosocial domains reported more positive experiences, in terms of the practices and products that are likely to lead to careers in research and academe, non-HBCU students appear to have certain advantages.

MULTIVARIATE ANALYSES

The above differences could derive from other social and academic differences between HBCU and non-HBCU students rather than from real differences between institutions. Thus we also investigated the extent to which HBCU attendance is a significant predictor in several of our regression models. (We simply used a dummy variable, coded 1 if the student was attending a historically black college or university, coded 0 otherwise.) Recall that only 62 percent of HBCU students in our sample were African American (weighted). The small numbers of HBCU African American students in certain fields precluded using a separate dummy variable representing African Americans at HBCUs in the regressions.

Students in sciences and mathematics at HBCUs reported more positive experiences with their advisers and higher regard for their faculty, even after controlling for the other predictors in the model. Interestingly, HBCU social sciences students reported increased levels (.5 SD) of student interaction compared with their non-HBCU peers; no differences existed in other fields. Holding constant their social and academic differences, HBCU and non-HBCU students reported statistically similar levels of satisfaction.

With the logistic regression analyses, HBCU and non-HBCU students were equally likely to have incurred debt during doctoral study and to have stopped out at some point (controlling for the other predictors). As suggested in the simple descriptive analyses, even after controlling for the other predictors in the model, HBCU students in education were four times less likely, and in engineering and social sciences roughly ten times less likely, than non-HBCU students to have received fellowships. However, across all fields, non-HBCU and HBCU doctoral students were equally likely to have served as a teaching or research assistants. Interestingly, HBCU students in the social sciences were four times as likely as non-HBCU students to have some research productivity (no differences existed across the other fields).

In terms of the proportion of students who had completed their doctorates by 2001, there were no differences between HBCU and non-HBCU students (controlling for the other predictors in the model). However, in terms of time to degree, among sciences and mathematics students who had finished by 2001, HBCU students took an average of almost one year less to graduate. On average, social sciences HBCU students finished more than two years sooner than their non-HBCU peers.

PREDICTING EXPERIENCES
AND PERFORMANCE REGRESSION TABLES

Table F.1

Regression Analysis of Predictors of Receiving a Fellowship Offer (Single or Multiyear) on Entry to Doctoral Program, by Field

Independent Variable[a]	Education[b]			Engineering			Humanities			Sciences and Mathematics			Social Sciences		
	Odds	Inverse Odds	Odds SE	Odds	Inverse Odds	Odds SE	Odds	Inverse Odds	Odds SE	Odds	Inverse Odds	Odds SE	Odds	Inverse Odds	Odds SE
GRE verbal (100s of points)	1.287**		0.105	1.190**		0.079	1.593***		0.195	1.267***		0.070	1.628***		0.127
GRE quantitative (100s of points)	1.050		0.086	1.369		0.222	1.293*		0.150	1.209*		0.108	1.113		0.100
GRE analytical (100s of points)	1.086		0.091	1.069		0.098	0.945	1.058	0.117	1.042		0.073	1.081		0.095
Male	0.997	1.003	0.145	0.726	1.378	0.120	0.725	1.379	0.130	0.660***	1.516	0.068	0.986		0.129
African American[c]	3.808***		0.880	2.722**			14.920***		6.572	5.468***		1.900	8.722***		2.352
Hispanic	5.665***		1.406	2.013			13.500***		6.572	7.245***		2.821	10.930***		3.724
Asian															
American Indian	2.415***		0.617	0.923	1.083	0.176	3.739***		1.399	1.141		0.187	1.733*		0.457
International	0.737	1.357	0.223	0.398***	2.511	0.067	2.632*		1.050	0.726*	1.377	0.101	1.136		0.220
Age at start of doctoral program (1 yr.)	0.983	1.018	0.010	0.930***	1.075	0.020	0.977	1.023	0.017	0.957**	1.045	0.015	0.939***	1.065	0.015
Master's upon entry	1.136		0.175	0.706*	1.416	0.105	0.506***	1.975	0.098	1.004		0.152	0.725*	1.379	0.111
Selective undergraduate institution	1.505**		0.219	0.920	1.087	0.139	0.978	1.022	0.183	0.904	1.106	0.103	1.218		0.171
Private graduate school	1.693***		0.226	1.159		0.153	3.205***		0.585	0.997	1.003	0.104	1.797***		0.228
Full-time student when first enrolled	7.987***		1.805	3.461**		1.569	6.599**		4.395	2.133		2.225	4.834***		0.860
Constant	0.005		0.003	0.038		0.052	0.002		0.002	0.064		0.053	0.006		0.005
n (unweighted)	1,504			797			1,171			1,635			2,187		
Likelihood ratio test	273.90***			209.20***			195.58***			162.52***			289.30***		
McFadden pseudo R^2	0.158			0.115			0.188			0.058			0.154		

Source: Survey of Doctoral Student Finances, Experiences, and Achievements.

[a] Parents' SES was not a significant predictor in at least one model and was dropped from the models.

[b] Dependent measure is dichotomous (no = 0, yes = 1). Odds ratio coefficients. Inverse odds ratio (1/odds ratio) presented for odds ratios less than 1.

[c] All racial groups and international students are compared with whites.

$* p < .05; ** p < .01; *** p < .001$

Table F.2
Regression Analysis of Predictors of Receiving a Teaching Assistantship Offer (Single or Multiyear) on Entry to Doctoral Program, by Field

Independent Variable[a]	Education[b]			Engineering			Humanities			Sciences and Mathematics			Social Sciences		
	Odds	Inverse Odds	Odds SE	Odds	Inverse Odds	Odds SE	Odds	Inverse Odds	Odds SE	Odds	Inverse Odds	Odds SE	Odds	Inverse Odds	Odds SE
GRE verbal (100s of points)	1.128		0.094	1.034		0.063	0.994	1.006	0.147	1.006		0.053	1.266***		0.086
GRE quantitative (100s of points)	1.112		0.094	0.952	1.050	0.130	1.112		0.112	1.012		0.093	1.224*		0.098
GRE analytical (100s of points)	0.931	1.075	0.080	0.877	1.140	0.071	0.988	1.012	0.110	1.130		0.066	1.005		0.088
Male	0.915	1.093	0.138	0.837	1.195	0.136	0.661**	1.513	0.105	1.397**		0.144	1.130		0.116
African American[c]	1.420		0.344	0.255**	3.928	0.118	3.395***		1.198	0.511*	1.958	0.161	0.957	1.045	0.354
Hispanic	1.111		0.310	0.330*	3.034	0.144	2.122*		0.790	0.690	1.450	0.216	1.469		0.352
Asian American	0.873	1.145	0.245	0.868	1.152	0.162	1.826		0.608	1.120		0.195	0.881	1.136	0.216
International	0.445*	2.245	0.140	0.518***	1.929	0.074	1.892		0.625	0.896	1.116	0.114	0.853	1.173	0.141
Age at start of doctoral program (1 yr.)	0.971**	1.030	0.010	0.949***	1.054	0.017	0.966*	1.035	0.014	0.947***	1.056	0.012	0.938***	1.066	0.012
Private graduate school	1.296		0.178	0.685**	1.459	0.088	0.821	1.194	0.137	0.821	1.218	0.086	0.641***	1.560	0.076
Full-time student when first enrolled	5.016***		1.127	2.670*		1.067	2.479**		1.674	6.153***		0.821	3.519*		2.961
Constant	0.059		0.038	0.041		3.959	1.526		0.040	0.024		1.134	2.241		0.020
n (unweighted)	1,550			815			1,199			1,693			2,241		
Likelihood ratio test	109.87***			64.12***			59.02***			75.34***			178.08***		
McFadden pseudo R^2	0.073			0.035			0.055			0.028			0.089		

Source: Survey of Doctoral Student Finances, Experiences, and Achievements.
[a] Parents' SES was not a significant predictor in at least one model and was dropped from the models.
[b] Dependent measure is dichotomous (no = 0, yes = 1). Odds ratio coefficients. Inverse odds ratio (1/odds ratio) presented for odds ratios less than 1.
[c] All racial groups and international students are compared with whites.
*$p < .05$; **$p < .01$; ***$p < .001$

Table F.3
Regression Analysis of Predictors of Receiving a Research Assistantship Offer (Single or Multiyear) on Entry to Doctoral Program, by Field

Independent Variable[a]	Education[b]			Engineering			Humanities[c]			Sciences and Mathematics			Social Sciences		
	Odds	Inverse Odds	Odds SE	Odds	Inverse Odds	Odds SE	Odds	Inverse Odds	Odds SE	Odds	Inverse Odds	Odds SE	Odds	Inverse Odds	Odds SE
GRE verbal (100s of points)	1.079		0.098	1.231***		0.072	0.983	1.017	0.176	1.034		0.054	0.869	1.151	0.073
GRE quantitative (100s of points)	0.993	1.007	0.089	1.306*		0.172	0.802	1.246	0.139	0.787**	1.271	0.066	1.324**		0.134
GRE analytical (100s of points)	0.970	1.031	0.089	0.838*	1.193	0.064	1.078		0.206	0.940	1.064	0.061	1.007		0.097
Male	1.120		0.178	1.098		0.172	0.949	1.053	0.266	1.062		0.106	0.773	1.294	0.113
African American[d]	1.069		0.288	0.368***	2.719	0.142	0.744	1.345	0.474	0.252***	3.973	0.090	1.063		0.303
Hispanic	1.484		0.403	0.488	2.048	0.188	1.185		0.717	0.803	1.245	0.253	0.927	1.079	0.329
Asian American	1.098		0.315	0.733	1.363	0.134	1.536		0.765	1.339		0.217	0.721	1.387	0.219
International	0.493*	2.029	0.169	0.576***	1.736	0.086	2.195		1.149	1.005	0.995	0.130	0.568*	1.762	0.125
Age at start of doctoral program (1 yr.)	0.960***	1.041	0.011	0.919***	1.088	0.015	0.970	1.031	0.029	0.930***	1.076	0.013	0.948**	1.055	0.017
Selective undergraduate institution	1.138		0.184	0.721*	1.387	0.104	1.586		0.487	1.034		0.115	1.167		0.182
Full-time student when first enrolled	4.965***		1.258	2.109*		0.696	110,428,763.663		785,402,057,348.821	2.513**		0.934	2.777*		1.430
Constant	0.135		0.094	0.781		0.832	0.000			16.733		13.036	0.157		0.155
n (unweighted)	1,513			797			1,177			1,641			2,197		
Likelihood ratio test	103.57***			95.16***			12.89			70.69***			53.24***		
McFadden pseudo R^2	0.077			0.048			0.029			0.025			0.037		

Source: Survey of Doctoral Student Finances, Experiences, and Achievements.

[a] Parents' SES, private graduate school, and master's upon entry were nonsignificant predictors in all fields and were dropped from the models.

[b] Dependent measure is dichotomous (no = 0, yes = 1). Odds ratio (1/odds ratio) presented for odds ratios less than 1.

[c] The model is not statistically significantly different from the null model. This suggests that there is no relationship among the predictors and receiving a research assistantship. The extremely large odds ratio for full-time student when enrolled may be attributed to the fact that there is no maximum likelihood estimate, which is supported by the fact that only one humanities student who was offered a research assistantship was not a full-time student.

[d] All racial groups and international students are compared with whites.

$*p < .05; **p < .01; ***p < .001$

Table F.4
Regression Analysis of Predictors of Receiving a Fellowship over the Course of Doctoral Study, by Field

Independent Variable[a]	Education[b]			Engineering			Humanities			Sciences and Mathematics			Social Sciences		
	Odds	Inverse Odds	Odds SE	Odds	Inverse Odds	Odds SE	Odds	Inverse Odds	Odds SE	Odds	Inverse Odds	Odds SE	Odds	Inverse Odds	Odds SE
Male	0.937	1.067	0.120	0.451***	2.215	0.078	0.707	1.415	0.082	0.702**	1.424	0.137	1.161		0.156
African American[c]	2.414***		0.511	6.089**		3.620	4.575**		1.556	4.461***		2.296	5.256***		1.928
Hispanic	3.640***		0.951	6.523**		3.888	11.206***		5.449	10.938***		8.090	11.564***		6.868
Asian American	2.131**		0.571	0.827	1.209	0.163	2.359		0.345	0.949	1.054	1.041	1.236		0.168
International	1.402		0.352	0.470***	2.127	0.076	2.138		0.363	0.558***	1.791	0.963	1.828**		0.080
Parents' SES[d]	0.889	1.125	0.058	1.072		0.076	1.119		0.071	1.152*		0.122	0.988	1.012	0.065
Household income ($1,000s)	0.996*	1.004	0.002	0.997	1.003	0.003	0.997	1.003	0.002	1.001		0.004	0.995*	1.005	0.003
Age at start of doctoral program (1 yr.)	0.976**	1.025	0.009	0.941**	1.063	0.019	0.971	1.030	0.014	0.942***	1.061	0.018	0.960**	1.042	0.015
GRE verbal (100s of points)	1.312***		0.094	1.055		0.067	1.166		0.109	1.320***		0.151	1.423***		0.077
GRE quantitative (100s of points)	0.940	1.064	0.066	1.011		0.148	1.273		0.077	1.008		0.157	0.905	1.106	0.092
GRE analytical (100s of points)	1.054		0.079	1.053		0.087	0.915	1.093	0.104	1.079		0.122	1.243**		0.077
Master's upon entry	0.772	1.295	0.111	0.707*	1.414	0.101	0.543**	1.842	0.102	1.233		0.106	0.696*	1.437	0.192
Selective undergraduate institution	1.635***		0.223	1.354*		0.209	1.187		0.166	1.006		0.242	1.139		0.125
Private graduate school	2.234***		0.276	1.052		0.139	2.401***		0.311	0.985	1.015	0.529	2.326***		0.111
Always full-time doctoral student	1.752***		0.235	1.275		0.245	1.405		0.242	1.582*		0.361	1.299		0.299

(table continues)

281

Table F.4 (*continued*)

Independent Variable[a]	Education[b]			Engineering			Humanities			Sciences and Mathematics			Social Sciences		
	Odds	Odds SE	Inverse Odds	Odds	Odds SE	Inverse Odds	Odds	Odds SE	Inverse Odds	Odds	Odds SE	Inverse Odds	Odds	Odds SE	Inverse Odds
Ever was a teaching assistant	1.732***	0.229		1.005	0.125		1.368	0.300		0.684**	0.080	1.463	0.899	0.128	1.112
Ever was a research assistant	2.128***	0.284		0.462***	0.080	2.165	2.059***	0.433		0.494***	0.057	2.022	1.123	0.145	
Time in doctoral program (yrs.)	1.013	0.023		1.119**	0.041		1.088*	0.040		1.078*	0.032		1.107***	0.034	
Expect first job to be faculty or postdoctoral position	0.760*	0.095	1.316	1.835***	0.251		1.239	0.264		1.346**	0.135		1.449**	0.187	
Constant	0.193	0.101		6.458	7.543		0.228	0.237		0.950	0.753		0.084	0.063	
n (unweighted)	1,435			774			1,113			1,590			2,071		
Likelihood ratio test	314.08***			260.24***			126.61***			285.07***			229.07***		
McFadden pseudo R²	0.151			0.135			0.148			0.105			0.127		

Source: Survey of Doctoral Student Finances, Experiences, and Achievements.

[a] Married or domestic partner and children under eighteen were nonsignificant predictors in all fields and were dropped from the models.

[b] Dependent measure is dichotomous (no = 0, yes = 1). Odds ratio coefficients. Inverse odds ratio (1/odds ratio) presented for odds ratios less than 1.

[c] All racial groups and international students are compared with whites.

[d] Parents' SEs is a composite of educational attainment and occupational prestige.

*$p < .05$; **$p < .01$; ***$p < .001$

Table F:5
Regression Analysis of Predictors of Being a Teaching Assistant over the Course of Doctoral Study, by Field

Independent Variable[a]	Education[b]			Engineering			Humanities			Sciences and Mathematics			Social Sciences		
	Odds	Odds SE	Inverse Odds	Odds	Odds SE	Inverse Odds	Odds	Odds SE	Inverse Odds	Odds	Odds SE	Inverse Odds	Odds	Odds SE	Inverse Odds
Male	0.797	0.106	1.255	0.650**	0.106	1.539	0.740	0.144	1.352	1.198	0.136		1.270	0.172	
African American[c]	0.690	0.162	1.450	0.278***	0.105	3.601	0.898	0.360	1.114	0.564	0.184	1.774	1.017	0.261	
Hispanic	0.600*	0.154	1.666	0.387**	0.140	2.583	0.699	0.300	1.431	1.067	0.374		0.684	0.208	1.463
Asian American	0.872	0.218	1.147	0.627*	0.116	1.594	0.892	0.358	1.122	0.702	0.127	1.425	1.157	0.330	
International	0.446**	0.115	2.240	0.511***	0.074	1.955	0.925	0.344	1.081	0.679**	0.099	1.472	1.656**	0.320	
Married or domestic partner	1.698***	0.252		1.206	0.162		1.210	0.273		0.914	0.114	1.094	1.286	0.195	
Household income ($1,000s)	0.990***	0.002	1.010	0.991**	0.003	1.009	1.000	0.004	1.000	0.995	0.003	1.005	0.994*	0.003	1.006
Age at start of doctoral program (1 yr.)	0.971**	0.009	1.030	0.946**	0.018	1.058	0.936***	0.017	1.069	0.970**	0.015	1.031	0.962**	0.013	1.040
Always full-time doctoral student	2.064***	0.286		1.418	0.254		2.121**	0.537		1.041	0.206		1.689**	0.319	
GRE verbal (100s of points)	1.207*	0.089		1.174**	0.069		1.400**	0.174		1.063	0.063		1.235**	0.092	
GRE quantitative (100s of points)	1.052	0.077		0.802	0.107	1.248	0.977	0.117	1.023	1.338**	0.119		1.011	0.086	
GRE analytical (100s of points)	0.955	0.073	1.047	0.901	0.070	1.109	0.901	0.120	1.110	0.968	0.071	1.033	1.202*	0.101	
Master's upon entry	0.823	0.115	1.215	0.849	0.114	1.178	1.025	0.213		0.964	0.151	1.038	0.664*	0.097	1.507
Private graduate school	1.053	0.132		0.757*	0.094	1.321	0.408***	0.082	2.451	0.772*	0.088	1.295	0.765*	0.102	1.307

(table continues)

283

Table F.5 (continued)

Independent Variable[a]	Education[b]			Engineering			Humanities			Sciences and Mathematics			Social Sciences		
	Odds	Inverse Odds	Odds SE	Odds	Inverse Odds	Odds SE	Odds	Inverse Odds	Odds SE	Odds	Inverse Odds	Odds SE	Odds	Inverse Odds	Odds SE
Ever received a fellowship	1.656***		0.212	0.993	1.007	0.120	1.448		0.307	0.697**	1.434	0.080	0.926	1.080	0.129
Ever was a research assistant	1.897***		0.243	1.239		0.194	1.664*		0.351	1.277*		0.144	1.931***		0.246
Time in doctoral program (yrs.)	1.118***		0.026	1.159***		0.040	1.165***		0.046	1.032		0.032	1.253***		0.040
Expect first job to be faculty or postdoctoral position	2.018***		0.251	1.404**		0.179	1.156		0.248	0.855	1.170	0.091	1.900***		0.243
Constant	0.159		0.088	20.837		22.448	1.294		1.286	0.927		0.704	0.082		0.061
n (unweighted)		1,509			806			1,167			1,673			2,193	
Likelihood ratio test		327.34***			142.94***			100.44***			102.87***			281.94***	
McFadden pseudo R^2		0.161			0.071			0.119			0.043			0.154	

Source: Survey of Doctoral Student Finances, Experiences, and Achievements.
[a] Parents' SES, children under eighteen, and selective undergraduate institution were nonsignificant predictors in all fields and were dropped from the models.
[b] Dependent measure is dichotomous (no = 0, yes = 1). Odds ratio coefficients. Inverse odds ratio (1/odds ratio) presented for odds ratios less than 1.
[c] All racial groups and international students are compared with whites.
*$p < .05$; **$p < .01$; ***$p < .001$

Table F.6
Regression Analysis of Predictors of Being a Research Assistant over the Course of Doctoral Study, by Field

Independent Variable[a]	Education[b]			Engineering			Humanities			Sciences and Mathematics			Social Sciences		
	Odds	Odds SE	Inverse Odds	Odds	Odds SE	Inverse Odds	Odds	Odds SE	Inverse Odds	Odds	Odds SE	Inverse Odds	Odds	Odds SE	Inverse Odds
Male	0.808	0.108	1.238	0.999	0.218	1.001	0.904	0.157	1.107	0.973	0.109	1.027	0.780*	0.096	1.282
African American[c]	0.458***	0.108	2.182	0.225***	0.087	4.448	0.873	0.323	1.146	0.293***	0.104	3.416	0.743	0.178	1.346
Hispanic	0.578*	0.150	1.730	0.955	0.490	1.047	0.626	0.256	1.598	1.049	0.359		0.769	0.227	1.300
Asian American	1.034	0.266		0.672	0.172	1.489	0.723	0.259	1.382	0.940	0.171	1.063	0.915	0.233	1.093
International	0.541**	0.122	1.847	0.594**	0.114	1.684	0.681	0.259	1.469	0.854	0.110	1.170	0.730*	0.108	1.370
Married or domestic partner	0.934	0.148	1.071	1.877**	0.368		1.119	0.230		0.939	0.119	1.064	1.238	0.173	
Household income ($1,000s)	0.998	0.002	1.002	0.987***	0.004	1.013	1.001	0.004		0.991**	0.003	1.009	0.996	0.003	1.004
Children under eighteen	0.944	0.139	1.059	0.458***	0.103	2.183	1.134	0.306		1.283	0.231		0.815	0.142	1.228
Age at start of doctoral program (1 yr.)	0.956***	0.009	1.046	0.949*	0.023	1.054	0.966	0.018	1.035	0.942***	0.015	1.061	0.964**	0.013	1.038
Always full-time doctoral student	2.583***	0.357		1.269	0.297		1.240	0.311		1.996***	0.384		1.279	0.226	
GRE quantitative (100s of points)	1.019	0.058		1.221	0.170		0.999	0.086	1.001	0.968	0.075	1.033	1.216**	0.079	
Master's upon entry	0.797	0.112	1.255	0.519***	0.094	1.927	0.835	0.163	1.197	0.771	0.119	1.297	1.036	0.143	
Private graduate school	0.528***	0.067	1.896	1.256	0.219		1.026	0.188		0.806	0.090	1.240	0.647***	0.079	1.545

(table continues)

Table F.6 (continued)

Independent Variable[a]	Education[b]			Engineering			Humanities			Sciences and Mathematics			Social Sciences		
	Odds	Odds SE	Inverse Odds	Odds	Odds SE	Inverse Odds	Odds	Odds SE	Inverse Odds	Odds	Odds SE	Inverse Odds	Odds	Odds SE	Inverse Odds
Ever received a fellowship	2.352***	0.304		0.455***	0.076	2.197	2.258***	0.479		0.510***	0.057	1.962	1.123	0.140	
Ever was a teaching assistant	1.847***	0.238		1.291	0.205		1.749*	0.383		1.289*	0.148		1.963***	0.251	
Time in doctoral program (yrs.)	1.066**	0.024		1.145**	0.053		1.045	0.035		1.305***	0.043		1.090**	0.030	
Expect first job to be faculty or postdoctoral position	1.102	0.142		0.808	0.135	1.237	1.145	0.222		0.795*	0.083	1.258	1.337*	0.158	
Constant	1.082	0.544		8.194	10.741		0.287	0.257		6.692	5.138		0.369	0.235	
n (unweighted)	1,509			783			1,121			1,640			2,148		
Likelihood ratio test	372.81***			161.20***			51.83***			210.62***			157.20***		
McFadden pseudo R^2	0.1833			0.125			0.056			0.082			0.081		

Source: Survey of Doctoral Student Finances, Experiences, and Achievements.
[a] Parents' SES, GRE verbal scores, GRE analytical scores, and selective undergraduate institution were nonsignificant predictors in all fields and were dropped from the models.
[b] Dependent measure is dichotomous (no = 0, yes = 1). Odds ratio coefficients. Inverse odds ratio (1/odds ratio) presented for odds ratios less than 1.
[c] All racial groups and international students are compared with whites.
*p < .05; **p < .01; ***p < .001

Table F.7
Regression Analysis of Predictors of Incurring Education Debt over the Course of Doctoral Study, by Field

Independent Variable[a]	Education[b]			Engineering			Humanities			Sciences and Mathematics			Social Sciences		
	Odds	Inverse Odds	Odds SE	Odds	Inverse Odds	Odds SE	Odds	Inverse Odds	Odds SE	Odds	Inverse Odds	Odds SE	Odds	Inverse Odds	Odds SE
Male	1.045		0.149	0.896	1.116	0.252	1.137		0.210	0.960	1.042	0.156	0.955	1.047	0.131
African American[c]	1.687*		0.391	2.046		1.207	0.899		0.355	1.372		0.560	0.899	1.113	0.236
Hispanic	1.293		0.355	0.314	3.180	0.271	0.646	1.548	0.281	1.137		0.457	0.568	1.762	0.181
Asian American	0.563*	1.778	0.152	0.791	1.264	0.245	0.708	1.413	0.269	0.407**	2.458	0.119	0.841	1.189	0.224
International	0.050***	20.156	0.022	0.210***	4.755	0.061	0.191***	5.245	0.092	0.060***	16.800	0.020	0.126***	7.915	0.030
Parents' SES[d]	0.937	1.067	0.067	0.728**	1.373	0.082	0.805*	1.243	0.083	0.829*	1.206	0.070	0.842*	1.188	0.063
Household income ($1,000s)	0.982***	1.018	0.002	0.978***	1.023	0.005	0.981***	1.019	0.005	0.979***	1.022	0.005	0.988***	1.012	0.003
Age at start of doctoral program (1 yr.)	0.972**	1.029	0.009	1.051		0.031	0.998	1.002	0.018	1.010		0.021	0.999	1.001	0.014
Married or domestic partner	1.259		0.213	2.809***		0.738	1.318		0.290	1.759**		0.326	1.192		0.190
Children under eighteen	1.166		0.178	2.358**		0.658	0.702	1.424	0.200	1.320		0.323	0.709	1.410	0.142
GRE quantitative (100s of points)	0.771**	1.298	0.063	0.468***	2.138	0.103	0.816	1.226	0.099	0.752*	1.330	0.096	0.734***	1.363	0.066
GRE analytical (100s of points)	1.066		0.085	1.340*		0.175	0.953	1.049	0.114	0.780*	1.283	0.076	1.020		0.089
Selective undergraduate institution	0.954	1.048	0.137	1.232		0.279	0.791	1.263	0.153	0.555***	1.801	0.090	0.680**	1.470	0.098
Private graduate school	2.068***		0.280	0.674	1.484	0.149	0.678*	1.474	0.131	0.575**	1.739	0.108	1.320*		0.183

(table continues)

Table F.7 (*continued*)

Independent Variable[a]	Education[b]			Engineering			Humanities			Sciences and Mathematics			Social Sciences		
	Odds	Odds SE	Inverse Odds	Odds	Odds SE	Inverse Odds	Odds	Odds SE	Inverse Odds	Odds	Odds SE	Inverse Odds	Odds	Odds SE	Inverse Odds
Ever received a fellowship	1.441**	0.195		0.578**	0.120	1.731	0.546**	0.113	1.832	1.164	0.185		0.878	0.124	1.138
Ever was a research assistant	1.177	0.169		4.421***	1.736		1.343	0.253		0.964	0.161	1.037	1.005	0.136	
Ever was a teaching assistant	1.420*	0.200		2.179***	0.468		1.399	0.302		2.392***	0.477		0.965	0.142	1.037
Time in doctoral program (yrs.)	1.047	0.026		1.054	0.059		1.112**	0.038		1.075	0.043		1.123***	0.034	
Constant	7.419	4.277		0.507	0.878		8.307	7.895		6.076	6.232		7.967	5.945	
n (unweighted)	1,213			673			979			1,450			1,875		
Likelihood ratio test	294.51***			167.35***			91.35***			259.45***			205.76***		
McFadden pseudo R^2	0.167			0.183			0.104			0.171			0.126		

Source: Survey of Doctoral Student Finances, Experiences, and Achievements.

[a] Master's upon entry, GRE verbal scores, and always being full-time were nonsignificant predictors in all fields and were dropped from the models.

[b] Dependent measure is dichotomous (no = 0, yes = 1). Odds ratio coefficients. Inverse odds ratio (1/odds ratio) presented for odds ratios less than 1.

[c] All racial groups and international students are compared with whites.

[d] Parents' SES is a composite of educational attainment and occupational prestige.

$* p < .05; ** p < .01; *** p < .001$

Table F.8
Regression Analysis of Predictors of Having Peer Interactions, by Field

Independent Variable[a]	Education[b] Odds	SE	Engineering Odds	SE	Humanities Odds	SE	Sciences and Mathematics Odds	SE	Social Sciences Odds	SE
Male	0.117*	0.058	−0.094	0.069	−0.238**	0.075	−0.132**	0.044	−0.134*	0.052
African American[c]	0.029	0.094	0.232	0.159	0.197	0.159	−0.072	0.134	0.083	0.099
Hispanic	0.036	0.118	0.263	0.154	0.381*	0.175	0.184	0.136	0.079	0.128
Asian American	−0.057	0.118	−0.048	0.080	0.206	0.158	−0.013	0.070	0.105	0.110
International	−0.019	0.115	−0.160**	0.062	0.287	0.150	−0.407***	0.054	−0.057	0.074
Parents' SES[d]	0.012	0.029	0.072*	0.028	0.023	0.040	0.038	0.022	0.011	0.028
Household income ($1,000s)	0.000	0.001	−0.001	0.001	0.000	0.002	−0.003**	0.001	0.002	0.001
Married or domestic partner	−0.066	0.067	−0.091	0.060	−0.059	0.088	−0.023	0.048	−0.279***	0.059
Age at start of doctoral program (1 yr.)	−0.001	0.004	−0.044***	0.008	−0.009	0.007	−0.027***	0.006	−0.026***	0.005
Children under eighteen	−0.155**	0.059	−0.017	0.076	−0.095	0.107	−0.116	0.067	−0.111	0.071
GRE verbal (100s of points)	−0.015	0.032	−0.027	0.025	0.070	0.049	0.037	0.023	0.063*	0.030
GRE quantitative (100s of points)	−0.155***	0.031	−0.075	0.057	−0.005	0.047	−0.131***	0.035	−0.114***	0.033
GRE analytical (100s of points)	0.059	0.034	0.021	0.033	0.071	0.051	0.009	0.028	0.072*	0.033
Master's upon entry	−0.024	0.069	−0.123*	0.057	−0.075	0.080	−0.032	0.059	−0.043	0.058
Private graduate school	0.113*	0.055	−0.019	0.052	−0.092	0.078	0.128**	0.044	0.108*	0.052
Always full-time doctoral student	0.388***	0.062	0.128	0.075	−0.012	0.099	0.023	0.074	0.140*	0.071

(table continues)

Table F.8 (continued)

Independent Variable[a]	Education[b]		Engineering		Humanities		Sciences and Mathematics		Social Sciences	
	Odds	SE	Odds	SE	Odds	SE	Odds	SE	Odds	SE
Expect first job to be faculty or postdoctoral position	-0.135*	0.056	-0.025	0.054	0.230**	0.081	-0.013	0.040	-0.047	0.051
Ever received a fellowship	0.229***	0.057	0.151**	0.051	0.049	0.082	0.103*	0.042	0.165**	0.053
Ever was a research assistant	0.077	0.065	0.159*	0.065	0.029	0.076	0.153***	0.044	0.022	0.051
Ever was a teaching assistant	0.203**	0.063	0.033	0.049	0.269**	0.085	0.219***	0.045	0.121*	0.055
Time in doctoral program (yrs.)	-0.003	0.008	0.018	0.014	-0.007	0.013	-0.011	0.011	-0.024*	0.010
Constant	0.291	0.237	1.556	0.446	-0.873	0.396	1.386	0.297	0.659	0.277
n (unweighted)	2,504		883		1,323		1,850		2,461	
R^2	0.104		0.140		0.097		0.155		0.146	

Source: Survey of Doctoral Student Finances, Experiences, and Achievements.
[a] Selective undergraduate institution was not a significant predictor in any field and was dropped from the models.
[b] Unstandardized regression coefficients; dependent measure is standardized ($M = 0$, $SD = 1$).
[c] All racial groups and international students are compared with whites.
[d] Parents' SES is a composite of educational attainment and occupational prestige.
* $p < .05$; ** $p < .01$; *** $p < .001$

290

Table F.9
Regression Analysis of Predictors of Having a Mentor, by Field

Independent Variable[a]	Education[b]			Engineering			Humanities[c]			Sciences and Mathematics			Social Sciences		
	Odds	Inverse Odds	Odds SE	Odds	Inverse Odds	Odds SE	Odds	Inverse Odds	Odds SE	Odds	Inverse Odds	Odds SE	Odds	Inverse Odds	Odds SE
Male	1.031		0.117	1.176	1.24	0.195	0.658	1.52	0.117	0.827	1.21	0.090	0.808	1.24	0.102
African American[d]	0.827	1.21	0.154	0.810	1.39	0.324	0.678	1.48	0.242	0.392**	2.55	0.124	0.943	1.06	0.233
Hispanic	1.357		0.317	0.720	2.07	0.277	1.161		0.504	0.567	1.76	0.182	0.805	1.24	0.238
Asian American	1.251		0.300	0.484***		0.091	1.214		0.484	0.808	1.24	0.137	0.825	1.21	0.218
International	0.666*	1.50	0.136	0.632**	1.58	0.091	1.013		0.376	0.909	1.10	0.117	0.856	1.17	0.147
Parents' SES[e]	1.110		0.062	1.219**		0.083	1.059		0.101	1.163**		0.062	1.173*		0.078
GRE verbal (100s of points)	0.970	1.03	0.055	0.893*	1.12	0.048	0.872	1.15	0.096	1.085		0.054	1.008		0.066
GRE quantitative (100s of points)	1.038		0.054	0.996	1.00	0.123	1.154		0.107	0.769**	1.30	0.062	1.024		0.069
Private graduate school	0.813*	1.23	0.085	1.211		0.158	0.729	1.37	0.131	0.785*	1.27	0.083	0.796	1.26	0.097
Constant	2.162		0.771	5.232		4.675	4.331		3.108	13.482		7.462	2.684		1.286
n (unweighted)	1,617			815			1,190			1,676			2,204		
Likelihood ratio test	17.93*			32.47***			13.29			44.69***			18.18*		
McFadden pseudo R²	0.008			0.018			0.015			0.017			0.011		

Source: Survey of Doctoral Student Finances, Experiences, and Achievements.
[a]Age at start of doctoral program, selective undergraduate institution, GRE analytical scores, master's upon entry, and first or only choice of doctoral program were nonsignificant predictors in all fields and were dropped from the models.
[b]Dependent measure is dichotomous (no = 0, yes = 1). Odds ratio coefficients. Inverse odds ratio (1/odds ratio) presented for odds ratios less than 1.
[c]The model is not statistically significantly different from the null model. This suggests that there is no relationship among the predictors and having a faculty mentor.
[d]All racial groups and international students are compared with whites.
[e]Parents' SES is a composite of educational attainment and occupational prestige.
*p < .05; **p < .01; ***p < .001

291

Table F.10
Regression Analysis of Predictors of Student-Faculty Social Interactions, by Field

Independent Variable[a]	Education[b]		Engineering		Humanities		Sciences and Mathematics		Social Sciences	
	Odds	SE	Odds	SE	Odds	SE	Odds	SE	Odds	SE
Male	0.198***	0.054	0.337***	0.064	0.094	0.074	0.043	0.044	0.124*	0.055
African American[c]	-0.121	0.088	-0.249	0.146	0.160	0.158	-0.381**	0.137	-0.034	0.105
Hispanic	-0.062	0.110	-0.126	0.144	0.046	0.173	-0.164	0.137	-0.026	0.135
Asian American	-0.151	0.112	0.139	0.075	-0.128	0.157	-0.056	0.071	0.045	0.117
International	-0.003	0.108	0.120*	0.057	0.036	0.148	0.007	0.054	-0.071	0.077
Married or domestic partner	-0.004	0.061	0.088	0.053	-0.133	0.086	0.062	0.048	-0.224***	0.061
Age at start of doctoral program (1 yr.)	0.005	0.003	-0.008	0.006	0.010	0.006	0.014**	0.005	0.006	0.005
Household income ($1,000s)	0.002*	0.001	0.002	0.001	0.004*	0.002	-0.001	0.001	0.002	0.001
GRE verbal (100s of points)	-0.111***	0.030	-0.062**	0.023	-0.093	0.049	-0.069**	0.023	-0.057	0.031
GRE quantitative (100s of points)	-0.035	0.029	0.150**	0.052	0.055	0.046	-0.005	0.036	0.037	0.035
GRE analytical (100s of points)	0.026	0.032	0.044	0.031	0.029	0.051	0.075**	0.028	0.027	0.035
Private graduate school	0.001	0.051	0.057	0.049	-0.298***	0.078	-0.126***	0.045	-0.270***	0.055
Always full-time doctoral student	-0.171**	0.057	0.257***	0.070	0.056	0.098	-0.071	0.075	-0.040	0.076
Time in doctoral program (yrs.)	-0.015	0.008	-0.037**	0.013	-0.040**	0.012	-0.064***	0.011	-0.058***	0.011
First or only choice of doctoral program	0.302***	0.072	0.203***	0.050	0.162*	0.071	0.031	0.041	0.312***	0.053
Ever received a fellowship	0.003	0.053	0.083	0.048	0.049	0.081	0.102*	0.043	-0.007	0.057
Ever was a teaching assistant	-0.038	0.059	-0.044	0.046	-0.169*	0.084	-0.093*	0.046	-0.088	0.058
Has a mentor	0.630***	0.051	0.501***	0.049	0.576***	0.081	0.436***	0.044	0.574***	0.058
Expect first job to be faculty or postdoctoral position	0.163**	0.053	0.049	0.050	0.204**	0.082	0.081*	0.041	0.042	0.054
Constant	-0.150	0.225	-1.851		-0.804		-0.425		-0.700	
n (unweighted)	2,469		884		1,317		1,834		2,444	
R^2	0.138		0.151		0.146		0.086		0.138	

Source: Survey of Doctoral Student Finances, Experiences, and Achievements.
[a] Parents' SES, children under eighteen, selective undergraduate institution, master's upon entry, and ever was a research assistant were nonsignificant predictors in all fields and were dropped from the models.
[b] Unstandardized regression coefficients; dependent measure is standardized (M = 0, SD = 1).
[c] All racial groups and international students are compared with whites.
$*p < .05$; $**p < .01$; $***p < .001$

292

Table F.11
Regression Analysis of Predictors of Student-Faculty Academic Interactions, by Field

Independent Variable[a]	Education[b]		Engineering		Humanities		Sciences and Mathematics		Social Sciences	
	Odds	SE	Odds	SE	Odds	SE	Odds	SE	Odds	SE
Male	0.146*	0.057	0.158*	0.063	-0.013	0.074	0.016	0.042	0.079	0.057
African American[c]	-0.092	0.093	-0.221	0.143	0.118	0.157	-0.192	0.130	0.009	0.108
Hispanic	-0.126	0.116	-0.033	0.140	-0.069	0.170	-0.134	0.130	-0.066	0.139
Asian American	-0.247*	0.118	0.235**	0.074	-0.155	0.153	0.019	0.067	-0.021	0.120
International	-0.077	0.116	0.106	0.060	0.005	0.149	0.109*	0.054	0.025	0.083
Parents' SES[d]	-0.028	0.028	0.063*	0.025	-0.004	0.040	-0.006	0.021	-0.011	0.030
Household income ($1,000s)	0.002*	0.001	0.002	0.001	0.005**	0.002	0.000	0.001	0.001	0.001
Married or domestic partner	0.041	0.064	0.108*	0.051	-0.082	0.084	0.053	0.045	-0.145*	0.063
GRE verbal (100s of points)	-0.097**	0.031	-0.081***	0.023	-0.062	0.048	-0.082***	0.022	-0.032	0.032
GRE quantitative (100s of points)	-0.003	0.031	0.174***	0.051	0.064	0.046	0.002	0.035	0.057	0.036
GRE analytical (100s of points)	0.007	0.032	0.040	0.030	-0.014	0.049	0.070**	0.026	-0.015	0.035
Selective undergraduate institution	-0.157*	0.062	-0.112*	0.057	-0.149	0.078	0.019	0.047	0.009	0.063
Private graduate school	0.026	0.055	0.186***	0.048	-0.148	0.076	-0.036	0.043	-0.170**	0.057
Always full-time doctoral student	-0.085	0.061	0.319***	0.068	0.118	0.097	0.030	0.071	-0.043	0.077
First or only choice of doctoral program	0.278***	0.076	0.156**	0.049	0.185**	0.070	0.151***	0.039	0.274***	0.054

(table continues)

293

Table F.11 (continued)

Independent Variable[a]	Education[b]		Engineering		Humanities		Sciences and Mathematics		Social Sciences	
	Odds	SE	Odds	SE	Odds	SE	Odds	SE	Odds	SE
Has a mentor	0.718***	0.055	0.540***	0.048	0.724***	0.080	0.448***	0.042	0.730***	0.060
Ever was a research assistant	0.008	0.064	0.048	0.059	−0.062	0.075	0.039	0.042	0.143*	0.056
Ever received a fellowship	−0.002	0.057	0.122**	0.047	0.095	0.080	0.125**	0.041	0.007	0.058
Ever was a teaching assistant	−0.054	0.063	−0.110*	0.045	−0.092	0.083	−0.051	0.044	−0.061	0.060
Time in doctoral program (yrs.)	−0.009	0.008	−0.035**	0.012	−0.027*	0.012	−0.055***	0.011	−0.060***	0.011
Expect first job to be faculty or post-doctoral position	0.193***	0.056	0.099*	0.049	0.319***	0.080	0.123**	0.039	0.182**	0.056
Constant	−0.280	0.200	−2.062	0.348	−0.637	0.318	−0.494	0.237	−0.757	0.241
n (unweighted)	2,415		875		1,296		1,814		2,393	
R^2	0.147		0.187		0.183		0.102		0.175	

Source: Survey of Doctoral Student Finances, Experiences, and Achievements.
[a] Children under eighteen and age at start of doctoral program were nonsignificant predictors in all fields and were dropped from the models.
[b] Unstandardized regression coefficients; dependent measure is standardized (M = 0, SD = 1).
[c] All racial groups and international students are compared with whites.
[d] Parents' SES is a composite of educational attainment and occupational prestige.
* $p < .05$; ** $p < .01$; *** $p < .001$

294

Table F.12
Regression Analysis of Predictors of Student Interactions with Faculty Adviser, by Field

Independent Variable[a]	Education[b]		Engineering		Humanities		Sciences and Mathematics		Social Sciences	
	Odds	SE	Odds	SE	Odds	SE	Odds	SE	Odds	SE
Male	0.110	0.062	0.130	0.083	0.015	0.079	0.001	0.052	−0.044	0.062
African American[c]	0.026	0.102	−0.174	0.181	0.044	0.169	−0.049	0.159	0.104	0.117
Hispanic	−0.129	0.129	−0.116	0.182	−0.022	0.195	−0.166	0.165	0.007	0.156
Asian American	−0.172	0.129	0.019	0.095	−0.069	0.172	0.019	0.085	−0.147	0.135
International	−0.120	0.117	0.036	0.071	−0.165	0.165	−0.049	0.062	−0.039	0.084
Parents' SES[d]	0.032	0.031	0.071*	0.033	0.044	0.044	0.054*	0.026	−0.005	0.034
Household income ($1,000s)	0.001	0.001	0.005***	0.001	0.001	0.002	0.000	0.001	−0.001	0.001
GRE verbal (100s of points)	−0.059*	0.030	−0.030	0.025	−0.097*	0.045	−0.051*	0.024	−0.018	0.031
Private graduate school	−0.131*	0.061	0.059	0.062	−0.085	0.085	−0.088	0.054	−0.080	0.064
First or only choice of doctoral program	0.222**	0.085	0.106	0.064	0.117	0.079	0.032	0.050	0.136*	0.062
Time in doctoral program (yrs.)	0.001	0.009	−0.011	0.016	0.012	0.014	−0.033*	0.014	−0.037***	0.013
Always full-time doctoral student	0.016	0.068	0.346***	0.092	0.030	0.109	0.049	0.093	−0.032	0.088
Ever received a fellowship	0.140*	0.062	0.058	0.060	−0.037	0.091	0.124*	0.052	0.061	0.065
Ever was a research assistant	0.122	0.069	−0.032	0.078	0.064	0.085	−0.025	0.054	0.177***	0.061
Expect first job to be faculty or postdoctoral position	0.186**	0.061	0.184**	0.063	0.233*	0.092	0.106*	0.049	0.177***	0.062
Adviser as mentor	0.891	0.058	0.660***	0.069	0.871***	0.080	0.757***	0.054	0.888***	0.061
Constant	−0.516	0.199	−1.041	0.224	−0.126	0.335	−0.321	0.191	−0.531	0.228
n (unweighted)	2,370		844		1,136		1,645		2,168	
R^2	0.199		0.136		0.225		0.148		0.220	

Source: Survey of Doctoral Student Finances, Experiences, and Achievements.
[a]Married or domestic partner, children under eighteen, age at start of doctoral program, GRE quantitative, GRE analytical, selective undergraduate institution, and ever was a teaching assistant were nonsignificant predictors in all fields and were dropped from the models.
[b]Unstandardized regression coefficients; dependent measure is standardized (M = 0, SD = 1).
[c]All racial groups and international students are compared with whites.
[d]Parents' SES is a composite of educational attainment and occupational prestige.
*p < .05; **p < .01; ***p < .001

295

Table F.13
Regression Analysis of Predictors of Overall Student Research Productivity, by Field

Independent Variable[a]	Education[b]			Engineering			Humanities			Sciences and Mathematics			Social Sciences		
	Odds	Inverse Odds	Odds SE	Odds	Inverse Odds	Odds SE	Odds	Inverse Odds	Odds SE	Odds	Inverse Odds	Odds SE	Odds	Inverse Odds	Odds SE
Male	1.009		0.120	2.277***		0.395	1.027		0.178	1.328*		0.147	0.869	1.151	0.109
African American[c]	0.809	1.236	0.159	1.379		0.581	0.915	1.093	0.336	0.406*	2.462	0.158	0.593*	1.687	0.144
Hispanic	0.909	1.100	0.209	0.510	1.962	0.215	0.831	1.203	0.329	0.631	1.585	0.224	0.648	1.544	0.200
Asian American	1.216		0.296	1.072		0.225	0.638	1.566	0.220	1.008		0.179	0.634	1.577	0.175
International	0.789	1.267	0.166	0.941	1.063	0.161	0.751	1.332	0.269	0.884	1.131	0.124	0.802	1.246	0.133
Children under 18	1.008		0.120	0.609**	1.642	0.105	1.043		0.268	1.007		0.168	0.912	1.096	0.153
Master's upon entry	1.109		0.143	1.112		0.156	1.630**		0.305	1.109		0.164	1.174		0.158
GRE quantitative (100s of points)	1.041		0.053	0.944	1.059	0.121	0.882	1.134	0.076	0.910	1.098	0.072	0.832**	1.202	0.055
Selective undergraduate institution	1.026		0.128	0.695*	1.439	0.115	1.051		0.191	0.944	1.060	0.114	1.022		0.140
Private graduate school	0.803	1.245	0.090	1.502**		0.216	1.106		0.205	1.132		0.127	0.799	1.251	0.100
Ever received a fellowship	1.536***		0.180	1.046		0.145	1.121		0.220	1.546***		0.167	1.296*		0.167
Ever was a research assistant	2.154***		0.262	1.782***		0.298	1.020		0.183	2.706***		0.308	1.879***		0.230
Ever was a teaching assistant	1.261		0.152	1.073		0.140	1.990***		0.401	0.623***	1.606	0.073	1.260		0.170
Has a mentor	1.447**		0.172	1.704***		0.236	2.134***		0.415	1.398*		0.158	2.171***		0.303
Time in doctoral program (yrs.)	1.114***		0.022	1.738***		0.078	1.291***		0.048	1.551***		0.050	1.263***		0.036
Expect first job to be faculty or postdoctoral position	1.550***		0.177	0.994	1.006	0.144	1.383		0.265	1.136		0.117	1.937***		0.241
Constant	0.165		0.058	0.132		0.133	0.229		0.134	0.186		0.107	0.352		0.160
n (unweighted)	1,502			774			1,118			1,591			2,131		
Likelihood ratio test	181.13***			280.50***			120.62***			423.52***			243.03***		
McFadden pseudo R²	0.084			0.157			0.122			0.152			0.1260		

Source: Survey of Doctoral Student Finances, Experiences, and Achievements.
[a] Parents' SES, married or domestic partner, age at start of doctoral program, household income, GRE verbal, and GRE analytical were nonsignificant predictors in all fields and were dropped from the models.
[b] Dependent measure is dichotomous (no = 0, yes = 1). Odds ratio coefficients. Inverse odds ratio (1/odds ratio) presented for odds ratios less than 1.
[c] All racial groups and international students are compared with whites.
*p < .05; **p < .01; ***p < .001

296

Regression Analysis of Predictors of Presenting a Paper at a National Conference (Sole or Joint Authorship), by Field

Independent Variable[a]	Education[b]			Engineering			Humanities			Sciences and Mathematics			Social Sciences		
	Odds	Inverse Odds	Odds SE	Odds	Inverse Odds	Odds SE	Odds	Inverse Odds	Odds SE	Odds	Inverse Odds	Odds SE	Odds	Inverse Odds	Odds SE
Male	1.041		0.135	1.821***		0.310	0.880	1.137	0.152	1.283*		0.155	0.873	1.146	0.115
African American[c]	1.109		0.241	1.351		0.540	0.743	1.346	0.280	0.578	1.731	0.269	0.737	1.358	0.192
Hispanic	1.046		0.256	0.601	1.664	0.253	0.568	1.759	0.227	0.341*	2.935	0.153	0.962	1.040	0.300
Asian American	1.078		0.279	1.211		0.244	0.619	1.615	0.217	1.225		0.228	0.846	1.182	0.240
International	0.850	1.177	0.224	1.251		0.211	0.396*	2.526	0.154	1.086		0.172	0.814	1.229	0.158
Married or domestic partner	1.134		0.147	1.234		0.165	1.380		0.239	1.356**		0.153	1.006		0.130
Children under 18	0.988	1.012	0.135	0.506***	1.978	0.091	0.919	1.088	0.237	0.936	1.069	0.163	0.802	1.247	0.146
GRE verbal (100s of points)	1.165*		0.082	0.992	1.008	0.065	0.871	1.148	0.100	0.865*	1.156	0.054	1.002		0.075
GRE quantitative (100s of points)	0.977	1.023	0.070	0.909	1.100	0.129	0.871	1.148	0.097	0.849	1.179	0.084	0.781**	1.281	0.065
GRE analytical (100s of points)	1.010		0.072	1.176*		0.096	1.042		0.123	1.070		0.079	1.062		0.089
Selective undergraduate institution	1.020		0.135	0.678*	1.476	0.109	0.857	1.167	0.155	1.109		0.145	0.978	1.022	0.139
Private graduate school	0.745*	1.343	0.090	1.722***		0.233	1.129		0.207	0.756*	1.323	0.095	0.746*	1.340	0.098
Ever received a fellowship	1.612***		0.205	1.115		0.147	1.342		0.261	1.572***		0.185	1.288		0.175
Ever was a research assistant	2.192***		0.283	1.929***		0.318	0.921	1.086	0.164	2.709***		0.368	1.705***		0.220
Ever was a teaching assistant	1.274		0.162	0.976	1.025	0.122	2.252***		0.466	0.741*	1.349	0.091	1.236		0.179
Has a mentor	1.460**		0.190	1.769***		0.239	1.940***		0.381	1.156		0.143	1.935***		0.295
Always full-time doctoral student	0.934	1.070	0.128	0.619*	1.617	0.123	1.147		0.274	0.948	1.055	0.184	1.203		0.220
Time in doctoral program (yrs.)	1.131***		0.026	1.573***		0.064	1.240***		0.045	1.354***		0.044	1.244***		0.037
Expect first job to be faculty or post-doctoral position	1.604***		0.194	1.352*		0.188	1.255		0.244	0.880	1.136	0.097	1.927***		0.255
Constant	0.056		0.025	0.061		0.059	0.450		0.346	0.220		0.144	0.213		0.117
n (unweighted)	1,451			769			1,110			1,585			2,119		
Likelihood ratio test	190.93***			275.52***			116.58***			253.06***			198.16***		
McFadden pseudo R²	0.097			0.145			0.117			0.106			0.111		

Source: Survey of Doctoral Student Finances, Experiences, and Achievements.

[a]Parents' SES, household income, age at start of doctoral program, and master's upon entry were nonsignificant predictors in all fields and were dropped from the models.

[b]Dependent measure is dichotomous (no = 0, yes = 1). Odds ratio coefficients. Inverse odds ratio (1/odds ratio) presented for odds ratios less than 1.

[c]All racial groups and international students are compared with whites.

*$p < .05$; **$p < .01$; ***$p < .001$

297

Table F.15
Regression Analysis of Predictors of Publishing a Research Article (Sole or Joint Authorship), by Field

Independent Variable[a]	Education[b]			Engineering			Humanities			Sciences and Mathematics			Social Sciences		
	Odds	Inverse Odds	Odds SE	Odds	Inverse Odds	Odds SE	Odds	Inverse Odds	Odds SE	Odds	Inverse Odds	Odds SE	Odds	Inverse Odds	Odds SE
Male	1.121		0.138	1.632**		0.261	1.409		0.262	1.344**		0.137	0.998	1.002	0.132
African American[c]	0.464**	2.156	0.116	0.379	2.637	0.421	1.164		0.210	0.309***	3.237	0.127	0.434**	2.305	0.126
Hispanic	0.772	1.295	0.200	0.633	1.580	0.530	1.455		0.307	0.795	1.257	0.264	0.466*	2.147	0.179
Asian American	1.252		0.292	0.657	1.522	0.219	1.198		0.293	0.998	1.002	0.165	0.546	1.832	0.177
International	0.763	1.310	0.181	1.038		0.136	1.037		0.408	0.889	1.124	0.109	0.731	1.367	0.128
Age at start of doctoral program (1 yr.)	1.006		0.008	0.957**	1.045	0.014	1.026		0.016	1.005		0.013	0.997	1.003	0.012
Selective undergraduate institution	1.137		0.149	0.610***	1.639	0.085	0.995	1.005	0.198	0.969	1.032	0.109	0.858	1.166	0.126
Private graduate school	0.685***	1.461	0.083	0.903	1.108	0.138	0.742	1.348	0.154	1.245*		0.132	1.051		0.144
Ever received a fellowship	1.171		0.149	1.160		0.107	1.264		0.274	1.384**		0.141	1.184		0.167
Ever was a research assistant	1.737***		0.231	1.584**		0.243	1.281		0.250	2.806***		0.313	1.673***		0.229
Ever was a teaching assistant	1.340*		0.174	1.014		0.114	1.897*		0.481	0.674***	1.483	0.074	1.024		0.153
Has a mentor	1.517**		0.202	1.353*		0.164	1.412		0.327	1.313*		0.141	2.045***		0.344
Time in doctoral program (yrs.)	1.066***		0.018	1.314***		0.042	1.135***		0.032	1.422***		0.040	1.112***		0.027
Expect first job to be faculty or postdoctoral position	1.418**		0.171	1.216		0.150	1.327		0.289	1.143		0.111	1.568**		0.218
Constant	0.065		0.022	0.448		0.230	0.019		0.013	0.071		0.029	0.075		0.034
n (unweighted)	2,303			844			1,260			1,733			2,330		
Likelihood ratio test	125.79***			137.95***			49.17***			379.06***			102.87***		
McFadden pseudo R^2	0.060			0.066			0.062			0.126			0.064		

Source: Survey of Doctoral Student Finances, Experiences, and Achievements.
[a] Parents' SES, married or domestic partner, children under eighteen, household income, GRE verbal, GRE analytical, GRE quantitative, master's upon entry, and always being full-time were nonsignificant predictors in all fields and were dropped from the models.
[b] Dependent measure is dichotomous (no = 0, yes = 1). Odds ratio coefficients. Inverse odds ratio (1/odds ratio) presented for odds ratios less than 1.
[c] All racial groups and international students are compared with whites.
*p < .05; **p < .01; ***p < .001

Table F.16
Regression Analysis of Predictors of Overall Satisfaction with Doctoral Program, by Field

Independent Variable[a]	Education[b]		Engineering		Humanities		Sciences and Mathematics		Social Sciences	
	Odds	SE	Odds	SE	Odds	SE	Odds	SE	Odds	SE
Male	0.044	0.041	0.127*	0.052	0.041	0.057	-0.005	0.035	0.057	0.043
African American[c]	-0.003	0.067	-0.219	0.116	-0.092	0.125	-0.197	0.108	-0.067	0.081
Hispanic	0.101	0.084	-0.035	0.116	-0.041	0.136	-0.017	0.111	-0.038	0.108
Asian American	-0.028	0.086	0.036	0.061	-0.140	0.125	-0.118*	0.057	-0.041	0.095
International	-0.038	0.079	-0.038	0.045	-0.021	0.119	-0.127**	0.043	-0.024	0.061
Married or domestic partner	0.075	0.040	0.096**	0.037	0.103	0.057	0.067*	0.033	0.044	0.043
GRE verbal (100s of points)	0.026	0.019	0.000	0.015	-0.027	0.033	-0.038*	0.016	-0.019	0.022
Private graduate school	0.018	0.040	-0.088*	0.040	0.066	0.061	0.048	0.037	0.002	0.044
Always full-time doctoral student	0.065	0.045	-0.011	0.056	0.063	0.075	0.249***	0.060	0.031	0.059
Time in doctoral program (yrs.)	-0.015*	0.006	-0.045***	0.010	-0.001	0.010	0.010	0.009	-0.020*	0.009
First or only choice of doctoral program	0.194***	0.056	0.059	0.041	0.059	0.057	0.072*	0.034	0.163***	0.044
Expect first job to be faculty or postdoctoral position	0.003	0.041	0.082*	0.041	0.150*	0.066	0.180***	0.033	0.108*	0.044
Ever was a teaching assistant	-0.059	0.045	-0.049	0.037	-0.047	0.067	0.028	0.038	-0.094*	0.046
Incurred education debt as doctoral student	-0.012	0.041	-0.002	0.057	-0.073	0.058	-0.120*	0.049	-0.008	0.046
Peer interaction	0.083***	0.019	0.123***	0.020	0.115***	0.030	0.075***	0.018	0.132***	0.023
Student-faculty social interactions	0.303***	0.031	0.249***	0.029	0.278***	0.042	0.234***	0.025	0.192***	0.031
Interactions with faculty adviser	-0.005	0.023	0.059*	0.026	-0.029	0.035	0.105***	0.020	0.055*	0.025
Academic interactions with faculty	0.417***	0.032	0.397***	0.035	0.438***	0.046	0.389***	0.029	0.457***	0.033
Constant	-0.331	0.128	0.004	0.130	-0.061	0.247	0.128	0.004	0.014	0.157
n (unweighted)	2,501		886		1,323		1,850		2,161	
R²	0.530		0.496		0.526		0.459		0.513	

Source: Survey of Doctoral Student Finances, Experiences, and Achievements.
[a]Parents' SES, age at start of doctoral program, children under eighteen, household income, selective undergraduate institution, GRE quantitative, GRE analytical, master's upon entry, ever received a fellowship, ever was a research assistant, and having a mentor were nonsignificant predictors in all fields and were dropped from the models.
[b]Unstandardized regression coefficients; dependent measure is standardized (M = 0, SD = 1).
[c]All racial groups and international students are compared with whites.
*p < .05; **p < .01; ***p < .001

299

Table F.17
Regression Analysis of Predictors of Stopping Out of a Doctoral Program

Independent Variable[a]	Odds	Inverse Odds	Odds SE
Sciences and mathematics[b]	0.384***	2.606	0.048
Social sciences	0.717**	1.395	0.078
Humanities	1.078		0.137
Engineering	0.469***	2.132	0.062
Parents' SES[c]	0.884**	1.131	0.034
Household income ($1,000s)	1.011***		0.001
Married or domestic partner	0.655***	1.528	0.061
Children under 18	1.641***		0.143
First or only choice of doctoral program	1.373***		0.126
Ever was a research assistant	0.704***	1.421	0.059
Peer interaction	0.836***	1.196	0.031
Overall satisfaction with doctoral program	0.733***	1.364	0.025
Constant	0.337		0.054
n (unweighted)	8,235		
Likelihood ratio test	685.806***		
McFadden pseudo R^2	0.117		

Source: Survey of Doctoral Student Finances, Experiences, and Achievements.
[a]Sex, race-ethnicity, age at start of doctoral program, masters' upon entry, GRE quantitative, GRE verbal, GRE analytical, selective undergraduate institution, private graduate school, ever was a teaching assistant, ever received a fellowship, student-faculty social interaction, student-faculty academic interaction, interaction with faculty adviser, has a mentor, incurred education debt as a doctoral student, and expect first job to be faculty or postdoctoral position were nonsignificant predictors in all fields and were dropped from the models.
[b]Dependent measure is dichotomous (no = 0, yes = 1). Odds ratio coefficients. Inverse odds ratio (1/odds ratio) presented for odds ratios less than 1.
[c]All fields are compared with education.
[d]Parents' SES is a composite of educational attainment and occupational prestige.
*$p < .05$; **$p < .01$; ***$p < .001$

Table F.18
Regression Analysis of Predictors of Rate of Progress in Doctoral Program, by Field

Independent Variable[a]	Education[b]		Engineering		Humanities		Sciences and Mathematics		Social Sciences	
	Odds	SE	Odds	SE	Odds	SE	Odds	SE	Odds	SE
Male	-0.024	0.065	-0.248**	0.087	0.058	0.065	-0.035	0.043	0.063	0.043
African American[c]	-0.077	0.108	0.058	0.189	0.144	0.144	0.105	0.134	0.069	0.086
Hispanic	-0.127	0.136	-0.187	0.189	-0.077	0.159	-0.112	0.137	-0.069	0.111
Asian American	-0.169	0.136	0.146	0.099	-0.004	0.144	-0.038	0.070	-0.181	0.095
International	0.118	0.128	0.136	0.077	0.315*	0.139	0.104	0.054	0.129*	0.063
Parents' SES[d]	0.089**	0.034	0.051	0.035	0.039	0.036	0.040	0.022	0.063**	0.024
Household income ($1,000s)	0.000	0.001	-0.003*	0.001	-0.001	0.001	-0.002*	0.001	0.000	0.001
Children under 18	0.013	0.065	-0.267***	0.089	-0.086	0.095	-0.176**	0.066	-0.228***	0.060
Age at start of doctoral program (1 yr.)	0.017***	0.004	0.053***	0.010	0.012*	0.006	0.022***	0.006	0.004	0.004
GRE verbal (100s of points)	-0.222***	0.036	-0.086**	0.031	-0.033	0.045	-0.056*	0.023	-0.119***	0.025
GRE analytical (100s of points)	0.103**	0.033	0.033	0.037	0.057	0.040	0.066**	0.025	0.055*	0.025
Master's upon entry	0.140	0.079	0.027	0.070	0.097	0.073	-0.030	0.060	0.134**	0.050
Private graduate school	0.165*	0.064	0.027	0.065	-0.020	0.071	0.158***	0.044	0.093*	0.045
Always full-time doctoral student	0.586***	0.068	0.315***	0.090	0.478***	0.086	0.356***	0.072	0.358***	0.059
Ever received a fellowship	0.101	0.066	-0.125*	0.063	-0.016	0.075	0.083*	0.042	-0.001	0.046
Ever was a teaching assistant	-0.166*	0.071	-0.027	0.061	-0.002	0.078	-0.013	0.046	0.027	0.047
Had some research productivity	-0.080	0.062	-0.121	0.064	0.004	0.067	-0.170***	0.040	-0.084	0.043
Incurred education debt as doctoral student	-0.000	0.067	-0.068	0.094	-0.054	0.068	-0.047	0.060	-0.165***	0.046
Has a mentor	0.182**	0.063	0.176**	0.065	0.229**	0.075	-0.010	0.043	0.047	0.048
Constant	-0.482	0.271	-0.952	0.399	-1.097	0.359	-0.817	0.255	-0.242	0.234
n (unweighted)	2,419		861		1,309		1,806		2,426	
R^2	0.108		0.091		0.094		0.062		0.120	

Source: Survey of Doctoral Student Finances, Experiences, and Achievements.
[a] Married or domestic partner, selective undergraduate institution, GRE quantitative, ever was a research assistant, and academic interactions with faculty were not significant predictors in any field and were dropped from the models.
[b] Unstandardized regression coefficients; dependent measure is standardized ($M = 0$, $SD = 1$).
[c] All racial groups and international students are compared with whites.
[d] Parents' SES is a composite of educational attainment and occupational prestige.
*$p < .05$; **$p < .01$; ***$p < .001$

Table F.19
Regression Analysis of Predictors of Doctoral Degree Completion by 2001 for Students beyond the First Year, by Field

Independent Variable[a]	Education[b]			Engineering			Humanities			Sciences and Mathematics			Social Sciences		
	Odds	Inverse Odds	Odds SE	Odds	Inverse Odds	Odds SE	Odds	Inverse Odds	Odds SE	Odds	Inverse Odds	Odds SE	Odds	Inverse Odds	Odds SE
Male	0.801	1.248	0.098	0.702	1.424	0.142	0.931	1.074	0.163	0.947	1.056	0.120	1.084		0.133
African American[c]	0.707	1.415	0.145	0.150***	6.686	0.061	0.936	1.068	0.373	0.511	1.956	0.197	0.790	1.265	0.197
Hispanic	0.704	1.421	0.169	0.407*	2.459	0.167	0.852	1.174	0.369	0.585	1.709	0.240	0.521*	1.919	0.161
Asian American	0.972	1.029	0.253	0.558**	1.791	0.122	1.110		0.404	0.645*	1.551	0.134	0.806	1.241	0.218
International	1.304		0.308	1.219		0.241	1.547		0.605	0.999	1.001	0.164	1.612**		0.282
Age at start of doctoral program (1 yr.)	0.993	1.007	0.009	0.931**	1.074	0.022	1.019		0.018	0.984	1.016	0.018	0.977	1.024	0.013
Married or domestic partner	1.294*		0.163	2.167***		0.346	1.247		0.228	1.306*		0.166	1.181		0.148
Children under 18	0.756*	1.322	0.101	1.031		0.246	1.333		0.371	0.889	1.125	0.190	0.860	1.162	0.156
GRE verbal (100s of points)	0.831**	1.203	0.059	0.821**	1.218	0.062	0.870	1.149	0.107	0.979	1.022	0.069	0.814**	1.228	0.059
GRE analytical (100s of points)	0.889	1.124	0.056	0.907	1.102	0.083	1.072		0.117	0.974	1.026	0.076	1.198*		0.086
Master's upon entry	1.433*		0.201	0.973	1.028	0.164	1.162		0.230	1.052		0.198	1.177		0.169
Private graduate school	1.025		0.120	1.092		0.181	1.355		0.266	1.500**		0.204	1.052		0.134
Selective undergraduate institution	1.149		0.153	1.213		0.222	1.303		0.247	1.365*		0.202	1.202		0.166
First or only choice of doctoral program	1.187		0.181	1.444*		0.223	0.919	1.089	0.163	1.503***		0.183	1.251		0.151

Predictor[a][b][c]	Model 1 OR	SE	Model 2 OR	SE	(add'l)	Model 3 OR	SE	Model 4 OR	SE	Model 5 OR	SE
Always full-time doctoral student	1.649***	0.218	1.374	0.308		2.761***	0.723	3.984***	0.936	1.868***	0.337
Time in doctoral program (yrs.)	1.166***	0.028	1.261***	0.059		1.318***	0.053	1.624***	0.070	1.285***	0.042
Ever received a fellowship	1.381**	0.171	1.091	0.168		1.074	0.221	1.100	0.142	1.072	0.141
Ever was a research assistant	1.142	0.153	1.284	0.229		1.125	0.210	1.379*	0.179	1.240	0.154
Ever was a teaching assistant	1.482**	0.193	0.757	0.110	1.320	1.877**	0.424	1.054	0.146	1.252	0.170
Has a mentor	1.390**	0.169	1.675***	0.249		1.352	0.290	1.185	0.152	1.491**	0.204
Expect first job to be faculty or postdoctoral position	1.285*	0.154	0.829	0.132	1.206	1.181	0.242	1.615***	0.194	1.356*	0.170
Had some research productivity	1.800***	0.215	2.733***	0.413		3.021***	0.555	3.895***	0.515	1.556***	0.197
Constant	0.964	0.509	11.004	11.221		0.014	0.015	0.044	0.035	0.132	0.093
n (unweighted)	1,436		769			1,107		1,581		2,105	
Likelihood ratio test	207.43***		219.33***			183.52***		552.10***		216.30***	
McFadden pseudo R^2	0.101		0.144			0.185		0.235		0.114	

Source: Survey of Doctoral Student Finances, Experiences, and Achievements.

[a] Parents' SES, household income, GRE quantitative, and incurred education debt as a doctoral student were nonsignificant predictors in all fields and were dropped from the models.

[b] Dependent measure is dichotomous (no = 0, yes = 1). Odds ratio coefficients. Inverse odds ratio (1/odds ratio) presented for odds ratios less than 1.

[c] All racial groups and international students are compared with whites.

* $p < .05$; ** $p < .01$; *** $p < .001$

Table F.20
Regression Analysis of Predictors of Elapsed Time to Degree for Doctoral Degree Completers by 2001, by Field

Independent Variable[a]	Education[b]		Engineering		Humanities		Sciences and Mathematics		Social Sciences	
	Odds	SE	Odds	SE	Odds	SE	Odds	SE	Odds	SE
Male	-0.071	0.221	0.155	0.139	-0.085	0.260	0.110	0.085	-0.265	0.154
African American[c]	0.200	0.387	-0.032	0.388	-1.155	0.615	0.249	0.329	-0.128	0.328
Hispanic	-0.239	0.466	0.695*	0.348	0.105	0.661	0.370	0.287	0.869	0.443
Asian American	-0.103	0.435	-0.172	0.168	-0.119	0.569	0.362**	0.139	0.877*	0.342
International	-0.114	0.422	-0.136	0.130	-0.147	0.557	0.012	0.114	-0.087	0.225
Parents' SES[d]	-0.217	0.113	-0.167***	0.056	0.062	0.147	-0.017	0.044	-0.243**	0.086
Household income ($1,000s)	0.006	0.003	0.009***	0.002	0.009	0.006	0.012***	0.002	0.003	0.003
Married or domestic partner	-0.245	0.263	-0.375***	0.120	-0.670*	0.315	-0.345***	0.098	-0.107	0.177
Children under 18	-0.217	0.232	0.558***	0.148	0.863*	0.356	0.134	0.135	0.805***	0.213
Age at start of doctoral program (1 yr.)	-0.047**	0.015	-0.028	0.016	-0.017	0.026	-0.019	0.013	-0.016	0.016
GRE verbal (100s of points)	0.691***	0.119	0.171***	0.050	0.081	0.176	0.255***	0.045	0.398***	0.088
GRE analytical (100s of points)	-0.434***	0.108	-0.067	0.058	-0.097	0.156	-0.130**	0.050	-0.278**	0.089
Selective undergraduate institution	0.030	0.240	0.384**	0.123	0.210	0.289	-0.163	0.097	-0.248	0.177
Private graduate school	0.300	0.214	0.389***	0.103	0.272	0.276	-0.236**	0.087	0.339*	0.153
Master's upon entry	-0.768**	0.267	-0.304**	0.112	-0.164	0.283	0.064	0.123	-0.203	0.178
Always full-time doctoral student	-1.860***	0.225	-0.333*	0.146	-1.906***	0.338	-0.674***	0.151	-1.273***	0.220
Has a mentor	-0.294	0.220	-0.152	0.109	-0.762*	0.320	-0.111	0.090	-0.469**	0.176
Incurred education debt as doctoral student	0.111	0.229	-0.082	0.150	0.375	0.266	0.182	0.120	0.676***	0.163
Constant	7.866	0.911	5.442	0.606	9.725	1.372	6.068	0.519	7.392	0.816
n (unweighted)	1,304		650		610		1,299		1,281	
R^2	0.179		0.113		0.189		0.079		0.203	

Source: Survey of Doctoral Student Finances, Experiences, and Achievements.
[a]GRE quantitative, ever was a research assistant, ever received a fellowship, ever was a teaching assistant, and had some research productivity were nonsignificant predictors in all fields and were dropped from the models.
[b]Unstandardized regression coefficients; dependent measure is standardized (M = 0, SD = 1).
[c]All racial groups and international students are compared with whites.
[d]Parents' SES is a composite of educational attainment and occupational prestige.
*p < .05; **p < .01; ***p < .001

Table F.21
Statistically Significant and Nonsignificant Predictors in the Twenty Regression Models

Predictor Variable	(1)	(2)	(3)	(4)	(5)	(6)	(7)	(8)	(9)	(10)	(11)	(12)	(13)	(14)	(15)	(16)	(17)	(18)	(19)	(20)
Male	+	+	+	+	+	+	+	+	+	+	+	+	+	+	+	+	−	+	+	+
Race-ethnicity	+	+	+	+	+	+	+	+	+	+	+	+	+	+	+	+	−	+	+	+
Parents' SES	−	−	−	+	−	−	+	+	+	−	+	+	−	−	−	−	+	+	−	+
Age at start of doctoral program (1 yr.)	+	+	+	+	+	+	+	+	−	+	−	+	−	−	+	−	−	+	+	+
Married or domestic partner				−	+	+	+	+		+	+	−		+	−	+	+	−	+	+
Children under 18				−	−	+	+	+		−	−	−	+	+	−	−	+	+	+	+
Household income ($1,000s)				+	+	+	+	+	−	+	+	+	−	−	−	−	+	+	−	+
GRE verbal (100s of points)	+	+	+	+	+	−	−	+	+	+	+	+	−	+	+	+	−	+	+	+
GRE quantitative (100s of points)	+	+	+	+	+	+	+	+	+	+	+	−	+	+	−	−	−	−	−	−
GRE analytical (100s of points)	+	+	+	+	+	−	+	+	−	+	+	−	−	+	−	−	−	+	+	+
Selective undergraduate institution	+		+	+	+	−	+	−	−	−	+	−	+	+	+	−	−	+	+	+
Master's upon entry	+		−	+	+	+	−	+	−	−	+	−	+	−	−	−	−	+	+	+
First or only choice of doctoral program									−	+	+	+				+	+		+	
Full-time when first enrolled	+					+			+	+	+	+								
Private graduate school	+	+	+	+	+	+	+	+	+	+	+	+	+	+	+	+	−	+	+	+
Ever received a fellowship	+	+	−	+	+	+	+	+		+	+	+	+	+	+	−	−	+	+	−
Ever was a teaching assistant				+	+	+	+	+		+	+	−	+	+	+	+	−	+	+	−
Ever was a research assistant				+	+	−	+	+		−	+	+	+	+	+	−	+	−	+	−
Incurred education debt as doctoral student			+		+						+					+	−	+	−	+

(table continues)

305

Table F.21 (*continued*)

Predictor Variable	(1)	(2)	(3)	(4)	(5)	(6)	(7)	(8)	(9)	(10)	(11)	(12)	(13)	(14)	(15)	(16)	(17)	(18)	(19)	(20)
Always full-time doctoral student				+	+	+	−	+		+	+	+	+	+	−	+		+	+	+
Time in doctoral program (yrs.)				+	+	+	+	+		+	+	+	+	+	+	+		+	+	+
Peer interaction																	+	+		
Has a mentor										+			+	+	+	−	−	+	+	+
Student-faculty social interactions																+	−			
Adviser as mentor												+								
Academic interactions with faculty																+	−	−		
Interactions with faculty adviser																+	−			
Had some research productivity																+				
Overall satisfaction with doctoral program																		+	+	−
Expect first job to be faculty or postdoctoral position					+	+		+		+	+	+	+	+	+	+	+	+	+	

Source: Survey of Doctoral Student Finances, Experiences, and Achievements.

Note: A plus sign (+) indicates that the predictor variable was included in the final regression models; the predictor variable may not be statistically significant in all fields. A minus sign (−) indicates that the predictor variable was included in the preliminary models but was not a significant predictor in any of the five fields of study. Column heads are as follows: (1) fellowship at entry; (2) teacher assistantship at entry; (3) research assistantship at entry; (4) ever received a fellowship; (5) ever received a teaching assistantship; (6) ever received a research assistantship; (7) incurred education debt while a doctoral student; (8) peer interaction; (9) had a mentor; (10) student-faculty social interaction; (11) academic interaction with faculty; (12) interaction with faculty adviser; (13) research productivity; (14) presented paper at national conference; (15) published research article; (16) satisfaction with doctoral program; (17) stopped out of doctoral program; (18) rate of progress; (19) completed doctoral program; (20) time to degree.

[a] Separate field regressions were not run for stopping out of a doctoral program.

[b] Sex and race-ethnicity were included in every model.

GRADUATE RECORD EXAMINATION SCORES: MISSING DATA AND DISTRIBUTIONS

Table G.1 indicates the proportion of doctoral students (n = 9,036) in each of the five major fields. (All analyses here are unweighted.)

An important issue with these data is the significant proportion of students in education who are missing Graduate Record Examination (GRE) General Test scores. As the data in tables G.2, G.3, and G.4 suggest, GRE analytical, verbal, or quantitative scores are missing for roughly one-third of education students in the sample. Conversely, less than 8 percent of students in each of the other four fields are missing GRE data. Considering the large number of education students with missing data, the question arises whether entire education schools or departments are removed from analyses employing listwise deletion of data. An investigation of GRE analytical scores (table G.2) reveals that, surprisingly, the answer is no; in no education departments are all cases missing data. However, roughly half of all education doctoral students at Temple, Maryland, and Teachers College are missing GRE analytical scores. (We can extrapolate this to GRE quantitative and GRE verbal, in that only 1 percent of students who are missing GRE analytical data have either GRE quantitative or GRE verbal data.)

Table G.1
Unweighted Distribution of Respondents across the Five Major Fields

Field	No.	%[a]
Education	2,507	28
Engineering	886	10
Humanities	1,326	15
Sciences/mathematics	1,853	21
Social sciences	2,464	27
Total	9,036	100

[a]Column adds up to more than 100 percent because of rounding.

Table G.2
Analysis of Missing GRE Analytical Data, by Field

	Education	Engineering	Humanities	Sciences and Mathematics	Social Sciences	Total
Not missing						
No.	1,614	835	1,225	1,737	2,287	7,698
%	64.4	94.2	92.4	93.7	92.8	85.2
Missing						
No.	893	51	101	116	177	1,338
%	35.6	5.8	7.6	6.3	7.2	14.8
Total no.	2,507	886	1,326	1,853	2,464	9,036

Table G.3
Analysis of Missing GRE Verbal Data, by Field

	Education	Engineering	Humanities	Sciences and Mathematics	Social Sciences	Total
Not missing						
No.	1,680	838	1,237	1,737	2,301	7,793
%	67.0	94.6	93.3	93.7	93.4	86.2
Missing						
No.	827	48	89	116	163	1,243
%	33.0	5.4	6.7	6.3	6.6	13.8
Total no.	2,507	886	1,326	1,853	2,464	9,036

Table G.4
Analysis of Missing GRE Quantitative Data, by Field

	Education	Engineering	Humanities	Sciences and Mathematics	Social Sciences	Total
Not missing						
No.	1,676	838	1,233	1,742	2,301	7,790
%	66.9	94.6	93.0	94.0	93.4	86.2
Missing						
No.	831	48	93	111	163	1,246
%	33.1	5.4	7.0	6.0	6.6	13.8
Total no.	2,507	886	1,326	1,853	2,464	9,036

REFERENCES

Abedi, Jamal, and Ellen M. Benkin. 1987. The effects of students' academic, financial, and demographic variables on time to the doctorate. *Research in Higher Education* 27, no. 1: 3–14.

Allen, Walter R., Angela Haddad, and Mary Kirkland. 1984. *Preliminary report: 1982 graduate professional survey, National Study of Black College Students.* Ann Arbor: University of Michigan, Center for Afroamerican and African Studies.

America's best graduate schools. 1995. *U.S. News and World Report.* March 20.

Andrieu, Sandra Carlin, and Edward P. St. John. 1993. The influence of prices on graduate student persistence. *Research in Higher Education* 34, no. 4: 399–425.

Arce, Carlos H., and W. H. Manning. 1984. *Minorities in academic careers: The experience of Ford Foundation fellows.* New York: Ford Foundation.

Astin, Alexander W. 1982. *Minorities in American higher education: Recent trends, current prospects, and recommendations.* San Francisco: Jossey-Bass.

Astin, Helen S. 1969. *The woman doctorate in America.* New York: Russell Sage Foundation.

Attiyeh, Gregory M. 1999. *Determinants of persistence of graduate students in Ph.D. programs.* Research Report ETS RR-99-04. Princeton, N.J.: Educational Testing Service.

Baird, Leonard L. 1976. Who goes to graduate school and how they get there. In *Scholars in the making,* ed. Joseph Katz and Rodney T. Hartnett, 19–48. Cambridge, Mass.: Ballinger Publishing.

———. 1978. Students' expectations and the realities of graduate and professional schools. *College and University* 54, no. 1: 68–73.

———. 1985. *Field trial of a user-oriented adaptation of the inventory of documented accomplishments as a tool in graduate admissions.* Research Report ETS-RR-85-13. Princeton, N.J.: Educational Testing Service.

———. 1986. What characterizes a productive research department? *Research in Higher Education* 25, no. 3: 211–25.

———. 1990a. Disciplines and doctorates: The relationships between program characteristics and the duration of doctoral study. *Research in Higher Education* 31, no. 4: 369–85.

———. 1990b. The melancholy of anatomy: The personal and professional development of graduate and professional school students. In vol. 6 of *Higher Education: Handbook of Theory and Research,* ed. John C. Smart, 361–92. New York: Agathon Press.

———. 1992. The stages of the doctoral career: Socialization and its consequences. Paper presented at the annual meeting of the American Educational Research Association, San Francisco.

———. 1993a. Studying graduate student retention and degree attainment: Resources for researchers. In *Increasing graduate student retention and degree attainment,* ed. Leonard L. Baird, 81–90. New Directions for Institutional Research 80. San Francisco: Jossey-Bass.

——. 1993b. Using research and theoretical models of graduate student progress. In *Increasing graduate student retention and degree attainment,* ed. Leonard L. Baird, 3–12. New Directions for Institutional Research 80. San Francisco: Jossey-Bass.

——. 1997. Completing the dissertation: Theory, research, and practice. In vol. 25 of *Rethinking the dissertation process: Tackling personal and institutional obstacles,* ed. Lester F. Goodchild, Kathy E. Green, Elinor Kluever, and Raymond C. Katz, 99–105. San Francisco: Jossey-Bass.

Baker, Joe G. 1998. Gender, race, and Ph.D. completion in natural sciences and engineering. *Economics of Education Review* 17, no. 2: 179–88.

Bargar, Robert R., and Jane Mayo-Chamberlain. 1983. Advisor and advisee issues in doctoral education. *Journal of Higher Education* 54, no. 4: 407–32.

Barron's profiles of American colleges and universities. 1999. Woodbury, N.Y.: Barron's Educational Series.

Bean, John P. 1982. A causal model of faculty research productivity. Paper presented at the annual meeting of the American Educational Research Association, New York.

Benkin, Ellen M. 1984. Where have all the graduate students gone?: A study of doctoral attrition at UCLA. Ph.D. diss., University of California, Berkeley.

Berelson, Bernard. 1960. *Graduate education in the United States.* New York: McGraw-Hill.

Berg, Helen M., and Marianne A. Ferber. 1983. Men and women graduate students: Who succeeds and why? *Journal of Higher Education* 54, no. 6: 629–48.

Berkner, Lutz, and Andrew G. Malizio. 1998. *Student financing of undergraduate education: 1995–1996, with an essay on student loans.* NCES 98-076. Washington, D.C.: U.S. Department of Education, National Center for Education Statistics.

Biglan, Anthony. 1973. The characteristics of subject matter in different academic areas. *Journal of Applied Psychology* 57, no. 3: 195–209.

Blackwell, James E. 1981. *Mainstreaming outsiders: The production of black professionals.* Dix Hills, N.Y.: General Hall.

——. 1987. *Mainstreaming outsiders: The production of black professionals.* 2d ed. Dix Hills, N.Y.: General Hall.

——. 1993. *Networking and mentoring: A study of cross-generational experiences by blacks in graduate and professional schools.* Atlanta: Southern Educational Foundation.

Bodian, Lester Hal. 1987. Career instrumentality of degree completion as a factor in doctoral student attrition. Ph.D. diss., University of Maryland–College Park.

Bowen, William G., and Derek C. Bok. 1998. *The shape of the river: Long-term consequences of considering race in college and university admissions.* Princeton, N.J.: Princeton University Press.

Bowen, William G., and Neil L. Rudenstine. 1992. *In pursuit of the Ph.D.* Princeton, N.J.: Princeton University Press.

Brazziel, Marian E., and William F. Brazziel. 1987. Impact of support for graduate study on program completion of black doctorate recipients. *Journal of Negro Education* 56, no. 2: 145–51.

Breneman, David W. 1977. *Efficiency in graduate education: An attempted reform; A report to the Ford Foundation.* Rev. ed. New York: Ford Foundation, Education and Research Division.

Brubacher, John Seiler, and Willis Rudy. 1968. *Higher education in transition: A history of American colleges and universities, 1636–1976.* New York: Harper and Row.

Bryk, Anthony S., and Stephen W. Raudenbush. 1992. *Hierarchical linear models: Application and data analysis methods.* Advanced Techniques in the Social Sciences. Thousand Oaks, Calif.: Sage Publications.

Buchanan, Anne L., and Jean-Pierre V. M. Hérubel. 1995. *The doctor of philosophy degree: A selected, annotated bibliography.* Westport, Conn.: Greenwood Press.

Buchmueller, Thomas C., Jeff Dominitz, and W. Lee Hansen. 1999. Graduate training and the early career productivity of Ph.D. economists. *Economics of Education Review* 18, no. 1: 65–77.

Carrington, Christine H., and William E. Sedlacek. 1976. *Attitudes and characteristics of black graduate students.* College Park, Md.: University of Maryland, Cultural Study Center.

Cartter, Allan. 1976. *Ph.D.'s and the academic labor market: A report prepared for the Carnegie Commission n Higher Education.* New York: McGraw-Hill.

Choy, Susan P., Sonya Geis, and Andrew G. Malizio. 2002. *Student financing of graduate and first-professional education, 1999–2000: Profiles of students in selected degree programs and their use of assistantships.* NCES 2002-166. Washington, D.C.: U.S. Department of Education, National Center for Education Statistics.

Clark, Mary Jo, and John A. Centra. 1982. *Conditions influencing the career accomplishments of PhDs.* Research Report GREB-76-2R. Princeton, N.J.: Educational Testing Service.

Clark, Shirley M., and Mary E. Corcoran. 1986. Perspectives on the professional socialization of women faculty: A case of cumulative disadvantage? *Journal of Higher Education* 57, no. 1: 20–43.

Clemente, Frank. 1973. Early career determinants of research productivity. *American Journal of Sociology* 79, no. 2: 409–19.

———. 1974. Race and research productivity. *Journal of Black Studies* 5, no. 2: 157–66.

Clewell, Beatriz Chu. 1987. *Retention of black and Hispanic doctoral students.* Research Report ETS RR-87-10. Princeton, N.J.: Educational Testing Service.

Clewell, Beatriz Chu, and Myra S. Ficklen. 1987. Improving minority retention in higher education: A search for effective institutional practices. *Journal of College Admissions* 57, no. 116: 7–13.

Cohen, Audrey, and Alida Mesrop. 1972. *Women and higher education: Creating the solutions.* Washington, D.C.: American Psychological Association, Task Force on the Status of Women.

Committee on Science, Engineering, and Public Policy (CSEPP). National Academy of Sciences. National Academy of Engineering. Institute of Medicine. 1995. *Reshaping the graduate education of scientists and engineers.* Washington, D.C.: National Academies Press.

Cook, Marlene M., and Austin Swanson. 1978. The interaction of student and program variables for the purpose of developing a model for predicting graduation from graduate programs over a 10-year period. *Research in Higher Education* 8, no. 1: 83–91.

Cordasco, Francesco. 1973. *The shaping of American graduate education: Daniel Coit Gilman and the protean Ph.D.* Totowa, N.J.: Rowman and Littlefield.

Council of Graduate Schools. 1990. *A policy statement: The doctor of philosophy degree.* Washington, D.C.: Council of Graduate Schools.

Creager, J. A. 1971. *The American college student: A normative description.* Washington, D.C.: American Council on Education.

Creswell, John W. 1985. *Faculty research performance: Lessons from the sciences and the social sciences.* ASHE-ERIC Higher Education Report 4. Washington, D.C.: Association for the Study of Higher Education.

Creswell, John W., and John P. Bean. 1981. Research output, socialization, and the Biglan model. *Research in Higher Education* 15, no. 1: 69–91.

Cronan-Hillix, Terry, L. K. Gensheimer, William Allen Cronin-Hillix, and William S. Davidson. 1986. Students' views of mentoring in psychology graduate training. *Teaching of Psychology* 13, no. 3: 123–27.

Daniels, Arlene Kaplan. 1975. A survey of research concerns on women's issues. Washington, D.C.: American Association of Colleges.

Devine, Betsy, and Joel E. Cohen. 1992. *Absolute zero gravity: Science jokes, quotes, and anecdotes.* New York: Simon and Schuster.

Dissertation Abstracts International. www.lib.umi.com/dissertations/gateway ?return=http%3A%2F%2fwwwlib.umi.com%2Fdissertations%2Fsearch.

Dolph, Robert Frank. 1983. Factors relating to success or failure in obtaining the doctorate. Ph.D. diss., Georgia State University, Atlanta.

Ehrenberg, Ronald G., and Panagiotis G. Mavros. 1995. Do doctoral students' financial support patterns affect their times-to-degree and completion probabilities? *Journal of Human Resources* 30, no. 3: 581–609.

Enright, Mary K., and Drew Gitomer. 1989. *Toward a description of successful graduate students.* Research Report GREB-85-17R. Princeton, N.J.: Educational Testing Service.

Ethington, Corinna A., and Anoush Pisani. 1993. The RA and TA experience: Impediments and benefits to graduate study. *Research in Higher Education* 34, no. 3: 343–54.

Feldman, Saul D. 1973. Impediment or stimulant? Marital status and graduate education. *American Journal of Sociology* 78, no. 4: 982–94.

———. 1974. *Escape from the doll's house: Women in graduate and professional school education.* New York: McGraw-Hill.

Frierson, Henry T., Jr. 1986. Black North Carolina medical students' perceptions of peer and faculty interactions and school environments. Paper presented at the annual meeting of the Southern Sociological Society, New Orleans.

Gilbert, Lucia A., June M. Gallessich, and Sherri L. Evans. 1983. Sex of faculty role model and students' self-perceptions of competency. *Sex Roles* 9, no. 5: 597–607.

Gilbert, Marvin G. 1982. The impact of graduate school on the family: A systems view. *Journal of College Student Personnel* 23, no. 2: 128–35.

Gillingham, Lisa, Joseph J. Seneca, and Michael K. Taussig. 1991. The determinants of progress to the doctoral degree. *Research in Higher Education* 32, no. 4: 449–68.

Gilula, Zvi, and Shelby J. Haberman. 2001. Analysis of categorical response profiles by informative summaries. *Sociological Methodology* 31, no. 1: 129–87.

Girves, Jean E., and Virginia Wemmerus. 1988. Developing models of graduate student degree progress. *Journal of Higher Education* 59, no. 2: 163–89.

Girves, Jean E., Virginia Wemmerus, and Janet Rice. 1986. Financial support and graduate student degree progress. Paper presented at the twenty-sixth annual meeting of the Association for Institutional Research, Orlando, Fla.

Glenn, Norval D., and Wayne Villemez. 1970. The productivity of sociologists at 45 American universities. *American Sociologist* 5, no. 3: 244–52.

Golde, Chris M. 1998. Beginning graduate school: Explaining first-year doctoral attrition. In *The experience of being in graduate school: An exploration,* ed. Melissa S. Anderson, 55–64. San Francisco: Jossey-Bass.

———. 2000. Should I stay or should I go? Student descriptions of the doctoral attrition process. *Review of Higher Education* 23, no. 2: 199–227.

Golde, Chris M., and Timothy M. Dore. 1997. Gaps in the training of future faculty: Doctoral student perceptions. Paper presented at the annual meeting of the Association for the Study of Higher Education, Albuquerque, N.M.

———. 2001. *At cross purposes: What the experiences of today's doctoral students reveal about doctoral education.* Philadelphia: Pew Charitable Trusts.

Goldstein, Elyse. 1979. Effect of same-sex and cross-sex role models on the subsequent academic productivity of scholars. *American Psychologist* 34, no. 5: 407–10.

Graduate Record Examinations Board. 1972. *The prediction of doctorate attainment in psychology, mathematics and chemistry: Preliminary report.* Research Report GREB-69-6aR. Princeton, N.J.: Educational Testing Service.

Gregg, Wayne E. 1972. Several factors affecting graduate student satisfaction. *Journal of Higher Education* 43, no. 6: 483–98.

Haberman, Shelby J. 1982. Analysis of dispersion of multinomial responses. *Journal of the American Statistical Association* 77, no. 379: 568–80.

Hagedorn, Linda S. 1999. Factors related to retention: Research, theory, and practice of female graduate students over 30. *Journal of College Student Retention* 1, no. 2: 99–114.

Hagedorn, Linda S., and Susan K. Doyle. 1993. Female doctoral students: How age differentiates institutional choice, retention, enhancement, and scholarly accomplishments. ERIC document ED 377809. Washington, D.C.: Association for the Study of Higher Education.

Hamovitch, William, and Richard D. Morgenstern. 1977. Children and the productivity of academic women. *Journal of Higher Education* 48, no. 6: 633–45.

Harmon, Lindsey R. 1978. *A century of doctorates: Data analyses of growth and change.* Washington, D.C.: National Academy of Sciences.

Hartnett, Rodney T. 1976. Environments for advanced learning. In *Scholars in the making,* ed. Joseph Katz and Rodney T. Hartnett, 49–82. Cambridge, Mass.: Ballinger Publishing.

———. 1981. Sex differences in the environments of graduate students and faculty. *Research in Higher Education* 14, no. 3: 211–27.

Hartnett, Rodney T., and Warren W. Willingham. 1979. *The criterion problem: What measure of success in graduate education?* Research Report GREB-77-4R. Princeton, N.J.: Educational Testing Service.

Hauptman, Arthur M. 1986. *Students in graduate and professional education: What we know and need to know.* Washington, D.C.: Association of American Universities.

Hawley, Peggy. 1993. *Being bright is not enough: The unwritten rules of doctoral study.* Springfield, Ill.: Charles C. Thomas.

Heins, Marilyn, S. N. Fahey, and L. I. Leiden. 1984. Perceived stress in medical, law, and graduate students. *Journal of Medical Education* 59, no. 3: 169–79.

Higher Education General Information Survey (HEGIS). 1980. Fall enrollment in colleges and universities. U.S. Department of Education, National Center for Education Statistics. http://caspar.nsf.gov (February 8, 2003).

———. 1977–1985. Degrees and other formal awards conferred. U.S. Department of Education, National Center for Education Statistics. http://caspar.nsf.gov (February 8, 2003).

———. 1977–2001. Completion surveys. National Science Foundation. http://caspar.nsf.gov/ (February 8, 2003).

Hite, Linda McNeil. 1985. Female doctoral students: Their perceptions and concerns. *Journal of College Student Personnel* 26, no. 1: 18–22.

Hockey, John. 1994. New territory: Problems of adjusting to the first year of a social science PhD. *Studies in Higher Education* 19, no. 2: 177–90.

Hoffer, Thomas B., Bernard L. Dugoni, Allen R. Sanderson, Scott Sederstrom, Rashna Ghadialy, and Peter Rocque. 2001. *Doctorate recipients from United States universities: Summary report 2000.* National Opinion Research Center, Chicago.

Holmstrom, Engin I., and Robert W. Holmstrom. 1974. The plight of the woman doctoral student. *American Educational Research Journal* 11, no. 1: 1–17.

hooks, bell. 2000. Black and female: Reflections on graduate school. In *Women in higher education: A feminist perspective,* ed. Judith Glazer-Raymo, Estela M. Bensimon, and Barbara K. Townsend, 2d ed., 386–90. Boston: Pearson Custom Publishing.

Howard, George S., and Scott E. Maxwell. 1980. Correlation between student satisfaction and grades: A case of mistaken causation? *Journal of Educational Psychology* 72, no. 6: 810–20.

Hurtado, Sylvia. 1994. Graduate school racial climates and academic self-concept among minority graduate students in the 1970s. *American Journal of Education* 102, no. 3: 330–51.

Ibarra, Robert A. 1996. *Latino experiences in graduate education: Implications for change; A preliminary report.* Enhancing the Minority Presence in Graduate Education 7, ed. Nancy Gaffney. Council of Graduate Schools, Washington, D.C.

Integrated Postsecondary Education Data System (IPEDS). 1986–2002. Enrollment surveys. U.S. Department of Education, National Center for Education Statistics. http://nces.ed.gov/ipeds (February 8, 2003).

———. 1986–2001. Completion surveys. U.S. Department of Education, National Center for Education Statistics. http://caspar.nsf.gov (February 8, 2003).

Isaac, Paul D., Roy A. Koenigsknecht, Gary D. Malaney, and John E. Karras. 1989. Factors related to doctoral dissertation topic selection. *Research in Higher Education* 30, no. 4: 357–73.

Jacks, Penelope, Daryl E. Chubin, Alan L. Porter, and Terry Connolly. 1983. The ABCs of ABDs: A study of incomplete doctorates. *Improving College and University Teaching* 31, no. 2: 74–81.

James, William. 1971 (1941). The Ph.D. octopus. In *Memories and studies,* ed. Henry James, 329–47. Westport, Conn.: Greenwood Press.

Kaplan, Susan Romer. 1982. A feminist Cinderella tale: Women over thirty in graduate and professional school. *Journal of the NAWDAC* 45, no. 3: 9–15.

Kennedy, Donald. 1997. *Academic duty.* Cambridge: Harvard University Press.

Kim, Jae-On, and Charles W. Mueller. 1978. *Introduction to factor analysis: What it is and how to do it.* Newbury Park, Calif.: Sage Publications.

Knapp, Laura G., Janice E. Kelly, Roy W. Whitmore, Shiying Wu, Lorrain M. Gallego, Eric Grau, and Susan G. Broyles. 2002. Postsecondary institutions in the United States, Fall 2000, and degrees and awards conferred, 1999–2000. NCES 2002-156. Washington, D.C.: U.S. Department of Education, Office of Educational Research and Improvement.

Kuh, George D. 2001. College students today: Why we can't leave serendipity to chance. In *In defense of American higher education,* ed. Philip G. Altbach, Patricia J. Gumport, and D. Bruce Johnstone, 277–303. Baltimore: Johns Hopkins University Press.

Levin, R. B., and A. L. W. Franklin. 1984. Needs assessment and problem identification of first-year and second-year medical students. *Journal of Medical Education* 59, no. 11: 908–10.

Lindahl, Ronald, Martin Rosenzweig, and Warren W. Willingham. 1974. Success in graduate school. *Science* 186, no. 4160: 196–98.

Long, J. Scott. 1983. *Confirmatory factor analysis.* Sage University Paper Series on Quantitative Application in the Social Sciences 07-033. Beverly Hills, Calif.: Sage Publications.

Long, J. Scott, Paul D. Allison, and Robert McGinnis. 1979. Entrance into the academic career. *American Sociological Review* 44, no. 5: 816–30.

Lovitts, Barbara E. 2001. *Leaving the ivory tower: The causes and consequences of departure from doctoral study.* Lanham, Md.: Rowman and Littlefield.

Lozoff, Marjorie M. 1976. Interpersonal relations and autonomy. In *Scholars in the making,* ed. Joseph Katz and Rodney T. Hartnett, 141–68. Cambridge, Mass.: Ballinger Publishing.

Lynch, Kathryn. 2002. An immodest proposal: Have children in graduate school. *Chronicle of Higher Education* 48, no. 39: 85.

Madden, Margaret E., and Linda Carli. 1981. Students' satisfaction with graduate school and attributions of control and responsibility. Paper presented at the annual meeting of the Eastern Psychological Association, New York.

Malaney, Gary D. Who receives financial support to pursue graduate study? *Research in Higher Education* 26, no. 1: 85–97.

Malcom, Shirley M. 1990. Reclaiming our past. *Journal of Negro Education* 59, no. 3: 246–59.

Malcom, Shirley M., Paula. Q. Hall, and Janet W. Brown. 1975. *The double bind: The price of being a minority woman in science.* Paper presented at the Conference of Minority Women Scientists, Warrenton, Va.

Marsh, Herbert, and John Hattie. 2002. The relation between research productivity and teaching effectiveness: Complementary, antagonistic, or independent constructs? *Journal of Higher Education* 73, no. 5: 603–41.

McCormick, James M., and E. Lee Bernick. 1982. Graduate training and productivity: A look at who publishes. *Journal of Politics* 44, no. 1: 212–17.

McFadden, Daniel. 1973. Conditional logit analysis of qualitative choice behavior. In *Frontiers in econometrics,* ed. Paul Zambreka, 104–42. New York: Academic Press.

Menard, Scott. 1995. *Applied logistic regression analysis.* Quantitative Applications in the Social Sciences 106. Newbury Park, Calif.: Sage Publications.

Millett, Catherine M. 2003. How undergraduate loan debt affects application and enrollment in graduate or first professional school. *Journal of Higher Education* 74, no. 3: 386–427.

Mooney, J. D. 1968. Attrition among Ph.D. candidates: An analysis of a cohort of recent Woodrow Wilson fellows. *Journal of Human Resources* 3, no. 1: 47–62.

Morgan, David R., and Michael R. Fitzgerald. 1977. Recognition and production among American political science departments. *Western Political Quarterly* 30, no. 3: 342–50.

Morrison, Todd, and Melanie Morrison. 1995. A meta-analytic assessment of the predictive validity of the quantitative and verbal components of the Graduate Record Examination with graduate grade point average representing the criterion of graduate success. *Educational and Psychological Measurement* 55, no. 2: 309–16.

Moses, Yolanda T. 1989. *Black women in academe: Issues and strategies.* Washington, D.C.: Association of American Colleges and Universities.

National Association of Graduate-Professional Students Survey Team (NAGPS). 2001. The national doctoral program survey: Executive summary. National Association of Graduate and Professional Students. http://survey.nagps.org/about/execsummary.php (March 16, 2003).

National Board on Graduate Education. 1976. *Minority group participation in graduate education.* Washington, D.C.: National Academies Press.

National Center for Education Statistics (NCES). 2000. *High School and Beyond.* Washington, D.C.: U.S. Department of Education. CD-ROM.

———. 1992a. *Baccalaureate and Beyond Longitudinal Study.* Washington, D.C.: U.S. Department of Education. CD-ROM.

——. 1992b. *Beginning Postsecondary Students Longitudinal Study.* Washington, D.C.: U.S. Department of Education. CD-ROM.

——. 1994. *Digest of education statistics, 1994.* NCES 94-115, by Thomas D. Snyder. Washington, D.C.: U.S. Department of Education.

——. 1995. *1991 Survey of Recent College Graduates Restricted.* Washington, D.C.: U.S. Department of Education. CD-ROM.

——. 1998. *National Postsecondary Student Aid Study.* Washington, D.C.: U.S. Department of Education. CD-ROM.

——. 2002. *Digest of education statistics, 2001.* NCES 2002-130, by Thomas D. Snyder. Washington, D.C.: U.S. Department of Education.

——. 2003. *National Education Longitudinal Study of 1988.* Washington, D.C.: U.S. Department of Education. CD-ROM.

National Research Council (NRC). 1995. *Minority science paths: National Science Foundation Minority Graduate Fellows of 1979–1981.* Washington, D.C.: National Academies Press.

——. 1996. *The path to the PhD: Measuring graduate attrition in the sciences and humanities.* Washington, D.C.: National Academies Press.

National Science Board. 2002. *Science and engineering indicators 2002.* NSB-02-1. Arlington, Va.: National Science Foundation.

National Science Foundation (NSF). 1996. *Indicators of science and mathematics education, 1995.* Edited by Larry E. Suter. NSF 96-52. Arlington, Va.: National Science Foundation, Division of Research, Evaluation, and Communication, Directorate for Education and Human Resources.

National Science Foundation (NSF), National Institutes of Health, National Endowment for the Humanities, United States Department of Education, and United States Department of Agriculture. Survey of earned doctorates. www.nsf.gov/sbe/srs/ssed/start.htm.

Naylor, Paul D., and Timothy R. Sanford. 1982. Intra-institutional analysis of student retention across student levels. *College and University* 57, no. 2: 143–59.

Nerad, Maresi, and Joseph Cerny. 1991. From facts to action: Expanding the educational role of the graduate division. *Communicator* (May): 1–12.

——. 1993. From facts to action: Expanding the graduate division's educational role. In *Increasing graduate student retention and degree attainment,* ed. Leonard L. Baird, 1–12. New Directions for Institutional Research 80. San Francisco: Jossey-Bass.

Nerad, Maresi, and Debra Sands Miller. 1996. Increasing student retention in graduate and professional programs. In *Assessing graduate and professional education: Current realities and future prospect,* ed. Jennifer Grant Hayworth, 61–76. San Francisco: Jossey-Bass.

Nettles, Michael T. 1986. Doctoral student survey. Princeton, N.J.: Educational Testing Service.

——. 1989. *Comparing the backgrounds, educational experiences and outcomes of black, Hispanic, and white doctoral students.* College Park, Md.: National Center for Postsecondary Governance and Finance.

——. 1990a. *Black, Hispanic, and white doctoral students: Before, during, and after enrolling in graduate school.* Princeton, N.J.: Educational Testing Service.

——. 1990b. Success in doctoral programs: Experiences of minority and white students. *American Journal of Education* 98, no. 4: 494–522.

Nieves-Squires, Sarah. 1991. *Hispanic women: Making their presence on campus less tenuous.* Washington, D.C.: Association of American Colleges and Universities.

Noboa-Ríos, Abdín. 1982. An analysis of Hispanic doctoral recipients from U.S. universities (1900–1973) with special emphasis on Puerto-Rican doctorates. *Metas* 2, no. 2: 1–32.

Ott, Mary Diederich, and Theodore S. Markewich. 1985. Logit analysis of graduate student retention and graduation. Paper presented at the twenty-fifth annual meeting of the Association for Institutional Research, Portland, Ore.

Ott, Mary Diederich, Theodore S. Markewich, and Nancy L. Ochsner. 1984. Logit analysis of graduate student retention. *Research in Higher Education* 21, no. 4: 439–59.

Padilla, Amado M. 1994. Ethnic minority scholars, research, and mentoring: Current and future issues. *Research News and Comment* 23, no. 3: 24–27.

Patterson-Stewart, Karen E., Martin H. Ritchie, and Eugene T. W. Sanders. 1997. Interpersonal dynamics of African American persistence in doctoral programs at predominantly white universities. *Journal of College Student Development* 38, no. 5: 489–98.

Pearson, Willie, Jr. 1985. *Black scientists, white society, and colorless science: A study of universalism in American science.* Millwood, N.Y.: Associated Faculty Press.

Peters, Dianne S., and Margaret Peterson. 1987. Rites of passage for doctoral students in higher education. Paper presented at the annual conference of the Association for the Study of Higher Education, Baltimore

Prior, Moody E. 1962. A manifesto on graduate education. *Journal of Higher Education* 33, no. 283–87.

Pruitt, Anne S., and Paul D. Isaac. 1985. Discrimination in recruitment, admission, and retention of minority graduate students. *Journal of Negro Education* 54, no. 4: 526–36.

Pyke, Sandra W., and Peter M. Sheridan. 1993. Logistic regression analysis of graduate student retention. *Canadian Journal of Higher Education* 23, no. 2: 44–64.

Reskin, Barbara F. 1979. Academic sponsorship and scientists' careers. *Sociology of Education: Journal of Educational Sociology* 52, no. 3: 129–46.

Roaden, Arliss L., and Blaine R. Worthen. 1976. Research assistantship experiences and subsequent research productivity. *Research in Higher Education* 5, no. 2: 141–58.

Robey, John S. 1979. Political science departments: Reputations versus productivity. *Political Science and Politics* 12, no. 2: 202–9.

Rock, Donald A. 1972. *The prediction of doctorate attainment in psychology, mathematics, and chemistry: Preliminary report.* Research Report GREB-69-6aR. Princeton, N.J.: Educational Testing Service.

Rosen, Bernard C., and Alan P. Bates. 1967. The structure of socialization in graduate school. *Sociological Inquiry* 37, no. 1: 71–84.

Rudd, Ernest. 1985. *A new look at postgraduate failure.* Surrey, Eng.: SRHE and NFER-Nelson.

———. 1986. The drop-outs and the dilatory on the road to the doctorate. *Higher Education in Europe* 11, no. 4: 31–36.

Rudolph, Frederick. 1990. *The American college and university.* Athens, Ga.: University of Georgia Press.

Sandler, Bernice R. 1991. *The campus climate revisited: Chilly for women faculty, administrators, and graduate students.* Washington, D.C.: Association of American Colleges.

Sanford, Timothy R., and Paul D. Naylor. 1984. Educational maturity, race, and student persistence in college. Paper presented at the twenty-fourth annual forum of the Association for Institutional Research, Fort Worth.

Schrader, William B. 1978. *Admissions test scores as predictors of career achievement in psychology.* Research Report GREB-76-1R. Princeton, N.J.: Educational Testing Service.

———. 1980. *GRE scores as predictors of career achievement in history.* Research Report GREB-76-1bR. Princeton, N.J.: Educational Testing Service.

Sheridan, Peter M., and Sandra W. Pyke. 1994. Predictors of time to completion of graduate degrees. *Canadian Journal of Higher Education* 24, no. 2: 68–88.

Smallwood, Scott. 2003. American women surpass men in earning degrees. *Chronicle of Higher Education* 50, no. 16: A10.

Smart, John C. 1987. Student satisfaction with graduate education. *Journal of College Student Personnel* 28, no. 3: 218–22.

Smith, Bruce L. R. 1985. Graduate education in the United States. In *The state of graduate education,* ed. Bruce L. R. Smith, 1–30. Washington, D.C.: Brookings Institution Press.

Smith, Earl, and Joyce Tang. 1994. Trends in science and engineering doctorate production, 1975–1990. In *Who will do science? Educating the next generation,* ed. Willie Pearson Jr. and Alan Fechter, 96–124. Baltimore: Johns Hopkins University Press.

Smith, Emilie P., and William S. Davidson III. 1992. Mentoring and the development of African-American graduate students. *Journal of College Student Development* 33, no. 6: 531–39.

Solmon, Lewis C. 1976. *Male and female graduate students: The question of equal opportunity.* New York: Praeger Books.

Sorenson, Garth, and David Kagan. 1967. Conflicts between doctoral candidates and their sponsors. *Journal of Higher Education* 38, no. 1: 17–24.

Southwick, Ron. 2002. Fewer foreign students, more women earn science and engineering doctorates in U.S., report finds. *Chronicle of Higher Education,* May 1. http://chronicle.com/prm/daily/2002/05/2002050103n.htm.

Spurr, Stephen Hopkins. 1970. *Academic degree structures: Innovative approaches; Principles of reform in degree structures in the United States.* New York: McGraw-Hill.

Steele, Claude M. 1992. Race and the schooling of black Americans. *Atlantic* 269, no. 4: 68–78.

Stein, Elizabeth L., and John C. Weidman. 1989a. Graduate student scholarly activities: Gender and perceived program support. Paper presented at the annual meeting of the American Educational Research Association, San Francisco.

———. 1989b. Socialization in graduate school: A conceptual framework. Paper presented at the annual meeting of the Association for the Study of Higher Education, Atlanta.

———. 1990. The socialization of doctoral students to academic norms. Paper presented at the annual meeting of the American Education Research Association, Boston.

Sternberg, Robert J., and Wendy M. William. 1997. Does the Graduate Record Examination predict meaningful success in the graduate training of psychology? A case study. *American Psychologist* 52, no. 6: 630–41.

St. John, Edward P., and Sandra Carlin Andrieu. 1995. The influence of price subsidies on within-year persistence by graduate students. *Higher Education* 29, no. 2: 143–68.

Storr, Richard J. 1953. *The beginnings of graduate education in America.* Chicago: University of Chicago Press.

Suzuki, Bob H. 1989. Asian Americans as the "model minority": Outdoing whites or media hype? *Change* 21, no. 6: 12–20.

Theil, Henri. 1970. On the estimation of relationships involving qualitative variables. *American Journal of Sociology* 76, no. 1: 103–54.

Thomas, Gail E. 1980. Race and sex group equity in higher education: Institutional and major field enrollment statuses. *American Educational Research Journal* 17, no. 2: 171–81.

Thomas, Gail E., Beatriz Chu Clewell, and Willie Pearson Jr. 1987. Case study of major doctoral producing institutions in recruiting, enrolling, and retaining black and Hispanic graduate students. In *Minorities in Graduate Education: Pipeline, Policy, and Practice,* 94–99. Princeton, N.J.: Educational Testing Service.

Tinto, Vincent. 1975. Dropout from higher education: A theoretical synthesis of recent research. *Review of Educational Research* 45, no. 1: 89–125.

———. 1993. Toward a theory of doctoral persistence. In *Leaving college: Rethinking the causes and cures of student attrition,* 230–43. 2d ed. Chicago: University of Chicago Press.

Tucker, Allan, David Gottlieb, and John Pease. 1964. *Factors related to attrition among doctoral students.* Ph.D. diss., Michigan State University–East Lansing.

Tuckman, Howard P., Susan L. Coyle, and Yupin Bae. 1989. The lengthening of time to completion of the doctorate degree. *Research in Higher Education* 30, no. 5: 503–16.

———. 1990. *On time to the doctorate: A study of the increased time to complete doctorates in science and engineering.* Washington, D.C.: National Academies Press.

Ulku-Steiner, Beril, Beth Kurtz-Costes, and C. Ryan Kinlaw. 2000. Doctoral student experiences in gender-balanced and male-dominated graduate programs. *Journal of Educational Psychology* 92, no. 2: 296–307.

U.S. Census Bureau. 2000. Current Population Study. March. www.census.gov/population/socdemo/education/p20-536/tab01.pdf (February 2, 2003).

Valentine, Nancy L. 1987. Factors related to attrition from doctor of education programs. Paper presented at the twenty-seventh annual forum of the Association of Institutional Research, Kansas City, Mo.

Veysey, Laurence. 1978. Graduate education in an age of stasis. In *The philosophy and future of graduate education,* ed. William K. Frankena, 177–200. Ann Arbor: University of Michigan Press.

Wanner, Richard A., Lionel S. Lewis, and David I. Gregorio. 1981. Research productivity in academia: A comparative study of the sciences, social sciences and humanities. *Sociology of Education: Journal of Educational Sociology* 54, no. 4: 238–53.

Waters, Lindsay. 2001. Rescue tenure from the tyranny of the monograph. *Chronicle of Higher Education* 147, no. 32: B7–B10.

Weidman, J. C., D. J. Twale, and E. L. Stein. 2001. *Socialization of graduate and professional students in higher education: A perilous passage.* ASHE-ERIC Higher Education Report 28, no. 3. Washington, D.C.: Association for the Study of Higher Education.

Weiler, William C. 1991. The effect of undergraduate student loans on the decision to pursue postbaccalaureate study. *Educational Evaluation and Policy Analysis* 13, no. 3: 212–20.

———. 1993. Post-baccalaureate educational choices of minority students. *Review of Higher Education* 169, no. 4: 439–60.

Wilder, Gita Z., and Nazli Baydar. 1991. A study of decisions about graduate education: A two-year longitudinal study of GRE takers. Paper presented at the annual meeting of the American Educational Research Association, Chicago.

Williams, Ellouise E., Judith Ann Gallas, and Susan Quiriconi. 1984. Addressing the problem of dropouts among graduate students. *Journal of College Student Personnel* 25, no. 2: 173–74.

Williamson, Madeline J., and Robert H. Fenske. 1994. Mexican American and American Indian student satisfaction with their doctoral programs. In vol. 2. of *Advances in program evaluation,* ed. Stafford Hood and Henry T. Frierson Jr., 85–120. Greenwich, Conn.: JAI Press.

Willie, Charles V., Michael K. Grady, and Richard O. Hope. 1991. *African-Americans and the doctoral experience: Implications for policy.* New York: Teachers College Press.

Willingham, Warren W. 1974. Predicting success in graduate education. *Science* 183, no. 4122: 273–78.

Wilson, Kenneth M. 1965. *Of time and doctorate.* Atlanta: Southern Regional Education Board.

Wong, Herbert Y., and Jimy M. Sanders. 1983. Gender differences in the attainment of doctorates. *Sociological Perspectives* 26, no. 1: 29–49.

Wright, Benjamin F. 1957. The PhD stretch-out. In *Vital issues in education: A report of the twenty-first educational conference held under the auspices of the Educational Records Bureau and the American Council on Education, New York City,* ed. Arthur E. Traxler, 140–51. Washington, D.C.: American Council on Education.

Wright, Charles R. 1964. Success or failure in earning graduate degrees. *Sociology of Education* 38 (Fall): 73–97.

Zwick, Rebecca. 1991. *Differences in graduate school attainment patterns across academic programs and demographic groups.* Princeton, N.J.: Educational Testing Service.

Zwick, Rebecca, and Henry I. Braun. 1988. *Methods for analyzing the attainment of graduate school milestones: A case study.* Research Report GREB-86-3P. Princeton, N.J.: Educational Testing Service.

INDEX

National Science Foundation, 2, 4,
15n, 24, 32, 46, 55, 130, 141, 216
Native Americans, 40
Naylor, Paul D., 122n
Nerad, Maresi, 3, 27, 38, 53, 120, 121,
122, 123n, 127, 128, 135, 221
Nettles, Michael, 41, 57n, 72, 77, 81,
86, 95, 98, 117, 193, 209, 218
New York University, 39
Nieves-Squires, Sarah, 218
Noboa-Rios, Abdin, 47
Northwestern University, 41

Ochsner, Nancy L., 48n, 122n
Ohio State University, 39, 41
Ott, Mary Diedrich, 48n, 68, 122n

Padilla, Amado M., 213
parents of doctoral students, 49–51;
educational attainment, 49–50;
socioeconomic status, 50–51, 221–
222, 267
as predictor of: academic interaction
with faculty, 161–163; ever received fellowship, 145–148; has a
mentor, 157–159; incurred education debt, 153–155; interaction
with faculty adviser, 163–164;
peer interaction, 155–157; rate of
progress, 171–172; stopping out of
a doctoral program, 170–171; time
to degree, 174–176
part-time enrollment. See enrollment
status
Patterson-Stewart, Karen E., 123n
Pearson, Willie, Jr., 27, 49, 77, 105,
107, 122, 134
Pease, John, 123n
peer interaction, xix, 92–94, 216, 218,
220–222, 267, 270–271, 289–290;
predictors of, 155–157
as predictor of: satisfaction with program, 168–170; stopping out,
170–171
performance: academic self-ranking,
118–119; grade point average, xx,
117–118
persistence. See degree completion;
stopping out
Peters, Dianne S., 123n
Peterson, Margaret, 123n
Ph.D. Octopus, The (James), 1, 9
physical sciences, 40
Pisani, Anoush, 27, 71, 105, 188
political science, 40
presented a paper, xxii–xxiv, 109, 212–
213, 217–218, 267, 297; predictors
of, 167–168

Princeton University, 39
private vs. public doctoral program, 60,
267
as predictor of: academic interaction
with faculty, 163–164; doctoral degree completion, 172–174; ever received fellowship, 148–150; ever
was a research assistant, 153–155;
ever was a teaching assistant, 150–
153; fellowship at entry, 139–141;
has a mentor, 159–161; incurred
education debt, 155–157; interaction with faculty adviser, 164–
168; peer interaction, 157–159;
presented a paper, 167–168; published an article, 168–170; rate of
progress, 172–174; research productivity, 167–168; satisfaction
with doctoral program, 171–172;
student/faculty social interaction,
161–163; teaching assistantship at
entry, 141–143; time to degree,
174–176
Pruitt, Anne S., 27, 81, 96, 213
psychology, 40
published article, xix, xxi, xxiii–xxiv,
109–111, 212–213, 217–218, 267,
298; predictors of, 167–168
Pyke, Sandra W., 123n, 130

Quiriconi, Susan, 123n

race/ethnicity, xix–xx, xxiii–xxiv, 46–
47, 208–216
as predictor of: academic interaction
with faculty, 161–163; doctoral degree completion, 172–174; ever received fellowship, 145–148; ever
was a research assistant, 150–153;
ever was a teaching assistant, 148–
150; fellowship at entry, 139–141;
has a mentor, 157–159; incurred
education debt, 153–155; interaction with faculty adviser, 163–164;
peer interaction, 155–157; presented a paper, 167–168; published an article, 167–168; rate of
progress, 171–172; research assistantship at entry, 143–145; research productivity, 164–168; satisfaction with doctoral program,
168–170; student/faculty social interaction, 159–161; teaching assistantship at entry, 141–143; time
to degree, 174–176
rate of progress, xx–xxiv, 37, 127–130,
200–202, 268–270, 301; predictors
of, 171–172